Market Response Models: Econometric and Time Series Analysis

International Series in Quantitative Marketing

Editor:
Jehoshua Eliashberg
The Wharton School
University of Pennsylvania
Philadelphia, Pennsylvania, U.S.A.

Previously published books in the series:

L. Cooper and M. Nakanishi: Market Share Analysis

Market Response Models: Econometric and Time Series Analysis

Dominique M. Hanssens
University of California, Los Angeles

Leonard J. Parsons
Georgia Institute of Technology

Randall L. Schultz
University of Iowa

Kluwer Academic Publishers
Boston/Dordrecht/London

Distributors

for North America: Kluwer Academic Publishers
101 Philip Drive, Assinippi Park, Norwell, MA 02061 U.S.A.

for all other countries: Kluwer Academic Publishers Group,
Distribution Centre, P.O. Box 322, 3300 AH Dordrecht, The
Netherlands

Library of Congress Cataloging-in-Publication Data

Hanssens, Dominique M.
   Market response models: econometric and time
series analysis / Dominique M. Hanssens,
Leonard J. Parsons, Randall L. Schultz.
     p. cm.—(International series in quantitative marketing)
   Bibliography: p.
   Includes index.
   ISBN 0-7923-9013-X
   1. Marketing surveys—Econometric models. 2. Sales
forecasting—Econometric models. 3. Time series analysis.
I. Parsons, Leonard J. II. Schultz, Randall L. III. Title.
IV. Series.
HF5415.3.H36 1989
658.8′3′028—dc19   89-2670
                                         CIP

To the memory of Dr. and Mrs. Germain
Hanssens. D.M.H.

To Margaret and Robert Grieve, and Marion and
Leonard Parsons, in honor of their 50th wedding
anniversaries. L.J.P.

To Irene K. Schultz and the memory of Robert
L. Schultz. R.L.S.

Contents

Preface

This book reports over a decade's worth of research on the development of empirical response models that have important uses for generating marketing knowledge and improving marketing decisions. Some of its contributions to marketing are the following:

1. It integrates state-of-the art technical material with discussions of its relevance to management.
2. It provides continuity to a research stream over 20 years old.
3. It illustrates how marketing generalizations are the basis of marketing theory and marketing knowledge.
4. It shows how the research can be applied to marketing planning and forecasting.
5. It presents original research in marketing.

The book addresses both marketing researchers and marketing managers. This can be done because empirical decision models are helpful in practice and are also based on theories of response. Econometric and time series analysis (ETS) is one of the few areas in marketing where there is little, if any, conflict between the academic sphere and the world of professional practice.

Market Response Models is a sequel to *Marketing Models and Econometric Research*, published in 1976. It is rare for a research-oriented book in marketing to be updated or to have a sequel. Unlike many other methodologies, ETS research in marketing has stood the test of time. It remains the main method for discovering relations among marketing variables.

What constitutes marketing knowledge? In our view, marketing generalizations provide the empirical basis for marketing theory and hence define marketing knowledge. Rather than dwelling on terminology or philosophical considerations, this book presents ideas about knowledge generation that are understandable and that work. It also presents research findings in the form of marketing generalizations, so it contributes to marketing knowledge.

Market Response Models offers an approach to planning and forecasting that is implementable in any marketing organization. Unlike books that are compendiums of techniques, this book shows how its subject matter can be used to improve marketing planning and forecasting through a logical, analytical framework. The fact that the kind of models reported are used regularly in business lends credibility to the analysis.

Finally, since the book is a research contribution to the marketing and management science literature, it contains original material. It bridges gaps in current research and offers suggestions for future research. To a large extent, the integration of ETS research as presented in this book is also original.

The book begins with an overview of response models and their use for research and management. This is followed by a discussion of the methodology of econometric and time series analysis. Next, empirical results on response models are presented, together with ways in which they can be applied. The book concludes by exploring how such models can be implemented to achieve scientific and management goals.

Although there is a good deal of technical material in this book, it was written to appeal to managers as much as researchers. If a manager feels uncomfortable with some of the mathematics, a researcher can be called in to execute the model building. If a researcher doesn't understand the management problem, a manager can explain the need for the research. A book written to serve only one of these two essential audiences would fail in its mission; only by integrating the material—and the people involved—can the book achieve its purpose.

Acknowledgments

We thank the Morris Hite Center for Product Development and Marketing Science at the University of Texas at Dallas for financial support in the preparation of this book. We thank Danny Boston, Kong Chu, and Frank Houston for their comments on portions of this book. We also thank the secretaries and teaching assistants at UCLA, UT-Dallas, and Iowa who helped us complete this project.

INTRODUCTION

1 RESPONSE MODELS IN MARKETING

Econometric and time series analysis (ETS) in marketing is the process of building models of marketing systems that delineate relations between organizations and markets through flows of communication and exchange. These models, called *market response models*, are useful for understanding the behavior of markets and for predicting the impact of marketing actions. The purpose of this book is to explain how ETS models are created and used.

The principal focus of ETS analysis in marketing is on the relation between controllable variables, such as price and distribution, and performance measures, such as sales or market share. Such relations are of considerable interest to both marketing managers and marketing scientists. Managers want to know how they can control sales, which decision variables have more impact than others, and, in general, how to plan and forecast better. Because sales response is a marketing phenomenon, scientists want to know how to explain it. Unlike many other areas of marketing and management science, there is virtually no conflict in ETS research between theoretical and applied matters. Thus, we do not create an artificial distinction between the theory of response, the measurement of response, or the practical use of models of response. What follows is an introduction to econometric and time series research in marketing that joins research and managerial issues precisely because they are inseparable in practice.

We begin this chapter with an example of how a simple marketing system can be modeled. Next, we define empirical response models and discuss various modeling approaches. The relation of marketing management tasks to marketing models is then discussed. Finally, we present an approach to planning and forecasting based on response models and show how ETS is instrumental to it.

Modeling Marketing Systems

As a point of departure, we consider the simplest form of marketing system, in which there is no competition, so that the firm and industry are identical. Figure 1–1 illustrates such a simple marketing system. The system is made up of two primary elements: the marketing organization or firm and the market or consumers. Linking these elements are three communication flows and two physical flows of exchange. The firm communicates to the market through various marketing actions, such as distributing its products or services, setting prices, and so forth. The consumers in the market respond to the

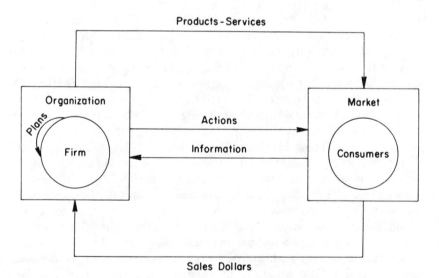

Figure 1–1. A Simple Marketing System. *Source*: Parsons and Schultz (1976, p. 4).

firm's actions through sales (or the lack of sales), and this information is sought by the firm. In an internal flow of communication, the firm makes plans for future actions on the basis of current and past information. The physical flows are the movement of products or services to consumers and the simultaneous movement of sales dollars to the firm. The process of physical exchange is characteristic of all commercial trade. The process of communication flows is the distinguishing characteristic of modern marketing systems.

If a firm had only one marketing decision variable (or instrument) that was thought to influence demand, say advertising, a positive model of its market behavior might be the *sales response function*

$$Q_t = f(A_t, E_t), \tag{1.1}$$

where

Q_t = firm's sales in units at time t,

A_t = firm's advertising expenditures at time t,

E_t = environmental factors at time t.

In this model, the geographic market is considered to be well defined, for example, a consolidated metropolitan statistical area (CMSA), and the environmental factors are taken to include all uncontrollable factors affecting demand, for example, population and income.

If this firm had, in addition, a *decision rule* for setting its advertising budget at time t equal to some percentage of the prior period's sales revenue, this heuristic could be represented as

$$A_t = f(P_{t-1} \cdot Q_{t-1}), \tag{1.2}$$

where

A_t = firm's advertising expenditures at time t,

P_t = price of the product at time $t - 1$,

Q_t = firm's sales in units at time $t - 1$.

This type of decision rule, or some variation of it in terms of current or expected sales, is a descriptive statement of management behavior. Ultimately, we may be interested in some expression for A^*, the optimal advertising budget, which would be a normative decision rule for managers to follow.

Functions 1.1 and 1.2 completely specify the marketing system model in this case. The system works in the following manner. We start with some *firm* offering a product at a specific price. Its marketing *action* at time t is advertising. The *market* responds to this action in some manner. The *consumers* may become aware of the product, develop preferences for it, purchase it, or react negatively to it. This *information* on consumer behavior, including sales, is obtained by the firm either directly or through marketing research. If purchases have been made, physical exchange has taken place. On the basis of its sales in period t, the firm makes marketing *plans* for period $t + 1$. In this case, the advertising budget is planned as a percentage of the prior period's sales. This decision rule yields a new level of advertising expenditure, which is the marketing action of the firm for period $t + 1$. Thus, the process is continued for all t.

Despite the obvious simplifications involved, this model can be thought of as a representation of a marketing system. In ETS research, models of this kind (and more complex versions) can be formulated, estimated, and tested in order to discover the structure of marketing systems and explore the consequences of changes in them. For example, suppose a researcher wants to model the demand structure for a cable television system. As a starting point, the preceding model is adopted, since it captures the essential characteristics of the marketing situation. The firm offers a product, cable television, to a well-defined geographic market, say a CMSA, at a regulated and hence (strictly) uncontrollable price. Since the product is homogeneous and the price is fixed, advertising is seen as the only marketing instrument. Although there are competitive sources for a television signal, the analyst concentrates on the demand for cable TV, and so there is no competition; industry and firm demand are identical in this monopoly situation. The analyst completes the model by specifying environmental factors, say income and population, and a decision rule for advertising.

To simplify further, the analyst assumes that the relations in the model will be linear and stochastic.[1] The linearity assumption may be one of convenience but the stochastic representation is necessitated both by (possible) omitted variables and by truly random disturbances (even a percent-of-sales decision rule will be subject to managerial discretion). The analyst is now ready to write the model of the cable television company as an *econometric model*, so that it can be checked with empirical data. In this way, the analyst seeks to test whether or not the model is any good and also to estimate the parameters of marketing action and reaction. The model to be tested is

$$Q_t = \gamma A_t + \beta_1 Y_t + \beta_2 N_t + \beta_3 + U_{t1} \qquad (1.3)$$

$$A_t = \beta_4 S_{t-1} + U_{t2}, \qquad (1.4)$$

where, in addition to the variables already defined,

Y_t = disposable personal income for the CMSA at time t,

N_t = population of the CMSA at time t,

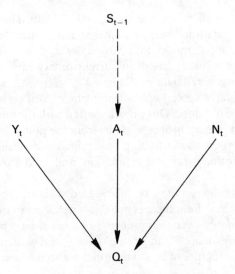

Figure 1-2. Causal Ordering of a Simple Econometric Model. Solid arrows represent causal links; dashed arrow, a decision rule. *Source*: Parsons and Schultz (1976, p. 8).

S_{t-1} = firm's sales revenue at time $t-1$, $S = PQ$,

γ = parameter of an endogenous variable,

β = parameter of a predetermined variable,

U_t = random disturbance.

This model includes two endogenous variables, Q_t and A_t, which means that they are determined within the system at time t. The predetermined variables include the purely exogenous variables Y_t and N_t and the variable S_t, which is a lagged endogenous variable but is exogenous at time t. The causal ordering of this econometric model is shown in figure 1-2.

The theory of identification, estimation, and testing of econometric models is explained in the remainder of the book, and so we can just hint at the analyst's next steps. If the analyst can assume that the structural disturbances, U_{t1} and U_{t2}, are independent, the model is a special kind of econometric model called a *recursive model*. In such a model, the equations are identified and ordinary least-squares estimates are consistent and unbiased. This simplifies the statistical problem, and if a time series of sufficient length is available, these data can be used to test the model. With some luck, the analyst will end up with a model that describes the demand for cable television and yields estimates of advertising effect, income effect, and so forth. The model may have value for forecasting future sales and for designing better decision rules.

Another form for a model involving sales and advertising, where the advertising decision rule is based on current or expected sales, would be a *simultaneous equation system*. Besides being different in a substantive sense, such a model requires special estimation techniques if consistent parameter estimates are to be obtained. Our preoccupation with the quality of estimates, especially the consistency property, stems from the policy implications of the parameters, e.g., their use in finding an optimal advertising budget. These issues of model form, parameter estimation, and model use unfold in subsequent chapters.

Our example assumes quite a bit of knowledge about the market situation being modeled. Many times there is not this much a priori information about which variables should be in the model or how they should be related. In such instances, *time series analysis* can be employed to deal with questions of causal ordering and the structure of lags. This topic is also discussed in the chapters that follow.

Most marketing systems are not as simple as this illustration. The effects of competition, more than one marketing decision variable, multiple products, distribution channels, and so forth make the task of modeling complex marketing systems a difficult one.

Empirical Response Models

A *response model* shows how one variable depends on one or more other variables. The so-called dependent variable could be company sales, company market share, consumer awareness, or any other variable of interest to marketing managers. The explanatory variables are those thought to produce changes in the dependent variable. Together, dependent and explanatory variables make up the systems of equations that are used to model market behavior. When such models include competitive reaction functions, vertical market structures, cost functions, or other behavioral relations, they are referred to as *models of market mechanisms* (Parsons 1981). A response model based on time series or cross-section data is called an *empirical response model* (Parsons and Schultz 1976). This is the category of response models that is the subject matter of this book. We do not deal with situations where no historical data are available; hence we do not deal with new products or established products with no data. However, a lack of historical data may be remedied through experimentation, including test marketing.[2]

Equation 1.1 is a response model that we have called a sales response function. Equation 1.2 is also a response model, in this case called a decision rule. We can also consider response models such as this:

$$AW_t = f(A_t), \tag{1.5}$$

where AW_t is percent awareness at time t, and A_t is promotional expenditures at time t. This is an example of an intermediate-level response model where the dependent variable is not sales but some intermediate state of consumer behavior between a stimulus such as promotion and an ultimate response such as sales.

Another example of an intermediate-level response model would be this:

$$N_t = f(RD_t), \tag{1.6}$$

where N_t is contract bids at time t, and RD_t is firm's R & D expenditures at time t. A model like this could describe one aspect of the marketing performance of an industrial company.

Sales response analysis refers to the study of factors that determine the sales of a product using response models. The dependent variable in such an analysis might be sales or market share (both being indicators of sales performance) measured at the brand, product, product line, company, or industry level of aggregation. The explanatory variables include marketing mix variables such as price and distribution as well as variables covering competition and the macroeconomic environment. Since for every product there must be some unknown process generating sales, the objective of sales response analysis is to discover this process.

In a way, this is like solving a mystery: what are the factors that determine sales? Each "case" of sales response is different and yet all have common features. Researchers want to generalize about response models across products and markets. Managers want to specialize response models to meet their particular planning and forecasting needs. Fortunately, as we have noted, these interests are complementary.

Research Uses

The main research use of response models is the generation of marketing *knowledge*, which constitutes validated findings about marketing behavior. Much marketing research assumes that marketing generalizations grow out of marketing theory, viz.,

theory → generalizations.

But marketing theory should be based on marketing generalizations that represent marketing knowledge.[3] This implies the relation

generalizations → theory.

In other words, we need to know *how* marketing variables are related before we can speculate on *why* they are related. Indeed, the rich descriptive base of most sciences is constructed in just this way.

Management Uses

The main management use of response models is for building marketing *decision models*, which are designed to aid managers in planning and forecasting. Most organizations make forecasts of industry and company sales and then make marketing plans, viz.,

forecasts → plans.

But we know that company plans can influence company sales. This implies the relation

plans → forecasts.

Thus, company plans should precede company sales forecasts. Companies could forecast industry sales, make company plans, and then on the basis of a response model relating company plans to company sales, forecast company sales. Alternatively, companies could make plans and then, using a response model that incorporates industry factors, forecast company sales.

Decision models are aids to management judgement. They are sometimes referred to as normative models or prescriptive models, since they indicate to managers what ought to be done under certain conditions. The optimization models of operations research are decision models because their output can be considered to be a recommendation to management on how to make the best choice from a number of decision alternatives. Some decision models are designed to generate alternatives or to suggest actions leading to better decisions. In all these cases, the models serve as aids to management judgment based on variables over which the manager has a measure of control.

The relation between response models and decision models is one of dependence of the latter on the former. Every decision model must incorporate some representation of response, and this representation is, in effect, a theory about market behavior. The quality of the representation is vital to the success of the response model and hence the decision model. This is why we stress the complementary nature of scientific issues and management issues in sales response research.

Table 1–1. Econometric, Time Series, and ETS Approaches to Market
Response Modeling

Econometrics	*Time Series Analysis*	*ETS*
Focus on relations between variables (interstructure)	Focus on relations within variables over time (intrastructure)	Recognizes relations between variables and within variables over time
Easily applied to theory building and marketing planning	Often superior forecasting performance	Uses econometric or time series techniques depending on the modeling task
Time series data and cross-section data	Time series data only	Accommodates forecasting and marketing planning objectives

Modeling Approaches

There are several different approaches to the development of empirical response models that vary in their ability to meet research and management needs (table 1–1).

Time Series Analysis

Time series analysis is an approach to modeling response behavior over time with the emphasis on the lag structures of variables and disturbances. Its main concern is to explain the variability *within* one or more variables over time (the intrastructure). Univariate time series methods include exponential smoothing, moving averages, autoregressive processes, and combinations of these, such as the Box-Jenkins technique. The approach, almost completely empirical, usually rests on the assumption that realizations of a response variable are outcomes from a stationary stochastic process, which is partly predictable from its own past. Management actions are not explicitly accounted for in such models.

Univariate time series analysis can yield useful forecasts for management, but it is weak as a method for producing knowledge about response behavior. The major limitation of univariate time series analysis in modeling sales response is its "world view." The approach does not reflect the belief of management that a performance measure like sales can be controlled by manipulating decision variables like price and sales effort; in fact, in univariate time series analysis, the only presumed determinant of sales would be sales itself, taking into account various lags.

Multivariate time series analysis examines the behavior of more than one time series and thus moves toward accommodating control variables. However, many multivariate time series models do not require an a priori distinction between response and decision variables, and their specification is completely empirical. This approach by itself is not well suited for modeling response behavior in marketing.

Regression Analysis

Regression analysis is based on the assumption that market response is a function of certain explanatory variables and error. This approach assumes that management control, environmental, and other variables affect response in a direct way, either correlational or causal: it focuses on the relations *between* variables (the interstructure). Regression analysis is a good way to meet knowledge and forecasting needs. It has a solid world view—some things are controllable, some not—and has contributed to marketing knowledge. Most marketing generalizations about response have been found using regression analysis. Still, the technique is often abused by atheoretical use. Econometrics, based on regression analysis but imposing an explicit causal structure, rates as a superior modeling approach.

Econometrics refers to the use of structural regression models based on theories of response behavior. Response can be explained by equations or sets of equations that represent causal connections between variables. The approach is thus a combination of theory, empirical analysis, and uncertainty that mirrors both management and scientific thinking. Econometrics is the best theoretical approach to modeling response models. As a form of regression analysis, it shares the same ideal world view. The proof that it can contribute to knowledge is the vast empirical content of economics. The major limitation of econometrics is model specification in the face of limited market or management information. Another consideration is that causal (econometric) models may not be required to forecast future values of some explanatory variables in a decision model. Finally, regression models often lack realism in describing behavior of the response variable that is not accounted for by the explanatory variables. Time series analysis can help in all of these cases.

ETS

ETS is a combination of econometric and time series analysis that provides response models best suited to research and management needs. Econometrics provides the framework for developing response models that represent theories of market behavior and the means for subjecting the response component of a decision model to a rigorous test of its validity. Time series analysis is used to help specify the response mechanism when little a priori information is available. It also plays an important role in forecasting the values of certain explanatory variables in response models, especially environmental variables like household income or gross national product. Finally, ETS models explain the systematic behavior of a response variable over time as a function of explanatory variables (interstructure) *and* the past values of the response variable (intrastructure).

ETS is a proven method for developing empirical response models. Since about 1970, hundreds of models have been developed with it, most of which are not published because they were built directly for corporations. Fortunately, there is also a large literature on response analysis in marketing ensuring a level of public scrutiny that has made ETS response models both scientifically and professionally legitimate.

Marketing Models and Management

Although the importance of technology to the advancement of organizations and markets is well understood, the significance of a special form of technology, *decision-making technology*, is not widely appreciated. Most companies are eager to improve their operations by investing in new technology. They adopt innovations such as robotics, computer-aided design, telecommunications, word processing, and other forms of production technology on a regular basis. But in the area of decision making there is much more resistance to change despite the fact that a wide array of management decision technology is available.

Empirical decision models are one form of this decision-making technology. Other forms include operations research and management science models, management information systems, decision support systems, and expert systems. The use of empirical decision models to improve marketing decision making requires an understanding of how companies go about marketing planning and forecasting. It also requires an understanding of the general tasks of marketing management, since planning and forecasting are only two of many tasks for a marketing manager.

Marketing Success

What makes a company or product successful? Apart from the overall quality of a company's management, its skill in production, finance, and the implementation of policy, or even plain luck, the key ingredient of corporate success is marketing strategy: the right products being sold to the right customers at the right time. This is more basic, hence strategic, to a product's success than tactical concerns like price, promotion, or distribution. Thus, to a very real extent, marketing strategy dominates marketing tactics.

Empirical decision models are designed to improve corporate success, but they are not so broad as to include the strategy formulation process. For this reason, we examine marketing tasks and models—and later planning, forecasting, and decision making—*given* an overall company or product strategy. If the company or product does not have the right strategic positioning, we do not contend that empirical decision models will correct this problem.[4] However, we do believe (and experience shows) that sales response analysis can lead to improved company planning and forecasting, improved insight into the market situation, and an improvement in tactical decision making that can feed back to better corporate strategy. In this way, marketing decision models can have an important impact on company success.

In general, marketing management is concerned with decisions regarding new or established products. The two kinds of products are closely related, since any new product that is successful becomes an established product, and all established products move through life cycles that ultimately end in other new products. In a dynamic environment like this, there are five primary tasks of marketing management. Related to these tasks are seven kinds of marketing models. The various tasks and models are shown in figure 1–3.

Marketing Tasks

The primary tasks of marketing management are development and introduction for new products, and planning, allocation, and control for established products. These are called tasks because they are things that must be done by marketing managers. Whether they are done well or not, of course, is another matter.

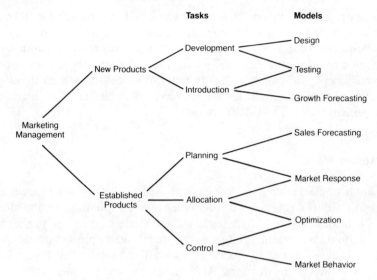

Figure 1-3. Marketing Management Tasks and Models.

New product development is the lifeblood of any company. A company is defined by its products, and its success depends on the success of the company's original (new) product and its successor products in a changing environment. The product development process ends with a decision to go or not go with a new product. A decision to market a product leads directly to the introduction task of marketing management. The fact that new product failure rates are so high for both consumer and industrial products reminds us that these tasks are not easy to master. Indeed, very few companies have sustained a record of new product success over long periods of time.

The management of established products requires attention to the marketing tasks of planning, allocation, and control. In some respects, planning is the most important of these, since it must be based on an understanding of the factors that determine sales and must provide both an agenda for action and a forecast of market outcomes. To maximize the effectiveness of plans, marketing managers turn to the tasks of allocation and control. Allocation refers to the distribution of company resources to carry out plans and achieve goals. Control refers to the checking of outcomes against plans and goals.

The tasks of marketing management can be accomplished using experience alone. But management judgment often fails, particularly in the face of task complexity, interaction, and change (Hogarth and Makridakis 1981). In this situation, models offer a supplement to experience. From the early work on consistency in decision making (Bowman 1963) to the more recent developments in aided decision making (Sjöberg 1982), the message is clear: models help managers.[5] In marketing, many types of models have been developed over the past two decades to aid managers with the tasks of marketing management (Schultz and Zoltners 1981).

Marketing Models

The kinds of marketing models include those for design, testing, forecasting of growth, modeling of response, forecasting of sales, optimization, and modeling of behavior. Figure 1–3 shows how these models are related to the tasks of marketing management. Product design models aid the product development process, and market testing models help with both new product development and new product introductions. Also related to new product introduction decisions are so-called growth models that forecast new product sales. New product models are discussed by Urban and Hauser (1980), Wind, Mahajan, and Cardozo (1981), Assmus (1981), and Lilien and Kotler (1983).

Response models aid the planning process for established products, as do sales forecasting models. The allocation task of marketing management is helped by market response models and optimization models. Finally, the control task benefits from optimization models and models of consumer, competitive, and market behavior. Response models are discussed by Parsons and Schultz (1976), Naert and Leeflang (1978), and Parsons (1981). Sales forecasting models are discussed by Makridakis and Wheelwright (1977), Armstrong (1985), and Fildes (1985).[6] Of course, response and sales forecasting models are the subject of this book.

Optimization models are discussed by Zoltners (1981) and Lilien and Kotler (1983). Models of market behavior, by which we mean any model that attempts to explain consumer choice, market segments, or the economic structure of markets, are not discussed in a single source. By explaining behavior, however, they clearly relate to control, since they deal with the outcomes of market actions. Some examples of the seven kinds of models are given in table 1–2.

Although all the kinds of marketing models that we have discussed are related to decision making, only design, testing, and optimization models are usually thought of as decision models. The other models are more properly known as forecasting models, response models, or models of behavior. A

Table 1-2.   Examples of Marketing Models

Kind	Examples
Design	Shocker and Srinivasan (1974); Urban (1975)
Testing	Silk and Urban (1978); Blattberg and Golanty (1978)
Growth forecasting	Fourt and Woodlock (1960); Parfitt and Collins (1968); Bass (1969a)
Response	Bass and Parsons (1969); Schultz (1971a); Hanssens (1980b)
Sales forecasting	Dalrymple and Haines (1970); Staelin and Turner (1973); Leone (1983)
Optimization	Dorfman and Steiner (1954); Lambin, Naert, and Bultez (1975); Dolan and Jeuland (1981); Horsky and Simon (1983)
Behavior	Ehrenberg (1972); Herniter (1973); McGuire and Staelin (1983); Moorthy (1984)

special case is that of empirical decision models, which we have already defined as planning models based on empirical response models.

Planning and Forecasting

All companies want to know how to forecast performance and how performance is affected by factors under their control. They can define certain performance measures of relevance, such as earnings, sales, or market share, at certain levels of planning, such as company, division, or product. They can also identify certain factors that influence the performance measures, such as marketing mix, competition, and environmental variables. The performance measures, factors, and organizational level of planning define the planning and forecasting tasks for the company.

There is a natural precedence relation between planning and forecasting: marketing plans should precede sales forecasts. Meaningful forecasts can only be made on the basis of a firm's plans and expectations regarding environmental conditions or competitive reactions. For example, suppose a sales response equation shows a relation between market share and distribution share. To forecast market share, the firm's plans and competitors' plans with respect to distribution expenditures must be known or at least estimated. If total industry demand is known, the firm can forecast its sales from these data. Although this prescription may seem straightforward, many firms reverse the functions, first forecasting company sales and then determining distribution expenditures. Familiar percent-of-sales decision rules for marketing expenditures imply this reverse order. It is only when plans precede forecasts that the logical nature of the dependence is maintained.

Model-Based Planning and Forecasting

One approach to planning and forecasting that incorporates this logic is shown in figure 1–4. It suggests a general process for planning and forecasting that many companies say they use, so it is easy for managers to grasp the procedure. But it goes quite far beyond what managers typically do because

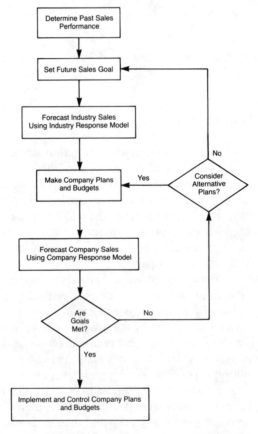

Figure 1–4. Model-Based Planning and Forecasting.

it includes empirical response models to provide a link between management information (experience) and market information (data). We call the approach model-based planning and forecasting.[7]

The model-based approach begins with determining past sales performance. As we will see, the process can be expanded to include other performance measures, say profit, but even in these cases, increasing sales is a subgoal or co-goal of considerable management, shareholder, or public interest. If increasing sales is the goal, a future sales goal will usually be set by top management. In addition to past performance, market opportunity will have a leading role in determining this figure. Some companies will work through what they call a planning process from the bottom up to arrive at this sales goal. But often, when this "planning" process is done, the outcome is just a company sales *forecast*; goal and forecast have become one and the same. No wonder so many top managers are pleased at the beginning of each year.

The model-based approach maintains the strict logical relation between planning and forecasting. It tries not to confuse goals and forecasts. Thus, the next step after goal setting is forecasting total market or industry sales using an industry response model.[8] This is where factors typically beyond the control of the firm are related to total market sales, or if industry sales is not a focus of the research, to the environment determining company sales. An industry response model does not give a rote forecast; rather, managers are presented with various scenarios of industry demand (cf. Naylor 1983). The industry sales forecast becomes the one associated with the most likely scenario. Since there is a model on which to base the forecasts, managers can see how the forecasts depend on their own assumptions about the leading factors determining industry sales.

Given an industry sales forecast, the company makes plans and converts the plans into budgets. These are not just general plans, but the plans associated with specific marketing control variables identified in a sales response analysis as being part of the company's sales response model. If price and advertising are factors determining company sales, the company must have specific planned levels of price and advertising before it can use a company response model to forecast company sales. There is a big difference between this approach and the one alluded to earlier, in which the company's plans may be vague and related to goals rather than to expected sales. Plans can be made directly from management judgment or through the use of decision rules based on previous management experience. Another way to develop marketing plans is through normative models or optimization (see chapter 8). Company plans, together with estimates of competitive response based on models or management experience, are then used in a company response model to forecast company sales.

Given a company sales forecast, the company evaluates whether goals are met. If they are, company plans and budgets are implemented and then controlled. If they are not, the company would decide if it should consider alternative plans that might meet the sales goal or if it should change the sales goal. Alternative plans could be generated through formal methods such as decision theory, optimization, game theory, and simulation. This would result in another run through the company planning and forecasting segment to produce new company sales forecasts. If goals simply cannot be achieved, they should be revised to make them more realistic. Then the model-based planning process would start over again.

Performance Measures and Factors

The model-based approach to planning and forecasting is quite robust. It accommodates different performance measures and factors, different planning levels, and different organizational arrangements for planning and forecasting. The most commonly used performance measures in planning are sales revenue, market share, and earnings. Since most companies serve multiple markets, market share is typically used only as a measure of *product* performance. Division or companywide planning typically requires the common denominator of sales revenue or earnings. For this same reason, sales measured in units must usually be restricted to product-level analysis.

Other aspects of the performance measures chosen for a study are the time, space, and entity dimensions. Typically we think of increasing the sales of a product over time; the performance measure in this case would be "product sales over time," and hence a time series analysis would be indicated. But sales can also be expanded across geographic territories or by increasing the sales of other products in the product line. In these cases, the performance measures would define a planning and forecasting task involving cross-section data. We see that by choosing a performance measure we also choose between time series, cross-section, or combined time series and cross-section analysis.

The most appropriate performance measure depends on the particular company and industry. Some examples of response studies with which we are familiar can illustrate this point. Company A competes in a consumer market where industry data are not available. In this case, the performance measure used was company sales. Company B sells a commercial product in a market where almost all competitors have small market shares; it is also very difficult to track company marketing variables. In this study, the dependent variable was industry sales. Another company, C, has a 10% share of a high-technology market with both company and industry sales data available. In this case, two performance measures became the focus of analysis: industry sales and company market share. Finally, company D manufactures an industrial product sold in different engineered forms to different applications markets. Here the analysis centered on total company sales and sales by market segment.

Each of these studies also involved an appropriate set of factors that explained the performance measures. The factors typically include marketing mix, competition, and environmental variables. The performance measures and the factors considered at a particular level of product aggregation define the planning and forecasting task for a company, i.e., the nature and scope of any real model-based planning and forecasting study.

Planning Levels

Just as the model-based approach accommodates different performance measures, it also accommodates different planning levels. The process shown in figure 1–4 can be used for product planning, division planning, or corporate planning. The highest level of product aggregation to be pursued in a response analysis usually defines the most logical performance measure. For example, if an analysis were to focus on both product sales *and* company sales, a problem with nonhomogeneous products would be overcome by using the common denominator of sales revenue. Similarly, an aggregation of divisional products would require a performance measure based on revenue.

The planning and forecasting task for any one company, then, is unique with respect to the particular variables being studied but general in the overall process of planning. In our experience, model-based planning and forecasting is usually more effective when it covers companywide planning activity and begins with top management support. Still, there are many examples of response studies that have aided planning at the brand or product level alone.

Organization

A final element of flexibility of model-based planning and forecasting is that it can be used with different organizational arrangements for planning and forecasting. A dedicated forecasting staff, for example, could easily develop and maintain the response models that underlie the model-based planning procedure. This staff would also be responsible for producing forecasts and doing whatever further analysis was needed. They would interact with planners as a true decision support system. Alternatively, product managers could be given the responsibility for maintaining response models developed by in-house or outside consultants. The models and associated software would be sufficiently user-friendly so that only periodic help would be needed to run them.

Although the model-based approach is essentially a top-down forecasting method, nothing precludes incorporating bottom-up forecasts or, as we have seen, bottom-up goals based on market opportunity. Indeed, nothing in the approach precludes management from overriding the model-produced forecasts. Such disagreements, however, would have to be based on good reasons.

The ETS Method

ETS is the modeling technology behind model-based planning and forecasting. The empirical response models for model-based planning are obtained through ETS and a combination of market information, or data, and management information, or experience. By utilizing both market and management information, the ETS method seeks the best possible answer to the question of what determines a company's performance.

Market Information

Two principal kinds of data are used in ETS research: time series data and cross-section data. These correspond to the time series and cross-section analyses discussed in connection with defining a specific planning or forecasting task. A time series is a set of observations on a variable representing one entity over t periods of time. A cross-section is a set of observations on n entities at one point in time. Sales of a product for ten periods is an example of a time series. Prices for 25 goods during one month is an example of a cross-section. Since our interest focuses on response models, showing relations among variables, we almost always deal with what can be called *multiple* time series or cross-sections.

Time series and cross-section data are empirical in that they are observed outcomes of an experiment or some natural process. This can be contrasted with data that are subjective in that they are obtained from managers as judgments based on experience. As will be seen, ETS utilizes judgment in a peripheral way. Management experience shapes every aspect of response research and its application to planning and forecasting. But response itself is not parameterized through judgment; rather, it is data-driven.

Another aspect of market information relevant to ETS research is the

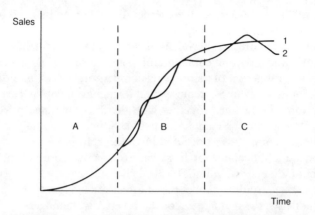

Figure 1–5. Sales Growth and Variability over Time.

growth and variability of a performance measure such as sales over time. Figure 1–5 shows two sales curves: (1) a standard S-shaped growth curve, and (2) a growth curve showing increased sales variability over time, i.e., increased variability resulting from an economic rather than a growth process. Planning and forecasting in stage A can only be accomplished with growth models because very few historical data are available. In stage B, growth and ETS models should be used together to produce plans and forecasts. Finally, in stage C, the growth process is exhausted and ETS becomes the natural method for modeling response and producing plans and forecasts.

Management Information

ETS research relies on management information in five important ways.[9] First, managers help to define the modeling task. In the case of response analysis or model-based planning and forecasting, managers can suggest the major variables of interest, including performance measures, factors, and the appropriate planning level. The fact that a study may be done on industry sales for a division of an industrial company with a focus on sales effort across territories may be due to management judgment.

Second, managers help to specify the models. Their experience is used to decide which variables are candidates as explanatory factors and what lags, if any, could occur in the process. This judgment ensures that the subsequent empirical analysis conforms to reality and is not a statistical artifact. At the same time, managers do not tell how the response takes place. They are not very good at this (cf. Naert and Weverbergh 1981b), and so the burden of proof falls on the empirical data.

Third, managers forecast the values of certain independent variables, such as competitive and environmental variables, if necessary. A model in which a firm's sales are a function of its price, its competitors' prices, and disposable personal income, for example, requires that its management forecast the price of competition and income. Together with the firm's planned price, then, a forecast of its sales can be made. Alternatively, time series analysis could be used to forecast competitive price and income, or, in some cases, the econometric model could account for these variables.[10] In these instances, direct management judgment would not be needed.

Fourth, managers adjust model-based forecasts as required. Response and planning models serve managers, not the reverse, so managers are asked to evaluate model output as if the model were another expert. Response modeling, model-based planning, and ETS do much to lay out the logic of analysis before managers. For this reason, as we have stated before, managers are more likely to face questions of bias and uncertainty directly.

The fifth way in which ETS research relies on management information is that managers evaluate alternatives for action. The end product of model-based planning is the plan itself. Response models give managers insight on what factors influence their sales and in addition provide an approach to planning and forecasting that integrates response with decision making. Still, the buck stops with managers. ETS can blend market and management information in a formidable mix of decision technology, but the *responsibility* for decision making falls on the managers, not the models.

Summary

Before we turn to more technical matters, let us review the basic argument of this book. This chapter has established that marketing systems can be modeled with ETS. These models are called empirical response models; by definition, they require history and thus exclude new products and established products with no data. Empirical response models have two major uses: (1) research, to develop scientific generalizations, and (2) management, to aid in planning and forecasting. These uses are complementary, since empirical decision models for planning and forecasting are necessarily based on empirical response models. Several approaches are available to specify and estimate empirical response models; ETS is the best.

The management use of empirical response models requires an understanding of how companies go about planning, forecasting, and accomplishing certain marketing tasks. Companies want to know how to forecast their performance and how their performance is affected by factors under their control. They can define certain performance measures of relevance, such as sales, market share, or earnings, for one or several products or territories at certain levels of planning, such as company, division, or brand. They can also identify certain factors that influence the performance measures. The performance measures, factors, and organizational level of planning define the planning and forecasting task for a company. A general process for planning and forecasting includes goal setting, industry forecasts, company plans, and company forecasts. This process can be improved when plans are evaluated with empirical response models. Such model-based planning and forecasting is very flexible; it accommodates different performance measures, different planning levels, and different organizational structures. ETS is a modeling technology behind model-based planning and forecasting that combines market and management information. Market data are used to discover response behavior; management experience is used to help define the modeling task, to help specify the models, to forecast independent variables if necessary, to adjust model-based forecasts, and to evaluate alternatives for action. Finally, the results of an ETS analysis include generalizations, theory, insight, plans, and forecasts.

Part II of this book discusses the techniques of econometric and time series model building. Part III shows how ETS research has led to generalizations about sales response, competitive behavior, and dynamic effects, shows how marketing decisions can be improved, and shows how an actual ETS study is done. In part IV, the book concludes with a discussion of how ETS relates to marketing science and practice.

Notes

1. Response models can be linear or nonlinear. The choice is typically based on theory or prior knowledge, e.g., diminishing returns to marketing effort.

2. Also excluded, for substantive reasons, are response models based on subjective estimates of model parameters. See Naert and Weverbergh (1981b).

3. This argument appears in Parsons and Schultz (1976) and Leone and Schultz (1980).

4. The relation between strategic variables such as positioning and market response is just beginning to be explored. See Moore and Winer (1987).

5. To help managers, models must be used, and to be used they must have certain characteristics. See Schultz and Henry (1981) and chapter 10 in this book.

6. A very useful reference is the special issue on "Forecasting in Marketing" of the *International Journal of Forecasting* [3 (3/4, 1987)].

7. ETS is the methodology behind the approach. For a complementary view of marketing forecasting, see exhibit 1 in Armstrong, Brodie, and McIntyre (1987).

8. Industry variables could be incorporated directly into a company response model; in this case, company planning and budgeting would be the next step.

9. Some market response models have been developed without direct or indirect management input; however, to do the kind of comprehensive modeling described in this book, such input is required.

10. In many cases, the forecasts of macroeconomic or industry variables are purchased directly from forecasting services.

II ECONOMETRIC AND TIME SERIES MODEL BUILDING

2 DESIGN OF RESPONSE MODELS

The design of response models involves variables, relations among variables, functional forms, and data. Variables represent the building blocks of a response study. An analysis of price elasticity, for example, would require at least two variables, price and unit sales. Relations are the connections among variables. To answer a question about the magnitude of price elasticity, it would be necessary to examine the special relation of price to unit sales. Functional forms refer to the nature of a relation. One form of a relation between price and sales could be linear; a form like this would give both mathematical and substantive meaning to the relation. Finally, data are the actual realizations of variables. Taken together, these four elements provide the materials for building a response model.

This chapter examines these four basic elements. We first discuss the choice of variables for a response model. Next, we examine how relations among variables can be established. Third, we show how each relation can be made concrete by stating its functional form in detail. Finally, we look at the central role played by the type of data available for estimating and testing response models.

Variables

A number of issues related to the variables in a system are important for understanding response models.[1] First, all the variables in a system must be defined. Sometimes, not all variables that could be included in a system are in fact included; in this case, we have an *omitted variable problem*. Second, since the variables represent theoretical constructs, they require operational definitions. For example, advertising could be defined as expenditures, as media units like advertising minutes or pages, or as gross rating points. Third, the variables must be measured and recorded accurately: if they are not, measurement errors result. The second and third problems are often viewed as special cases of a more general problem type, the *errors-in-variables problem*. Fourth, not all the variables may be observable, giving rise to the *unobservable variable problem*. Before addressing these issues in detail, we must introduce some nomenclature for describing variables.

Classification of Variables

Within a dynamic simultaneous equation model, it is possible to make several distinctions among the variables. As an illustration, consider a simple three-equation system involving a brand's unit sales, Q_t; retail availability, R_t; and advertising expenditures, A_t. This system can be represented as

$$Q_t = f(R_t, A_t, Q_{t-1}, P_t, U_{1t}) \qquad (2.1)$$

$$R_t = f(A_t, Q_{t-1}, U_{2t}) \qquad (2.2)$$

$$A_t = f(Q_t, A_{t-k}, P_t, U_{3t}), \qquad (2.3)$$

where

Q_{t-1} = unit sales in the previous period,

A_{t-k} = advertising k periods ago (usually $k = 1$, i.e., the previous period),

P_t = price per unit,

U_t = random disturbance.

At least four distinctions can be made among the variables. The first is whether the variables pertain to the present time period (Q_t, R_t, A_t, P_t) or to previous time periods (Q_{t-1}, A_{t-k}). The presence of lagged variables makes a system dynamic. The second distinction is whether the values of the variables are independent of the operation of the model (P_t) or determined by the model

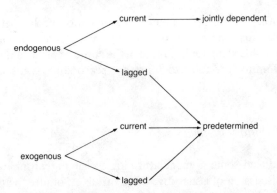

Figure 2–1. Distinguishing Predetermined Variables. *Source*: Naert and Leeflang (1978, p. 62).

$(Q_t, Q_{t-1}, R_t, A_t, A_{t-k})$. The former are called *exogenous variables*; the latter, *endogenous variables*. Third, is the variable stochastically independent of all current and future disturbances in the model? If yes, they are called *predetermined variables* (Q_{t-1}, A_{t-k}, P_t), if no, *current endogenous variables* (Q_t, R_t, A_t). The predetermined variables include lagged endogenous variables as well as both current and lagged exogenous variables. This partitioning is diagramed in figure 2–1.

The fourth distinction is whether within a given equation, say (2.1), the variable is to be explained. If it is, it is a *dependent variable*; if not, it is an *explanatory variable*. When an equation contains only one current endogenous variable, it is the dependent variable. When an equation like (2.1) contains more than one current endogenous variable, one must be the dependent variable (Q_t) while the others are classified as explanatory variables (R_t, A_t) along with the predetermined variables (Q_{t-1}, P_t).

A qualitative variable like quality of advertising copy may be represented by a *dummy variable*. In this case, there would be one dummy variable for each characteristic, such as old copy or new copy. For statistical reasons, if a model contains a constant intercept, it must represent one of the characteristics. When the characteristic is present, the value of the dummy variable is 1; if it is absent, the value of the dummy variable is 0. Arnold et al. (1987), in a study of the role of advertising quality in sales response models, used dummy variables to control for three product reformulations made over a nine-year period. Blattberg and Levin (1987) used a dummy variable in their study of trade promotion to represent the offering of a fall premium to a manufacturer's sales force every September. Wildt, Parker, and Harris (1987) used one set of dummy variables to represent contest periods and another set to designate postcontest periods. There were no dummy variables for precontest periods, because salespeople were not informed of the contests prior to their beginning. The use of dummy variables to represent seasonality is discussed later in this chapter.

Issues Concerning Variables

Having introduced some nomenclature for classifying variables, we now return to our discussion of issues involving variables: omitted variables, errors in variables, and unobservable variables.

Omitted Variables. Sometimes we may not recognize the importance of a variable and unintentionally omit it from our analysis. More likely, we recognize the importance of a variable but have failed to obtain observations on it. Perhaps there is no economical way to collect the information. In any case, an omitted variable will handicap our ability to estimate relations among variables. The consequences of an omitted variable are discussed in chapter 3.

Sometimes another variable is used in place of the omitted variable. Such a measured variable is called a *proxy variable*. For example, Hogarty and Elzinga (1972) wanted to account for the impact of differences in taste on U.S. beer demand. They conjectured that immigrants were more prone to beer drinking than native drinkers. The proxy variable they used was the percentage of each state's population that was foreign-born. Typically, a proxy variable is treated as the true variable with measurement error. Some technical aspects of proxy variables are discussed in the section on stochastic regressors in chapter 3.

Errors in Variables. Errors in variables means that one or more variables have been measured or recorded inaccurately. As almost anyone who has worked with marketing data knows, variables are often measured with considerable uncertainty. We can consider three kinds of measurement problems: (1) problems of definition, (2) problems of operationalization, and (3) errors of measurement.

Definitional problems arise whenever theory or observation suggests a concept for analysis. For example, in the study of sales response to advertising, what is included in the concept "sales" and what in the concept "advertising"? Sales might be factory shipments, distributor warehouse withdrawals, or retail sales (or equivalently, consumer purchases). Advertising could imply a broad spectrum of activities from public relations to point of purchase, the definition usually focuses on media expenditures. And yet "advertising impact" comes closer than other concepts to representing the factor that we seek to relate to sales. Does "impact" include advertising expenditures, impressions, or what?

Once advertising has been defined, problems of operationalization arise. Suppose we operationalize the concept-definition of advertising as mass media expenditures on advertising in a certain time and space frame. Of course, by varying time, space, or the selection of media, other operationalizations of the same concept-definition would be possible.

No matter what the operationalization, we are still faced with problems of measurement. Each company knows its own media expenditures, but for the expenditures of all other companies it must usually rely on some other method for *estimating* advertising. The most common form is the so-called media-counting technique which, as the name suggests, is a method of counting advertisements and adding up their (presumed) market value.

To the list of measurement errors, we could add mere errors of transcription and other mechanical mistakes. In any event, it should be apparent that an assumption of error-free variables in marketing is likely to be unfounded.[2]

Unobservable Variables.   Marketing studies often contain observations on quantity of goods sold, dollar expenditures on advertising, prices, and so on. These kinds of variables tend to have well-defined meanings and measurements. However, a number of other marketing variables, such as attitudes about products, intentions to purchase, and feelings of cognitive dissonance, are unobservable in any direct way. For such psychological variables, we seek observable correlates of behavior through instruments of measurement.

Unobservable variables may play important roles in certain sales response models. For example, advertising often affects future demand for a product as well as present demand. Advertising can be viewed as an investment in advertising capital. We call this advertising capital goodwill. Goodwill is an unobservable. Note that demand is also an unobservable variable—what we observe are sales.

There are two fundamental solutions to the problem of unobservable variables. First, they can be omitted from the analysis. A study on the relation between advertising and sales, for example, could omit the intermediate and unobservable levels of the "hierarchy of effects" and focus simply on the observable variables sales and advertising. The second solution would be to devise instruments to measure the unobservable variables, either directly or as a function of observable variables. Which solution is chosen depends on the purpose of the research.

The impact of advertising spending is mediated by advertising quality. Buzzell (1964b) and Buzzell, Kolin, and Murphy (1965) explained market share by Schwerin Research Corporation pre-, post-, and norm theater test scores as well as by advertising expenditures. Buzzell (p. 31) concluded that "advertising message quality is more important than the level of advertising expenditure." Eastlack and Rao (1986, p. 259), in an investigation of a new creative approach to advertising "V-8" Cocktail Vegetable Juice, similarly concluded that "the creative component of advertising has been found to be far more important than the actual spending rates or patterns."

Sales response functions probably should be driven by quality-adjusted advertising spending, an unobservable variable, rather than simply by advertising expenditures, an observable variable. Parsons and Schultz (1976, p. 85) suggested that survey data on awareness or attitude might be used to define a qualitative adjustment factor, θ_t, such that

$$A_{Q',t} = \theta_t A_t,\qquad(2.4)$$

where $A_{Q',t}$ is the unobservable quality-adjusted advertising spending at time t.

Arnold et al. (1987) formally treated the intuitive notion of Parsons and Schultz. They posited that the quality adjustment factor is a function of quality attributes of the copy:

$$\theta_t = g(q_{1t},\ldots,q_{kt},\ldots,q_{Kt}),\qquad(2.5)$$

where q_{kt} is the kth quality attribute.[3] Technically, this is an example of systematic parameter variation, which we discuss later in this chapter. A questionnaire was developed to capture two broad dimensions of advertising quality. One dimension was the extent to which advertising strategies and production values were met by the commercial, and the other dimension was the performance of each commercial against the target audience. Their results (p. 111) indicated that "the sales affect of a 1% change in the advertising quality attribute 'creative device' rating is 20 times as large as that of a 1% increase in advertising spending." Little (1975a, p. 637) has recommended that qualitative adjustment in advertising spending should take into account media efficiency as well as copy effectiveness.

Another example of devising a way to measure an unobservable variable is Winer's (1986) discussion of reference price. In making a purchase, a customer often compares an actual market price with the price he or she anticipated paying (the reference price). A marked difference between the two is sometimes called sticker shock. Winer discussed two processes for price formation. In the *extrapolative expectations hypothesis,* perception of the current price of a brand is formed by the most recently observed price and trend. In the *rational expectations hypothesis,* perception of the current price is determined by the customer's model of how management sets prices. Under either hypothesis, reference prices are expressed in terms of observables.

Relations among Variables

A firm may simply be interested in how its advertising and prices effect its sales; this firm needs to know about a single relation—its sales response function. Its sales, the dependent variable, are determined by a set of independent variables, advertising and price. The set of independent variables might be expanded to include environmental variables as well as other decision variables of the firm. The environmental variables might represent competitors' actions and autonomous macroeconomic variables.

Decomposition of the Sales Response Function

Sometimes a firm might find it advantageous to decompose its sales response function into two relations. One relation would describe how various factors influence industry sales; the second, how various factors, which may or may not include some or all of those factors affecting industry sales, influence the firm's market share.

Many firms evaluate their relative success in terms of selective demand position or market share. Two reasons for this are suggested: (1) trends in primary demand are frequently out of the control of the firm and affect the industry as a whole (cf. Kleinbaum 1988); and (2) marketing instruments, in particular advertising, may have minimal impact on total industry sales; instead, the setting of managerial decision variables serves to allocate this total amount among the competing firms.

In many cases, however, a single relation between a firm's sales, its own actions, and environmental variables will be preferred. Decomposition, like many design alternatives in response modeling, depends on the nature of the response problem.

Models of Market Mechanisms

Multiple relations also arise when a firm wants to describe a more complete model of a market mechanism.[4] In such a model, not only will there be a sales response function but there also may be competitive reaction functions, vertical market structures, cost functions, and other behavioral relations. A market mechanism specifies the connections among these relations as well as among individual variables.

In many situations, a firm must be able to forecast the levels for competitors' marketing instruments. If competitors make their decisions without regard to the firm's actions, then time series analysis (chapter 4) might be used to project future values for their marketing activities. If competitors react to the firm's actions, then reaction functions (chapter 6) should be taken into account. If both the firm and its competitors are simultaneously trying to optimize their results in light of their opponents' likely behaviors, then game theory (chapter 8) might be appropriate.

Most firms do not sell directly to their customers. Usually one or more intermediaries exist in a channel of distribution. For example, a channel for a consumer packaged good might look like this:

$$\text{factory} \xrightarrow[\text{shipments}]{} \text{chain/distributor} \xrightarrow[\text{withdrawals}]{} \text{retail} \xrightarrow[\text{sales}]{} \text{customer}$$
$$\text{warehouse} \qquad\qquad \text{store}$$

Each channel member has its own sales response function. For example, Blattberg and Levin (1987) studied the effectiveness and profitability of trade promotions using a market mechanism containing two relations—one for shipments and another for consumer sales. Factory shipments will respond to trade promotions. Shipments will increase sharply during the interval when an allowance is given on product purchases. Shipments will fall markedly after the promotion is over. A similar pattern occurs just before a major price increase as the trade stocks up on a product at the existing price. Peaks and valleys in retail sales occur in response to the presence or absence of temporary sales promotions such as price features, special displays, and coupons. Findley and Little (1980) noted that dynamics of warehouse withdrawals tend to be smoother than factory shipments and retail sales. They argued that this smoothing is mainly due to the buffer effect of retail inventories. We formally discuss lead and lag effects later in this chapter.

In many applications, a product's cost per unit, exclusive of marketing costs, is assumed to be constant. This is a satisfactory approximation in most circumstances. However, there are times when more attention should be given to the cost function. For instance, price promotions typically cause both consumer sales and factory shipments to be uneven. Irregular factory shipments often mean higher production or inventory costs. Another exception occurs in the case of technological innovations, including consumer durables. For these products, total unit costs usually decline as experience with producing a product is gained (Hall and Howell 1985). Total unit costs also tend to decline in response to competitive entry. As new brands enter a market, the resultant growth of industry output forces price downward, and consequently, costs must be reduced if profitability is to be maintained (Devinney 1987).

Functional Forms

A relation is made concrete by specifying its functional form. A functional form should exhibit the same properties as the relation is known to possess. Possible properties of a sales response function include what happens to sales when marketing effort is zero or very large; rate of change in sales as marketing activity increases, e.g., diminishing returns to scale; threshold effects like a minimum advertising investment; parameter variation, such as might occur over different market segments; and asymmetric response, such as a different response by competitors to a decrease or increase in price. Reaction functions, since they usually represent decision rules, may be less complex.

Shape of a Reaction Function

The shape of a reaction function is usually fairly simple. In most cases, a firm will respond either to an absolute change or to a relative change in a competitor's marketing instrument. For example, a firm might price its brand at $120 and a competitor its brand at $100. For simplicity, suppose that the firm matches competitive action. If this competitor cuts its price to $90, the firm would reduce its price to $110 ($120 + [$90 − $100]), if it reacts to absolute changes in competitive price levels, or to $108 ($120 + {[$90 − $100]/$100} × $120), if it reacts to relative changes.

A simple absolute change reaction involving a marketing instrument X is

$$dX_{us} = \beta_1 \, dX_{them}, \tag{2.6}$$

which yields the linear reaction function

$$X_{us} = \beta_0 + \beta_1 X_{them}. \tag{2.7}$$

A simple relative change reaction is

$$\frac{dX_{us}}{X_{us}} = \beta_1 \left(\frac{dX_{them}}{X_{them}} \right), \tag{2.8}$$

which yields a reaction function that is linear in logarithms

$$\ln(X_{us}) = \beta_0 + \beta_1 \ln(X_{them}). \tag{2.9}$$

This model (2.9) is, in turn, equivalent to

$$X_{us} = e^{\beta_0} X_{them}^{\beta_1}, \tag{2.10}$$

which is a nonlinear model. This power function also happens to be the most common model for a sales response function, for reasons we shall see in the next section.

Shape of a Sales Response Function

The shape of sales response to a particular marketing instrument, holding the other factors affecting sales constant, is generally concave. In a few instances, it may be convex or S-shaped.

Diminishing Returns to Scale.   When sales always increase with increases in marketing effort, but each additional unit of marketing effort brings less in incremental sales than the previous unit did, a sales response curve is said to exhibit diminishing returns to scale.

One concave sales response function is the *semilogarithmic model*:

$$Q = \beta_0 \ln X. \tag{2.11}$$

Constant *absolute* increments in sales require constant *percentage* increases in marketing effort.[5] Wildt (1977) and Lambin (1969) used the semilog model of sales response to advertising for branded consumer products. Simon (1982) elaborated upon this model in his study of wearout and pulsation.

Another functional form that meets this requirement, provided that $0 < \beta_1 < 1$, is the *power model*:

$$Q = e^{\beta_0} X^{\beta_1}. \tag{2.12}$$

This model has the attractive property that the power coefficient of the marketing instrument can be directly interpreted as that instrument's elasticity.[6] The model can be extended to take into account all the *interactions* among marketing decision variables. The most general version of this model for three marketing instruments is

$$Q = e^{\beta_0} + e^{\beta_{01}} X_1^{\beta_1} + e^{\beta_{02}} X_2^{\beta_2} + e^{\beta_{03}} X_3^{\beta_3}$$
$$+ e^{\beta_{12}} X_1^{\beta_3} X_2^{\beta_4} + e^{\beta_{13}} X_1^{\beta_5} X_3^{\beta_6} + e^{\beta_{23}} X_2^{\beta_7} X_3^{\beta_8} + e^{\beta_{123}} X_1^{\beta_9} X_2^{\beta_{10}} X_3^{\beta_{11}}. \tag{2.13}$$

The full interaction model can quickly become unwieldy when all the possible interactions among marketing decision variables are taken into account. Because of small sample sizes or estimation problems, this model is usually simplified by having some of the parameters equal each other and often equal 0 or 1 as well. Prasad and Ring (1976), for example, looked at four main effects plus only the six pairwise interactions. The most popular sales response function retains only the highest-order interaction, i.e.,

$$Q = e^{\beta_0} X_1^{\beta_1} X_2^{\beta_2} \dots X_J^{\beta_J}. \tag{2.14}$$

This model is known as the *multiplicative model*. It maintains the property of (2.12), that the power parameters can be interpreted directly as elasticities. Hanssens and Levien (1983) specified multiplicative functional forms for the relations in their econometric model of recruitment marketing in the U.S. Navy.

When there is only a single instrument, then (2.13) reduces to only its first two terms. If, in addition, β_1 lies between 0 and 1, the resultant model is called the *fractional-root model*. A special case of the fractional-root model is the *square-root model*, in which $\beta_1 = \frac{1}{2}$. Another special case is the *power model* (2.12), for which β_0 in (2.13) equals minus infinity and consequently the additive constant disappears.

Increasing Returns to Scale. Although sales response to most marketing variables exhibits diminishing returns to scale, sales response to decreases in price may exhibit increasing returns to scale. One functional form that can be used is the *exponential model*:

$$Q = Q^o e^{-\beta_0 X}, \beta_0 > 0, \tag{2.15}$$

where Q^o is saturation sales. When price becomes large, sales tend to zero. Cowling and Cubbin (1971) used this functional form to explain the United Kingdom market for cars in terms of quality-adjusted price.

S-Shaped Response. Sometimes a response function might be S-shaped.[7] Initially, sales may exhibit increasing returns to scale and then diminishing returns to higher levels of marketing effort. A functional form that meets this requirement is the *log-reciprocal model*:

$$Q = \exp\left(\beta_0 - \frac{\beta_1}{X} \right), \qquad \beta_0 > 0, \tag{2.16}$$

or

$$\ln Q = \beta_0 - \frac{\beta_1}{X}. \tag{2.17}$$

Bemmaor (1984) considered this model in his study of the advertising threshold effect. The inflection point, the point at which the change from increasing to decreasing marginal returns occurs, is $X = \beta_1/2$. Even though the response function is S-shaped, the elasticity of the marketing instrument decreases as

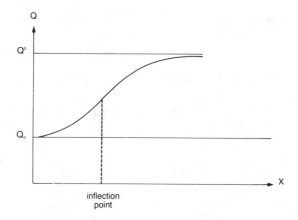

Figure 2–2. S-Shaped Response Function with Minimum and Maximum Sales.

efforts increase.[8] Other S-shaped response functions are discussed next in the context of minimum and maximum sales potential.

Minimum and Maximum Sales Potential. Even when marketing effort is zero, a firm might still have sales due to loyal buyers, captive buyers, or impulse buyers. Neither functional form (2.12) nor (2.16) allows for sales when marketing effort is zero. These functional forms can be modified by adding a positive constant, say K, to the functional form, as was done in (2.13), where $K = e^{\beta_0}$. Metwally (1980) added a positive constant to (2.16). The resulting relation is intrinsically nonlinear. This relation is shown in figure 2–2. Alternatively, a positive constant could be added to each marketing instrument. Sales when marketing effort is zero, Q_0, would be given by

$$Q_o = e^{\beta_0} K^{\beta_1} \quad \text{and} \quad Q_o = e^{\beta_0 - \beta_1 / K}$$

respectively, for (2.12) and (2.16). For convenience, K is often specified as 1.

Saturation means that no matter how much marketing effort is expended, there is a finite achievable upper limit to the sales. Buyers become insensitive to the maketing stimulus or find themselves purchasing at their capacities or capabilities. The power model (2.12) does not not have a finite upper limit, but the S-shaped model (2.16) does. As $X \to \infty$, $Q \to \exp(\beta_0)$.

The saturation level, Q^o, is explicitly represented in the *modified exponential model*:

$$Q = Q^o(1 - e^{-\beta X}). \tag{2.18}$$

This functional form was used by Buzzell (1964a) in his analysis of the optimal number of salespeople, by Shakun (1965) for the study of advertising expenditures in coupled markets, by Holthausen and Assmus (1982) in a probe of advertising budget allocation across territories, and by Rangan (1987) in an investigation of the effects of channel effort.

A *logistic model* can also depict an S-shaped function while taking into account market saturation. One version of the logistic function is

$$Q = \frac{Q^o}{1 + \exp\left[-\left(\beta_0 + \sum_{j=1}^{J} \beta_j X_j\right)\right]} \tag{2.19}$$

This relation can be rewritten as

$$\ln\left(\frac{Q}{Q^o - Q}\right) = \beta_0 + \sum_{j=1}^{J} \beta_j X_j. \tag{2.20}$$

This S-shaped curve is symmetric around the inflection point, $Q = Q^o/2$.

A nonsymmetric S-shaped curve may be more appropriate in many marketing applications. One such logistic function would be

$$\ln\left(\frac{Q - Q_o}{Q^o - Q}\right) = \ln \beta_0 + \sum_{j=1}^{J} \beta_j \ln X_j, \tag{2.21}$$

where Q_o is the intercept ($0 \le Q_o \le Q^o$). The independent variables are assumed to be positive. The dependent variable Q may vary between a lower limit Q_o and the saturation level Q^o.

The saturation level Q^o must be specified a priori in both the log-linear model (2.20) and the double-log model (2.21). In the latter model, the intercept must also be specified. When the dependent variable is a proportion such as market share, the most common assumption is that $Q^o = 1$ and $Q_o = 0$. Johansson (1973) used survey data to estimate the intercept and the saturation level for a new women's hair spray. His estimate of the intercept was the proportion of repeaters, and his estimate of the saturation level was the trial proportion.

When a priori information is not available, we must use a functional form that allows the intercept and saturation level to be estimated. One such functional form was used by Little (1970) in his ADBUG model:

$$Q = \beta_0 + (\beta_1 - \beta_0)\frac{X^{\beta_2}}{\beta_3^{\beta_2} + X^{\beta_2}}, \tag{2.22}$$

where

$$\beta_0 = \text{intercept},$$

$$\beta_1 = \text{saturation level},$$

$$\beta_2, \beta_3 = \text{shape parameters}.$$

An additional phenomenon has been theorized, *supersaturation*. Supersaturation results when too much marketing effort causes a negative response; for example, a buyer might feel that an excessive number of visits by a salesperson is intolerable. The simplest functional form that represents this effect is the quadratic:

$$Q = \beta_0 + \beta_1 X - \beta_2 X^2. \tag{2.23}$$

The value of Q starts declining for values of $X > \beta_1/2\beta_2$.

Threshold. A threshold occurs when some positive amount of marketing effort is necessary before any sales impact can be detected. The expenditure of only one thousand dollars in a highly competitive mass market is unlikely to show a sales effect. If the threshold marketing effort is X_o, we can use the functional form of our choice with X, marketing effort, replaced by $(X - X_o)$.

The fact that the quantity sold must be non-negative (ignoring the possibility that returned product exceeds product sales) implies that some functional forms have thresholds built into them. For example, the saturation model with decreasing returns,

$$Q = \beta_0 - \beta_1 X^{-\beta_2}, \tag{2.24}$$

is only valid if all the observations on X are greater than, or equal to, $(\beta_1/\beta_0)^{1/\beta_2}$. This restriction must be checked after the model is estimated. A special case of (2.24) is the *reciprocal model*, in which $\beta_2 = 1$. Ward (1975) applied a reciprocal model to the processed-grapefruit industry.

Interaction. We have already discussed one way to model marketing mix interactions; i.e., (2.14). Perhaps a more general way is the *transcendental logarithmic (translog) model*. The translog model for three marketing instruments is

$$\ln Q = \beta_0 + \beta_1 \ln X_1 + \beta_2 \ln X_2 + \beta_3 \ln X_3$$
$$+ \beta_{12} \ln X_1 \ln X_2 + \beta_{13} \ln X_1 \ln X_3 + \beta_{23} \ln X_2 \ln X_3$$
$$+ \beta_{11} (\ln X_1)^2 + \beta_{22} (\ln X_2)^2 + \beta_{33} (\ln X_3)^2. \tag{2.25}$$

The translog functional form is a quadratic approximation to any continuous function. The elasticities of the marketing instruments vary with changes in the entire marketing mix. For example, the elasticity of X_1 in (2.25) is

$$\varepsilon_{Q,X_1} = \beta_1 + \beta_{12} \ln X_2 + \beta_{13} \ln X_3 + 2\beta_{11} \ln X_1. \tag{2.26}$$

A constant elasticity model is a special case in which $\beta_{12} = \beta_{13} = \beta_{23} = 0$. Jagpal, Sudit, and Vinod (1982) estimated a translog model for Lydia Pinkham sales and advertising.

Special cases of the translog model include the multiplicative nonhomogeneous model and the multiplicative model. The *multiplicative nonhomogeneous model* is defined by letting $\beta_{11} = \beta_{22} = \beta_{33} = 0$ in (2.25):

$$\ln Q = \beta_0 + \beta_1 \ln X_1 + \beta_2 \ln X_2 + \beta_3 \ln X_3$$
$$+ \beta_{12} \ln X_1 \ln X_2 + \beta_{13} \ln X_1 \ln X_3 + \beta_{23} \ln X_2 \ln X_3. \quad (2.27)$$

Jagpal, Sudit, and Vinod (1979) illustrated this model with Palda's (1964) Lydia Pinkham data. Jagpal (1981) also used it in his investigation of cross-product media advertising affects for a commercial bank. The *multiplicative model* is obtained by setting $\beta_{12} = \beta_{13} = \beta_{23} = 0$ in the multiplicative non-homogeneous model:

$$\ln Q = \beta_0 + \beta_1 \ln X_1 + \beta_2 \ln X_2 + \beta_3 \ln X_3. \quad (2.28)$$

Economists are familiar with this functional form as the Cobb-Douglas production function (Zellner, Kmenta, and Dréze 1966).

Asymmetry in Response. The magnitude of sales response to a change in a marketing instrument might be different, depending on whether the change is upward or downward. The effect is beyond any that might be explained by the nonlinearity of the sales response function. Sales might rise quickly under increased advertising but stay the same or decline slowly when the advertising is removed. This phenomenon, termed *hysteresis* by Little (1979a), is shown in figure 2–3.

Parsons (1976) gave this explanation of the phenomenon: higher advertising expenditures create more customers through greater reach as well as greater frequency. Under the customer holdover paradigm (discussed later in this chapter), these new customers subsequently repurchase the product. Thus, if advertising is cut back, sales will fall by less than would be the case in the absence of this carryover effect.

Sales response to price may also be asymmetric because of habit formation. The sales response function will be kinked. A price rise would be less elastic than a price fall. Scitovsky (1978) calls this *addiction asymmetry*.

Asymmetry in response is captured by *rachet models*. There are two types of rachet models. The first is saw-toothed in appearance, as shown in figure 2–4a. The sales response function is kinked at the prevailing level of a marketing instrument, irrespective of past changes in the instrument. Segments of the adjustment path for increases in level are parallel; segments for decreases are also parallel to each other. The second resembles a bird's footprint in appearance, as shown in figure 2–4b. Purchasing habits that were developed by use of a product under a condition of record-breaking marketing activity will not be broken easily if marketing effort recedes.

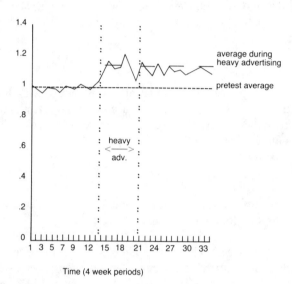

Figure 2–3. Fast Learning, Slow Forgetting. *Source*: Little (1979a, p. 633).

There are various formulations of a rachet model. We consider only linear models. Sales could be a function of cumulative increases and cumulative decreases in marketing activity:

$$Q_t = \beta_0 + \beta_1 XI_t + \beta_2 XD_t, \qquad \beta_1 > \beta_2, \qquad (2.29a)$$

where XI_t (XD_t) represents the sum of all period-to-period increases (decreases) in a marketing instrument. Using the decomposition $X_t = X_0 + XI_t + XD_t$, suggested by Wolffram (1971), yields

$$Q_t = (\beta_0 - \beta_2 X_0) + (\beta_1 - \beta_2)XI_t + \beta_2 X_t. \qquad (2.29b)$$

This relation could be expressed in terms of XD_t instead of XI_t. Young (1983) used this model in a study of the response of cigarette sales to price changes.

Formulation of the second type of rachet model involves creating a record marketing effort variable equal to $\max(X_i)$, $i = 1, \dots, t$ (or $\min(X_i)$ in the case of price):

$$Q_t = \beta_0 + \beta_1 X_t + \beta_2 [\max(X_i)]. \qquad (2.30)$$

This approach was used by Parsons (1976) in his rachet model of advertising carryover effects and by Young (1983) as an alternative model in his cigarette sales-price investigation.

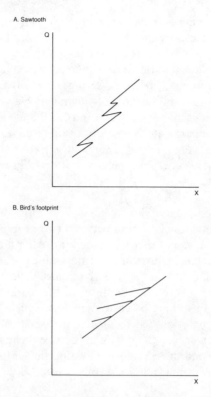

Figure 2–4. Alternative Forms of a Rachet Model.

A related model displaying asymmetry is

$$Q_t = \beta_0 + \beta_1 X_t + \beta_2 \max(0, \Delta X), \qquad (2.31)$$

where $\Delta X = X_t - X_{t-1}$. (Again, for price, the min operator would replace the max operator.) Simon's (1982) ADPULS model is in the spirit of this formulation. Just considering increases in marketing effort, the same magnitude of the marketing instrument X_t can have different responses, depending on its previous value, X_{t-1}. This would not seem to be a very desirable property, but Simon (p. 355) argued that this property is necessary when trying to reproduce the advertising wearout phenomenon correctly. Asymmetric models may be considered a special case of coefficient variation.

Coefficient Variation. The effectiveness of each controllable marketing instrument is frequently treated as having the same value over time. However, market response to managerial decision variables might change because of the impact of marketing actions by either a company or its competitors or because of shifts in the environment.

If structural changes occur at known points in time, the changes in the coefficients of the relevant variables can be represented by dummy variables. Unfortunately the timing of structural changes is rarely known.

The parameters in a response function might vary between each time period rather than only between a few time periods. If the parameters follow some random process, the parameter variation is said to be *stochastic*. If the parameters themselves are functions of observable variables, the parameter variation is said to be *systematic*. Parameter variation is discussed in more detail later in this chapter.

Error Structure.   Our discussion of functional forms has emphasized the specification of a functional relation between two or more variables. Such a functional relation does not explain everything. After all, it is only a model incorporating the salient features of some marketing phenomenon. Moreover, only the deterministic part of the underlying mechanism has been specified. There may be some inherent randomness in the marketplace; for instance, unpredictable variety seeking by customers. Consequently, any specification of a relation must be expanded to include a *random disturbance term* that captures *equation error*, i.e., the difference between actual observations of a dependent variable and those predicted by a particular functional relation.

The equation for a single relation can be written as

$$y = f(X, U; \beta), \tag{2.32}$$

where

y = column vector of n observations on single endogenous variable,

$X = n \times k$ matrix of n observations on k predetermined variables,

U = column vector of n observations on disturbances,

β = column vector of k (unknown population) parameters.

The random disturbances are realizations of a stationary probability distribution:[9]

$$U \sim f(\theta). \tag{2.33}$$

Many distribution functions can be characterized by their first two moments, that is, $\theta = (\mu, \sigma^2)$.

In situations where the data represent observations from a combination of a cross-section and a time series, the disturbance term is sometimes partitioned into three components:

$$U_{it} = \mu_i + \tau_t + \nu_{it}. \tag{2.34}$$

The components are the individual or cross-section effect, μ_i, the temporal effect, τ_t, and the remaining effects, which vary over both individuals and time periods, ν_{it}. Parsons (1974) and Moriarty (1975) used variants of this variance components formulation. Parsons studied the advertising, retail availability, and sales of new brands of ready-to-eat cereals. Moriarty studied regional fluctuations in the effectiveness of marketing decision variables for a single brand.

When a single equation is the ith equation in a larger system, it is often written as

$$f(y_i, Y_i, X_i; \alpha_i) = U_i \tag{2.35}$$

and the covariance matrix among disturbances in *different* equations is Σ, the contemporaneous covariance matrix.

Specification of Market Share Models

When the dependent variable in a response function is market share, an additional complication is introduced. A desirable property of any market share model is that it be *logically consistent* (McGuire et al. 1968; Naert and Bultez 1973; McGuire and Weiss 1976; Bultez 1978; Koehler and Wildt 1981). This means that the model produces an estimate of a brand's market share that lies between 0 and 1 when market share is expressed as a fraction. Furthermore, the sum of these estimated market shares for all brands in any given period must equal 1. Violations of the range or sum constraints expose the internal inconsistencies of a model.

A model that must be logically consistent is one based upon the definition of market share.

$$MS_i = \frac{Q_i}{\sum\limits_{j=1}^{N} Q_j} = \frac{f_i(X, U_i; \beta_i)}{\sum\limits_{j=1}^{N} f_j(X, U_j; \beta_j)}. \tag{2.36}$$

This model has been called an *attraction model* (Bell, Keeney, and Little 1975). Monahan (1987) used this model in a theoretical study of profit-maximizing competitive resource allocations in a duopoly. By including competitors' marketing instruments in the set of explanatory variables X for each sales response function, *cross-competitive* (market share) *effects* can be modeled. When the multiplicative form (2.14) is used for each sales response function, the model (2.36) is known as the *MCI* (Multiplicative Competition Interaction) *model* (Nakanishi and Cooper 1974, 1982). The MCI model also assumes that all brands have the same coefficients ($\beta_{ik} = \beta_{jk} = \beta_k$ for all i, j). In effect, a prototype brand rather than a specific brand is being estimated.[10] Karnani (1985) has studied the strategic implications of such a model. He found that at equilibrium, each active competitor must have a market share above a certain minimum threshold value. This value is a function of both the cost structure of the firms and the demand structure of the market. The assumption that each firm has the same coefficient has been relaxed in the *differential-effects MCI model* ($\beta_{ik} \neq \beta_{jk}$ for $i \neq j$):

$$MS_{ti} = \frac{\beta_{0i} \prod_{k=1}^{K} X_{tik}^{\beta_{ik}} U_{ti}}{\sum_{j=1}^{N} \beta_{0j} \prod_{k=1}^{K} X_{tjk}^{\beta_{jk}} U_{tj}}, \tag{2.37}$$

where N is the number of brands in a market, and K is the number of explanatory variables needed for all the sales response functions. Carpenter et al. (1984) point out that differential effects can arise for four reasons: (1) differences in marketing effectiveness, (2) differences in competitive vulnerability, i.e., relative positions in the market structure, (3) differences in marketing objectives, and (4) differences in timing of marketing efforts. The differential-effects MCI model was used by Urban (1969) in studying interdependencies among brands in a firm's product line, by Bultez and Naert (1975) in investigating competitive marketing activities in the market for an inexpensive European consumer durable, and by Carpenter et al. (1988) in exploring an Australian household-product market.

Specification Issues in Dynamic Models

Marketing for a firm rarely takes place in a static environment. Customers and competitors anticipate or react to the firm's actions. Their adjustment processes are one basis for believing market mechanisms should be dynamic. We first discuss specification issues in dynamic models, then examine in some detail discrete models of carryover. Substantive results are covered in chapter 7.

The specification of a dynamic model begins with the choice of the appropriate time measure, discrete or continuous. Then any anticipation (lead) or carryover (lag) effects must be identified.

Continuous-Time Versus Discrete-Time Models.   The main issue in the specification of a dynamic model is whether to formulate a continuous-time model using differential equations, a discrete-time model using difference equations, or a mixed model using differential-difference equations. Before discussing this issue, it is necessary to make a distinction between instantaneous (stock) variables and flow variables.

An *instantaneous variable* is a variable that is measurable at a point in time. Prices, distribution coverage, and interest rates are examples of instantaneous variables in marketing. A *flow variable* is a variable that is not measurable at a point in time. Unit sales and advertising expenditures are examples of flow variables in marketing. The rate of change in an instantaneous variable is also treated as a flow variable. If τ is the length of an observation period, an observation on a flow variable at time t corresponds to the integral

$$X_t = \frac{1}{\tau} \int_{t-\tau}^{t} X(\theta) d\theta. \tag{2.38}$$

If X were an instantaneous variable, this integral would not be observable.

The primary advantage of a continuous-time model is that *its estimated parameters are independent of the observation period*. This does not hold for a discrete-time model. A discrete-time model estimated on weekly data will be different from one estimated on annual data. This important point is addressed in chapter 7.

The two primary advantages of a discrete-time model are that it can capture discontinuous phenomena and that most econometric techniques, such as those that discussed in chapter 3, were developed from estimating it. Since most models to date have been discrete-time models, we begin by discussing them.

Leads and Lags. Current expenditures on marketing instruments usually do not have their full impact on sales in the same accounting period. Moreover, their impact on sales may extend well into the future. The influence of current marketing expenditures on sales in future periods is called the *carryover effect*. It is possible to extend marketing dynamics to include *anticipations* as well as carryover. Leads occur when customers or competitors anticipate a marketing action and adjust their behavior even before the action takes place. Therefore, sales may react to marketing efforts in the future.

Two forms of carryover effects have been identified by Kotler (1971). The *delayed response effect* arises when there is an interval between making the marketing expenditure and realizing the associated sale. For instance, a salesperson may wait some time between making an initial call and consummating the deal. The *customer holdover effect* arises because the marketing expenditure may create a new customer who not only will make an initial purchase but also will repurchase in future periods. Thus, the current marketing effect must receive some credit for these subsequent sales. Some credit should also be given to purchase experience reinforcement (Givon and Horsky 1986), but we postpone discussion of this refinement until chapter 7.

Sales may not react fully and immediately to changes in marketing inputs but may do so in a more gradual manner. Advertising can create new customers; however, the timing of the first purchases by these new customers will vary according to each buyer's shopping and usage behavior. Moreover, repeat purchases will also depend on usage rates.

In order to assess properly the effectiveness of marketing instruments, the fraction of total sales in the current period and each succeeding period that are attributable to the current marketing effort must be measured. The duration of the carryover effect induced by this effort must also be determined.

Discrete-Time Models of Carryover.   Sales, Q_t, may respond to marketing expenditures with lag k. A linear model of this relation might be

$$Q_t = \beta_0 + \beta_{k+1} X_{t-k}. \tag{2.39}$$

This model represents a *simple* lag of the exogenous variable (X_t). The effect of a marketing expenditure in period $t - k$ occurs only, and completely, within period t. Often, the effect of a marketing variable is *distributed* over several time periods. Consequently, sales in any period are a function of the current and previous marketing expenditures:

$$Q_t = \beta_0 + \sum_{k=0}^{\infty} \beta_{k+1} X_{t-k}, \tag{2.40}$$

where

$$\sum_{k=0}^{\infty} \beta_{k+1} = \text{constant} = \beta < \infty. \tag{2.41}$$

This restriction (2.41) ensures that even if a finite change in the level of marketing expenditures persists indefinitely, it will cause only a finite change in sales.

The general distributed lag model cannot be estimated, because it contains an infinite number of parameters. Even if the maximum lag is known a priori to be finite, so that

$$Q_t = \beta_0 + \sum_{k=0}^{T} \beta_{k+1} X_{t-k}, \tag{2.42}$$

the exact value of the maximum lag, T, is rarely known. In any case, the number of parameters to be estimated still may be large and the exogenous variables highly collinear. Additional assumptions usually must be imposed to obtain estimates.

The Lag Structure as a Set of Probabilities. A very useful assumption, and one that is usually plausible in marketing situations, is that the coefficients of the marketing decision variable all have the same sign. The general distributed lag can now be written as

$$Q_t = \beta_0 + \beta \sum_{k=0}^{\infty} \omega_k X_{t-k}, \tag{2.43}$$

where

$$\omega \geq 0 \quad \text{and} \quad \sum_{k=0}^{\infty} \omega_k = 1. \tag{2.44}$$

The sequence of omegas (ω's) describes the shape of the lag over time. More importantly, the omegas can be regarded as probabilities of a discrete-time distribution.

This probability formulation permits easy interpretation of some of the properties of the empirical response function. Properties like the average lag between making a marketing expenditure and obtaining a sales response, or the degree to which the impact is concentrated in an interval of short duration or diffused over an extended period, can be calculated using the moments of the probability distribution.

The *geometric distributed lag model* is the one most commonly used in marketing. The maximum impact of marketing expenditures on sales is registered instantaneously. Then the influence declines geometrically to zero; that is, if a past expenditure has an impact in a particular period, its impact in subsequent periods will only be a constant fraction of that impact. This constant fraction is called the *retention rate*. This approach was popularized in marketing by Palda (1964) in his attempt to measure the cumulative effects of advertising.

If the retention rate is λ, the geometric distribution gives

$$\omega_k = (1 - \lambda)\lambda^k, \qquad k = 0, 1, 2, \ldots \tag{2.45}$$

where $0 < \lambda < 1$. Thus, the specification of the sales response function becomes

$$Q_t = \beta_0 + \beta(1 - \lambda) \sum_{k=0}^{\infty} \lambda^k X_{t-k}. \tag{2.46}$$

This relation is nonlinear in the parameter λ. In the case of more than one independent variable, the same rate of decline could apply to different variables. This assumption was made by Frank and Messy (1967) and Montgomery and Silk (1972). However, it is more probable that different rates of decline apply to different variables. Peles (1971a) found that advertising expenditures by a firm and advertising expenditures by competitors exhibited different carryover effects on the firm's sales of beer.

The monotonically decreasing pattern of coefficients in the geometric lag structure may be inappropriate in some marketing situations. The effect of marketing expenditures may be small initially, increase to a peak, and then decline. The geometric lag can be modified so that the geometric decline does not start immediately in the first period but rather starts at the jth period. The modification can be represented by

$$Q_t = \beta_0 + (1 - \lambda) \sum_{k=0}^{j-2} \beta_{k+1} X_{t-k} + \beta_j (1 - \lambda) \sum_{k=j}^{\infty} \lambda^{k-j} X_{t-k+1}. \qquad (2.47)$$

Bass and Clarke (1972), Lambin (1972b), and Montgomery and Silk (1972) have incorporated this extension into their models. Alternatively, the negative binomial distribution, which is a flexible two-parameter distribution, can represent such an effect:

$$\omega = \frac{(r + k - 1)!}{(r - 1)!k!} (1 - \lambda)^r \lambda^k, \qquad k = 0, 1, 2, \ldots \qquad (2.48)$$

where $0 < \lambda < 1$, and r is a positive integer. For $r = 1$, the negative binomial reduces to the geometric distribution.

Rational Lag Structures. Advanced work in dynamics is facilitated by the use of the lag or delay operator. The lag operator L is the transformation

$$LX_t = X_{t-1} \qquad (2.49a)$$

and it can be applied k successive times, so that

$$L^k X_t = X_{t-k}. \qquad (2.49b)$$

Then the general rational lag structure can be written as

$$B(L)Q_t = B(L)\beta_0 + A(L)X_t, \quad \text{or} \quad Q = \beta_0 + \frac{A(L)}{B(L)} X_t, \qquad (2.50)$$

where

$$A(L) = \sum_{i=0}^{I} a_i L^i, \qquad B(L) = \sum_{j=0}^{J} b_j L^j, \qquad b_0 = 1.$$

This formulation permits us to extend the geometric lag function to higher-order lag functions.

The finite lag structure and the negative binomial lag function are special cases of the general rational lag. In the former, the correspondence is

$$B(L) = I, \qquad (2.51)$$

where I is an operator that, when applied to an element, yields that element; and in the latter

FUNCTION	EXPLANATION	BEHAVIOR
1 STEADY STATE	Simple effect	
2 POSITIVE LAG	Distributed lag	
3 NEGATIVE LAG	Stocking	
4 POSITIVE LEAD	Anticipation	
5 NEGATIVE LEAD	Regret reduction	
6 NEGATIVE LEAD & LAG	Opportunistic	

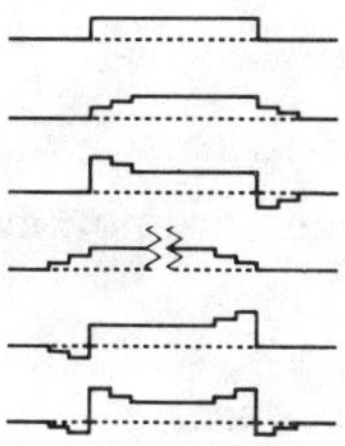

Figure 2–5. A Taxonomy of Dynamic Models. *Source*: Doyle and Saunders (1985, p. 57).

$$A(L) = \beta(1 - \lambda)^r \quad \text{and} \quad B(L) = (1 - \lambda L)^r. \qquad (2.52)$$

Setting $r = 1$ yields the geometric distributed lag function.

Recent advances in time series analysis have made the rational lag structure model much easier to use. We argue in chapter 4 that the statistical version of this model, *the transfer function*, is a sufficiently general model to accommodate the dynamic aspects of markets and marketing efforts. Working with transfer functions offers the distinct advantage that the data can be used to specify the dynamic structure of a market. Since different markets can have very different dynamic patterns, this approach offers considerable opportunity for marketing planning, forecasting, and theory testing.

A Taxonomy of Leads and Lags. An interesting catalog of lead/lag effects (figure 2–5) has been provided by Doyle and Saunders (1985). By distinguishing between a steady state and a transient component of the effect of marketing on sales, they propose the following reduced forms for marketing dynamics.

Case 1. Steady State.

$$Q_t = \beta_0 + \beta_1 X_t, \qquad (2.53a)$$

a pure static model of sales versus marketing effort.

Case 2. Positive Lag.

$$Q_t = \beta_0 + \beta_1 X_t + \sum_{k=1}^{T} \beta_{-k} X_{t-k}, \qquad (2.53b)$$

the typical distributed lag model introduced earlier.

Case 3. Negative Lag.

$$Q_t = \beta_0 + \beta_1 X_t - \sum_{k=1}^{T} \beta_{-k} X_{t-k}, \qquad (2.53c)$$

in which smart and opportunistic customers stockpile when the brand is on deal. After the promotional campaign, sales temporarily sink below the steady-state level.

Case 4. Positive Lead.

$$Q_t = \beta_0 + \beta_1 X_t + \sum_{k=1}^{L} \beta_k X_{t+k}, \qquad (2.53d)$$

in which customer anticipation causes a gradual buildup of sales before the marketing event takes place. For example, sales of child restraint seats for automobiles increased before laws making them mandatory went into effect.

Case 5. Negative Lead.

$$Q_t = \beta_0 + \beta_1 X_t - \sum_{k=1}^{L} \beta_k X_{t+k}, \qquad (2.53e)$$

in which even smarter and more opportunistic customers than in case 3 anticipate the promotion period and reduce current consumption before the event.

Case 6. Negative Lag and Lead.

$$Q_t = \beta_0 + \beta_1 X_t - \sum_{k=-T}^{L} \beta_k X_{t+k}, \qquad (2.53f)$$

which is a combination of cases 3 and 5.

Continuous-Time Dynamic Models.   Continuous-time dynamic models are often used to derive policy implications of marketing actions. An example would be Sethi's logarithmic model (Sethi 1975). The rate of change of sales is explained by a sales response coefficient β, the logarithm of a marketing instrument X, a sales decay coefficient γ, and unit sales, Q:

$$\frac{dQ}{dt} = \beta \ln X - \gamma Q, \qquad Q(0) \text{ known.} \qquad (2.54)$$

The logarithmic model does not assume any saturation level. Sethi imbedded this model in a profit function and then used optimal control theory to find the optimal advertising rate over both finite and infinite planning horizons.

Jørgensen (1982) extended Sethi's model to the case of a duopoly differential game.

Perhaps the best known of the continuous-time models is the Vidale-Wolfe (1957) model. The rate of change of sales does experience a saturation effect in the form of untapped potential $(Q^o - Q)/Q^o$. Thus, their model is

$$\frac{dQ}{dt} = \beta X \left(\frac{Q^o - Q}{Q^o} \right) - \gamma Q, \qquad 0 \le Q \le Q^o. \tag{2.55}$$

This model has a number of desirable properties. It takes into account saturation (Q^o), exhibits asymmetry (β, γ), and the steady-state response is concave. Its major drawback is that it does not consider competition. The steady-state response has zero sales at zero marketing effort. The differential equation (2.55) can be solved analytically when X is a constant. It has been used to analyze advertising pulsing strategies.

Advertising dynamics have been studied by Nerlove and Arrow (1962). They argued that advertising drives sales through goodwill, G, and that goodwill depreciates at a rate δ:

$$\frac{dG}{dt} = A - \delta G. \tag{2.56}$$

In their model, the resultant sales response function is not asymmetric (unlike Vidale-Wolfe), and competition is ignored (as in Vidale-Wolfe).

In passing, we should note that the geometric distributed lag model is a discrete-time version of the Nerlove-Arrow model. Rewrite (2.56) as

$$G_t - G_{t-1} = A_t - \delta G_{t-1}, \tag{2.57}$$

and the stock of goodwill can now be expressed as

$$G_t = \sum_{k=0}^{\infty} (1 - \delta) A_{t-k}. \tag{2.58}$$

Thus, the depreciation rate equals 1 less the retention rate. Picconi and Olson (1978) make use of this approximation. Approximating a continuous-time model by a discrete-time model still presents the problem of choosing the correct time interval.

For new durables, diffusion market growth models have been used. A general formulation has been proposed by Dockner and Jørgensen (1988):

$$\frac{dQ}{dt} = [\beta_1 + \beta_2 f(X) + \beta_3 Q + \beta_4 f(X)Q](Q^o - Q). \tag{2.59}$$

The first term represents adoption uninfluenced by either marketing efforts or other adopters; the second, adoption stimulated marketing effort only; the third, adoption prompted by interactions with previous adopters, usually word of mouth; and the fourth, adoption stimulated by both marketing effort and interaction with previous adopters. The model is inspired, in part, by the diffusion model of Stigler (1961) and the contagion model of Ozga (1960). The market growth model of Bass (1969a) occurs when $\beta_2 = \beta_4 = 0$, and then β_1 is interpreted as the innovation coefficient and β_3 as the imitation coefficient.

The Vidale-Wolfe monopoly model has been extended to the duopoly conflict situation by Deal (1979). The model of the market mechanism now has two sales response functions:

$$\frac{dQ_1}{dt} = \beta_1 X_1 \left(\frac{Q^o - Q_1 - Q_2}{Q^o} \right) - \gamma_1 Q_1, \tag{2.60a}$$

$$\frac{dQ_2}{dt} = \beta_2 X_2 \left(\frac{Q^o - Q_1 - Q_2}{Q^o} \right) - \gamma_2 Q_2, \tag{2.60b}$$

There is no direct effect of a brand's effort on its competitors' sales. The effect of competitive pressure is to reduce the effectiveness of a brand's marketing effort by decreasing the unsold portion of the market. This implies diminishing returns to marketing effort.

An alternative competitive generalization that is closely related to the Vidale-Wolfe model is the Lancaster model (Kimball 1957). In the Lancaster model, total sales are fixed. For the two-competitor case, it is written as

$$\frac{dQ_1}{dt} = \beta_{11} X_1 Q_2 - \beta_{12} X_2 Q_1, \tag{2.61a}$$

$$\frac{dQ_1}{dt} = \beta_{21} X_2 Q_1 - \beta_{22} X_1 Q_2. \tag{2.61b}$$

Its similarity to Vidale-Wolfe can be seen by letting $\beta_i = \beta_{i1} Q_T$ and $\delta_i = \beta_{i2} X_j$. Then it becomes

$$\frac{dQ_1}{dt} = \beta_1 X_1 \left(\frac{Q_T - Q_1}{Q_T} \right) - \delta_1 Q_1, \tag{2.62a}$$

$$\frac{dQ_2}{dt} = \beta_2 X_2 \left(\frac{Q_T - Q_1}{Q_T} \right) - \delta_2 Q_2. \tag{2.62b}$$

A brand's sales come from its competitors' customers rather than from untapped potential. Each brand's decay constant varies systematically with its competitors' advertising. The general issue of coefficient variation is discussed in the next section. Horsky (1977a; 1977b), Case (1979, p. 199), and Erickson

(1985) used variants of the Lancaster model. Horsky took into account carry-over effects, and Erickson allowed for market expansion.

Varying Coefficient Structures

The coefficients of the controllable marketing instruments and the uncontrollable environmental variables in sales response functions are almost invariably assumed to be constant for the analysis period. However, the longer the time interval, the more tenuous this assumption is likely to be. Our focus in this section is consequently on the time effectiveness of marketing decision variables. Coefficients can also vary over cross-section units.

The coefficient variation may be either nonstochastic or stochastic. Nonstochastic variation occurs when the coefficients change as a function of observable variables. This variation is often called systematic. Stochastic variation occurs when coefficients are random parameters from either a stationary or nonstationary process. Any model of stochastic parameter variation that assumes an autoregressive process is called a *sequentially varying parameter model*. The modeling of changing market environments has been critically reviewed by Wildt and Winer (1983).

Systematic Coefficient Variation.   Systematic variation can be expressed by a general model or by specific models for special cases. Specific models have been developed for situations where sample observations are generated by two or more distinct regimes. The seasonality model, discussed later in this chapter, is an example of these "switching" models.

General Systematically Varying Coefficient Model.   The parameter vector β in some models, such as $y = f(\beta, X_1)$, may exhibit variation, and this variation may be systematic. Systematic variation implies that the parameter vector can be written as

$$\beta = f(\alpha, X_2). \tag{2.63}$$

The parameters β are expressed as a function of other parameters α and observable variables X_2. This set of variables may include some of the variables in X_1. Marketing applications include those by Parsons (1975a), Arora (1979), Simon (1979), Shoemaker (1986), and Parsons and Vanden Abeele (1981). These researchers analyzed systematic variations in advertising, price, and sales call elasticities. Simon and Sebastian (1987) allowed the innovation or imitation coefficients in the Bass market growth model (2.59) to vary systematically with advertising.

The deterministic relation (2.63) can be made stochastic by adding a disturbance term, $\mathbf{V}$, or

$$\boldsymbol{\beta} = f(\boldsymbol{\alpha}, \mathbf{X}_2, \mathbf{V}), \tag{2.64}$$

When this relation is linear and it is imbedded in a linear response function, the resultant model,

$$\mathbf{Q}_t = \mathbf{X}'_{1t}\mathbf{X}_{2t}\boldsymbol{\alpha} + (\mathbf{X}'_{1t}\mathbf{V} + \mathbf{U}_t), \tag{2.65}$$

has a heteroscedastic disturbance term. Such a model was used by Gatignon (1984) to investigate the influence of advertising on a market's price sensitivity and by Gatignon and Hanssens (1987) to examine factors influencing sales force effectiveness.

Switching Models. If structural changes occur at *known* points in time, the changes in the coefficients of the relevant variables can be represented by dummy variables. Palda (1964) assumed that restrictions placed upon Lydia Pinkham's advertising copy by the Food and Drug Administration in 1914 and again in 1925 and by the Federal Trade Commission in 1940 could be captured by dummy variables. These dummy variables affect only the intercept of the sales response function. A somewhat more appropriate approach might have been to use the dummy variables to model changes in the slope coefficient, i.e., the effectiveness of advertising.

The switch from one regime to another may depend on time, but alternatively, it might depend on a threshold value for some variable or occur stochastically. In the two-regime case, the model can be written as

$$\text{Regime 1: } Q = f(\mathbf{X}_1; \boldsymbol{\beta}) \quad \text{if condition holds,}$$
$$\text{Regime 2: } Q = f(\mathbf{X}_2; \boldsymbol{\alpha}) \quad \text{if condition does not hold.} \tag{2.66}$$

Bemmaor (1984) tested for the existence of an advertising threshold effect using the stochastic version of this model. The first regime condition is "with probability θ" while the second regime condition is "with probability $1 - \theta$." Lee and Brown (1985) studied the impact of Florida Department of Citrus coupon promotional programs on the demand for frozen concentrated orange juice. Separate sales response functions were estimated for coupon users and nonusers. The probability of a household redeeming a coupon was itself a function of household characteristics, market conditions, and properties of various promotional programs.

Coefficients in a response function might vary between each time period rather than only between a few time periods. If cross-section observations were also available, we could use a random coefficients model (described in the next section). Otherwise, some a priori constraint must be imposed so that we may obtain unique estimates of the coefficients.

Stochastic Parameter Variation. The primary model involving random parameters from a stationary process is the random coefficients model, while that for random parameters from a nonstationary process is the Cooley-Prescott model.

Random Coefficients Model. The random coefficients model assumes that the parameters are stochastic and can be expressed as

$$\boldsymbol{\beta}_i = \bar{\boldsymbol{\beta}} + \mathbf{V}_i, \tag{2.67}$$

where

$\boldsymbol{\beta}_i$ = vector of random response coefficients for the ith individual unit,

$\bar{\boldsymbol{\beta}}$ = vector of mean response coefficients,

$\mathbf{V}_1$ = vector of random disturbances.

This model is very appealing when investigating cross-sectional data on a large number of microunits, for instance, a large consumer survey.

A generalization of the random coefficients model to time series data is the return-to-normality model. Parameters in this model are dynamic.

Return-to-Normality Model. Little (1966), whose work antedated econometric developments in this area, was the first to propose such a sales response function. The coefficient of promotion rate was assumed to be generated by a stochastic process:

$$\beta_t = (1 - \phi)\bar{\beta} + \phi\beta_{t-1} + V_t, \tag{2.68}$$

where $0 \leq \phi \leq 1$. The value of the parameter β in any time period will be a weighted average of its value in the previous period and its long-run average value plus a random disturbance. The term $1 - \phi$ represents a tendency to converge toward the mean value $\bar{\beta}$. As $\phi \to 1$, β_t becomes more dependent on β_{t-1} and wanders more freely from its mean value. On the other hand, as $\phi \to 0$, β becomes equal to the mean value plus a random coefficient, as in a random coefficients model. This model can be generalized by letting the process generating the parameters be an Auto Regressive Moving Average (ARMA) process, ARMA processes are discussed in chapter 4.

$$A(L)(\beta_t - \bar{\beta}) = B(L)V_t.$$

Cooley-Prescott Model. A model in which the parameters follow a nonstationary stochastic process is the random walk model. In this model, the parameters are assumed to adapt to permanent and transitory changes (Cooley and Prescott 1973). The transitory change of the parameter vector can be represented as

$$\beta_t = \beta_t^* + \tau_t, \tag{2.69}$$

where β_t^* is the permanent component of β_t, and τ_t is the vector of transient change in period t. In addition to transient changes, which are in effect for only one period, there are permanent changes, which persist into the future:

$$\beta_t^* = \beta_{t-1}^* + \xi_t, \tag{2.70}$$

where ξ_t is the permanent change vector.

The vectors τ and ξ are assumed to be identically and independently distributed normal variables with mean vectors zero and known covariance structures. These covariance structures are written as

$$E(\tau\tau') = (1 - \phi)\sigma^2\Sigma_\tau \tag{2.71}$$

and

$$E(\xi\xi') = \phi\sigma^2\Sigma_\xi, \tag{2.72}$$

where Σ_τ and Σ_ξ are known up to scale factors. The parameter ϕ indicates how fast the parameters are adapting to structural change. It is restricted to fall within the range $0 \le \phi \le 1$. In this formulation, if $\phi = 0$, we once again have a random coefficients model.

Certain simplifying assumptions are often made for estimation purposes. In the absence of information to the contrary, first, the relative importance of permanent and transitory changes is assumed to be the same for all random parameters; thus, $\Sigma_\tau = \Sigma_\xi$. Second, these changes are assumed to be uncorrelated among parameters. Consequently, the covariance matrices will be diagonal. The variances of the estimated parameters under the assumption of no temporal changes provide an estimate of the variances in these matrices.

Winer (1979) applied this approach to Palda's Lydia Pinkham data. While Palda maintained that the regulatory actions should produce discrete changes in the constant of the sales response function and should leave the effectiveness of advertising otherwise unchanged, Winer argued that the shock is likely to induce some continuous change in the constant, and in any event, the assumption of parameter constancy for the other coefficients is not valid. Winer estimated the sales response function

$$Q_t = \beta_{0t} + \beta_{1t}A_t + \beta_{2t}Q_{t-1} + U_t \tag{2.73}$$

subject to (2.69)–(2.72) and the simplifications covered in the last paragraph. His empirical results indicated that the interecept β_{0t} showed a strong non-discrete tendency to change over time, that the advertising coefficient β_{1t} showed an upward trend, and that the coefficient of sales in the previous period, β_{2t}, declined over time. The proportion of permanent parameter change, ϕ, was about 0.75 for these data.

An equation similar to (2.73) can be derived from a geometric advertising lag model provided that the coefficients are constant. In such a model, the coefficient of lagged sales will be equal to the advertising carryover parameter. It is not transparant that the same correspondence holds if the coefficients are time-varying. Since we consider the measurement of advertising carryover difficult in even favorable circumstances, we think that superimposing time-varying parameters on top of distributed lag models may well create insurmountable problems.

Data

We have already pointed out that there are two types of data: cross-section data and time series data. Individual units at a point in time are observed in cross-section data. The data may be on different sales territories, on different channel members such as retail outlets, on different individual customers, or on different brands. The same units at different points in time are observed in time series data. While these observations may take place at any interval, the most common intervals in marketing are monthly, bimonthly, quarterly, and annually. A data base may well contain a combination of cross-section and time series data. For instance, information may be available on a number of brands over a number of bimonths.

The choice among the three kinds of data bases should depend on the purpose of the research. The dynamic character of marketing activities can only be investigated by a time series. The generality of a sales response function may require a cross-section of territories, brands, or firms. Unfortunately, a choice may not exist, because of lack of some data. This is especially true in marketing, where good time series data may not be systematically recorded, or perhaps only recorded annually when the appropriate data interval would be quarterly or monthly. Cross-section studies in marketing are often limited by competitive consideration—sometimes data for all firms in an industry cannot be obtained.

Sources of Data

Marketing sales performance for consumer goods might be measured in terms of factory shipments, warehouse withdrawals, or retail sales. Factory shipment information is usually available from company records. Retail sales can be measured by collecting data from retail stores or their customers. The following discussion of data sources draws heavily on Findley and Little (1980) and Totten and Block (1987).

Factory Shipments.   A brand manager can usually find out how much product has been shipped. Unfortunately, shipments may not track consumer purchases very closely, especially if a high proportion of the product has been sold on deals. The trade will engage in forward buying, that is, it will stock up at lower prices and carry the product in inventory (Chevalier and Curhan 1976; Abraham and Lodish 1987, p. 108). Are there situations where trade inventories are low or nonexistent? If so, then shipments might make a good proxy for retail sales. This could happen when a product has a short shelf life, is expensive to store, or store-door delivered (Findley and Little 1980, p. 10). Ice cream, which is bulky and requires refrigeration, would be a good example.

Warehouse Withdrawals.   With the exception of products sold in supermarkets, data on products in the intermediate stages of a channel are sparse. For many products sold in supermarkets, Selling Areas Marketing, Inc. (SAMI) provides sales and distribution information for the national (U.S.) and approximately 50 individual markets. SAMI also reports the average of distributors' suggested retail prices. This information is obtained from supermarket chains and food distributors. To maintain confidentiality, chain-by-chain breakdowns are not available. The warehouse withdrawal method does not measure any product that is delivered directly to the store by the manufacture. Inventory control policies at the warehouse level tend to disguise the full impact of short-term marketing activities. Sales response studies using SAMI data include Wittink (1977b), Pekelman and Tse (1980), and Eastlack and Rao (1986).

Store Shelf Audit.   Retail sales of many consumer products for an audit period can be estimated from a stratified sample of food, drug, and mass merchandise stores. An auditor takes an inventory of the amount of product on the shelf and in any temporary storage area and collects records of any purchases by the store since the last audit. Retail sales can then be calculated as beginning inventory less ending inventory plus purchases less credits, returns, and transfers. Sales can be estimated by brand and package size. The leading supplier of syndicated retail audits is the A. C. Nielsen Company. Its audit period is every two months. Sales response studies that used Nielsen data include Kuehn, McGuire, and Weiss (1966); Bass and Parsons (1969); and Clarke (1973).

In addition to retail sales data, the store shelf audit provides estimates on average retail prices, wholesale prices, average store inventory, and promotional activity. Retail availability of a product can be calculated from the percentage of stores weighted by volume selling the product. Out-of-stock situations are also noted. Special promotional activities, such as premiums or bonus packs, may also be recorded.

Although store shelf audits capture trends very accurately, they do less well at detecting short-run effects. For example, the impact of a week-long in-store display would be dampened by looking at sales aggregated over an eight-week period. Moreover, not every store can be audited on the first day of a reporting period. Consequently, some audits are before or after the start of the period. The bias resulting from this is discussed in Shoemaker and Pringle (1980).

Store Scanner Data.   Retail sales on a store-level daily or weekly basis can be found using automated checkout scanners. A computer-controlled reader identifies each product from its universal product bar code; the computer matches the product with its price, already stored in the data base, and then records the purchase in the data base. The scanner method yields more precise information than the store shelf audit method. Information is available on the characteristics of the product or brand, the exact price paid, the amount bought, and the purchase data and time of day. Scanner data are provided by IRI (Information Resources, Inc.) and by Nielsen. Cooper (1988) employed a special case of three-mode factor analysis to construct competitive maps that described the structure underlying asymmetric cross-elasticities for market share attraction models estimated from IRI store-level data.

One problem with scanner data is that in most markets not all retail outlets are scanned. Shipment data, warehouse withdrawal data, store audit data, and scanner data all share a common problem—the lack of any information about the consumer. This precludes conducting any analyses at the segment level.

Mail Consumer Panels.   Consumer-level information is obtained by a consumer mail panel. Consumers report their purchase behavior by returning a purchase diary or recall questionnaire. The purchase diary is given to consumers before they buy, and they are to record each purchase as it is made. The recall questionnaire is given to consumers after they buy, and they are asked to recall purchases made during a specified period of time. Totten and Block (1987, p. 27) assert that the recall questionnaire method is currently the more popular method. Members of panels are asked to record the prices of their purchases and whether purchases were on promotion. This major advantage of mail panels is that information can be collected on any product. Sales response studies that used the Market Research Corporation of America (MRCA) consumer purchase diary panel include Urban (1969) and Nakanishi (1973).

There are problems with mail panels. They are subject to selection bias, attrition bias, response bias, and measurement bias. Not everyone agrees to participate in a mail panel when asked. Not everyone remembers past purchase behavior accurately. Not everyone records information completely, legibly, or accurately. Winer (1983, p. 185) notes: "For panels on which dropouts are replaced, ... replacement by household descriptors such as demographic/socioeconomic variables ensures a representative panel only in terms of those variables—not in terms of behavior variables such as purchase quantity."

Store Scanner Panels.   Store scanner panels combine the individual-level detail of the mail panel with the accuracy of the store scanner. Individuals are given special cards that can be read by the bar code reader in a store. Thus, information is available on all scannable purchases for a subset of households.

The latest advance is to provide panel members with their own bar code readers so that data can be obtained from stores without readers. Adtel, for instance, uses a bar code reader that looks like a large fountain pen and reads and records information.

Advertising Data.   Price, promotion, and distribution data are by-products of one or more of the sales performance data collection methods just discussed; however, advertising data are not. A firm knows its own advertising expenditures and can purchase reasonable estimates of competitors advertising from suppliers like Leading National Advertisers (LNA). Diary data can be collected in conjunction with a split-cable TV experiment like the one provided by Adtel (see, for example, Krishnamurthi and Raj 1985).

Broadbent (1979) used TV ratings (TVRs) taken over the same TV areas and periods. Commercials of different lengths were standardized on 30–seconds, increasing the TVRs for longer advertisements and decreasing them for shorter ones in proportion to their costs. Each period's actual TVRs were then replaced by a measure of the amount of advertising which was effective then. This measure he called *adstock*. Colman and Brown (1983), Broadbent (1984), and Broadbent and Colman (1986) have studied the relationship among adstock, awareness, and sales.

Eastlack and Rao (1986) focused on delivered advertising, measured as gross ratings points (GRPs), in modeling response to advertising changes for "V-8" Cocktail Vegetable Juice. Delivered GRPs were calculated for spot TV placements using quarterly sweeps of areas of dominant influence (ADI's) aggregated to SAMI markets conducted by the Nielson Station Index. Delivered GRPs for national TV placements were based on Nielsen Audimeter Data (NTI data). Spot radio delivered GRPs were based on Arbitron data, and network radio delivered GRPs were from RADAR.

Managerial Judgment Data. Sometimes historical data are insufficient or not available at all, as in the case of new products. In such situations, knowledgeable managers are asked how they expect the market to respond to marketing actions. For example, they might be asked: "Given the reference levels of your and your competitors' marketing efforts (perhaps last period's values) and given that all marketing instruments except one (say price) remain at these levels during the next period, what sales do you expect if competitors do not change their levels (prices) and your company effort (price) increases (decreases) by specified percentages?" The question is repeated for each instrument in the firm's marketing mix. Gijsbrechts and Naert (1984) collected subjective data for some industrial products sold by a multinational multiproduct firm.

The use of judgment-based marketing decision models is controversial (Chakravarti, Mitchell, and Staelin 1979; Little and Lodish 1981). Chakravarti, Mitchell, and Staelin have pointed out the dangers of relying on management judgment to estimate parameters, especially when the sales response function is nonlinear. Fraser and Hite (1988) advocate an adaptive utility approach to integrating information from managerial experience with that provided by marketing models.

Whether the data come from objective or subjective sources, the number of observations should be greater than the number of parameters. Even assuming that the appropriate data can be obtained, a number of important issues regarding the use of those data remain. These include pooling, adjustments to the data, and aggregation.

Consumer Durables, Industrial Goods, and Services. The sources of data for consumer durables, industrial goods, and service industries are somewhat different from those for consumer goods. Some consumer durables like automobiles or personal computers are shipped from the factory direct to dealers; some are shipped directly to final customers. For industrial goods, such direct channels of distribution are commonplace, and industrial goods may also be shipped to distributors or to value-added resellers. Finally, both consumer and industrial services may involve direct sales to customers. Fast-food restaurants and security services, for example, record only one level of sales, which we would not call shipments.

Although it is true that most market response studies focus on consumer nondurable goods, the techniques discussed in this book are perfectly generalizable to all types of products and services. Their use may require a little extra digging for appropriate data, but by combining company, industry association, business publication, and other sources, it should be possible to model any real-life marketing situation.

Table 2–1. Taxonomy of Pooling Models

	Assumptions about	
Model	*Intercept*	*Vector of Slope Coefficients*
I	Common for all i, t	Common for all i, t
II	Varying over i (or t)	Common for all i, t
III	Varying over i, t	Common for all i, t
IV	Varying over i (or t)	Varying over i (or t)
V	Varying over i, t	Varying over i, t

Pooling

Pooling time series and cross-section data raises some issues on how we specify a functional form. The simplest model, model I in table 2–1, assumes a common intercept and a common set of slope coefficients for all units for all time periods. A more usual assumption (model II) is to allow for individual differences by introducing separate dummy variables for each cross-section entity. In a similar manner, differences over time could be represented. Individual differences and temporal differences could each be represented by dummy variables in the same equation (model III). This results in a substantial loss of degrees of freedom. Moreover, interpretation of the dummy variables may be difficult. In addition, these dummy variables are likely to account for a large share of the explanatory power of the model. Consequently, a variance component model (2.34) is often used instead of the dummy variable technique. The models that we have discussed assume that the individual and time effects manifest themselves in differences in the intercept. These effects also have an impact on the slope coefficients (models IV and V). One way they are captured is by means of random coefficients models (2.67).

The notion of sequentially varying parameters can be incorporated into a cross-section–time series model. This combination is known as a *convergent parameter model* (Rosenberg 1973). The individual coefficient vectors follow first-order Markov processes subordinated to a tendency to converge to the population mean vector. The population mean vector will also evolve over time.

The individual parameter vector may contain both cross-varying parameters, which vary across the population, and cross-fixed parameters, which are the same for all individuals in any time period. The F cross-fixed parameters obey the relation

$$\beta_t = \beta_{t-1} + \tau_{t-1}. \tag{2.74}$$

The number of cross-fixed parameters, F, may be zero. The V cross-varying parameters are assumed to obey the relation

$$\beta_\alpha = \bar{\beta}_{\alpha-1} + \Delta_\phi(\beta_{\alpha-1,i} - \bar{\beta}_{\alpha-1}) + v_{\alpha-1,i}. \tag{2.75}$$

The convergence matrix Δ_ϕ is diagonal with entries ϕ_v. Each ϕ, $0 \le \phi_v < 1$, is the proportion of the individual divergence from the population mean that persists into the next period. If there are no cross-fixed parameters and the divergence rates are set equal to zero, the model reduces to a version of a random coefficients model.

Johansson (1974) represented the margarine market by a convergent parameter model. The individual, or cross-sectional, units were the 15 largest brands in the margarine market. The time units were 52 weeks. He focused on the relation between the price of the product and the quantity purchased:

$$Q_{ti} - Q_{t-1,i} = \beta_{1ti}(P_{ti} - P_{t-1,i}) + \beta_{2,ti}\left(\frac{P_{ti}}{\bar{P}_t} - \frac{P_{t-1,i}}{\bar{P}_{t-1}}\right) + U_{ti}, \tag{2.76}$$

where

Q_{ti} = per-capita quantity (in pounds) of brand i at time t,

P_{ti} = price (in dollars) of brand i at time t,

$\bar{P}_t$ = mean price in the market at time t.

Both coefficients in this model were postulated to be cross-varying parameters and to obey (2.75). The empirical results indicated that this model should be rejected. The coefficients were rarely significantly different from zero and, contrary to theory, often were positive in sign. Johansson suggested that one cause of these results might be misspecification, the omission of a deal promotion variable.

Adjustments to the Data

Patterns may exist in data that confound the relation between marketing effort and marketing results. The most common patterns are trend, seasonality, price-level changes, and population changes.

Trend. If a variable, say sales, is highly correlated with time, it is said to exhibit trend. In trying to explain sales behavior, we might introduce a linear trend variable (TREND = $1, 2, \ldots, T$) into the sales response function. Marketing applications include Ball and Agarwala (1969), Rao and Bass (1985), and Eastlack and Rao (1986). Be warned that conventional tests for trend are strongly biased toward finding trend even when none is present. The treatment of nonlinear trends and cycles involves classical time series analysis.[11] The introduction of a trend variable (or variables) may serve forecasting quite well, but if the model has explanatory purpose as well, the analyst would be advised to search further for the cause of the trend.

Seasonality.   If a variable follows a cyclical pattern within the year, it is said to exhibit seasonality. In some cases, seasonality makes successive time observations not comparable; for example, the sales in each month vary around different means. In that case, two solutions are available. First, the data can be seasonally adjusted, i.e., the effects of the seasonality can be removed from the data, primarily by employing some type of moving average. Second, dummy variables can be used to represent the seasons. For example, a quarterly sales response model might be expressed as

$$Q_t = \beta_0 + \beta_1 D_2 + \beta_2 D_3 + \beta_3 D_4$$
$$+ \beta_4 A_t + \beta_5 (D_2 A_t) + \beta_6 (D_3 A_t) + \beta_7 (D_4 A_t). \tag{2.77}$$

Because this model includes an intercept, we need only three dummy variables to represent the four quarters. As we have noted, the impact of one of the quarters, in this case the first, will be captured by this intercept. The other dummy variables will measure shifts from this (first-quarter) base. The coefficients β_1, β_2, β_3 capture shifts of the intercept β_0, and the coefficients β_5, β_6, β_7 capture shifts of the slope β_4.[12] Franke and Wilcox (1987), in their study of the relation between alcoholic beverage advertising and consumption, used one dummy variable to capture marked increases in beer consumption in the second and third quarters of each year and another dummy variable to represent a fourth-quarter peak in wine consumption. A more detailed description of seasonality, which is a very common feature of marketing data, is given in chapter 4.

Price-Level Change.   Another pattern that may exist in the data is inflation and hence the changing real value of the unit of currency. Price changes must be accounted for by adjusting current dollar figures to real dollar figures using some deflator or price index. Consumer prices could be deflated by the Consumer Price Index (CPI), since this series is designed to reflect price changes in a "market basket" of goods and services. Similarly, business prices might be deflated by the producer price index (PPI). Any other variables expressed in monetary terms should be deflated in a similar manner. For example, Franke and Wilcox (1987) deflated all advertising series using the McCann-Erickson cost-per-thousand price index for the appropriate medium.

The point of these adjustments is to ensure that the effect on sales of the variable being measured is due to true changes and not to artificial ones like changes in the price level.

Population Change. The final adjustment to the data is straightforward. Just as price levels change, so does population, and thus sales in all the models described may be more appropriately measured by per capita sales. Since Franke and Wilcox (1987) studied alcoholic beverage consumption over a long timespan, 21 years, they wanted to remove the effect of population growth. Per capita consumption figures were obtained by dividing total consumption of the beverages in gallons by the number of adults age 21 and older.

An example of the use of data adjustment is PROMOTER, a system for evaluating manufacturers' trade promotions (Abraham and Lodish 1987). This system requires the estimation of a baseline of what sales would have been had a promotion not been run. The variation of sales due to known factors is taken out by data adjustment for trend, seasonality, all commodity volume distribution, price increases, major competitive promotions, product improvements, and the like.

Aggregation

Closely related to the questions of model form and the variables to be used is the issue of the level of aggregation at which the analysis should take place. In practice, model-building efforts appear to exclude considerations about the level of aggregation, probably because of the constraints surrounding availability of data.

Various kinds of aggregation are possible in marketing—aggregation can take place over entities, time, space, or variables. The intersection of the various levels of aggregation for each of these dimensions defines the *aggregation space* of the response study. For example, the aggregation space of a study might be brand sales recorded as bimonthly data for metropolitan sales territories and advertising equal to television plus radio expenditures. It should be clear that the specification of the levels of aggregation has an important bearing on the nature of the relations that can be discovered.

Entity Aggregation. Aggregation over entities can be of two types, corresponding to the two basic types of entities in a marketing system. The first is aggregation over buyers, and the second is aggregation over product levels. Buyer aggregation occurs when individual buying units are added to obtain market segment sales, total brand sales, or industry sales of the product. Krishnamurthi, Raj, and Selvam (1988) have discussed the statistical and managerial issues in cross-sectional aggregation. Clements and Selvanathan (1988) have described how the Rotterdam model, a system of consumer demand equations, can be applied to aggregate data. Product aggregation occurs when individual brands are added to obtain larger product categories or total sales of a firm.

Temporal Aggregation.   Temporal aggregation refers to the collection of shorter observation periods into longer ones. Research regarding the relation between sales and marketing and other economic variables can be carried out on daily, monthly, bimonthly, quarterly, or annual data. To some extent, aggregation over time is unavoidable. In fact, the length of the time period that forms the basis of the analysis is often not determined by the researcher. The researcher simply uses the data made available for analysis. However, even if constrained in this respect, the researcher is not absolved of responsibility for considering the effect of temporal aggregation on the outcome of the analysis. Using the smallest possible time period allows proper investigation of the reasons for changes in the market position of a brand. If the average time between purchases for a given product is approximately one month, it is important to have, as a minimum, monthly data. Each time period would then reflect, on average, one purchase per customer. Using annual data for such a product instead would smooth the data, thereby not allowing the researcher to determine the reasons for changes on a month-to-month basis.

Spatial Aggregation.   Spatial aggregation means the gathering of smaller geographic areas into larger ones. Data describing the behavior of marketing variables over geographic areas are available in increasingly more detailed forms. This allows separate analyses to be carried out for each of the geographic areas or sales territories in which a firm is competing. Analysis at the national level will certainly not reveal information about marketing differences among such territories. Moreover, such an aggregate analysis is likely to be invalid if the relation between marketing variables is not the same for all areas. There are several reasons why this relation may differ across sales territories. At least in some industries, the structure of the market is not homogeneous across territories, that is, some brands are available in some areas and not in others. The market position of a selected brand may differ substantially across territories, partly as a result of differences in market structure. Futhermore, the characteristics of customers may vary substantially across territories. If the relation of interest depends on some of these characteristics or on the presence and extent of competition provided by competing brands, a certain amount of variation in the effectiveness of marketing decision variables can be expected.

Variable Aggregation. Sometimes variables are summed across their various components. For example, total advertising may be comprised of television advertising, radio advertising, magazine advertising, newspaper advertising, and outdoor advertising. Although each medium is measured on a common monetary basis, each may have a different effect on sales. A major problem that arises is that the "optimal" advertising budget derived from a sales response function based on total advertising is unlikely to be the same as the "optimal" advertising budget derived from a sales response function based on the individual advertising media.

The model builder has more flexibility in modeling, the more data are disaggregated. The model builder faces serious problems when temporal aggregation occurs in conjunction with a dynamic model.

Marketing Models and Prior Knowledge

We have described the elements that constitute a market response model. In any given situation, the model builder may or may not have advance knowledge of these factors. For example, the analyst may be able to identify the elements of the marketing mix but know very little about the functional form of the model. It is the task of careful empirical analysis, using econometric and time series methods, to advance the model builder to a higher state of knowledge.

ETS models are useful for scientific as well as managerial inference. The marketing manager uses ETS to build planning and forecasting models. The marketing scientist uses ETS to build theory from empirical generalizations. However, in both cases, the analysts may face different modeling tasks that are primarily a function of their prior knowledge and the ultimate objectives of the model.

Consider the following two marketing planning scenarios:

1. Company A markets a variety of products through different channels. It has, over the years, developed some simple decision rules for marketing mix allocations. Now, in the face of declining market shares and a squeeze on profit margins, the company needs hard facts on what is driving sales and profit performance.

2. Company B, a retailer, sells several hundred products via aggressive local advertising campaigns coupled with temporary price cuts. Man-

agement is well aware of the sales impact of advertising and lower prices but struggles with the question of the timing of promotional campaigns and the optimal combination of advertising budgets and profit margins.

Similarly, consider the following two marketing research scenarios:

1. In the 1970s, several authorities in industry and academia advanced the notion that larger market share leads to higher profitability. Although several appealing arguments exist for this theory, it is also possible to describe conditions leading to the reverse relation i.e., profitability leads to larger market share. More research is needed in this area.

2. The issue of distributed lag effects of advertising on sales is in more disarray than ever before. Major research papers have argued that the effects last for months, not years; that the results are a function of the chosen data interval; that "current effects" models are as good as lag models; and even that lag structures do not matter. Here, too, more research is needed.

As different as these scenarios are, they are similar in the amount of prior knowledge available to the manager or the scientist and in the objective of the model building. In the first two scenarios, an information set (i.e., a collection of relevant variables) is given and the task is to sort out the causal ordering among the variables. In the second two scenarios, the causal ordering is given, but there is a lack of knowledge about functional forms and lag structures in the response structures. This implies that different ETS methods are needed to develop and test response models in marketing.

Our knowledge about the modeling enviroment can be organized in the following way:

- Level 0: only the information set is known.
- Level 1: the causal ordering among variables is known.
- Level 2: the functional form, causal ordering, and lag structure are known.

ETS techniques are not appropriate to situations with less than level 0 knowledge. We must start with an information set developed from subject matter theory or directly from managers. For example, the concept of the marketing mix leads to a commonly used information set in market response modeling consisting of product sales, price, distribution, sales force, and communication efforts. Once a level 0 prior knowledge is obtained, ETS methods can make substantial contributions in moving the marketing scientist up the knowledge hierarchy.

Each of the following three chapters addresses model building at a different level of prior knowledge, starting with the highest level. At level 2, the model builder estimates the parameters of a fully specified model using econometric techniques. The model may then be used for forecasting or marketing planning. Alternatively, the analyst may verify the adequacy of the model via testing procedures. This is the content of chapter 3.

At level 1, the model builder is not ready to estimate parameters or predict sales. The functional form and dynamic structure of the model must first be specified. The latter may require a different set of techniques involving time series analysis. Chapter 4 starts with univariate techniques for lag structure specification and then discusses multiple time series methods.

At level 0, empirical methods should be used to establish the direction of causality among marketing variables. This can only be accomplished with time series data, because it requires the temporal ordering of events. Techniques for assessing the direction of causality are discussed in chapter 5.

Notes

1. The terms *response models* and *response systems* may be used interchangeably.

2. For this reason, causal models of consumer or managerial behavior often use techniques such as LISREL, which accommodate measurement error. See Bagozzi (1980).

3. Problems can arise when the independent variables in a regression analysis are interval-scaled, as they would most likely be in the case of quality attributes. Yi (1988) has recommended mean centering of interval variables used in regression models with interaction effects.

4. Additional discussion of models of market mechanisms can be found in Parsons (1981).

5. This can be seen by differentiating (2.11): $dQ = \beta_0(dX/X)$.

6. $\varepsilon_X = (dQ/Q)/(dX/X) = (dQ/dX)(X/Q)$, and for (2.12), $dQ/dX = \beta_1 Q/X$, $\therefore \varepsilon_X = \beta_1$.

7. More precisely, we are discussing "nicely convex-concave" functions (Ginsberg 1974).

8. $\varepsilon_X = (dQ/dX)(X/Q)$ and $dQ/dX = \beta_1 Q/X^2$, $\therefore \varepsilon_X = \beta_1/X$.

9. Stationarity is discussed in chapter 4.

10. Sometimes brands are allowed to have individual intercepts (Naert and Bultez 1973, p. 337).

11. Classical time series analysis is described in Armstrong (1985).

12. Wildt (1977) has pointed out that there is an inherent high degree of multicollinearity between seasonal slope and seasonal intercept variables for the same time period, which sometimes results in an inability to distinguish between the two forms of seasonal influence.

3 PARAMETER ESTIMATION AND MODEL TESTING

When the causal ordering, functional form, and lag structure are believed known, all that needs to be done is to estimate the model. Nonetheless, any assumptions underlying a model should be tested. In what follows, our discussion is primarily on a conceptual level. Technical details can be found in most leading econometric texts; Judge et al. (1985) is especially helpful in providing guidance for applied work.[1]

Steps in building market response models include specification, estimation, hypotheses testing, verification, and forecasting. While sound theory should always form the foundation of response models, marketing theory, at best, provides rough guidance to the specification of functional form. Moreover, rival theories may exist. Verification is consequently very important and may provide feedback to the specification step. Thus, we begin this chapter with a discussion of model selection. We next turn to model estimation. Finally, we cover model testing, including specification error analysis. Conventional tests for autocorrelation, heteroscedasticity, parameter constancy, and the like are model selection criteria inasmuch as models that fail such tests will be discarded.

Model Selection

The specification problem in econometric models has been described as one of choosing the correct variables and the correct form of the relation between them (Theil 1971). It is thus a problem of choice, and a research strategy should be designed to aid in this decision process. We are, of course, seeking the true model of some marketing phenomenon out of all possible models, and so we are appropriately concerned with how the correct specification (if it were known) differs from any number of incorrect specifications. For econometric research, this issue becomes one of investigating alternative regression models according to some criterion. The criterion can either be informal decision rule such as maximizing $\bar{R}^2$ or a formal decision rule involving hypothesis testing.

Informal Decision Rule

A frequently used measure of the adequacy of a single estimated linear regression model is R^2, the coefficient of determination. This R^2 measure varies between 0 and 1 and can be interpreted as the fraction of the variation in the dependent variable (typically unit sales in a market response study) explained by the model (usually a linear combination of controllable marketing instruments and uncontrollable environmental factors).

Not surprisingly, the most common decision rule for choosing among alternative linear models with nonstochastic exogenous variables is to select the model with the largest $\bar{R}^2$, an adjustment of R^2 that approximately corrects for the bias caused by the fact that R^2 can be increased simply by adding more variables:

$$\bar{R}^2 = R^2 - \frac{k-1}{n-k}(1 - R^2), \tag{3.1}$$

where k is the number of exogenous variables including the constant term and n is the number of observations. An equivalent rule is to select the model with the smallest residual variance. The probability that the decision rule will choose a particular model when it is the correctly specified model can be calculated. Ideally, this probability should be large.

The problem is to choose between two alternative models:

$$\text{(A1)} \qquad \mathbf{q} = \mathbf{X}\boldsymbol{\beta} + \boldsymbol{\varepsilon} \tag{3.2}$$

and

$$\text{(A2)} \qquad \mathbf{q} = \mathbf{Z}\boldsymbol{\gamma} + \boldsymbol{\eta}. \tag{3.3}$$

The number of independent variables in $\mathbf{X}$ is k_X and in $\mathbf{Z}$ is k_Z. The number of observations is n. The dependent variable, q, is assumed to have a multi-variate normal distribution with mean vector ξ and covariance matrix $\sigma^2 I_n$. The probability of choosing model A1 over model A2 by the maximum $\bar{R}^2$ criterion when model A1 is the correctly specified model is $\Pr(\bar{R}_X^2 > \bar{R}_Z^2) = \Pr(q'Aq < 0)$. The symmetric matrix A is defined as $M_X - \alpha M_Z$, where $M_X = I_n - X(X'X)^{-1}X'$, $M_Z = I_n - Z(Z'Z)^{-1}Z'$, and $\alpha = (n - k_X)/(n - k_Z)$. This result is due to Schmidt (1973) and Ebbeler (1974). This approach was utilized by Parsons (1976) in a market response study.

There are several valid uses for goodness of fit, especially as measured by $\bar{R}^2$. Comparing the fit of the same response model over several territories would be one example. It is a particularly appropriate measure of the extent to which a (true) model accounts for total variation or, in a sense, approximates the real phenomenon under study. In this case, $\bar{R}^2$ is a measure of the degree of approximation by which a generalization holds. For testing theories, however, a more powerful criterion is necessary (cf. Bass 1969a).

The major weakness of this criterion is fundamental—it does not work when none of the alternative specifications are correct. Moreover, since it only holds "on the average," there is no small chance that the wrong specification prevails. Since the objective of response modeling is to identify true response models and market mechanisms, a criterion that relies on the fortuitous inclusion of the correct model as one of the set under evaluation seems to be an inefficient way of conducting research. It is inefficient because the process does not encourage the development of models that are otherwise readily falsifiable, and therefore incorrect models are more easily accepted.

Moreover, this criterion assumes that the dependent variables of the models are identical. Sometimes, for instance, a marketing researcher may want to explore regressions with q and $\ln q$ as alternative forms of the sales dependent variable. In this case, the $\bar{R}^2$ criterion does not obtain directly; however, it can be determined by drawing on an alternative interpretation of R^2 as the square of the correlation between the actual and predicted values of the dependent variable. Thus, in comparing a set of linear market share models with a set of log-linear ones, Weiss (1969) used antilog conversions for the log-linear models and then calculated correlation of q with $\hat{q}$, instead of $\ln q$ with $\ln \hat{q}$, to evaluate relative goodness of fit. Now the goodness of fit numbers for different models were measuring the fit of the same thing.

Hypothesis Testing

The maximum $\bar{R}^2$ selection rule discussed in the last section is a methodological convention. It involves an implicit assumption that disagreement between the theoretical model and observations is a monotone decreasing function of $\bar{R}^2$. However, this convention can be in conflict with classical statistical inference. In classical statistical inference, the disagreement between the theoretical model and observations is a monotone decreasing function of the probability with which the observed event is supposed to occur.

The two conventions necessarily yield similar conclusions only if the *population* coefficient of determination, P^2, is equal to 1.0. The probability density function of the *sample* coefficient of determination is noncentral F, with $k - 1$, $n - k$ degrees of freedom and noncentrality parameter nP^2. This reduces to the familar central F (see equation 3.28) when the null hypothesis is $P^2 = 0$.

The following illustrates this distinction (Basmann 1964). Suppose we are able to derive, from a conjunction of the underlying behavioral marketing postulates and the given sample observations of size 20 on three exogenous variables, a statement that P^2 just lies between 0.3 and 0.4. Furthermore, suppose we obtain $R^2 = 0.75$ in the regression run. Under the first convention, we may well judge that this test statistic does not disagree with our model. However, since

$$\int_{0.75}^{1.0} f(R^2; 20P^2; 2)\, d(R^2) \leq 0.05, \tag{3.4}$$

under the second convention, we would decide that the observed sample coefficient of determination is *too large* to be in good agreement with our marketing postulates.

Embedded Alternatives.   Classical statistical inference can be used to compare two models when one model is a constrained version of the other. We consider the application of this approach to discriminating among nested models and to deciding whether to pool cross-section and time series data.

Nested Models.   One way to discriminate among linear models is to nest the specific alternative models within one general model. Hypotheses about the values of certain parameters of the general model can be deduced from the specific alternative models. For instance, suppose we want to choose between these two alternative specific models:

$$q_t = \beta_{10} + \beta_{11} x_t + \beta_{12} x_{t-1} + \varepsilon_{1t}, \tag{3.5}$$

and

$$q_t = \beta_{20} + \beta_{21} x_t + \beta_{22} q_{t-1} + \varepsilon_{2t}. \tag{3.6}$$

Then we can embed these two models in this general model:

$$q_t = \beta_0 + \beta_1 x_t + \beta_2 x_{t-1} + \beta_3 q_{t-1} + \varepsilon_t. \tag{3.7}$$

If at least one, but not both, of the last two parameters (β_2, β_3) in the general model is zero, then we can discriminate between the two models. If $\beta_2 = 0$, we will reject the model of (3.5). If $\beta_3 = 0$, we will reject the model of (3.6). Bass and Clarke (1972), Weiss and Windal (1980), and de Kluyver and Brodie (1987) applied this test to various nested models of advertising carryover. Weiss and Windal's work is discussed in the section on specifying marketing dynamics in chapter 7.

A robust procedure for testing a regression model against a nested alternative model can be derived using the likelihood ratio method. A nested model implies that s of the variables in a full regression model with k variables will have zero regression coefficients. Kendall and Stuart (1973, pp. 257–61) show that the appropriate test statistic is

$$F = \frac{n - k}{s} \frac{(\text{SSE}_r - \text{SSE}_f)}{\text{SSE}_f}, \tag{3.8}$$

where SSE_r and SSE_f are the least-squares residual sum of squares for the nested and full regression models, respectively. The nested model will be rejected if $\hat{F} > F(\alpha, s, n - k)$.

The nested approach to model discrimination has some limitations. It is difficult to use if the number of alternative models becomes too large. A large number of alternative models would likely require a general model with a large number of variables. This, in turn, would necessitate a large sample size as well as increase the potential for multicollinearity problems. Moreover, if one of the specific alternative models is the correct model, then the general model will involve specification error because of the presence of irrelevant variables. However, the specification error involved in inclusion of irrelevant variables is minor. The parameters and the mean–squared error are estimated correctly; only the precision of the estimates is affected. The standard errors of the parameter estimates will be larger than they should be. This will become a problem if the collinearity between the relevant included variables and the irrelevant included variables is large.

Pooling. The F-statistic (3.8) can be used to test whether or not to pool T time periods and N cross-sections of data. The problem is one of testing the conditions under which pooling is appropriate, since we know that the micro-parameter vectors (say, of the different sales territories) have to be equal to prevent aggregation or "pooling" bias. The basic procedure is described briefly. Perform *unconstrained* regression, viz.,

$$
\begin{bmatrix} q_1 \\ q_2 \\ \vdots \\ q_N \end{bmatrix} = \begin{bmatrix} \mathbf{X}_1 & 0 & \cdots & 0 \\ 0 & \mathbf{X}_2 & & \\ \vdots & & & \\ 0 & 0 & \cdots & \mathbf{X}_N \end{bmatrix} \begin{bmatrix} \boldsymbol{\beta}_1 \\ \boldsymbol{\beta}_2 \\ \vdots \\ \boldsymbol{\beta}_N \end{bmatrix} + \begin{bmatrix} \varepsilon_1 \\ \varepsilon_2 \\ \vdots \\ \varepsilon_N \end{bmatrix}, \tag{3.9}
$$

estimating $N \times k'$ parameters using $N \times T$ observations, and *constrained* regression, viz.,

$$
\begin{bmatrix} q_1 \\ q_2 \\ \vdots \\ q_N \end{bmatrix} = \begin{bmatrix} \mathbf{X}_1 \\ \mathbf{X}_2 \\ \vdots \\ \mathbf{X}_N \end{bmatrix} [\boldsymbol{\beta}] + \begin{bmatrix} \varepsilon_1 \\ \varepsilon_2 \\ \vdots \\ \varepsilon_N \end{bmatrix}, \tag{3.10}
$$

estimating k' parameters with $N \times T$ observations. The constrained regression amounts to pooling the observations from all sales territories, thereby constraining the coefficient vectors $\boldsymbol{\beta}_i$, $\boldsymbol{\beta}_j$ for all i, j to be equal. This would imply that the sales territories exhibit equivalent sales responsiveness. Unconstrained regression, on the other hand, allows each sales territory to behave differently in this regard. The null hypothesis is

$$
H_0: \boldsymbol{\beta}_1 = \boldsymbol{\beta}_2 = \cdots = \boldsymbol{\beta}_N = \boldsymbol{\beta}. \tag{3.11}
$$

To test the null hypothesis of equal response coefficients, covariance analysis may be used. The general framework in which this testing can take place will be discussed briefly. In general, let the model under investigation be

$$
q_i = \mathbf{X}_i \boldsymbol{\beta}_i + \varepsilon_i, \qquad i = 1, 2, \ldots, N \text{ (territories)}. \tag{3.12}
$$

Making the usual assumptions, the ordinary least squares (OLS) estimator of $\boldsymbol{\beta}_i$ is unbiased and efficient.

To determine whether the response coefficient vectors, $\boldsymbol{\beta}_i$, $\boldsymbol{\beta}_j$ for all i, j, differ significantly, we can proceed as follows. Assuming that

$$
\sigma^2_{\varepsilon_i} = \sigma^2_{\varepsilon_j}, \quad \text{for all } i, j,
$$

this hypothesis of overall homogeneity can be tested using the F-statistic (3.8) where $n = N \times T$, $k = N \times k'$, and $r = k' \times (n - 1)$. Leeflang and Reuyl (1986) used this test in examing entity aggregation in market share response models of the West German cigarette market.

A number of issues relevant to this procedure for investigating the homogeneity in the overall relation should be considered, however. A lack of overall homogeneity may be the result of differences in only one or two of the parameters across sales territories. It is possible to use mixed models in the sense that all but one or a few of the parameters are constrained to be equal while the other parameters are allowed to be different. Similarly, it may be argued that some of the cross-sections have the same relation while others behave differently. Although it would be possible to segment sales territories according to similarity in the relation using some heuristic (Wittink 1973), it is not possible, in a strict sense, to test the appropriateness of such a procedure.

The F-statistic suggested to test the existence of homogeneity in the relation is based on several assumptions. First, the model is assumed to be correctly specified. If it is argued that it is never possible to include all relevant variables in a model, then the null hypothesis of homogeneity can always be rejected as long as the sample size is large enough. Wallace (1972, p. 690) has argued for constrained estimation (pooling) even when the null hypothesis is rejected, because "even if the restriction is strictly invalid, the constrained estimators have smaller variances and one might be willing to make a trade-off, accepting some bias in order to reduce variances."

A second assumption involves the homogeneity of disturbance variances. When comparing the relation across sales territories using covariance analysis, it is assumed that the variances are homogeneous. This assumption can be relaxed, but only asymptotic tests (using the estimated disturbance variances) can be used to investigate the homogeneity of relations under conditions of heterogeneous variances (Swamy 1971, pp. 124–26). Furthermore, the appropriateness of the F-test for the purpose of comparing response coefficient vectors for each of the sales territories is also conditional upon the existence of homogeneity in the relation over time. The validity of each of these assumptions should be established. In addition, different pooling methods should be considered and compared, from both theoretical and empirical viewpoints (Bass and Wittink 1975).

Disparate Alternatives.   Rust and Schmittlein (1985) reviewed some methods for comparing non-nested models; that is, models in which there is no relation between the models' parameter spaces. These methods included Atkinson's supermodel, split-half cross-validation, Akaike's maximum likelihood criterion, and Bayesian. Atkinson (1970) discussed how earlier notions of Cox (1961; 1962) could be implemented for discriminating among models. A supermodel is constructed that is an exponentially weighted product of the competing models:

$$\text{supermodel} = (\text{model specification } 1)^\theta (\text{model specification } 2)^{1-\theta}, \quad (3.13)$$

where $0 \leq \theta \leq 1$. When $\theta = 1$, the supermodel reduces to the first model specification, and when $\theta = 0$, to the second. Split-half cross-validation involves estimating the models on one sample and then calculating error statistics on the holdout sample. This method should be used for time series data only with extreme caution, as we shall discuss shortly. One form of Akaike's information criterion, AIC (Stone 1979, p. 276), is

$$AIC = \log(\text{maximum likelihood}) - (\text{number of estimated parameters}). \quad (3.14)$$

The decision rule is to choose the model with the largest AIC. Bayesian methods generate posterior probabilities that might be interpreted as probabilities of model correctness (Atkinson 1978; Smith and Spiegelhalter 1980). Rust and Schmittlein (1985) concluded by proposing a new method, a Bayesian cross-validated likelihood method, and illustrating how it could be applied.

MacKinnon (1983) reviewed model specification tests against non-nested alternatives in the context of regression models. He noted that non-nested hypothesis tests are tests of model specification rather than of model selection criteria. While it may be that one of two rival models will be rejected and the other not, it could also be that both models, or neither model, will be rejected. He has warned that the results of non-nested hypothesis tests should be interpreted with caution when the sample size is small and that these tests should be used only when both models have similar numbers of parameters.

Predictive Testing.   The notion of predictive testing, in which the predictions of a theory are tested against empirical data, falls within long-established traditions of scientific inquiry. For this reason, the fact that predictive tests are not used more widely in marketing is somewhat surprising. The primary development of the ideas of predictive testing in econometric research is due to Basmann (1964; 1965; 1968). Initial studies involving predictive testing in marketing have been made by Bass (1969a) and Bass and Parsons (1969). The concept has been further discussed by Bass (1969b; 1971).

Horsky (1977a) provides an example of predictive testing. He derived a model of market share response to advertising:

$$Y_1 = K_1 X_1 + K_2 X_2 + \lambda_1 X_3 + \lambda_1^2 X_4 + K_1 \lambda_1 X_5 + K_2 \lambda_1 X_6, \quad (3.15)$$

where the definition of variables is not important to our discussion. He then estimated the model:

$$Y_1 = \beta_1 X_1 + \beta_2 X_2 + \beta_3 X_3 + \beta_4 X_4 + \beta_5 X_5 + \beta_6 X_6. \quad (3.16)$$

The theoretical model predicts relations among the parameters. In particular, the hypotheses $\beta_4 = \beta_3^2$, $\beta_5 = \beta_1 \beta_3$, and $\beta_6 = \beta_2 \beta_3$ must be tested.

An explanatory marketing model, such as a sales response function, is comprised of theoretical marketing premises and justifiable factual statements of initial conditions. From the model, a set of prediction statements that attribute definite probabilities to specified observable marketing events can be deduced. Deductive analysis of an explanatory marketing model should result in a statement of the exact finite sample joint distribution function of parameter estimates and test statistics.

Discourses on the scientific method usually consider a predictive test to be conducted under experimental conditions. Often it is implied that initial conditions appropriate for a particular theory are thoroughly known. Then an effective technology for controlling these initial conditions is assumed to exist and to have been used.

It is true, nevertheless, that careful consideration of initial conditions cannot be omitted when developing a marketing model. Since the model can be falsified by unsuccessful predictions, close attention must be given to substantiating statements that claim that external influences are negligible during the historical period analyzed.

A statement of initial conditions is really a combination of three statements. One statement specifies the observed values of the exogenous variables explicitly included in the structural relations of the model. Another statement specifies the statistical distribution of the random disturbances explicitly included in the structural relations. In addition, one statement asserts that relevant external conditions stay approximately constant during the historical period under consideration.

What we are saying is that in the marketing environment uncontrollable changes can be anticipated to cause the structure of a relation to change. Thus, we need to know how a theory can be tested in a situation where its structural form is not invariant to time. The necessary additional information is clearly a precise statement of the environmental conditions under which the theory is assumed to hold. In effect, we must guard against sampling from the wrong temporal population when testing a particular model; otherwise, we may falsely reject a theory.

The predictive test of an explanatory marketing model is implemented by specifying an observable event (the critical region for the test) with a very small probability of occurring if the conjunction of initial conditions and substantive premises is discredited. If factual investigation justifies the statement of initial conditions, then at least one, and maybe only one, of the marketing premises is discredited.

Note that forecast and prediction are not synonymous. Important and pragmatic statements about future occurrences can be made without deducing these statements from initial conditions with the aid of a model. A forecast is an extrapolation from statistical parameter estimates obtained in one historical period to observations generated in another historical period. Therefore, while forecasts *seem* to provide information concerning a hypothesis, neither "good" nor "bad" forecasts supply any relevant evidence in themselves (Brunner 1973). Forecasts do not satisfy the logical requirements of a test statement. Similar arguments would seem to hold for the application of split-half cross-validation methods to time series data.

Managerial Usefulness

Market response models are usually formulated, estimated, and tested in terms of aggregated data. One exception is the work of Blattberg and Jeuland (1981b). They built an advertising response model starting with microrelations and then derived a macromodel for estimation and testing purposes.[2] The problem is that the macrovariables do not relate to each other in the same way microvariables do. The macromodel is likely to be quite complex unless very restrictive assumptions are made. Even worse, there may not even be an exact relation based only on macrovariables. Thus, when a macromodel is thought of as an aggregation of microrelations, it should be considered an approximation rather than an exact specification (cf. Clements and Selvanathan 1988). In this sense, a model may be more appropriately assessed in terms of its usefulness.

Perhaps too much emphasis is placed on significance tests. The model builder should always keep in mind the purpose for fitting the model in the first place. Consideration should be given to the consequences of erroneously choosing one model specification when a competing specification might be the true one. Thus, a broader concept of model adequacy is perhaps required. Fortunately, as we shall see in chapter 8, the consequences in terms of deviation from the optimal level of discounted profits that arise from misspecifying market response is usually not great.

Observational Equivalence

Discrimination among alternative models is impossible if they are *observationally equivalent*. This occurs when two or more theories yield exactly the same implications about observable phenomena in all situations. Under such conditions no sample, no matter how large, can resolve the issue.

We use the term *observational equivalence* loosely to cover any observed space in which the models under consideration are not observationally distinguishable. Saunders (1987, pp. 27–29) applied different functional forms to the same data sets and all fit quite well. He concluded:

> It is evident that good fit does not mean that an expression [functional form] gives the right shape. This is particularly true if an expression is used to fit data that only

covers a small portion of the curve. In such cases it is not safe to draw conclusions about the shape that an expression gives beyond the limits of the data.

This warning should be kept in mind when implementing marketing policies based upon an estimated sales response function.

Observational equivalence is an inherent problem with the hypothetico-deductive method of science. We can conclusively reject theories but cannot have the same confidence about their acceptance. The fact that a model cannot be rejected does not imply that every other model describing a sales response function is incorrect.

Even when we are able to set the values of variables for best discrimination among models, we should be aware that these values will not in general be those that give the best parameter estimation for the correct model. The impact, or the lack thereof, of sample size should also be noted. A model's total error can be partitioned into modeling error and estimation (sampling) error. Model error refers to the discrepancy between the particular parametric specification being estimated and the true model. Estimation error is sampling error arising from the fact that estimation is being done on one of many possible data sets. Rust and Schmittlein (1985, p. 23) have stated:

> As the sample size is increased the estimation error for a model may be decreased to any desired level, but modelling error cannot be reduced in this way. Using an incorrect parametric ... means that there is always a discrepancy between the estimated model and the true process, regardless of sample size. When compared with parsimonious models, complex models which include more effects (and more parameters) will generally have a smaller modelling error and a larger estimation error. ... Akaike's information criterion is a Bayes solution for trading off these modelling and estimation errors in choosing models.

Estimation

Our focus is on finding estimates of the unstandardized parameters in a sales response function, or, more generally, in a market mechanism. This information will allow a marketing manager to evaluate the possible consequences of a marketing action. In this setting, the use of standardized parameter estimates, sometimes called beta weights, is not appropriate. Wittink (1983a) has demonstrated that "beta weights are meaningless for applications involving managerial decision making" by showing that "although beta weights allow for comparisons between predictor variables when the variables are measured in different units, they have no actionable interpretation to managers."

To make estimation as easy as possible and to ensure that any resultant parameter estimates have desirable statistical properties, simplifying assumptions are made about the error structure. A set of generally accepted assumptions is the starting point. If one or more of these assumptions is not reasonable, estimation is usually still possible but may be more difficult.

Generally Accepted Assumptions

There are eight assumptions underlying classical estimation of a single-equation model. These are shown in table 3–1. When a response system or market mechanism involves more than one equation, additional assumptions are required. The first assumption, linearity, is now expressed as a linear simultaneous equation system:

$$Q\Gamma + XB = E. \qquad (3.17)$$

When a model contains as many equations as current endogenous variables, the system is said to be complete. The generally accepted assumption is that an equation system is complete. Consequently, the matrix Γ, which contains the coefficients of the current endogenous variables in each equation, is square. The matrix Γ is assumed to be nonsingular. Each equation in the model is

Table 3–1. Classical Ordinary Least Squares (OLS) Assumptions

Assumption	Violation
1. Linearity $q = \beta_1 x_1 + \beta_2 x_2 + \cdots + \beta_k x_k + \varepsilon$ $= X\beta + \varepsilon$	Nonlinearity (see table 3–2)
2. Constant coefficients β	Varying or random coefficients (see table 3–3)
3. Nonstochastic regressor matrix X	Contemporaneous correlations of regressor and disturbance (see table 3–4)
4. Zero mean for disturbances $E(\varepsilon) = 0$	Nonzero mean for disturbances (see table 3–5)
5. Constant variance σ^2 for disturbances	Heteroscedasticity (see table 3–6)
6. Pairwise uncorrelated disturbances $E(\varepsilon\varepsilon') = \sigma^2 I$	Autocorrelation (see table 3–7)
7. Influence of each regressor distinguishable rank $X = k$	Multicollinearity (see table 3–8)
8. Disturbances distributed multivariate normal $\varepsilon \sim N(0, \sigma^2 I)$	Non-normality (see table 3–9)

assumed to be identifiable; that is, the a priori information necessary to distinguish the model from other models capable of generating the observed data exists.

Estimation Methods

General methods for obtaining point estimators for the unknown parameters of a model include (1) the least-squares method, (2) the maximum likelihood (ML) method, and (3) the statistical decision theory approach, and (4) the Bayesian method. The method of least squares involves finding the values of the parameters that make the sum of squares of the deviations of the predictions of the estimated function from the actual observations as small as possible. The maximum likelihood method involves finding the values of parameters that make the probability of obtaining the observed sample outcome as high as possible. The statistical decision theory approach chooses a decision rule that makes the risk of not knowing the values of the parameters as small as possible. The Bayesian method uses sample information to update any knowledge that may exist about the probability distribution on a parameter before sample information is observed.

Choosing an Estimation Method

Identification is logically prior to estimation. Econometrics texts discuss the requirements for identification. A marketing illustration on evaluation of the identifiability of a model is given in Parsons and Schultz (1976, pp. 58–64). If the identifiability condition is met, the parameters of a model can then be estimated. There are many alternative techniques for estimation. Most techniques have been developed for the case where only sample information is available; occasionally, prior information is also available.

Sample Information Only. The choice among alternatives will be made primarily on the basis of the nature of the matrix of coefficients of the current endogenous variables Γ and the contemporaneous matrix Σ. This choice process is shown in figure 3–1. An introduction to the estimation procedures covered in figure 3–1 can be found in Parsons and Schultz (1976, pp. 67–78). They briefly discussed the model, the estimation procedure, and properties of estimators for each technique. Lack of knowledge of the exact finite sample properties of estimators means that we cannot be sure we have made the correct choice in situations involving small samples.

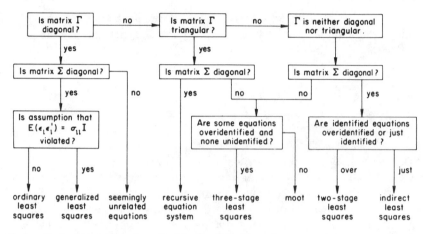

Figure 3–1. Selection of an Estimation Method. *Source*: Parsons and Schultz (1976, p. 65).

The first step is to examine the matrix Γ. If the matrix Γ is diagonal, the matrix Σ is examined. If the matrix Σ is diagonal, determine whether $E(\varepsilon\varepsilon') = \mathbf{V} = \sigma^2\mathbf{I}$ or not. If it does, use ordinary least squares (OLS); if not, use generalized least squares (GLS) if $\mathbf{V}$ is known. If $\mathbf{V}$ is not known, use a consistent estimate of $\mathbf{V}$ instead, in which case the technique is known variously as estimated, approximate, or feasible generalized least squares (EGLS). If lagged dependent variables or autocorrelated residuals are present, use iterative generalized least squares (IGLS). If the matrix Σ is not diagonal, use disturbance related equations regression—also called seemingly unrelated equations regression (SURE). When Σ is not known, an iterative procedure is again required.

If the matrix Γ is triangular and the matrix Σ diagonal, apply ordinary least squares directly to the recursive model. For the remaining categories involving the matrix Γ, if the matrix Σ is not diagonal and some equations are overidentified while none are not identified, use three-stage least squares (3SLS). When Σ is not known, an iterative procedure is once again required (I3SLS). If these conditions are not met, use indirect least squares if an equation is just identified or two-stage least squares (2SLS) if an equation is overidentified.

There are numerous applications of econometrics to a single linear estimating equation in marketing. Some examples of ordinary least squares estimation include Wierenga (1981), relating the number of visitors in a recreational park to advertising effort; Wildt, Parker, and Harris (1987), analyzing sales contests; and Hagerty, Carman, and Russell (1988), estimating elasticities with

PIMS (Profit Impact of Market Strategies) data. Generalized least squares was used by Franke and Wilcox (1987) to take into account autocorrelation in their study of industrywide advertising and consumption of alcoholic beverages.

Utilization of econometrics for multiple-equation systems is somewhat less common. Ordinary squares estimation of a recursive model was employed by Aaker and Day (1971) to study the communication process and by Moore and Winer (1987) to integrate information from joint space maps into market response models.

Disturbance related equations regression has been applied by Beckwith (1972), Wildt (1974), Houston and Weiss (1974), Picconi and Olson (1978), Takada (1986), and Nguyen (1985) to analyze the response of competing brands to advertising expenditures; by Reibstein and Gatignon (1984) to study the response of competing brands to prices; and by Parker and Dolich (1986) to understand retail strategy using cross-section rather than time series data. Clarke (1973) used an extension of the disturbance related equations regression procedure that takes into account autocorrelated disturbances in his investigation of sales-advertising cross-elasticities. Nakanishi and Cooper (1974); Bultez and Naert (1975); Naert and Weverbergh (1981a); Brodie and de Kluyver (1983); Ghosh, Neslin, and Shoemaker (1984); and Leeflang and Reuyl (1984) used ordinary least squares, generalized least squares, and iterative generalized least squares in conducting methodological comparisons of estimation methods for market share models.[3]

Any complete market share system is sum-constrained (by definition), and consequently its contemporaneous covariance matrix will be singular. In such a situation, one equation is deleted and disturbance related regression applied to the remaining equations. If the contemporaneous covariance matrix is known, the resulting parameter estimates are invariant as to which equation was deleted (McGuire et al. 1968). Gaver, Horsky, and Narasimhan (1988) have shown that when the contemporaneous covariance matrix is unknown, the parameter estimates may indeed depend on the equation deleted. They made recommendations for the estimation of market share systems that vary depending upon the balance of the error covariance structure and the correlation it exhibits.

The method of two-stage least squares is the most popular of the simultaneous equation estimating procedures. This method has been applied by Farley and Leavitt (1968) to a model of the distribution of branded personal products in Jamaica; by Bass (1969b) and Rao (1972) to models of the sales-advertising relation of cigarettes; by Bass and Parsons (1969) to the analysis of sales and advertising of ready-to-eat cereals; by Dalrymple and Haines (1970) in an investigation of market period demand-supply relations for a firm selling fashion products; by Samuels (1970–1971) to advertising and sales of household cleansers; by Cowling (1972) to advertising and sales of various products; and by Albach (1979) to pricing and sales of prescription drugs.

Three-stage least squares was used by Schultz (1971a) in an study of the airline industry; by Houston (1977b) in an econometric analysis of positioning; and, in two studies based on business-level (PIMS) data, by Carpenter (1987) in an investigation of competitive marketing strategies and by Tellis and Fornell (1988) in a examination of the relation of advertising and product quality over the product life cycle. Iterative three-stage least squares was employed by Lancaster (1984) to explore the relation of competitive brand advertising to industry, brand, and rival retail sales and market share in seven mature nondurable product categories.

Incorporating Other Information. Benefits may accrue from integrating marketing information from diverse sources (Parsons 1975a):

1. A source might provide information that is unique.
2. Even where alternative sources could provide the identical information, their costs may be quite different.
3. Different sources might provide complementary perspective of the same situation.
4. Different kinds of data are amenable to different types of analytical procedures.
5. Similar information from different sources is a basis for validation.
6. Together, different sources might improve the precision with which a structural relation can be measured.
7. Finally, but perhaps most importantly, there might be a theoretical connection among various information inputs.

These benefits justify developing methods for integrating various sources of marketing information. Our immediate concern is with methods for combining sample and nonsample information. This can be done either by traditional econometric approaches or by a Bayesian econometric approach.

The Traditional Approach. The basic econometric approach to incorporating extraneous information about some of the parameters in a linear relation is straightforward. The parameter vector is partitioned into two subvectors:

$$q = [X_1 \quad X_2]\begin{bmatrix} \beta_1 \\ \beta_2 \end{bmatrix} + \varepsilon. \tag{3.18}$$

If an outside unbiased estimate $\tilde{\beta}_1$ of β_1 is available, then the equation can be rearranged:

$$q - X_1\tilde{\beta}_1 = X_2\beta_2 + (\varepsilon - X_1\tilde{\varepsilon}), \qquad (3.19)$$

where $\tilde{\varepsilon} = \tilde{\beta}_1 - \beta_1$. Now the regression of $q - X_1\tilde{\beta}_1$ on the smaller set of explanatory variables X_2 can be run.

Exact nonsample information may not only be about a particular parameter but could also be about a linear combination of parameters. For instance, the sum of certain parameters may equal a known value, or two coefficients may be known to equal each other. All these various pieces of information can be expressed in the relation

$$R\beta = r, \qquad (3.20)$$

where R is a prespecified matrix of order $s \times k$ with $s \leq k$, and r is a prespecified s-element vector. The matrix R is often called the information design matrix. The least-squares method can be extended to take into account the linear equality restriction (3.20) by using classical Lagrangian procedures, in which case the method is known as *restricted least squares*.[4]

The estimates $\tilde{\beta}_1$ of the parameters β_1 often come from one sample, say, a cross-section sales response function, and are introduced into the subsequent equation, say, a time series sales response function, as if they were known with certainty. Thus, the parameter estimates obtained from the time series data are *conditional* upon the estimates obtained from the cross-section data. Consequently, sensitivity analysis, in which the values of $\tilde{\beta}_1$ are systematically varied, is often necessary. However, a better procedure would involve explicitly taking into account the random nature of $\tilde{\beta}_1$.

A more efficient procedure would also attempt to improve the estimate of β by taking into account the regression data. Thus, the two pieces of information can be combined, i.e.,

$$\begin{bmatrix} q \\ \tilde{\beta}_1 \end{bmatrix} = \begin{bmatrix} X_1 & X_2 \\ I & 0 \end{bmatrix} \begin{bmatrix} \beta_1 \\ \beta_2 \end{bmatrix} + \begin{bmatrix} \varepsilon \\ \tilde{\varepsilon} \end{bmatrix}, \qquad (3.21)$$

and then generalized least squares can be applied to this equation system as a whole.

The stochastic nonsample information can come from management judgment as well as from research findings. Suppose a manager believes that 0.5 is the most plausible value of a promotion elasticity and that the odds that this elasticity is in the interval (0.3, 0.7) are 20 to 1. Since the range is approximately equal to 4 standard deviations, the manager's judgment can be considered a point estimate of the elasticity equal to 0.5 with a standard error of 0.1.

Whatever the source, stochastic nonsample information can be expressed in more general form by modifying (3.21) to take into account η, an s-element normally distributed random vector

$$\mathbf{R}\boldsymbol{\beta} + \boldsymbol{\eta} = \mathbf{r}. \tag{3.22}$$

The generalized least squares estimation procedure that incorporates this restriction is called *stochastic restricted least squares*.

The estimation procedures discussed have involved two steps. First, estimate parameters from the first sample. Second, use these estimates as additional information for efficient estimation in the second sample. A logical extension is to combine the two samples. The relation would now be expressed as

$$\begin{bmatrix} \mathbf{q}_A \\ \mathbf{q}_B \end{bmatrix} = \begin{bmatrix} \mathbf{X}_{1A} & \mathbf{X}_{2A} & \mathbf{0} \\ \mathbf{X}_{1B} & \mathbf{0} & \mathbf{X}_{3B} \end{bmatrix} \begin{bmatrix} \boldsymbol{\beta}_1 \\ \boldsymbol{\beta}_2 \\ \boldsymbol{\beta}_3 \end{bmatrix} + \begin{bmatrix} \boldsymbol{\varepsilon}_A \\ \boldsymbol{\varepsilon}_B \end{bmatrix}, \tag{3.23}$$

where A and B denote observations from samples 1 and 2, respectively. There is one subset of variables and corresponding parameters that the two samples have in common, and there are two other subsets each of which is specific to a particular sample. The parameters are estimated by generalized least squares. The procedure is said to be balanced in that the a priori information from one sample is not assumed to be error-free.

Up to this point, a one-to-one correspondence between parameters from different samples has been assumed. Unfortunately, these parameters may not be directly comparable. The problem occurs when there is temporal interdependence in the time series relation or when there is contemporaneous interdependence in the cross-section relation. This necessitates formulating a more general model that incorporates these phenomena in order to establish the relation between parameters from different sources.

The Bayesian Approach.   A substantial amount of literature exists on Bayesian inference in econometrics, e.g., Zellner (1971; 1988a). Although this approach is not without its critics, Bayesian methodology does focus on integration of different data.

Bayesian inference might be used to combine initial information with new data. The initial information could result from previous studies, theoretical considerations, or casual observation. Initial information about a parameter is expressed as a prior probability density function. The new sample information is represented by its likelihood function. Bayes' theorem is then used to obtain a posterior probability density function, which incorporates both the initial information and sample information. This relation can be written for an unknown parameter vector $\boldsymbol{\theta}$ as

$$p(\boldsymbol{\theta}|\mathbf{q}) \propto p(\boldsymbol{\theta})l(\boldsymbol{\theta}|\mathbf{q}). \tag{3.24}$$

This approach can be used in the context of regression models.

When the initial information is vague, $\boldsymbol{\beta}$ and $\log \sigma$ are assumed to be independently and uniformly distributed. The prior distribution is thus

$$p(\boldsymbol{\beta}, \sigma) \propto \frac{1}{\sigma}, \tag{3.25}$$

where $-\infty < \beta_i < \infty$, and $0 < \sigma < \infty$.

The disturbances in regression usually are assumed to be normally distributed, in which case the likelihood function for the sample values is

$$l(\boldsymbol{\beta}, \sigma^2|\mathbf{q}) = \frac{1}{(2\pi\sigma^2)^{n/2}} * \exp\left(\frac{-(\mathbf{q} - \mathbf{X}\boldsymbol{\beta})'(\mathbf{q} - \mathbf{X}\boldsymbol{\beta})}{2\sigma^2}\right). \tag{3.26}$$

The joint posterior probability density function is

$$p(\boldsymbol{\beta}, \sigma|\mathbf{q}, \mathbf{X}) \propto \frac{1}{\sigma} * \frac{1}{\sigma^n} * \exp\left(-\frac{(\mathbf{q} - \mathbf{X}\boldsymbol{\beta})'(\mathbf{q} - \mathbf{X}\boldsymbol{\beta})}{2\sigma^2}\right). \tag{3.27}$$

In this case, the estimator for $\boldsymbol{\beta}$ is the same as that given for the classical maximum likelihood method.

Given the appropriate expression for diffuseness, that is, priors for the situation where our knowledge about model parameters is vague or diffuse, the Bayesian approach often yields similar results to that of the traditional approach. However, the interpretation will differ inasmuch as the Bayesian approach considers the parameters as random variables whereas the traditional approach views them as fixed numbers.

Bayesian analysts note that the traditional methods of introducing additional information about some coefficients in a regression model have only an asymptotic justification. In contrast, they argue, their approach yields "exact finite sample" results. However, these "exact finite results" are possible only through the introduction of a tractable continuous prior distribution. The arbitrariness in eliciting prior distributions remains a central problem of Bayesian analysis. Moreover, tractability requires that a priori opinion be represented by one of several special distributions. Nonetheless, the argument between Bayesians and traditionalists focuses on how prior information should be used and not on whether it should be used.

Testing

A broad set of tests can and should be applied to a model during its development and implementation. The evaluation of a model begins with the testing of its statistical assumptions. The model must be examined for problems such as nonlinearity, contemporaneous correlation of regressor and disturbance, omitted variables, heteroscedasticity, autocorrelation, multicollinearity, and non-normality. This portion of the evaluation is called specification error analysis. If no violations of the assumptions are found, the regression results can be tested. This involves tests of significance concerning each individual model and subsequently discrimination among alternative models. First, however, we consider some tests of significance that assume there is no specification error.

Tests of Significance

When the disturbances in the standard linear model are assumed to be normally distributed, we can conduct separate tests of hypotheses about each of the parameters of the model as well as a joint test on the significance of the entire linear relation. Various linear hypotheses about the elements of β can be tested using the relation (3.20). For instance, the hypothesis that $R = [0 \quad I_{k-1}]$ and $r = 0$ provides a test of the overall relation that assesses whether the independent variables have any influence upon the dependent variable. If b and e are the OLS parameter and residual vectors, then the test statistic

$$F = \frac{(Rb - r)'[R(X'X)^{-1}R']^{-1}(Rb - r)/s}{e'e/(n - k)} \tag{3.28}$$

is distributed as $F(s, n - k)$.

These tests of significance apply only to single-equation models. Except in a few special cases, the small-sample properties of various simultaneous equation estimators are unknown. We next turn to an examination of the maintained hypothesis that underlies the single-equation tests of significance.

Specification Error Analysis

A true model describes the distributional characteristics of a population. Specification error occurs when a model other than the true model is used. We view the distribution of the disturbance terms as an integral part of the model. Consequently, when an assumption about the error structure of a model is violated, the result is not merely being unable to obtain optimal properties for the estimators of the model parameters. Rather, the violation poses a fundamental challenge to the model. This section focuses on specification error tests constructed primarily for the single-equation standard linear model.

The common types of specification error are (1) omitted variables, (2) incorrect functional form, (3) simultaneous equation problems, (4) heteroscedasticity, (5) non-normality of the disturbance term, (6) autocorrelation, and (7) errors in variables. Tests for these errors can be either general or specific. A general test is one against a broad group of alternatives; a specific test is one against a limited alternative. For instance, we could use a general test against nonlinearity, or we might test against a specific alternative such as a quadratic relation:

$$y = \beta_1 + \beta_2 x + \beta_3 x^2 + \varepsilon. \tag{3.29}$$

The specific test would be the F-test for the null hypothesis $\mathbf{R} = [0 \ \ 0 \ \ 1]$ and $\mathbf{r} = 0$. In subsequent sections, we discuss general tests for specification error.

Residual Vectors. Specification error tests involve examination of the regression residuals. The least-squares residual vector

$$\mathbf{e} = \mathbf{q} - \mathbf{Xb} = [\mathbf{I} - \mathbf{X(X'X)}^{-1}\mathbf{X'}]\mathbf{q} = \mathbf{Mq} \tag{3.30}$$

provides one approximation to the disturbance vector. Unfortunately, even though the disturbances are stochastically independent and homoscedastic, the least-squares residuals are usually not. This causes problems in testing the distribution of the disturbance vector. Consequently, a residual vector is required that has a scalar covariance matrix when the disturbance vector does. The BLUS residual vector is such a vector. BLUS stands for Best Linear Unbiased Scalar covariance matrix. Theil (1971, pp. 202–10) defined the BLUS residual vector and describes its properties. One property of the BLUS residual vector is that the maximum number of independent residuals that can be obtained is $n - k$. Thus, we must choose which subset of residuals to use. Theil (1971, pp. 217–18) discussed this selection procedure.

The Impact of Specification Error. One approach to specification error analysis (Ramsey 1969; 1974) is to consider the impact of the various types of error. The null hypothesis is that a particular single-equation linear model is the true model. Under the usual assumptions, the BLUS residuals are normally distributed with mean zero and covariance matrix $\sigma^2 \mathbf{I}_{n-k}$. If an alternative model is true, use of this given model will result in specification error. Alternative models that would give rise to omitted variables, incorrect function form, or simultaneous equation problems lead to the BLUS residuals being normally distributed with a nonzero mean and covariance matrix $\mathbf{V}$. Thus, if the estimator were unbiased, the error creates bias, or if the estimator were biased but consistent, this error brings about a different bias and inconsistency.

The recognition of the presence of at least one of these errors is accomplished by regressing the BLUS residuals against a polynomial (usually of degree 2 or 3) in transformed least-squares estimates of the dependent variable:

$$\hat{\varepsilon} = \alpha_1 + \alpha_2(\mathbf{C}\hat{\mathbf{q}}) + \alpha_3(\mathbf{C}\hat{\mathbf{q}}^2) + \cdots. \tag{3.31}$$

Under the null hypothesis of no specification error, the alphas should all be zero. Unfortunately, if the null hypothesis is rejected, we do not know which of the three types of errors caused this shift in the central tendency of the estimator.

Alternative models that would give rise to heteroscedasticity result in the BLUS residuals being normally distributed with mean zero and a diagonal covariance matrix with unequal nonzero elements. If the alternative hypothesis is that the BLUS residuals are distributed as $\sigma^2\chi^2$, then Bartlett's M-test can be used.

General tests exist for most of the specification errors we might encounter. We now turn to a discussion of these tests. Each test is for one specification error in the absence of other specification errors.

Nonlinearity. Linear models are computationally easy to estimate. Unfortunately, most marketing phenomena are nonlinear. For example, a sales response function is believed to exhibit diminishing returns to scale over most, if not all, of its range. Fortunately, many nonlinear functional forms can be transformed into linear ones for estimation purposes. Those that cannot be transformed must be estimated by nonlinear methods. The treatment of nonlinearity is summarized to table 3–2.

Transformations. Transformations are often used to convert linearizable nonlinear structural models into linear estimating equation. Consider the common sales response function (see equation 2.12) with a multiplicative disturbance

Table 3–2.   Nonlinearity

When It Occurs	*How to Detect*	*Possible Remedies*
Incorrect functional form	Plot residuals; look for systematic patterns.	Improve specification. Transform nonlinear model into linear model; otherwise use nonlinear least squares (NLS) or maximum likelihood (ML).

$$Q = e^{\beta_0} X^{\beta_1} e^{\varepsilon}. \tag{3.32}$$

A linear estimating equation for this function can be found by taking the logarithms of both sides of the relation, i.e.,

$$\ln Q = \beta_0 + \beta_1 \ln X + \varepsilon. \tag{3.33}$$

For example, di Benedetto (1985) applied this transformation to a multiplicative dynamic adjustment model of sales response to marketing mix variables. A problem arises when an observation on a variable, especially the dependent variable, is zero ($\ln[0] = -\infty$). To get around this problem, many researchers add 1 to each observation ($\ln[1] = 0$). Rao, Wind, and DeSarbo (1988, p. 132), for example, recommended adding a small positive number to all entries. Young and Young (1975) have recommended dropping observations rather than arbitrarily setting the log value of the dependent variable to be zero.

Another common transformation is the Koyck transformation for finding an estimating equation for geometric distributed lag models. This transformation is discussed in chapter 7.

Nonlinear Estimation.   Some functional forms are intrinsically nonlinear. For instance, if the sales response function (see equation 2.12) has an additive error instead of the multiplicative error assumed in (3.32), or

$$Q = e^{\beta_0} X^{\beta_1} + \varepsilon, \tag{3.34}$$

the relation cannot be transformed and its parameters must be found by nonlinear estimation techniques.

The least-squares principle can be applied to nonlinear models, although the computations will be more complex. *Nonlinear least squares* (NLS) in general provides biased estimates of the parameter vector **b**. A more serious problem is that the distribution of **b** is usually unknown even if the distribution of the disturbance term is known. Again, we must rely on asymptotic results. Under suitable conditions, the NLS estimator is consistent and asymptotically normally distributed. When the error term follows the standard normal distribution, the maximum likelihood estimator is the same as the least-squares estimator, as was the case for linear models. Horsky (1977a) used nonlinear regression to estimate market share response to advertising in the cigarette industry and Metwally (1980) used it to estimate sales response to advertising of eight Australian products.

Direct search can be used to fit parameters to complex models (Van Wormer and Weiss 1970). Srinivasan and Weir (1988) conducted a constrained search in the estimation of a version of the Koyck advertising-sales model (see

Table 3–3.   Nonconstant Coefficients

When It Occurs	How to Detect	Possible Remedies
Microunits in cross-section data respond differently. Environment changes over time.	Suspect systematic change: Split data into separate regimes, estimate, and compare results. Farley-Hinich-McGuire. Brown-Durbin-Evans. Suspect randomness: Breusch-Pagan.	Improve specification. If coefficients are systematic and deterministic, use OLS; if systematic plus a disturbance, use EGLS; if random, use EGLS; if return-to-normality, use ML; if Cooley-Prescott, use ML at point in time.

equation 7.2). The relation of interest was nonlinear in the advertising carry-over rate, which itself was constrained to lie between 0 and 1.

Nonconstant Coefficients.   The coefficients in the standard linear model are assumed to be constant. This may well not be true if microunits in a cross-section study respond differently or if the environment changes over time. The treatment of nonconstant coefficients is summarized in table 3–3.

If the changes are systematic and deterministic (see equation 2.63), OLS regression can be used. However, if the systematic changes also incorporate a random disturbance (see equation 2.64), then EGLS must be used because the error term will be heteroscedastic (see equation 2.65). Gatignon (1984) extends this approach to take into account constraints on some of the parameters in his model.

When the timing of a structural change is known, the data can be partitioned into separate regimes. Segments of a sales response function can fit separately by linear regression. This method is called *piecewise regression*. A more elegant counterpart of this methodology can be found in the theory of *splines* (Poirier 1973).

A major difficulty is defining the segments, since the timing of structural changes is rarely known. A procedure has been developed by Farley and Hinich (1970) and Farley, Hinich, and McGuire (1975) for determining if structural change has occurred. They create a set of interaction variables by multiplying each suspect explanatory variable by a time index. They then examine whether the coefficients of these interaction variables are zero or nonzero. Another test has been proposed by Brown, Durbin, and Evans (1975), which uses a *moving regression*.

The random coefficients model (see equation 2.67) can be shown to belong to the class of heteroscedastic error models in which the variance of the dependent variable is a linear function of a set of exogenous variables. These models will be discussed shortly, but we will use the results now. An appropriate test for randomness is the Breusch-Pagan test. The estimation technique will be EGLS.

The return-to-normality model (see equation 2.68) leads to serially correlated and heteroscedastic errors. In this case, the appropriate estimation method is maximum likelihood, conditional on ϕ and $\mathbf{V}$.

The Cooley-Prescott model (see equations 2.69–2.72) creates special problems because the process generating the parameters is not stationary. A maximum likelihood function can be constructed by focusing at a particular point in time, say one period past the sample.

Stochastic Regressors. The regressor matrix $\mathbf{X}$ has been assumed to be nonstochastic. This should be no problem in marketing experiments where the values of the explanatory variables can be set. However, most marketing information is nonexperimental and thus the assumption may well be violated.

Violations vary in their degree of complexity. In the simplest case, the regressor matrix $\mathbf{X}$ is stochastic but completely independent of the disturbance vector ε. The usual test statistics will not hold in finite samples, except in the unlikely case that we would want to limit any inferences made to the particular sample values of $\mathbf{X}$. Under certain conditions, the usual test statistics are asymptotically valid. The least-squares estimator $\mathbf{b}$ does provide a consistent estimate. The least-squares estimator will be the maximum likelihood estimator if the other standard assumptions hold.

A more complex case occurs when the stochastic regressors are only partly independent of the disturbance vector. This can occur in time series data when the explanatory variables include lagged values of the dependent variable. The tth observation on the regressor vector is independent of the tth and subsequent values of the disturbance term but not of past values of the disturbance term, so the least-squares estimator will be biased. The estimator is still consistent, however, and the usual test statistics are asymptotically valid.

The most complicated case (summarized in table 3–4) arises in situations where observations on some stochastic regressors are not even independent of the current disturbance. This can happen when lagged values of the dependent variable are coupled with serially correlated errors, when there are errors in variables, and when an equation is in actuality part of a larger simultaneous-

Table 3–4.   Contemporaneous Correlations of Regressor and Disturbance

When It Occurs	How to Detect	Possible Remedies
Lagged values of dependent variable coupled with serially correlated errors. Errors in measurement. Simultaneity.	Plot regressors against disturbances.	Improve specification. Use method of instrumental variables to get consistent but inefficient estimates.

Table 3–5.   Nonzero Mean Disturbances

When It Occurs	How to Detect	Possible Remedies
Omitted variable	Can only detect if not constant and repeated measures are available.	Improve specification. Use dummy variables.

equations system. The least-squares estimator will be biased and inconsistent in such cases. One solution is to replace the stochastic regressors with a new set of regressors, known as *instrumental variables*, which are correlated with the stochastic regressors but uncorrelated with the disturbance. The new estimates will then be consistent.

Sometimes a variable in a market mechanism is unobservable. A choice may arise between using a proxy variable in place of the unobserved variable and simply omitting the unobserved variable. Generally, the use of a poor proxy is better than omission of the unobserved variable. Qualifications to this conclusion are noted in Judge et al. (1985, pp. 710–11).

Nonzero Mean Disturbances.   The mean of the disturbances is expected to be zero. This will not be true if there is an omitted variable. However, as long as the mean is constant, say θ, and the equation contains a separate intercept, β_0, no major problem arises. The constant simply becomes part of the intercept, $(\beta + \theta)$. If the mean is not constant, then repeated measures become necessary. If the mean differs across microunits, then individual dummy variables can be used; i.e., we are now pooling time series and cross-section data. The treatment of nonzero mean disturbances is summarized in table 3–5.

Heteroscedasticity.   The variance of the disturbance term has been assumed to be constant. An alternative hypothesis is that this variance increases (de-

Table 3–6.   Heteroscedasticity

When It Occurs	How to Detect	Possible Remedies
Cross-section data	Bartlett	Improve specification. Use
Structural change	Breusch-Pagan	EGLS or ML.
in environment	Goldfeld-Quandt	
Change in accuracy	Szroeter	
in measurement	White	
Random coefficients model		

Alternative Error Model	Formula
No restriction on variance of y	$\mathbf{V} = \text{diag}\,(\sigma_1^2, \sigma_2^2, \ldots, \sigma_T^2)$
Variances constant within subgroups of observations	$\mathbf{V} = \text{blk diag}\,(\sigma_1^2\mathbf{I}, \sigma_2^2\mathbf{I}, \ldots, \sigma_m^2\mathbf{I})$
Standard deviation of y is a linear function of exogenous variables	$\sigma_t^2 = (\mathbf{z}_t'\boldsymbol{\alpha})^2$
Variance of y is a linear function of exogenous variables	$\sigma_t^2 = \mathbf{z}_t'\boldsymbol{\alpha}$
Variance of y is proportional to a power of its expectation	$\sigma_t^2 = \sigma^2(\mathbf{x}_t'\boldsymbol{\beta})^p$
The logarithm of the variance of y is a linear function of exogenous variables (multiplicative heterogeneity)	$\sigma_t^2 = \exp(\mathbf{z}_t'\boldsymbol{\alpha})$
Autoregressive conditional heteroscedasticity (ARCH)	$\sigma_t^2 = \xi_t(\alpha_0 + \alpha_1\varepsilon_{t-1}^2)^{1/2}$

creases) with increases in an explanatory variable in a cross-section study or over time in a time series study. If the disturbances are heteroscedastic, OLS estimates of the coefficients of the model will be unbiased but not efficient. The solution is to use estimated generalized least squares or maximum likelihood. The exact details of the estimation will depend on the alternative heteroscedastic error model posited. See table 3–6 for a summary of the treatment of heteroscedasticity.

General tests for heteroscedasticity have been proposed by Breusch-Pagan, Goldfeld-Quandt, Szoeter, and White. Historically, the most commonly used test has been Goldfeld-Quandt; currently, White's test seems to be in fashion. Kristensen (1984) used the Breusch-Pagan test in analyzing price/quantity relations.

Autocorrelation.   The standard linear model assumes that disturbances are independent, that is,

$$E(\varepsilon_t \varepsilon_{t-s}) = 0, \qquad s \neq 0. \tag{3.35}$$

The alternative hypothesis may be that two disturbances s periods apart are correlated. The correlation between these disturbances is called the *autocorrelation coefficient*, ρ.

Autocorrelation occurs most frequently with temporal data; however, it can occur in cross-section data if spatially close units are similar to one another (Dubin 1988). For example, adjacent sales territories may be more similar to one another than to more distant territories.[5]

Estimation of the covariance matrix $E(\varepsilon\varepsilon') = \mathbf{V}$ from any finite sample is not possible, as the number of parameters to be estimated will always exceed the number of observations available (Johnston 1974, p. 305). An alternative hypothesis is that the successive disturbances are positively (negatively) autocorrelated. In particular, the process is assumed to be first-order autoregressive AR(1):

$$\varepsilon_t = \varepsilon_{t-1} + \eta_t. \tag{3.36}$$

Although under this alternative hypothesis, the estimates of the regression coefficients are unbiased, the usual least-squares formula underestimates their sampling variance. Correspondingly, the usual F-statistic will be overestimated, and thus the model will seem to fit the data better than it actually does.

The test against autocorrelation is the modified von Neumann ratio. This test uses BLUS residuals. See table 3–7 for a summary of this and other tests of autocorrelation. A somewhat less powerful test, but one that is computationally simpler is the Durbin-Watson statistic, which uses least-squares residuals instead of BLUS residuals. The Durbin-Watson statistic has been used in numerous marketing studies.

The Durbin-Watson test assumes that the independent variables are fixed. Thus, the test cannot be used when lagged values of the dependent variable are present among the predetermined variables. An alternative statistic, known as Durbin h, can be used in this situation. The test statistic was used by Montgomery and Silk (1972), for example.

When one of these tests indicates the presence of first-order autocorrelation, a two-step estimation procedure is required. The first step involves obtaining an estimate of ρ by means of ordinary least squares (OLS) estimation. The second step requires that this estimate of ρ be used in an estimated generalized least squares (EGLS) regression. Marketing applications include Simon (1982) and Vanhonacker (1984).

Although AR(1) error models are the most common alternative specifications, the error structure could be a higher-order autoregressive process AR(p),

$$\varepsilon_t = \rho_1 \varepsilon_{t-1} + \rho_2 \varepsilon_{t-2} + \cdots + \rho_p \varepsilon_{t-p} + \eta_t, \tag{3.37}$$

Table 3–7. Autocorrelation

When It Occurs	Alternative Error Model	How to Detect	Possible Remedies
Omitted variable. Inherently smooth behavior of time series data.	First-order autoregressive errors AR(1)	von Neumann ratio. Durbin-Watson. Durbin h-statistic. Periodogram of residuals.	GLS EGLS NLS ML B
	Second- and higher-order autoregressive errors AR(p)	Periodogram of residuals	GLS EGLS NLS ML
	First-order moving-average errors MA(1)	Periodogram of residuals	GLS NLS ML B
	Higher-order moving-average errors MA(q)	Periodogram of residuals	NLS ML
	Autoregressive moving-average errors ARMA(p, q)	Periodogram of residuals	NLS ML

a moving-average process MA(q),

$$\varepsilon_t = \eta_t + \theta_1 \eta_{t-1} + \theta_2 \eta_{t-2} + \cdots + \theta_q \eta_{t-q}, \tag{3.38}$$

or an autoregressive moving-average process ARMA(p, q),

$$\varepsilon_t = \rho_1 \varepsilon_{t-1} + \rho_2 \varepsilon_{t-2} + \cdots + \rho_p \varepsilon_{t-p}$$
$$+ \eta_t + \theta_1 \eta_{t-1} + \theta_2 \eta_{t-2} + \cdots + \theta_q \eta_{t-q}. \tag{3.39}$$

These can be estimated by the nonlinear squares or maximum likelihood methods. ARMA processes are discussed in detail in chapter 4.

Wittink (1983b) reviewed autocorrelation and related issues in applications of regression analysis. In particular, he showed that residuals can be autocorrelated as a result of having a misspecified model.

Multicollinearity. Multicollinearity occurs when the predetermined variables are strongly related to each other; in this case, the influence of one is difficult to separate from that of another. Consequently, the explanatory

Table 3–8.   Multicollinearity

When It Occurs	How to Detect	Possible Remedies
Poor sample design, e.g., correlated explanatory variables.	Belsley-Kuh-Welsch	Collect better data. Introduce nonsample information. Use ridgelike/Stein-like estimators.

power of the regression is unaffected, but the estimates of the coefficients are not precise.

The determinant of $\mathbf{X}'\mathbf{X}$ becomes smaller as collinearity increases. Furthermore, this determinant can be expressed as the product of its eigenvalues:

$$|\mathbf{X}'\mathbf{X}| = \lambda_1 \lambda_2 \ldots \lambda_k. \tag{3.40}$$

This led Belsley, Kuh, and Welsch (1980) to propose two statistics for detecting multicollinearity, which they called the condition number and the regression coefficient variance decomposition.

The usual solution for multicollinearity is to drop one or more of the offending variables from the equation. The risk of doing this is that the relation between included and excluded variables might change over time. Thus, a better approach is to obtain new data or information that would resolve the multicollinearity issue. The treatment of multicollinearity is summarized in table 3–8. This might involve estimating some of the parameters in a time series model by a cross-section study. Then these estimates would replace the corresponding unknown parameters in the time series model. Finally, the remaining unknown parameters could be estimated using the time series data.

Another possible solution is to use *ridge regression*. The mean-square error of an estimator is equal to its variance plus its bias squared. The least-squares estimator has zero bias but has a large variance in the presence of multicollinearity. In ridge regression, some bias is accepted in order to reduce the variance. This trade-off is shown in figure 3–2. Marketing applications of ridge regression include Mahajan, Jain, and Bergier (1977), Erickson (1981b), and Ofir and Khuri (1986). Sharma and James (1981) and Krishnamurthi and Rangaswamy (1987) have recommended that latent root regression and equity estimator, respectively, be used for biased estimation instead of ridge regression. Shipchandler and Moore (1988), on the other hand, found ridge regression to be better than latent root regression.

Non-normality.   The previous specification error tests assume that the distribution of the disturbance terms is normal. One test for normality is the Shapiro-Wilk W-test. Table 3–9 summarizes the treatment of non-normality.

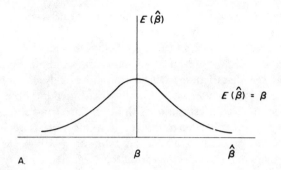

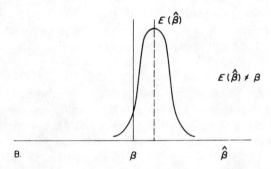

Figure 3-2. Bias and Variance in an Estimator. (A) Least-Squares Estimator: Zero Bias and a Large Variance. (B) Ridge Estimator: nonzero Bias and a Small Variance. *Source*: Parsons and Schultz (1976, p. 108).

Table 3-9. Non-normality

When It Occurs	How to Detect	Possible Remedies
Error distribution has fat tails. Distribution of dependent variable is skewed.	Shapiro-Wilk	If a priori information about form of non-normal distribution is known, use ML. Otherwise, if outliers in the error distribution are not likely, use OLS; if they are likely, use a robust estimator. When dependent variable has a skewed distribution, the Box-Cox transformation might be a solution.

The W-test can detect deviations from normality due to either skewness or kurtosis and is consequently superior to commonly used tests such as the chi-square and Kolmogorov-Smirnov tests. Shapiro and Wilk have tabulated critical values of W for values of $n - k$ between 3 and 50. For sample sizes larger than 50, the D-statistic by D'Agostino must be used.

When the disturbances are not normally distributed but do possess a finite variance, the least-squares estimators will be unbiased and consistent but not efficient or asymptotically efficient. Given that appropriate regularity conditions are met, the maximum likelihood estimators will be asymptotically efficient, but the usual tests on the estimated coefficients not be valid. If the distribution of the disturbances has an infinite variance, it will have fat tails and outliers will be common. Least-squares estimation is very sensitive to outliers, and all results will be very unreliable.

If a priori information about the form of the non-normal distribution is known, maximum likelihood estimation can be used. Otherwise, if outliers in the error distribution are not likely, ordinary least-squares regression can be used; if they are likely, it is necessary to use a robust estimator. When the dependent variable has a skewed distribution, the Box-Cox transformation might be a solution.

Robust Estimation.   One way to identify outliers is Cook's D-statistic. This test assesses whether there is a significant change in the regression coefficients if an observation is deleted from the sample. Cook's D statistic has been used in salesforce and retail store performance studies to determine if relatively large territories have an undue influence on the results.

Estimators have been developed that place less weight on outliers than the ordinary least squares method does. There are three classes of these so-called *robust estimators*: M-estimators, L-estimators, and R-estimators. M-estimators are maximum-likelihood–like estimators. L-estimators are based on linear combinations of the order statistics on the dependent variable. R-estimators are based on a ranking of the residuals in a linear model. Details and some marketing applications can be found in Mahajan, Sharma, and Wind (1984).

The Box-Cox Transformation.   Sometimes a model may be specified in which the dependent variable is not normally distributed but for which a transformation may exist that will result in the transformed observations being normally distributed. Box and Cox (1964) assume there exists a value λ such that

$$\frac{y_t^\lambda - 1}{\lambda} = \mathbf{x}_t'\boldsymbol{\beta} + \varepsilon_t, \qquad \lambda > 0, \tag{3.41}$$

where the ε_t's are normally distributed and homoscedastic.[6]

Although introduced here to address the problem of non-normality, the Box-Cox transformation is primarily applied to let the data determine the most appropriate functional form. For example, Kristensen (1984) performed an econometric analysis of an hedonic price function and concluded that the empirical result, $\hat{\lambda} = 0.59$, supported the hypothesis of a square-root model, $\lambda = 0.5$, and ruled out traditional specifications such as the linear and semilog models. Thus, the Box-Cox transformation is really a topic in functional form analysis, which is covered in chapter 4.

Systems of Equations. The analysis of specification error in simultaneous-equations models involves two additional problems. First, when an estimation technique that incorporates more information than is contained in an isolated single equation is employed, the effects of specification error can be transferred across equations. Second, the inclusion of irrelevant variables or the omission of a relevant variable is a specification error that may affect the identifiability of one or more of the equations in the system. In general, the discussion of these problems is beyond the scope of this book. We discuss just one test.

An *identifiability test statistic* should be used whenever the order and rank conditions for identifiability indicate an equation is overidentified. The purpose of the test is to determine if the a priori restrictions that caused the overidentifying conditions are correct. Usually the overidentifying condition arises from variables in the system as a whole being excluded from a particular equation. Thus, a statistical test is required to judge if these extra exclusions are correctly specified in view of the evidence provided by the sample data. Basmann (1965) discusses the construction of identifiability tests, and Parsons (1968) gives a marketing application of such tests.

Summary

At level 2 of prior knowledge, econometric methods can be applied to data to confirm or reformulate market response models. The focus of level 2 analysis is on estimation and testing.

Specification is a general problem of research strategy. It should be apparent that both scientific and creative talents are necessary to specify response models. Whether the level 2 knowledge involves market or management information, or both, the model builder's task is to specify a set of premises that imply that the model belongs to a small subset of all possible models, assuming that the model represents the true response phenomenon. The specification problem involves the procedures required to identify marketing variables and relations. Specification analysis is also concerned with the consequences of incorrect specifications on the interpretation of research results.

This chapter has emphasized *confirmatory* methods of data analysis; the next two chapters will stress *exploratory* methods of data analysis. Suppose sales of a brand are conjectured to be related to some explanatory variables, such as marketing instruments and socioeconomic variables, but there is no information about the shape of the relation. In such cases, exploratory data analysis can be used to probe the data for patterns that might justify testing in future studies.

Notes

1. Other econometric texts include Theil (1971), Maddala (1977), Harvey (1981), Pindyck and Rubinfeld (1981), Chow (1983), Johnston (1984), and Amemiya (1985).

2. Weinberg and Weiss (1986) have proposed an alternative estimation approach to the Blattberg and Jeuland model.

3. Naert and Weverbergh (1981a, p. 149) concisely explained the reason for using generalized least squares in market share models:

> When one of the market shares is overestimated, the error must be compensated for by an underestimation of one or more of the other brands. It follows that the error terms ... will be contemporaneously correlated, that is, error terms in different equations but with respect to the same time period will not be independent. Estimation efficiency therefore can be improved by explicitly accounting for this correlation in the estimation process.

4. Sometimes nonsample information will involve an inequality restriction rather than an equality restriction. In this case, the Kuhn-Tucker conditions can be used to construct an inequality-restricted least-squares estimator.

5. A major problem is the arbitrary nature of units of area. Openshaw and Taylor (1979) emphasize that "since the area over which data is collected is continuous, it follows that there will be numerous alternative ways in which it can be partitioned to form areal units for reporting the data."

6. Note that

$$\lim_{x \to 0} \left(\frac{y_t^\lambda - 1}{\lambda} \right) = \ln y_t.$$

4 DETERMINING FUNCTIONAL FORM AND LAG STRUCTURE

The techniques of parameter estimation, forecasting, and model testing set forth in chapter 3 can be used only when the market response model is fully specified. In a number of cases, however, full model specification is not possible without some preliminary data searches, in particular the search for a functional form and the specification of lag structures. In chapter 2, we referred to such cases as level 1 prior knowledge. In other words, we start from a situation where the causal ordering of a model is known but not its functional form or lag structure.

Selecting the shape of a market response function logically precedes lag specification. A functional form should be chosen with the objective of the marketing model in mind and may involve some empirical techniques, which are discussed in this chapter. Lag specification is more complex and has benefited from numerous recent developments in stochastic time series analysis. These techniques, by definition, can be applied only to longitudinal data bases.

There are many reasons why lag structures are important to marketing models. They are at the foundation of various buyer behavior theories, such as the linear learning model and the zero-order choice model. They separate short-term from long-term effects of marketing actions and thus help the manager decide what the optimal timing of marketing strategies should be. And they even make it possible to sort out the causal ordering of variables in a system.

Our discussion of lag specification starts with univariate time series analysis, where the behavior of a time series is studied strictly as a function of its own past.[1] Then, we study lag specification in single-equation models, known as transfer functions and intervention models. Finally, we discuss lag specification in systems of equations.

Specifying Functional Form

The functional form of a market response model is logically specified before the lag structures in the model. It is unlikely that different functional forms would occur at different lags; however, there is some empirical evidence that lag structures may be sensitive to functional form (e.g., Roberts and Nord 1985). Thus, it is a safe practice to choose the functional form of a market response model first.

Various shapes of market response were discussed in chapter 2. In choosing a functional form the marketing modeler should be guided by the following criteria:

1. *Theoretical insights.* Examples include diminishing returns to scale, threshold levels, and saturation level.
2. *The characteristics of the data sample.* For example, even though sales response to advertising may be concave, an approximately linear relation may exist within the range of advertising expenditures considered reasonable for the brand.
3. *The objective of the model.* A linear response model may be adequate for sales forecasting but not for setting optimal marketing budgets.
4. *Parsimony.* A large variety of mathematical forms could be used to fit marketing phenomena. Other things being equal, a simple functional form should be chosen over a more complex one: the parameter estimates are often more robust, and the results are easier to interpret in marketing terms.
5. *Empirical analysis of the data.* When a priori considerations still leave the model builder in doubt, some empirical methods may be useful. First and foremost, the model builder may visually inspect the data to infer the shape of the response function. Second, in some cases it may be possible to set up a formal hypothesis test to discriminate between competing functional forms. Finally, we can let the data select the

best functional form by examining properties of the response model residuals. The second and third alternatives are relatively new in marketing and are discussed in more detail.

Formal Tests for Functional Form

We have mentioned two frequently observed market response shapes: the concave function and the S-shaped function. The former is appropriate when additional marketing efforts have a less than proportional sales effect. The latter postulates that increasing returns to scale occur at a low level of marketing effort and that beyond some threshold level the response changes to decreasing returns.

An interesting method for a data-driven choice between the two functional forms was proposed by Johansson (1979). The principle is that of specifying a "super-model," i.e., a response function that accommodates both hypotheses. Concavity of the response function holds for one range of the parameter estimates and the S-shaped function holds for another range. Thus, it is possible to conduct a formal hypothesis test on the most likely shape of the response function.

Johansson's method is described in an advertising setting but can be logically extended to any marketing effort variable, X, and its effect on market performance, Y. The proposed supermodel is

$$\frac{Y - Y_0}{Y^0 - Y} = \beta_0 X^{\beta_1}, \tag{4.1}$$

where

β_0 = constant,

β_1 = sales response parameter,

Y_0 = base level of Y, i.e., when $X = 0$,

Y^0 = saturation level of Y, i.e., when $X \rightarrow \infty$.

Examination of the first and second derivatives of this function reveals that it is concave for $0 < \beta_1 < 1$ and S-shaped for $\beta_1 > 1$. The model is easily estimated with ordinary or weighted least squares when the base and saturation levels Y_0 and Y^0 are known a priori. When this is not the case, we can estimate the model with maximum likelihood or, more practically, with ordinary least squares using some trial values for Y_0 and Y^0. For example, when market performance is measured by market share, $Y_0 \geq 0$, and $Y^0 \leq 1$.

Johansson argues that choosing reasonable trial values for Y_0 and Y^0, along with ordinary least-squares estimates of the response coefficient, will quickly reveal whether the underlying response model is concave or S-shaped. An empirical test on the relation between market share and advertising exposures for three brands revealed two concave and one S-shaped function. Johansson's method was refined by the use of switching regression methods by Bemmaor (1984).

Formal tests for functional form need not be restricted to the choice between S-shaped and concave functions. This case, however, is the most relevant one in marketing to date because both forms are marketing-plausible and have important implications for the optimal level of marketing spending (e.g., Freeland and Weinberg 1980). Also, by focusing on the obtained value of a parameter, the supermodel technique avoids problems of ambiguity that often arise when model selection is based on goodness of fit.

Empirical Functional Form Specification

In some situations, the marketing modeler may not even have sufficient a priori knowledge or may otherwise not be willing to formulate candidate shapes of the response function. In that case, a functional form may be selected by transforming the data such that the following statistical criteria are met (Box and Cox 1964): (1) the response model is linear, (2) the model residuals are normally distributed, (3) the model residuals have a constant variance. Under these conditions, parameter estimation of the response model and hypothesis testing are straightforward. Box and Cox propose the following general class of transformations:

$$Z(\lambda) = \frac{Z^\lambda - 1}{\lambda}, \tag{4.2}$$

which is applied to both the explanatory and the dependent variables in the model. Some special cases of this transformation are

$\lambda = 1$: standard linear response model,

$\lambda = -1$: reciprocal function,

$\lambda = 0$: logarithmic, or constant-elasticity response model.

The search for an optimal transformation parameter is accomplished by maximum likelihood estimation of the following function:

$$Y(\lambda) = \beta_0 + \beta_1 X(\lambda) + \varepsilon. \tag{4.3}$$

Although only the asymptotic properties of the estimates are known, it has been reported that this estimation works well in small samples, in particular for forecasting purposes (Spitzer 1978). One disadvantage of this method, which may be a reason why it has not been used in marketing to date, is that the marketing interpretation of the response coefficients may be difficult unless, of course, λ takes on a simple value like 0 or 1.

In conclusion, the selection of a functional form is a very important task in response modeling and should be addressed early in the process. Unless prior theory dictates a response shape, the researcher may use data-driven methods ranging from simple graphs to formal tests of functional form or even transform the data via parameter estimation of a general class of functions. At the same time, it should be emphasized that the choice of a response shape is not independent of the objective of the model.

Lag Specification in the Univariate Case

There are a number of scenarios in model-based planning and forecasting that make it desirable to analyze a marketing time series strictly as a function of its own past. These scenarios can be organized in three categories:

1. We have developed a planning model relating, say, product prices to product sales. However, price may be determined partly from market factors outside the control of the firm, so it is necessary to forecast prices separately. These predictions are then used to obtain sales estimates. We refer to such situations as *forecasting exogenous variables*.
2. The product line is so large that building individual planning models for each product is prohibitive. Nevertheless, separate forecasts for each are needed. Perhaps the company will invest in a comprehensive marketing mix model for the four or five leading products and use extrapolative methods to handle the remaining 200 or so items. This would be an example of *forecasting performance variables*.
3. Sometimes it is useful to decompose a marketing time series, say, price, into a systematic, predictable part and a random, unpredictable part. For example, product sales may react differently to predictable price changes, say, those due to inflation adjustments, and to unpredictable price shocks, say, surprise deals offered by the manufacturer. This decomposition of the price variable produces a smooth, predictable price series and a residual price series, which is uncorrelated over time (white noise). This is an example of *prewhitening* a marketing time series.

The three scenarios apply only when marketing data over time are available. Furthermore, we assume that the data are collected in regular intervals (e.g., weekly or quarterly) and that they are sufficiently long for statistical modeling (i.e., a minimum of 30 uninterrupted observations).[2] Under these assumptions we can apply principles of univariate time series analysis in order to obtain extrapolative forecasts.

The time series analyst examines the behavior of data over time as a function of deterministic and stochastic elements:

1. Deterministic elements, whose outcome is perfectly predictable at any point of time. For example, the linear trend model on an arbitrary variable Z is

$$Z_t = \beta_0 + \beta_1 t, \tag{4.4}$$

where t is a time counter. For every new period, a fixed value β_1 is added to the base level β_0.

2. Random or stochastic components, whose effects cannot be predicted with certainty. If the random component is correlated over time, it may contribute to forecasting, although imperfectly. It is referred to as a systematic time series component. If it is uncorrelated, however, it is strictly an error term and is of no use for forecasting. These terms are known as white noise, shocks, or innovations. For example,

$$Z_t = \beta_2 Z_{t-1} + \alpha_t, \tag{4.5}$$

where $E(\alpha_t) = 0$, $E(\alpha_t^2) = \sigma_\alpha^2$, and $E(\alpha_t \alpha_{t-k}) = 0$ for all $k \neq 0$.

The first right-hand term is a systematic effect of the last period on the current period and is useful for forecasting. The second term is white noise; while it may affect the current Z significantly, it cannot be used for estimating future Z.

A time series model combining the deterministic and random elements might be

$$Z_t = \beta_0 + \beta_1 t + \beta_2 Z_{t-1} + \alpha_t. \tag{4.6}$$

Although model 4.6 is cast in a regression form, it does not have the straightforward interpretation of the more common marketing regression models, relating, for example, unit sales to prices. The focus of model 4.6 is on the fluctuations over time of the marketing variable, Z, rather than on the underlying causes of these movements. In many cases, though, the time series patterns have a plausible marketing explanation. For example, if Z is product sales, then market growth may explain a positive trend parameter. Also, brand

Table 4–1.   Time Series Components in Marketing Data

Time Series Component	Market Performance	Marketing Decisions	Environment
Deterministic	Agreement to buy a fixed amount over an extended period	Ad agency does not serve competing accounts	Obligation to close stores on Sundays
Systematic	Repeat purchase rates, diffusion of innovation	Percent-of-last-year decision rule in advertising	Fashion effects in clothing
White noise	Zero-order random market share fluctuations	Marketing director resigns	Earthquake destroys distribution center

loyalty may result in a constant fraction of buyers at time $(t - 1)$ who purchase the same brand at time t, which would explain a value for β_2 in the $(0, 1)$ interval. Other examples of deterministic, systematic, and pure random elements in market performance, marketing decisions, and market environment data are given in table 4–1.

In conclusion, situations exist in model-based planning and forecasting where strictly extrapolative predictions of marketing variables are needed. Such models are developed using principles of modern time series analysis, which pay particular attention to the deterministic, systematic, and pure random elements in marketing data. We now discuss the most important aspects of time series modeling: the philosophy of linear filters, the specification method due to Box and Jenkins, the estimation of parameters, and the use of the model for forecasting.

The Linear Time Series Filter

Suppose a time series of weekly sales volumes of a brand is observed over a two-year period (see figure 4–1). That series contains a definite upward trend and deviations from the trend, which may be systematic or random. If we are able to extract the deterministic and the systematic patterns from the series, the remaining fluctuations would be strictly random. The objective of the time series modeler is to find the mechanism that converts an observed time series of data to a series of serially uncorrelated values called white noise. This

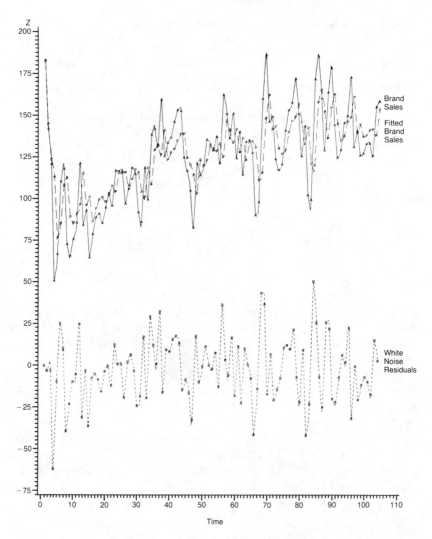

Figure 4–1. Brand Sales and Time Series Filter.

mechanism, or *filter*, does not change over time, and thus it can be used to predict future values of the time series strictly from its own past. The filter should be chosen so that all deterministic and systematic parts of the time series are captured, leaving only the white noise component unaccounted for. Schematically,

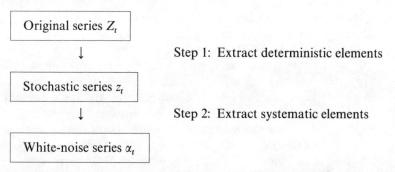

Step 1: Extract deterministic elements

Step 2: Extract systematic elements

The challenge, of course, lies in finding the filter that makes these transformations (steps 1 and 2) possible. Once specified and estimated, these filters are the basis for forecasting, because they contain the maximum amount of information about the future based on the past. Although the choice of filters is theoretically unlimited, a general class of linear filters introduced by Yule in the 1920s has become the standard.[3] Yule proposed that time series observations are generated by an underlying stochastic process:

$$p(z_1, z_2, \ldots, z_{t-1}, z_t, \ldots, z_T)$$

in such a way that each observation z_t is a linear combination of all previous shocks:

$$z_t = \alpha_t + \psi_1 \alpha_{t-1} + \psi_2 \alpha_{t-2} + \cdots + \psi_t \alpha_0. \tag{4.7}$$

This underlying stochastic process is assumed to be stationary, i.e., it remains the same over time. In practice, we check the stationarity assumption by verifying that the first two moments of the distribution, i.e., the mean and the variance, are constant:

$$E(Z_t) = \mu \tag{4.8a}$$

and

$$E(Z_t - \mu)^2 = \sigma^2. \tag{4.8b}$$

We explain how this is done later in this chapter.

The stationarity condition makes it possible to sample the time series between any two dates and draw a statistical inference. But it also rules out the presence of deterministic elements, since they typically change the moments of the distribution. Specifically, there are four types of deterministic influences:

1. *Trend* is defined as any smooth function of time. It shifts the mean of a time series upward or downward. For example, nominal prices may go up because of inflation.

2. *Seasonality* creates within-year patterns that are the same across years. In the extreme, every month of the year may have its own mean, for example, the sales levels of toys or suntan lotion.
3. *Cyclical patterns* may emerge over many years, for example, owing to cycles of economic activity. Unless very long time series of 30 years or more are available, cyclical patterns are not important in marketing models.
4. The variance may change over time, a condition called *heteroscedasticity*. For example, as retail promotion activities, such as couponing, expand in an industry, the volatility of the market shares of the competing brands may increase over time.

Yule's filter theory does not accommodate these phenomena, so they must be removed prior to analyzing the data. Techniques for removing nonstationarity are discussed later; we focus now on the analysis of stationary data z_t. These data can be transformed to white noise by means of two distinctive linear filters, the *autoregressive* (AR) *filter* and the *moving-average* (MA) *filter*.

Suppose a marketing manager allocates a yearly advertising budget as a fixed amount 100, plus 90% of the previous year's expenditure. The actual advertising, however, is also affected by random factors due to current market conditions and execution errors. Then, part of the resulting advertising time series would be predictable from its own past as follows:

$$\text{advertising}_t = 100 + 0.9* \text{advertising}_{t-1} + \text{random amount}_t. \quad (4.9)$$

To turn the scenario around, the analyst would have to discover the decision rule in order to transform the time series "advertising" to the white noise series "random amount":

$$\text{random amount}_t = -100 + \text{advertising}_t - 0.9* \text{advertising}_{t-1}. \quad (4.10)$$

The decision rule is linear and relates current values to previous values of the time series. All these previous observations will be correlated with the current value. This is an example of an autoregressive (AR) filter.

A moving-average filter may appear as follows: Suppose the advertising manager sets this year's advertising budget as 100 plus a fraction of the allocation error that was made last year. Indeed, many errors in execution are possible because of personnel changes, bankruptcies, limited ad space availability, unexpected competitive entry, and so on. As a result, last year's advertising target or budget was either exceeded or not met, and the manager may wish to build an adjustment factor to last year's budget error into this year's budget. Since execution errors will again occur this year, the resulting time series model on advertising may be

$$\text{advertising}_t = 100 + 0.5^* (\text{advertising}_{t-1} - \text{target}_{t-1})$$
$$+ \text{ random amount}_t. \tag{4.11}$$

Unlike the AR case, current values of the time series are not directly related to previous values but to previous unexpected values, or shocks. In the example, this rule results in current advertising being correlated with last year's advertising but not with previous years' expenditures. This is an example of a moving-average (MA) filter.

We are now in a position to introduce a formal notation for AR and MA filters. Yule's linear filter theory is represented as:

$$\text{White noise} \longrightarrow \boxed{\begin{array}{c} \text{Linear filter} \\ \Psi(L) \end{array}} \longrightarrow \text{Observed data}$$
$$\alpha_0 \alpha_1 \ldots \alpha_t \qquad\qquad\qquad\qquad z_t$$

Thus, the observed stationary series $z_t (t = 1, 2, \ldots, T)$ is generated by an unobservable white noise series $(\alpha_0, \alpha_1, \ldots, \alpha_t)$, filtered by the linear filter $\Psi(L)$:

$$z_t = \alpha_t + \psi_1 \alpha_{t-1} + \psi_2 \alpha_{t-2} + \cdots$$
$$= \alpha_t + \psi_1 L \alpha_t + \psi_2 L^2 \alpha_t + \cdots$$
$$= (1 + \psi_1 L + \psi_2 L^2 + \cdots) \alpha_t$$
$$= \Psi(L) \alpha_t, \tag{4.12}$$

where L is the lag operator, e.g., $L^k z_t = z_{t-k}$.

As explained earlier, an autoregressive filter relates current observations to previous observations, and a moving-average filter relates current observations to previous shocks. The AR filter is generally denoted by $\Phi(L)$ and operates on the left-hand side of the time series equation (z_t); the MA filter $\Theta(L)$ operates on the right-hand side (α_t). Thus, the basic univariate time series model is

$$\Phi(L) z_t = \Theta(L) \alpha_t. \tag{4.13}$$

Rearranging terms shows that the linear filter $\Psi(L)$ has been decomposed in an AR and MA component:

$$z_t = \frac{\Theta(L)}{\Phi(L)} \alpha_t = \Psi(L) \alpha_t. \tag{4.14}$$

In the example, if the manager uses both the AR and the MA decision rule, the resulting advertising time series model would be (omitting the constant for ease of presentation):

$$z_t = 0.9z_{t-1} + 0.5(z_{t-1} - \hat{z}_{t-1}) + \alpha_t, \tag{4.15}$$

where α_t is white noise, and $\hat{z}_{t-1}$ is the forecast value of z obtained in period $(t-1)$.

Although the equation is easy to understand, its form is not very efficient for time series analysis. A more common and much shorter notation is obtained by using the lag operator L, so the budgeting equation is rewritten as

$$z_t - 0.9z_{t-1} = 0.5(z_{t-1} - \hat{z}_{t-1}) + \alpha_t, \tag{4.16}$$

and since the forecast error in $(t-1)$ is the shock in that period,

$$z_t - 0.9z_{t-1} = 0.5\alpha_{t-1} + \alpha_t. \tag{4.17}$$

By introducing lag operators,

$$z_t - 0.9Lz_t = \alpha_t + 0.5L\alpha_t, \tag{4.18}$$

we obtain:

$$(1 - 0.9L)z_t = (1 + 0.5L)\alpha_t \tag{4.19}$$

This is a simple example of a linear filter with an AR and an MA component. Now, since we have carefully chosen the two parameters, we can also write:

$$z_t = (1 - 0.9L)^{-1}(1 + 0.5L)\alpha_t$$
$$= (1 + 0.9L + 0.81L^2 + 0.729L^3 + \cdots)(1 + 0.5L)\alpha_t, \tag{4.20}$$

by arithmetic expansion, and ultimately:

$$z_t = (1 + 1.4L + 1.26L^2 + 1.13L^3 + 1.02L^4 + \cdots)\alpha_t, \tag{4.21}$$

which is an expression in line with Yule's linear stochastic time series model. In this case, the linear filter $\Psi(L)$ is infinite. However, since α_t has a finite, constant mean and variance, the observed series will not "explode," because the influence of any shock α_t gradually declines. In other words, as long as the parameters of the model are within certain bounds, the resulting time series process will be stationary.

The example teaches some important properties of AR and MA filters. The AR filter is infinite, so its weights must converge in order to preserve stationarity. In the advertising case, this implies that the parameter ϕ must be less than 1 in absolute value:

$$(1 - \phi L)^{-1} = 1 + \phi L + \phi^2 L^2 + \phi^3 L^3 + \cdots \tag{4.22}$$

as long as $-1 < \phi < 1$. The MA filter is finite, so stationarity is always implied, although later we will argue that similar parameter restrictions may be applied to an MA filter as well. Most important, however, the example demonstrates that two conceptually different linear filters, one relating current data to previous data, the other relating current data to previous shocks, are compatible with Yule's general stochastic time series model.

We are now in the position to generalize the model to an autoregressive process of order p (AR(p)) and a moving-average process of order q (MA(q)). Let:

$$\Psi(L) = \frac{\Theta(L)}{\Phi(L)}, \tag{4.23}$$

where

$$\Phi(L) = 1 - \phi_1 L - \phi_2 L^2 - \cdots - \phi_p L^p,$$
$$\Theta(L) = 1 - \theta_1 L - \theta_2 L^2 - \cdots - \theta_q L^q.$$

The autoregressive filter $\Phi(L)$ models the dependence of the series on its p previous observations. The moving-average filter $\Theta(L)$ relates current observations to q previous shocks in the system. The combination produces an ARMA (p, q) model, which can be written as

$$\Phi(L)z_t = \Theta(L)\alpha_t, \tag{4.24}$$

or

$$(1 - \phi_1 L - \phi_2 L^2 - \cdots - \phi_p L^p)z_t = (1 - \theta_1 L - \theta_2 L^2 - \cdots - \theta_q L^q)\alpha_t. \tag{4.25}$$

The Autocorrelation and Partial Autocorrelation Function

The ARMA model relates current time series observations to previous observations and previous shocks. The order of the ARMA parameters, p and q, determines the *memory* of the series: the longer the memory, the longer the usable forecasting horizon of a series. AR models have an infinite memory, i.e., an observation contributes to the forecast of every future observation, although the strength of the contribution varies with p. Moving-average models have a finite memory of order q. The critical question, of course, is how to identify the order of the ARMA model for a given series.

Box and Jenkins (1976) have proposed two useful tools for the identification of ARMA models. The *autocorrelation* at lag k is simply the correlation of two data points that are k periods apart. The *partial autocorrelation* at lag k is a similar correlation, but it holds constant all $(k - 1)$ observations between the two data points. Box and Jenkins use these tools because every ARMA(p, q) model comes with a unique set of predefined autocorrelations and partial autocorrelations. Thus, the idea is to infer (p, q) from the behavior of the autocorrelation and partial autocorrelation functions (ACF and PACF) at various lags k. To do this, we must first explain the ACF and PACF analytically and then examine their behavior for AR, MA, and general ARMA models.

Formally, the autocovariance γ_k and the autocorrelation ρ_k of a *stationary* series at lag k are defined as

$$\gamma_k = E\{(z_t - Ez_t)(z_{t-k} - Ez_t)\}$$
$$= E\{(z_t - Ez_t)(z_{t+k} - Ez_t)\}, \qquad (4.26)$$

and

$$\rho_k = \frac{E(z_t - Ez_t)(z_{t-k} - Ez_t)}{E(z_t - Ez_t)^2} = \frac{E(z_t - Ez_t)(z_{t+k} - Ez_t)}{E(z_t - Ez_t)^2}, \qquad (4.27)$$

$$\rho_k = \frac{\gamma_k}{\gamma_0}. \qquad (4.28)$$

When viewed as a function of the lag index k, these definitions lead to the autocorrelation function (ACF) of a series. In practice, it is estimated as

$$r_k = \frac{\sum_{t=1}^{T-k} (z_t - \bar{z})(z_{t+k} - \bar{z})}{\sum_{t=1}^{T} (z_t - \bar{z})^2}, \qquad \forall k > 0, \qquad (4.29)$$

where $\bar{z}$ is the sample mean

$$\frac{\sum_{t=1}^{T} z_t}{T}.$$

Notice that the sample estimator is not unbiased, i.e., $E(r_k) \neq \rho_k$; however, it does produce a positive semidefinite matrix of autocorrelations, which will be useful later.

The ACF plays a predominant role in the identification of a time series filter $\Psi(L)$ via a *pattern recognition* of significant (nonzero) and zero elements for various lags k. Therefore, an expression for its variance is needed. Bartlett (1946) has provided the following approximation for a time series whose autocorrelations are zero beyond lag q:

$$\text{var}(r_k) \simeq \frac{1}{T}\left\{1 + 2\sum_{v=1}^{q} \rho_v^2\right\} \qquad (k > q). \tag{4.30}$$

This expression is quite useful, even though it is only an approximation. First, it shows that $\text{var}(r_k)$ is of the order T^{-1}, which is a simple yardstick. Second, under the assumption that higher-order autocorrelations are zero, we can always compute $\text{var}(r_k)$ from lower-order correlations. The expression further reveals that $\text{var}(r_k)$ increases with k.

In interpreting an ACF, it is assumed that $r_k \sim N(\rho_k, \text{var}(r_k))$, so that a classical t- or z-test of significance is possible. We must, however, be careful, because r_k and r_{k+s} $(s \neq 0)$ are correlated, so spurious autocorrelations may occur. This is one of the reasons why the identification of a time series process is supplemented with the *partial autocorrelation function* Φ_{kk}, or the PACF.

The partial autocorrelation of kth order is the correlation between two observations k lags apart, *holding constant all $(k - 1)$ intermediate observations*. As a simple example, consider the following sequence of observations and correlations:

$$\rho_{13}$$

$$z_1 \qquad z_2 \qquad z_3$$

$$\rho_{12} \qquad \rho_{23}$$

The partial correlation between z_1 and z_3, holding z_2 constant, is

$$\rho_{13.2} = \frac{\rho_{13} - \rho_{12}\rho_{23}}{\sqrt{(1 - \rho_{12}^2)(1 - \rho_{23}^2)}}, \tag{4.31}$$

following the general definition of partial correlation. Now, if the series z_t is stationary, $\rho_{12} = \rho_{23}$, and we can simplify as

$$\rho_{13.2} = \frac{\rho_2 - \rho_1^2}{1 - \rho_1^2} = \phi_{22}. \tag{4.32}$$

The example also shows that stationarity imposes restrictions on the permissible values of ρ_1 and ρ_2. For example, since $-1 < \phi_{22} < 1$, it follows that $2\rho_1^2 - 1 < \rho_2 < 1$.

The ACF and the PACF are the major statistical tools for identifying a time series model. How they should be used will become clear from a discussion of autoregressive (AR), moving-average (MA), and mixed (ARMA) models. In each case, we derive the *theoretical* behavior of the ACF and PACF so that their diagnostic value can be determined.

Autoregressive Models

There are many reasons for the autoregressive behavior of marketing time series, and indeed AR patterns are often found. An earlier example was the memory decay hypothesis as applied to advertising effects: If each period's retention level z_t is a constant function of the previous period's level, a smooth first-order autoregressive pattern may appear:

$$z_t = \delta + \phi z_{t-1} + \alpha_t, \tag{4.33}$$

or, in time series notation,

$$(1 - \phi L)z_t = \delta + \alpha_t, \tag{4.34}$$

The first-order autoregressive model is stationary only within a range of ϕ, $-1 < \phi < 1$. Under these conditions we can derive the first- and second-order moments. The AR(1) model may be written as:

$$z_t = \frac{\delta}{1 - \phi L} + \frac{1}{1 - \phi L} \alpha_t, \tag{4.35}$$

or

$$z_t = \frac{\delta}{1 - \phi} + \frac{1}{1 - \phi L} \alpha_t, \tag{4.36}$$

since the lag operator L does not affect a constant. Therefore,

$$E(z_t) = \frac{\delta}{1 - \phi}, \tag{4.37}$$

$$V(z_t) = \frac{1}{1 - \phi^2} \sigma_\alpha^2. \tag{4.38}$$

The autocorrelation function of an AR(1) process is particularly simple. Let $\tilde{z}_t = z_t - E(z_t)$. Then the autocovariance at lag k is

$$\gamma_k = E(\tilde{z}_t \tilde{z}_{t-k}) = \phi E(\tilde{z}_{t-1} \tilde{z}_{t-k}) + E(\alpha_t \tilde{z}_{t-k}) \tag{4.39}$$

$$= \phi \gamma_{k-1}.$$

Therefore,

$$\rho_1 = \frac{\gamma_1}{\gamma_0} = \phi, \tag{4.40}$$

$$\rho_2 = \frac{\gamma_2}{\gamma_0} = \frac{\phi \gamma_1}{\gamma_0} = \phi^2, \tag{4.41}$$

$$\rho_k = \phi^k = \rho_1^k. \tag{4.42}$$

The ACF pattern is intuitively clear: The AR(1) process is completely deter-

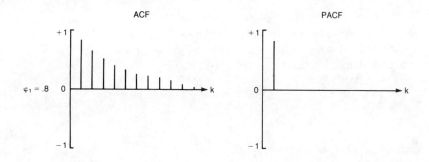

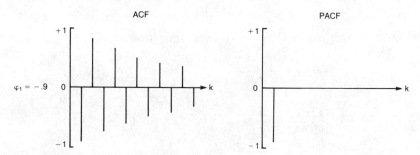

Figure 4–2. Autocorrelation Function and Partial Autocorrelation Function for an AR(1) Process.

mined by $\phi = \rho_1$; for $0 < \phi < 1$, the ACF dies out monotonically; and for $-1 < \phi < 0$, it oscillates toward zero. This behavior is illustrated in figure 4–2.

The behavior of the PACF is easily derived from its definition, i.e.,

$$\rho_{13.2} = \frac{\rho_2 - \rho_1^2}{1 - \rho_1^2}. \qquad (4.43)$$

Since $\rho_2 = \rho_1^2$, it follows that $\rho_{13.2} = 0$. Also, higher-order PACs can be shown to be zero, so that the general rule is

$$\phi_{kk} = \phi = \rho_1, \qquad k = 1, \qquad (4.44)$$

$$\phi_{kk} = 0, \qquad k > 1.$$

The PACF pattern is intuitively clear: The AR(1) process is fully explained by ϕ; therefore, if we hold constant all autocorrelations up to lag k, the

$(k + 1)$th autocorrelation has no explanatory power to add and is therefore zero. A graph of the PACF is also shown in figure 4–2.

The extension to higher-order autoregressive processes $(AR(p), p > 1)$ is straightforward. For example, the $AR(2)$ model,

$$z_t = \delta + \phi_1 z_{t-1} + \phi_2 z_{t-2} + \alpha_t, \tag{4.45}$$

or

$$(1 - \phi_1 L - \phi_2 L^2)z_t = \delta + \alpha_t, \tag{4.46}$$

has the following stationarity conditions:

$$\phi_1 + \phi_2 < 1, \tag{4.47}$$

$$\phi_2 - \phi_1 < 1, \tag{4.48}$$

$$|\phi_2| < 1. \tag{4.49}$$

When these are met, the critical moments of the process are

$$E(z_t) = \frac{\delta}{1 - \phi_1 - \phi_2}, \tag{4.50}$$

$$V(z_t) = \gamma_0 = \frac{1 - \phi_2}{1 + \phi_2} \frac{1}{[(1 - \phi_2)^2 - \phi_1^2]} \sigma_\alpha^2, \tag{4.51}$$

$$\gamma_k = \phi_1 \gamma_{k-1} + \phi_2 \gamma_{k-2}. \tag{4.52}$$

The ACF is more complex than in the $AR(1)$ case, but it will die out in a pattern dictated by ϕ_1 and ϕ_2. In particular, it can be shown that

$$\rho_1 = \phi_1 + \phi_2 \rho_1, \tag{4.53}$$

$$\rho_2 = \phi_1 \rho_2 + \phi_2, \tag{4.54}$$

$$\rho_k = \phi_1 \rho_{k-1} + \phi_2 \rho_{k-2}, \quad k > 2. \tag{4.55}$$

From $k = 2$ on, the autocorrelations are fully determined by their lower-order values and ϕ_1 and ϕ_2, so the partial autocorrelations are zero. Therefore, the $AR(2)$ process is characterized by a dying-out ACF and a PACF with nonzero values at $k = 1$ and $k = 2$ only.

The extension to the $AR(p)$ model follows logically:

$$(1 - \phi_1 L - \phi_2 L^2 - \cdots - \phi_p L^p)z_t = \delta + \alpha_t, \tag{4.56}$$

is stationary when the roots of $(1 - \phi_1 L - \phi_2 L^2 - \cdots - \phi_p L^p) = 0$ are greater than 1 in absolute value. The ACF will die out in a pattern dictated by the ϕ parameters, and the PACF will have p distinctive values, followed by zeros.

Moving-Average Models

The term *moving average* is generally accepted, although ill-chosen, for the class of models where current z_t depends on α_{t-k} $(k > 0)$. The simplest case is the first-order model (MA(1)):

$$z_t = \mu + \alpha_t - \theta\alpha_{t-1}, \tag{4.57}$$

or

$$z_t - \mu = (1 - \theta L)\alpha_t. \tag{4.58}$$

This model is always stationary because the linear filter relating z_t to α_t is finite. However, we must impose restrictions on the parameter θ if the model is to be *invertible*, that is, it can be written as

$$(1 - \theta L)^{-1}(z_t - \mu) = \alpha_t, \tag{4.59}$$

or

$$(1 + \theta L + \theta^2 L^2 + \theta^3 L^3 + \cdots)(z_t - \mu) = \alpha_t. \tag{4.60}$$

The invertibility condition is useful for parameter estimation. In the MA(1) model, invertibility requires that $-1 < \theta < 1$, which is similar to the stationarity condition on ϕ in an AR(1) process. By analogy with linear programming, invertibility is the "dual" of stationarity.

The important moments of an MA(1) process are

$$E(z_t) = \mu, \tag{4.61}$$

$$V(z_t) = \gamma_0 = (1 + \theta^2)\sigma_\alpha^2, \tag{4.62}$$

$$\gamma_k = E(\tilde{z}_t \tilde{z}_{t-k}) = E(\alpha_t - \theta\alpha_{t-1})(\alpha_{t-k} - \theta\alpha_{t-k-1}), \tag{4.63}$$

$$= -\theta\sigma_\alpha^2, \quad \forall k = 1,$$

$$= 0, \quad \forall k > 1,$$

and, therefore,

$$\rho_k = \frac{-\theta}{1 + \theta^2}, \quad k = 1,$$

$$= 0, \quad k > 1. \tag{4.64}$$

So, the ACF of an MA(1) model has one *spike* at lag 1, uniquely determined by θ, and zeros elsewhere. By contrast, the PACF *dies out* because an MA(1) model is equivalent to an AR(∞) process; therefore, each autocorrelation at lag k offers additional explanatory power beyond that explained by the $(k - 1)$

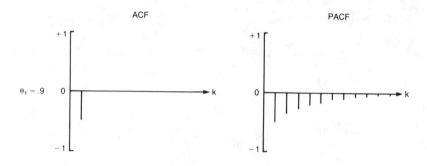

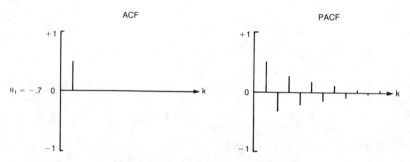

Figure 4–3. Autocorrelation Function and Partial Autocorrelation Function for an MA(1) Process.

lower-order autocorrelations. Examples of MA(1) correlograms are shown in figure 4–3.

The MA(1) model is readily extended to the MA(q) process:

$$z_t = \mu + \alpha_t - \theta_1 \alpha_{t-1} - \cdots - \theta_q \alpha_{t-q}, \tag{4.65}$$

or

$$z_t = \mu + (1 - \theta_1 L^2 - \cdots - \theta_q L^q) \alpha_t, \tag{4.66}$$

which is invertible if the roots of $\Theta(L) = 0$ are outside the unit circle. Its auto-correlations will show q spikes as determined by

$$\rho_j = -\frac{\theta_j + \theta_1 \theta_{j+1} + \cdots + \theta_{q-1} \theta_q}{1 + \theta_1^2 + \cdots + \theta_q^2}, \qquad j \le q, \tag{4.67}$$

followed by zeros ($j > q$). In other words, the *memory* of an MA(q) process is exactly q periods long. The PACF dies out according to the θ parameter values.

Mixed Autoregressive–Moving-Average Models

The well-known autoregressive–moving-average, or ARMA, process combines AR(p) and MA(q) parameters:

$$z_t = \delta + \phi_1 z_{t-1} + \cdots + \phi_p z_{t-p} + \alpha_t - \theta_1 \alpha_{t-1} - \cdots - \theta_q \alpha_{t-q}, \quad (4.68)$$

or

$$(1 - \phi_1 L - \cdots - \phi_p L^p)z_t = \delta + (1 - \theta_1 L - \cdots - \theta_q L^q)\alpha_t. \quad (4.69)$$

Stationarity requires that the roots of $\Phi(L)$ be outside the unit circle, and invertibility occurs when the roots of $\Theta(L)$ are outside the unit circle. In practice, the ARMA $(1, 1)$ is by far the most common of the mixed models, so we shall use it to illustrate the basic properties of mixed models. The ARMA $(1, 1)$ is

$$(1 - \phi_1 L)z_t = \delta + (1 - \theta_1 L)\alpha_t, \quad (4.70)$$

with

$$E(z_t) = \mu = \frac{\delta}{1 - \phi_1}, \quad (4.71)$$

$$V(z_t) = \gamma_0 = \frac{1 + \theta_1^2 - 2\phi_1\theta_1}{1 - \theta_1^2}\sigma_\alpha^2. \quad (4.72)$$

The ACF at lag 1 is complex because it is affected by both autoregressive and moving-average components:

$$\rho_1 = \frac{(1 - \phi_1\theta_1)(\phi_1 - \theta_1)}{1 + \theta_1^2 - 2\phi_1\theta_1}. \quad (4.73)$$

On the other hand, for $k > 1$, the only memory factors are contributed by the autoregressive side of the equation. Formally, it can be shown that

$$\rho_k = \phi_1 \rho_{k-1}, \quad k > 1. \quad (4.74)$$

Therefore, the ACF has a spike at lag 1, followed by a typical autoregressive decay pattern for $k > 1$. The PACF pattern is more difficult to predict, except for the fact that it dies out as k increases. Examples of ARMA $(1, 1)$ correlograms are shown in figure 4–4.

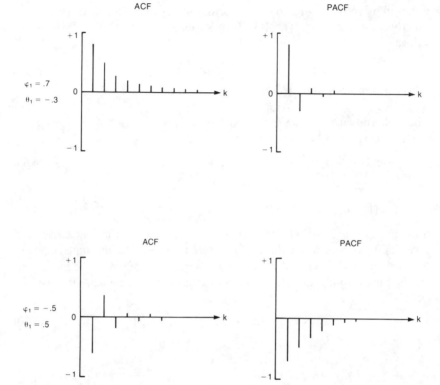

Figure 4–4. Autocorrelation Function and Partial Autocorrelation Function for an ARMA(1, 1) Process.

Extending these findings to the ARMA (p, q) process, we conclude that the ACF shows spikes for the first q lags, followed by a decay pattern. The PACF dies out in function of the $(p + q)$ model parameters.

The Method of Box and Jenkins

Now that we have derived the theoretical ACF and PACF behavior of any linear time series process, we are in a position to apply the well-known search heuristic due to Box and Jenkins (1976) for the identification of a model. First, let us summarize the key findings from the previous section:

Table 4–2. The Behavior of the Autocorrelation Function (ACF) and the Partial Autocorrelation Function (PACF)

	Autoregressive Process	Moving-Average Process	Mixed Process
ACF	Dies out	Cuts off	Dies out
PACF	Cuts off	Dies out	Dies out

- Autoregressive processes have a dying-out ACF pattern, which also implies that their memory is infinite. To determine the order of the process, we can simply count the number of spikes in the PACF, which has a cutoff pattern.
- The situation for a moving-average process, which has a finite memory, is the reverse: The ACF cuts off at a point equal to the order of the MA process. The PACF is less informative, except that it must die out, since an MA(q) is equivalent to an AR(∞).
- The mixed ARMA model is more difficult to identify, because both the ACF and the PACF die out. It will usually take more than one attempt to find the right model for such a process.

These findings are shown in table 4–2.

Box and Jenkins proposed a three-step modeling procedure, consisting of identification, estimation, and diagnostic checking (figure 4–5). First, the modeler selects a candidate ARMA process by inspecting the ACF-PACF of the original series. Next, the model's parameters are estimated and the residuals are stored. If the candidate model is adequate, i.e., if the proposed filter does whiten the data, then the ACF-PACF of the residuals should be flat. If not, then some spikes will remain and their pattern will suggest ways of improving the original model. Thus, the modeler uses the diagnostic checking phase to return to model identification if necessary.

The method of Box and Jenkins is tremendously popular. If used properly, it virtually guarantees success, i.e., a filter that whitens the data will be found. Furthermore, the method promotes parsimonious models—those that whiten the data with a minimum of parameters. Therefore, it is highly recommended to build time series models bottom-up by starting with simple candidates such as AR(1) and only adding parameters if certain patterns in the residual ACF-PACF call for it.

Some other tools for univariate time series modeling have been proposed, but an extensive discussion is beyond the scope of this book. Among the more

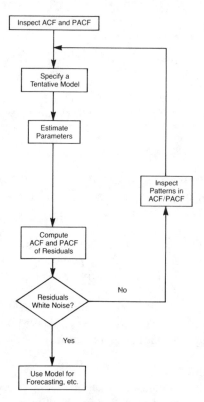

Figure 4–5. The Method of Box and Jenkins.

promising techniques are the inverse autocorrelation function (Cleveland 1972), the S-array (Gray, Kelly, and McIntire 1978), and the extended sample autocorrelation function (Tsay and Tiao 1984). Thus, the state-of-the-art in univariate time series analysis is such that virtually any time series can be transformed to white noise with a reasonable amount of effort.

One important assumption of the ARMA (p, q) is that the order (p, q) and the parameters are constant. However, in many marketing modeling situations, we may suspect that different ARMA processes hold for different regions or brands or that the ARMA parameters change over time. Moriarty and Adams (1979) have addressed this general problem in a territory sales forecasting context. For example, should a manager use one ARMA model for each region in the market or use separate models for separate regions? They proposed an interesting sequence of formal tests, which can be applied in a

Table 4–3. Moriarty-Adams ARMA Model Tests

Task	Test	Verdict
1. Are (p, q) the same?	t-test on model form	No: Build separate models. Yes: Continue.
2. Are the parameters the same?	F-test on coefficient equality	No: Estimate separately. Yes: Continue.
3. Is the error variance the same?	F-test on white noise variance equality	No: Estimate separately. Yes: Continue.
4. Is the forecasting accuracy affected?	Wilcoxon signed-ranks test on forecast errors	No: Use parsimonious model. Yes: Use separate parameters.

practical situation (table 4–3). The procedure is very useful in deciding how many different forecasting models are needed for optimal performance.

Dealing with Nonstationarity

As crucial as the stationarity assumption is to the theoretical analysis of time series, it is often violated in real-world data, notably marketing data. First, many marketing series exhibit *trend*, i.e., the mean changes smoothly over time. Examples include sales growth due to market expansion and price increases due to inflation. Second, the use of short-interval data in marketing makes many analyses subject to *seasonality*, e.g., different means may be applicable to different periods. Third, a number of marketing series are *heteroscedastic* (variance changes over time), for example, market shares may become more volatile over time as a result of aggressive marketing strategies. The last source of nonstationarity, *cyclicality*, is less influential in marketing: even though sales or price cycles may exist, they are typically not constant in length and thus pose less of a threat to stationarity.

Nonstationarity in Means and Variances. Nonstationarity in means (i.e., trend, seasonality, and cyclicality) is more serious than nonstationarity in variance (heteroscedasticity). The former may result in spurious correlations among the observations in a time series, because of a deterministic time factor common to all. Typically, the ACF of a series affected by trend or cycles will *fail to die out*, so that the usual identification techniques may not work. While the ACF of a heteroscedastic series will generally be well-behaved, parameter

estimation may be inefficient, comparable to the case of heteroscedastic disturbances in a regression model.

To start with the latter, Box and Jenkins have suggested taking the logarithm of a heteroscedastic series in order to obtain variance homogeneity:

$$w_t = \ln(Z_t + c), \tag{4.75}$$

where c is an additive constant that removes nonpositive data values. This
approach, while widely used, has been criticized for its arbitrariness (Chatfield
and Prothero 1973). A more general class of transformations was formulated
by Box and Cox (1964):

$$w_t = \frac{(Z_t + c)^\lambda - 1}{\lambda}, \qquad \lambda \neq 0, \tag{4.76}$$

$$w_t = \ln(Z_t + c), \qquad \lambda = 0. \tag{4.77}$$

As discussed earlier, the advantage of this method is that the transformation parameter λ is obtained empirically, usually by maximum likelihood.
Nevertheless, Box-Cox transformations seem to be used infrequently in time
series applications, perhaps because the transformed series is difficult to
interpret intuitively.

Nonstationarity in means is generally treated by appropriate differencing
of the data. Regular differencing of order d removes a trend polynomial of
order d:

$$z_t = (1 - L)^d Z_t. \tag{4.78}$$

Trends in marketing data are mostly linear, sometimes quadratic, so that d is
seldom greater than 2. The two most common transformations are linear
differencing ($d = 1$),

$$z_t = Z_t - Z_{t-1} = (1 - L)Z_t, \tag{4.79}$$

and quadratic differencing ($d = 2$),

$$z_t = (Z_t - Z_{t-1}) - (Z_{t-1} - Z_{t-2}) = (1 - L)^2 Z_t. \tag{4.80}$$

Seasonal differencing of order d_s is a natural extension of regular differencing to deal with seasonal nonstationarity:

$$z_t = (1 - L^s)^{d_s} Z_t, \tag{4.81}$$

where s is the season length (e.g., $s = 12$ for monthly data). This is the
equivalent of "same time last year" comparisons often made by marketing
practitioners. Again, d_s is seldom greater than 2 in practice.

Regular and seasonal differencing are simple, widely used transformations
to remove nonstationarity in means. Sometimes they are used excessively,

creating a condition known as *overdifferencing*. Suppose the stationary AR(1) series z_t is "accidentally" differenced with $d = 1$:

$$(1 - \phi_1 L)z_t = c + \alpha_t, \tag{4.82}$$

$$w_t = (1 - L)z_t \tag{4.83}$$

Substitution then reveals

$$(1 - \phi_1 L)w_t = c' + (1 - L)\alpha_t, \tag{4.84}$$

where c' is a different constant. Although the original AR(1) process is maintained, a spurious MA(1) process with parameter 1 is added. Therefore, overdifferencing may adversely affect the parsimony of the time series model (Plosser and Schwert 1977).

The most practical rule for detecting and thus avoiding overdifferencing is to inspect the ACF of the differenced series. Figure 4–6 compares the ACF of

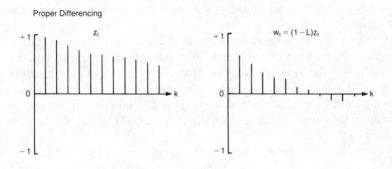

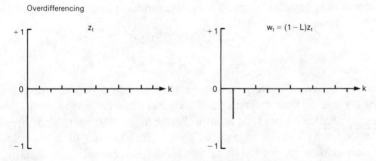

Figure 4–6. Autocorrelation Functions before and after Differencing.

a properly differenced series to the ACF of an overdifferenced series. The negative spike at lag 1 has a value around -0.5, which corresponds to a moving-average parameter of 1.0. Formal tests on overdifferencing can be found in the growing literature on unit-root testing (e.g., Dickey, Bell, and Miller 1986). The importance of ensuring the stationarity of longitudinal data before statistical modeling cannot be overemphasized.[4]

The Seasonal ARIMA Model.   Seasonal time series are not necessarily nonstationary and can exhibit seasonal patterns even after differencing. The Box-Jenkins model takes such patterns into account by adding seasonal autoregressive and moving-average parameters to the base equation:

$$\Phi(L)\Phi_s(L)(1 - L)^d(1 - L^s)^{d_s}Z_t = c + \Theta(L)\Theta_s(L)\alpha_t, \tag{4.85}$$

where $\Phi_s(L)$ denotes the seasonal autoregressive process and $\Theta_s(L)$ the seasonal moving-average parameters. The model is multiplicative and is generally represented as ARIMA $(p, d, q)(p_s, d_s, q_s)_s$, where s is the length of the season.

It is convenient to think of seasonal AR and MA processes as regular processes on a different time interval. For example, on quarterly data ($s = 4$), the ACF may die out over the interval $k = 4, 8, 12$, indicating a seasonal AR process, or it may display a single spike at lag $k = 4$, indicating a seasonal moving-average model. Of course, if the ACF fails to die out, we must transform the data to obtain stationarity. Figure 4–7 illustrates these different seasonal behaviors.

One of the best-known Box-Jenkins applications, the so-called airline model, illustrates these points. Many monthly airline passenger series have been found to follow an ARIMA $(0, 1, 1)(0, 1, 1)_{12}$ process, i.e.,

$$(1 - L)(1 - L^{12})Z_t = (1 - \theta_1 L)(1 - \theta_{12}L^{12})\alpha_t. \tag{4.86}$$

The forecasting equation derived from this model is insightful:

$$\hat{Z}_t = Z_{t-1} + Z_{t-12} - Z_{t-13} - \hat{\theta}_1(Z_{t-1} - \hat{Z}_{t-1})$$

$$- \hat{\theta}_{12}(Z_{t-12} - \hat{Z}_{t-12}) - \hat{\theta}_{13}(Z_{t-13} - \hat{Z}_{t-13}), \tag{4.87}$$

where $\hat{\theta}_1$, $\hat{\theta}_{12}$, and $\hat{\theta}_{13}$ are parameter estimates, and $\hat{z}_t$ denotes the one-step forecast value at time t. The model suggests that passenger levels can be optimally predicted from "last month," "same month last year," and "previous month last year" levels, as well as shocks (i.e., deviations from previous forecasts) in these periods. The airline model is a complex combination of

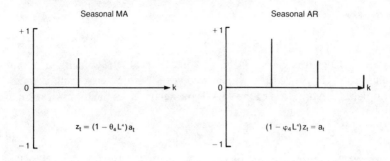

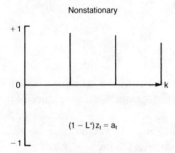

Figure 4–7. Autocorrelation Functions for Seasonal Processes (Quarterly Data).

regular and seasonal time series patterns that seemingly predicts air travel
very well (see, for example, Box and Jenkins 1976).

Parameter Estimation

The parameters of an adequately specified ARIMA model can be estimated
in a variety of ways. The simplest case involves the $AR(p)$ process, which can
be expressed in regression form as

$$z_t = c + \phi_1 z_{t-1} + \cdots + \phi_p z_{t-p} + \alpha_t. \tag{4.88}$$

Since α_t is white noise, the model can be parameterized with ordinary least
squares, which provides consistent estimates.

The situation is more complex when MA parameters are included. Even the simplest MA(1) model,

$$z_t = \alpha_t - \theta\alpha_{t-1}, \tag{4.89}$$

is difficult to estimate because α_{t-1} is unobservable. Typically, a maximum likelihood (ML) procedure, which involves a parameter search, is used. For example, ML estimation of the MA(1) model involves the minimization of the following sums-of-squares function:

$$s(\theta) = \sum [z_t + \theta\hat{\alpha}(\theta)_{t-1}]^2 = \sum \hat{\alpha}_t^2. \tag{4.90}$$

In order to execute a search, we need a starting value for α_0 so that we can subsequently compute $\hat{\alpha}_1 = z_1 + \theta\hat{\alpha}_0$, and so forth. The most obvious choice is to set $\hat{\alpha}_0 = 0$, i.e., to assume that there is no shock in the time series at its beginning. To the extent the assumption is wrong, the impact of the error will die out as long as the model is invertible, i.e., $|\theta| < 1$ in the MA(1) case. Indeed, we can write at time t:

$$\hat{\alpha}_t = z_t + \theta\hat{\alpha}_{t-1}$$
$$= z_t + \theta z_{t-1} + \cdots + \theta^{t-1}z_1 + \theta^t\hat{\alpha}_0. \tag{4.91}$$

Thus, for sufficiently long time series the effects of the initial observation die out exponentially as $\theta^t \to 0$. This example illustrates the importance of having invertible time series models.

Several variations of the likelihood method exist. A conditional likelihood approach for the ARMA (p, q) model assumes that $\alpha_t = 0$ for $p \le t \le (p + q - 1)$. An exact likelihood method estimates values for these α_t based on the exact likelihood derived by Newbold (1974). Furthermore, various nonlinear least-squares algorithms have been used, most notably the Gauss-Marquardt method. Issues in parameter estimation of ARMA models continue to receive attention in the statistical literature (e.g., Bustos and Yohai 1986).

Forecasting

It can be proved that the minimum squared-error forecast for a time series is obtained by a model that filters the data to white noise. Intuitively, whitening the data removes all systematic patterns so that only random error, which by definition cannot be forecast, remains. A poor time series model leaves auto-correlation in the data, which could have been used to improve the accuracy of the forecasts.

The quality of a forecast depends on σ_α^2, the residual variance of the ARIMA model, and on the forecasting horizon. Consider the MA(∞) expression of an ARMA model

$$z_t = \sum_{j=0}^{m} c_j \alpha_{t-j}, \qquad (4.92)$$

where m is infinite when AR parameters are present. An observation at time $(t + k)$ can be decomposed into a predictable part (i.e., known at time t) and a forecast error:

$$z_{t+k} = \sum_{j=k}^{m} c_j \alpha_{t+k-j} + \sum_{j=0}^{k-1} c_j \alpha_{t+k-j} \qquad (4.93)$$

or, more compactly,

$$z_{t+k} = f_{t,k} + e_{t,k}, \qquad (4.94)$$

where $f_{t,k}$ is a forecast made at time t. It follows that the forecast error is

$$e_{t,k} = z_{t+k} - f_{t,k} = \sum_{j=0}^{k-1} c_j \alpha_{t+k-j}, \qquad (4.95)$$

$$\text{var}(e_{t,k}) = \sigma_\alpha^2 \left[\sum_{j=0}^{k-1} c_j^2 \right]. \qquad (4.96)$$

Therefore, $\text{var}(e_{t,k}) \geq \text{var}(e_{t,k-1})$, or, the longer the forecasting horizon, the lower our confidence in the forecast.

The implication of this result is that frequent forecast updating will improve accuracy, at least theoretically. The options to the forecaster are to update the forecasts only, to update the parameter estimates and the forecasts, or to rebuild the model altogether.

Lag Specification with Multiple Time Series

The major limitation of univariate time series analysis for the marketing model builder is that it does not handle cause-and-effect situations, which are at the heart of marketing planning. Thus, if we are using time series analysis to specify the lag structure in a response model, we must extend the techniques of univariate extrapolation to the case of multiple time series. As it turns out, empirical lag specification in marketing models is important because little prior theory, or even conventional wisdom, is available in this area. In particular, there is a lack of understanding of the dynamic effects of marketing variables that are easy to manipulate, such as price and advertising.

There are two conditions for specifying lag structures on multiple time series:

1. Good time series data, i.e., sufficiently long time series (usually $T > 50$), collected at an appropriate data interval.
2. Statistical techniques that can effectively separate the lags between variables (the interstructure) from the lags within variables (the intrastructure).

In this chapter, we focus on the use of appropriate statistical methodology, assuming that we have sufficiently long time series and an adequate data interval. The data interval bias problem, which is very important in marketing and has received recent attention, is discussed in chapter 7.

Many of the advances in time series analysis in the 1970s pertained to lag specification. We start with the single-equation marketing model, for example a sales response model, as an application of transfer function analysis and intervention analysis. Next, we discuss the more difficult case of multiple-equation models, focusing on dynamic regression models and vector ARMA techniques.

The Transfer Function Model

Transfer function (TF) analysis is undoubtedly the most popular technique for analyzing multiple time series. It was first proposed by Box and Jenkins as a "dynamic" version of univariate analysis and has had numerous applications in the social and management sciences and in engineering. Helmer and Johansson (1977) introduced transfer functions in marketing for the purpose of modeling the sales-advertising relation. The basic model distinguishes an output series (Y) and one or more input series (X) in the following scheme:

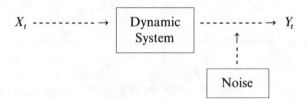

where the noise follows an ARIMA process independent of the input series. Thus, the model is (possibly after differencing x and y):

$$y_t = c + \frac{\omega(L)}{\delta(L)} L^b x_t + \frac{\Theta L}{\Phi(L)} \alpha_t, \qquad (4.97)$$

where

$$\omega(L) = \omega_0 + \omega_1 L + \omega_2 L^2 + \cdots + \omega_s L^s,$$

$$\delta(L) = 1 - \delta_1 L - \delta_2 L^2 - \cdots - \delta_r L^r,$$

$$\Theta(L) = 1 - \theta_1 L - \theta_2 L^2 - \cdots - \theta_q L^q,$$

$$\Phi(L) = 1 - \phi_1 L - \phi_2 L^2 - \cdots \phi_p L^p,$$

$$b = \text{delay operator.}$$

The order of the transfer function is said to be (r, s, b) and the added noise model is of order (p, q).

The transfer function is a straightforward extension of the ARMA model; for $\omega(L) = 0$, the model is equivalent to a univariate time series process. The transfer function parameters are interpreted as follows:

- The numerator parameters in $\omega(L)$ model the direct effects of changes in x on y over time. In the absence of denominator parameters (i.e., $\delta(L) \equiv 1$), the cumulative effect of x on y is simply the sum of these parameters:

$$\omega_0 + \omega_1 + \omega_2 + \cdots + \omega_s.$$

- The denominator parameters model the gradual adjustment of y to a change in x over time. Gradual adjustment occurs when a fraction of the direct effect carries over in subsequent periods. For example, an advertising campaign may induce purchases from new buyers in the same period. In every subsequent period, a fraction of these new buyers may repeat their purchase. The long-run effect of the advertising is then computed as

$$\frac{\omega_0 + \omega_1 + \cdots + \omega_s}{1 - \delta_1 - \delta_2 - \cdots - \delta_r}.$$

- The added noise model is of order (p, q).

The success of the transfer function in applied time series analysis is due in part to the fact that the traditional regression model is a special case of it. Indeed, if $\omega(L) = \omega_0$, and $\delta(L) = \Theta(L) = \Phi(L) \equiv 1$, we obtain:

$$y_t = c + \omega_0 x_t + \alpha_t. \tag{4.98}$$

However, the philosophy of transfer function modeling differs from traditional regression modeling in two important ways: (1) specific attention is paid to the dynamic relation between input and output, i.e., the response parameter is polynomial in time, and (2) the error term is allowed to exhibit systematic behavior, as represented by the added noise term. For example, marketing efforts are known to have instantaneous and delayed effects on product performance; also, product sales often exhibit autoregressive patterns due to customer loyalty, slowly changing distribution, and the like. The transfer function is a highly realistic model for incorporating these phenomena.

Transfer function analysis is a set of techniques for specifying the dynamic relation between an output variable Y_t and one or more input variables X_t, plus an added noise ARMA process. The approach is similar to the iterative Box-Jenkins method for univariate time series: identification, tentative model specification, parameter estimation, and diagnostic checking. However, since multiple time series are involved, we need to introduce a new statistical tool—the cross-correlation function (CCF). Then, we explain the Box-Jenkins identification method and a newer method, due to Liu and Hanssens (1982), which is more appropriate for multiple-input models. Finally, we cover some principles of intervention analysis, i.e., transfer functions where the input variable is binary.

The Cross-Correlation Function

Without loss of generality, the bivariate stochastic process (X_t, Y_t), which generates successive observations over time, is

$$(X_1, Y_1), (X_2, Y_2), \ldots, (X_T, Y_T).$$

Assume that a transformation such as differencing exists so that each series (x_t, y_t) is stationary. Then we may define the sample autocovariance at lag k of x or y as

$$c_{yy}(k) = E(y_t - \bar{y})(y_{t-k} - \bar{y}) = \frac{1}{T} \sum_{t=k+1}^{T} (y_t - \bar{y})(y_{t-k} - \bar{y}), \qquad (4.99)$$

$$c_{xx}(k) = E(x_t - \bar{x})(x_{t-k} - \bar{x}) = \frac{1}{T} \sum_{t=k+1}^{T} (x_t - \bar{x})(x_{t-k} - \bar{x}), \qquad (4.100)$$

the sample cross-covariance between x and y at lag k as

$$c_{xy}(k) = E(y_t - \bar{y})(x_{t-k} - \bar{x}) = \frac{1}{T} \sum_{t=k+1}^{T} (y_t - \bar{y})(x_{t-k} - \bar{x}), \qquad (4.101)$$

and the sample cross-correlation coefficient between x and y at lag k as

$$\gamma_{xy}(k) = \frac{E(y_t - \bar{y})(x_{t-k} - \bar{x})}{\sqrt{E(y_t - \bar{y})^2 \cdot E(x_t - \bar{x})^2}} = \frac{c_{xy}(k)}{\sqrt{c_{xx}(0) \cdot c_{yy}(0)}} \qquad (4.102)$$

Notice that while the autocovariance is symmetric around lag $k = 0$, the cross-covariance and cross-correlation coefficients are not, i.e., $\gamma_{xy}(k) \neq \gamma_{yx}(k)$, but $\gamma_{xy}(k) = \gamma_{yx}(-k)$.

The cross-correlation function is the natural extension of the autocorrelation function when more than one time series is considered. Its interpretation is also parallel with univariate time series analysis: spikes in the CCF denote moving-average or numerator parameters, and dying-out patterns suggest autoregressive or denominator parameters. The CCF is used in virtually all applications of multiple time series analysis as a diagnostic tool for statistical relations among series, sometimes referred to as *interstructure*. However, such inferences are often hampered by the existence of within-series patterns, known as *intrastructure*, i.e., the sign and magnitude of a cross-correlation may be affected by the autocorrelation in both series. Formally, this implies that the standard errors of the CCF are a function of the ACFs of the series, so that we may obtain nonsensical correlations among time series. This problem was discovered long ago (Yule 1926) but it remains one of the main challenges in the statistical analysis of time series. We discuss its implications in conjunction with the various multiple time series models that are of interest to marketing modelers.

Transfer Function Identification: Single-Input Models

A transfer function is identified when appropriate order values of the transfer function (r, s, b) and the added noise (p, q) have been set. This is a sufficiently complex task so that we prefer to work with a simplified version of the model, called the *impulse response form*:

$$y_t = c + (v_0 + v_1 L + v_2 L^2 + \cdots)x_t + n_t \tag{4.103}$$

or

$$y_t = c + V(L)x_t + n_t, \tag{4.104}$$

where n_t is a short notation for the added noise process and $V(L)$ is finite when $r = 0$ and infinite when $r > 0$. Box and Jenkins (1976) suggest using the CCF to obtain preliminary estimates of the impulse response weights v_j as follows:

- *Step 1.* Find the ARMA model for the input x and store the residuals of that model. This step is known as prewhitening the input:

$$\hat{\Phi}(L)x_t = \hat{\Theta}(L)\alpha_t, \tag{4.105}$$

$$\hat{\alpha}_t = \hat{\Theta}(L)^{-1}\hat{\Phi}(L)x_t. \tag{4.106}$$

- *Step 2.* Apply the *same* prewhitening filter to the output y and store the residuals:

$$\hat{\beta}_t = \hat{\Theta}(L)^{-1}\hat{\Phi}(L)y_t. \tag{4.107}$$

- *Step 3.* Compute the CCF between $\hat{\alpha}_t$ and $\hat{\beta}_t$. It can be shown that

$$\hat{v}_j = \frac{s_{\hat{\beta}}}{s_{\hat{\alpha}}} r_{\hat{\alpha}\hat{\beta}}(j), \tag{4.108}$$

implying that the CCF is directly proportional to the impulse response weights.

The variance of a cross-correlation coefficient when at least one of the series is white noise is of the order $1/T$. Thus, hypothesis testing becomes relatively easy. Furthermore, a CCF pattern analysis similar to ACF analysis can be used to identify the values r, s, and b. Figure 4–8 shows some common transfer functions and the shapes of the CCFs that would lead to their identification.

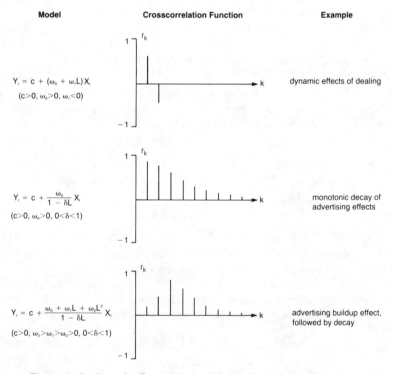

Figure 4–8. Transfer Functions and Cross-Correlation Patterns.

Once the values (r, s, b) are specified, the transfer function parameters can be estimated, usually by nonlinear least squares, and preliminary estimates of the noise series can be obtained:

$$\hat{n}_t = y_t - \hat{V}(L)x_t. \tag{4.109}$$

The ACF of the series $\hat{n}_t$ is now used to identify an appropriate added noise model. Finally, the complete transfer function-added noise model is estimated.

As in univariate analysis, the method includes built-in diagnostic checking. In this case, two checks are necessary:

1. The ACF of the residuals should be flat. Any remaining patterns are modeled via the added noise parameters $\Phi(L)$ and $\Theta(L)$.
2. The CCF of the residuals and the (prewhitened) input should be flat. A spike at, say, $k = 2$ would indicate that a response effect at lag 2 was omitted from the transfer function, which can be corrected by adding a parameter.

The prewhitening method for TF analysis has stood the test of time, as witnessed by its numerous applications. Nevertheless, there are a few weaknesses in this approach, which are due to the bivariate (pairwise) nature of the identification strategy. In multiple-input situations we must specify each transfer function separately, under the implicit assumption that the inputs are independent of one another. The method quickly becomes time-consuming and may produce conflicting results when the final model combining all inputs is estimated. Finally, some applications report that the results may be sensitive to the choice of a prewhitening model for x.

Transfer Function Identification: Multiple-Input Models

Multiple-input models are common in market response analysis. Indeed, most marketing decisions involve resource allocations among various activities, for example, media planning. The multiple-input transfer function allows for differences in the dynamic response of, say, sales to various marketing efforts.

Using the CCF method makes it necessary to individually prewhiten each explanatory variable in the model. If management uses one decision rule for advertising planning, another for price setting, and so on, substantially different ARMA models for these time series may be obtained. Furthermore, the sum of all these pairwise transfer functions may be different from the overall market response model. Regression analysis has long resolved the problems associated with pairwise correlations. The multiple regression model can be used in transfer function identification as long as we are particularly careful about the time series properties of the data. A least-squares regression method due to Liu and Hanssens (1982) offers the robustness and ease of use of multiple regression while avoiding the pitfalls of making inferences from autocorrelated data.

Suppose the following two-input transfer function model on stationary data is to be identified:

$$y_t = c + \frac{\omega_1(L)}{\delta_1(L)} L^{b_1} x_{1t} + \frac{\omega_2(L)}{\delta_2(L)} L^{b_2} x_{2t} + \frac{\Theta(L)}{\Phi(L)} \alpha_t. \qquad (4.110)$$

The impulse response form of the transfer function is

$$y_t = c + V_1(L)x_{1t} + V_2(L)x_{2t} + n_t. \qquad (4.111)$$

If the transfer function contains rational (denominator) parameters, the impulse response polynomials are infinite. However, since these parameters die out under the stationarity assumption, they can be approximated in practice with a finite number of terms, say k_1 and k_2. Thus, the identification model is a *direct-lag regression equation*:

$$y_t = c + (v_{10} + v_{11}L + \cdots + v_{1k_1}L^{k_1})x_{1t}$$
$$+ (v_{20} + v_{21}L + \cdots + v_{2k_2}L^{k_2})x_{2t} + u_t, \qquad (4.112)$$

where k_1 and k_2 are chosen sufficiently large to avoid truncation bias. The direct-lag regression model can be estimated by ordinary least squares, and the pattern of the OLS coefficients is used to identify cutoff versus dying-out patterns.

Two problems may arise in the least-squares procedure: (1) the lagged input variables may be highly collinear, and (2) the residuals of the model may not be white noise. It is well known that the first condition leads to unstable parameter estimates and the second condition makes OLS inefficient. Liu and Hanssens (1982) observe that collinearity results from highly autoregressive input series; for example, if x_{1t} is AR(1) with parameter 0.9, then each input variable is 0.9 correlated with the next variable. In contrast, if x_{1t} follows an MA(1) process with parameter 0.9, then the successive correlations in the data matrix would only be 0.45. Therefore, they propose to filter the data prior to OLS estimation, using a common filter that eliminates the AR factors close to 1. For example, if the ARMA processes for the inputs are

$$(1 - 0.8L)x_{1t} = (1 - 0.62L^2)\alpha_{1t}, \qquad (4.113)$$

$$(1 - 0.5L)(1 - 0.85L^4)x_{2t} = \alpha_{2t}, \qquad (4.114)$$

a common filter $(1 - 0.8L)(1 - 0.85L^4)$ would be recommended. The second problem, nonwhite residuals, can be handled by applying generalized least squares (GLS) estimates in lieu of OLS. The practical GLS application consists of two steps: (1) find the ARMA process underlying the residuals from OLS estimation, and (2) transform the data by these ARMA filters and re-estimate. It is seldom necessary to engage in such an iterative procedure, though, as the OLS identification results alone are typically satisfactory.

There are several variations on least-squares identification of transfer functions. For example, a study on distributed lag modeling proposes the use of ridge regression estimators to circumvent the problem of collinearity in direct-lag estimation (Erickson 1981b). Also, a transfer function identification method combining common filters and ridge regression was recently developed (Edlund 1984).

Intervention Analysis

Although many marketing variables like price, distribution, and communication expenditures are quantifiable, some are not, and yet their impact on market performance may be substantial. A qualitative change in advertising copy, the advent of a new government regulation, or the sudden presence of a foreign competitor in a market are but a few examples of nonquantifiable inputs in a marketing model. To the extent that the effects of such inputs are spread over time, multiple time series methods are needed to identify their impact and measure their magnitude. Intervention analysis is a dynamic version of dummy variable regression analysis that was specifically designed to handle such modeling tasks (Box and Tiao 1975). Qualitative events or interventions exist in two forms:

1. A pulse function, where the intervention occurs and disappears sometime in the future:

$$P_t = 0 \quad \text{for all } t < k, \text{ the intervention time,}$$

$$P_t = 1 \quad \text{for } k \leq t \leq k + l,$$

$$P_t = 0 \quad \text{for all } t > (k + l).$$

Marketing examples include airline strikes, discount periods, "happy hours," and advertising campaigns.

2. A step function, where the intervention is permanent once it has occurred:

$$S_t = 0 \quad \text{for all } t < k,$$

$$S_t = 1 \quad \text{for all } t \geq k.$$

Examples are a major product reformulation, the exit of a competitor, and the deregulation of an industry.

The general form of a pulse intervention model is

$$Y_t = c + \frac{\omega(L)}{\delta(L)} L^b P_t + \frac{\Theta(L)}{\Phi(L)} \alpha_t, \qquad (4.115)$$

where all parameters are as previously defined.

The difference between pulse and step interventions is important because it affects the shape of the intervention response function. Following Vandaele

MODEL

$y_t = c + \omega_o x_t$

$(c > 0, \omega_0 > 0)$

MODEL

$y_t = c + \frac{\omega_0}{1 - \delta L} x_t$

$(c > 0, \omega_0 > 0, 0 < \delta < 1)$

PULSE INPUT[1]

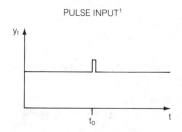

PULSE INPUT[1]

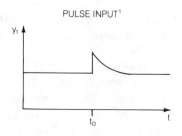

STEP INPUT[2]

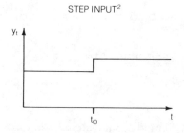

STEP INPUT[2]

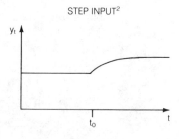

Example: Static sales response to product availability.

Example: Decaying sales effects of an advertising campaign.

[1]Intervention occurs at time $t = t_0$: $x_t = 0$ $(t \neq t_0)$, $x_t = 1$ $(t = t_0)$
[2]Intervention starts at time $t = t_0$: $x_t = 0$ $(t < t_0)$, $x_t = 1$ $(t \geq t_0)$

Figure 4–9. Intervention Scenarios.

(1983), we can classify intervention effects as having an abrupt or a gradual start and a permanent or a temporary duration. Price promotion effects on sales are typically abrupt, while some image advertising campaigns affect sales in a gradual way. Permanent effects in marketing are almost exclusively due to step interventions, such as product modification or new distribution channels. However, some step interventions may have only temporary effects, for example, consumers may initially react negatively to a price hike but eventually adjust to previous purchase levels.

Several intervention scenarios are shown graphically in figure 4–9. In interpreting these graphs it is important to realize that the first difference of a step is a pulse, i.e.,

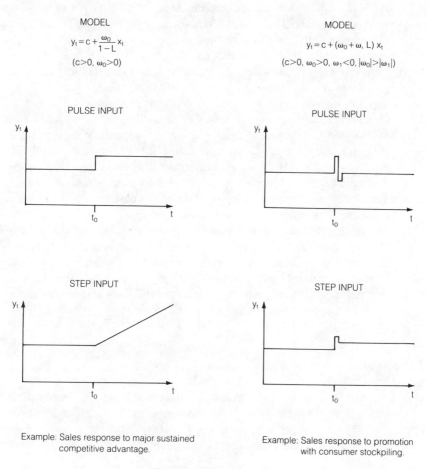

MODEL

$$y_t = c + \frac{\omega_0}{1 - L} x_t$$

$(c>0, \omega_0>0)$

PULSE INPUT

STEP INPUT

Example: Sales response to major sustained competitive advantage.

MODEL

$$y_t = c + (\omega_0 + \omega_1 L) x_t$$

$(c>0, \omega_0>0, \omega_1<0, |\omega_0|>|\omega_1|)$

PULSE INPUT

STEP INPUT

Example: Sales response to promotion with consumer stockpiling.

Figure 4–9 (*continued*)

$$(1 - L)S_t = P_t \qquad\qquad (4.116)$$

Thus, when a step intervention makes a time series nonstationary, we may model the change in the data (first differences) as a function of a pulse intervention.

The identification of intervention models usually requires some a priori notion of the shape of the effect (i.e., abrupt or gradual start, temporary or permanent duration), which is not difficult to obtain in a marketing context. However, the intervention may interfere with the univariate ARMA model underlying the data, so that we must be careful to separate the two. Three situations may arise:

1. There is a sufficiently long preintervention time series so that the ARMA model can be identified from ACF-PACF analysis of the pre-intervention data. Then the ARMA and intervention components are estimated jointly on the entire time series.
2. A separate time series exists that has not been affected by the intervention. For example, in a study of the effects of a communication campaign on city bus ridership, Tybout and Hauser (1981) used the time series of an adjacent city to establish a univariate model, which was then applied to the campaign city. The method is commonly known as interrupted time series analysis and is most popular in experimental design research (e.g., Cook and Campbell 1979). Krishnamurthi, Narayan, and Raj (1986) discuss intervention modeling techniques for measuring the buildup effect of advertising by experimental design.
3. Neither a long preintervention period nor an uninterrupted time series exist. Here the modeler is forced to specify one of the components first and to identify the other component from the residuals in the first step. We recommend starting the analysis with the dominant component; for example, an abrupt and permanent shift in the level of the data should be modeled first. Either way, careful judgment and prior knowledge must be used to specify the model, and the usual diagnostic checks should be applied to the residuals of the model.

Lag Specification in Multiple-Equation Models

Whether an a priori theoretical or an empirical method for model specification is used, it is possible that the ultimate marketing model contains multiple equations. Then the identification of lag structures and the estimation of parameters pose some special challenges. First, some marketing variables may be jointly endogenous, i.e., they are both caused by, and cause, other elements in the system. Second, the shocks in the system may not be white noise, in which case we must be careful not to confuse lagged-variable effects and lagged-error effects in estimation.

There are two basic approaches to lag specification in this case: we may try to find lag structures in the system as a whole, or we may work on each equation individually, treating it as a transfer function. The first method is generally referred to as vector ARMA analysis, first proposed by Tiao and Box (1981). The second method is based on least-squares analysis with instrumental variables on the rational structural form model (Hanssens and Liu 1983).

Vector ARMA Analysis. The multivariate ARMA model for a $k \times 1$ vector of stationary observations z_t is

$$\Phi(L)z_t = c + \Theta(L)\alpha_t, \qquad (4.117)$$

where

$c = k \times 1$ vector of constants;

$\Phi(L) = I - \phi_1 L - \cdots - \phi_p L^p$;   each matrix ϕ contains autoregressive parameters and is of order $k \times k$;

$\Theta(L) = I - \theta_1 L - \cdots - \theta_q L^q$;   each matrix θ contains moving average parameters and is of order $k \times k$;

$\alpha_t = k \times 1$ vector of white noise error terms generally assumed to be i.i.d. multivariate normal with $E(\alpha_t) = 0$ and $E(\alpha_t \alpha_t') = \Sigma$.

The vector ARMA (VARMA) model is a logical extension of univariate Box-Jenkins analysis to multiple time series. The diagonal elements of the matrices $\Phi(L)$ and $\Theta(L)$ contain within-series lagged effects. That makes it a very comprehensive model from a statistical perspective. Furthermore, the model does not require an a priori distinction between endogenous and exogenous variables.

The original specification method is due to Tiao and Box (1981), and subsequent improvements and variations were proposed by Tiao and Tsay (1983) and Tsay (1985). The two basic identification tools are as follows:

1. The sample cross-correlation matrix that contains the simple correlations among the series at various lags k. Tiao and Box (1981) use indicator symbols $+$, $-$, and 0 for positive, negative, and insignificant correlations instead of the actual values, in order to identify patterns

that are cutting off or dying out with increasing k. As in univariate modeling, the cutoffs indicate moving-average parameters (matrix $\Theta(L)$), and the dying-out patterns suggest an autoregressive process (matrix $\Phi(L)$).

2. Partial autocorrelation matrices $\mathbf{P}(l)$, which are obtained by fitting successively higher $AR(l)$ models to the data. They are interpreted in the same spirit as the PACF: as soon as the "true" AR order p is reached, the elements of $\mathbf{P}(l)$ for $l > p$ will be zero.

Once the model is identified, the parameters are estimated using conditional or exact likelihood procedures. Diagnostic checking of the residual cross-correlation matrices may reveal model inadequacies that can be correlated, as in the univariate diagnostic checking stage.

Vector ARMA modeling is a promising tool for forecasting multiple time series without regard to causal ordering in the system. For example, Moriarty (1985b) used it to illustrate the relative value of objective versus judgment forecasts in a marketing setting. On the other hand, the technique is of limited use in structural marketing modeling because the VARMA model is a "reduced form" model, so contemporaneous endogenous effects cannot be modeled other than through the residual covariance matrix. Furthermore, the use of correlational techniques on raw data carries the danger of modeling spurious effects and, in general, may cause overparameterized models. These problems make the technique less useful for hypothesis testing in marketing.

The Rational Distributed Lag Structural Form.   When the causal ordering of marketing variables is known, we can do simpler and more robust lag specification. The most general linear model for this purpose is the rational distributed lag structural form (RSF) (Wall 1976):

$$\Gamma(L)\mathbf{y}_t + \mathbf{B}(L)\mathbf{x}_t = \mathbf{\psi}(L)\alpha_t, \qquad (4.118)$$

where

Γ = rational matrix with endogenous parameters,

$\mathbf{B}$ = rational matrix with exogenous parameters,

$\mathbf{\psi}$ = rational matrix with added noise parameters.

The traditional static simultaneous equation model is a special case of the RSF, for example,

$$\Gamma\mathbf{y}_t + \mathbf{B}\mathbf{x}_t = \alpha_t. \qquad (4.119)$$

Again, it is possible to specify the dynamics of such a model via a combined use of econometric and time-series techniques. Without loss of generality, a dynamic simultaneous-equation system on stationary data with two endogenous variables y_1 and y_2 and two exogenous variables x_1 and x_2 is

$$y_{1t} = \beta_1(L)x_{1t} + \gamma_1(L)y_{2t} + \varepsilon_{1t}, \tag{4.120}$$

$$y_{2t} = \beta_2(L)x_{2t} + \gamma_2(L)y_{1t} + \varepsilon_{2t}, \tag{4.121}$$

Each equation in the system is similar to a transfer function except that the disturbance may be correlated with the endogenous variable. Hanssens and Liu (1983) propose to identify such a system by extending their OLS technique for transfer functions with instrumental variables:

1. Approximate y_{1t} and y_{2t} via lag regression over x_1 and x_2, using a sufficiently large number of lags,

    $$y_{1t} = c_1(L)x_{1t} + c_2(L)x_{2t} + e_{1t}, \tag{4.122}$$

    $$y_{2t} = c_3(L)x_{1t} + c_4(L)x_{2t} + e_{2t}, \tag{4.123}$$

    and store the estimates of y_{1t} and y_{2t}, say $\hat{y}_{1t}$ and $\hat{y}_{2t}$.
2. Apply the least-squares transfer function identification method (Liu and Hanssens 1982) to the model:

    $$y_{1t} = v_1(L)x_{1t} + v_2(L)\hat{y}_{2t} + \varepsilon'_{1t}, \tag{4.124}$$

    $$y_{2t} = v_3(L)x_{2t} + v_4(L)\hat{y}_{1t} + \varepsilon'_{2t}, \tag{4.125}$$

3. Identify the added noise from the residuals in step 2, and estimate the complete model with an appropriate estimator.

It can be shown that the proposed method provides consistent transfer function weights. Furthermore, it is implementable with standard statistical software. When compared to the VARMA method on an exercise in agricultural price setting, the method provided a similar goodness of fit with many fewer parameters and no marketing counterintuitive results (Hanssens and Liu 1983).

Summary

We have discussed techniques for specifying the dynamics of a model from a combined time series and structural perspective. First, in a number of cases, univariate time series extrapolation of marketing data is sufficient, in particular when the objective of marketing model building is strictly forecasting. The autoregressive–moving-average, or ARMA, filter first proposed by Yule was made practical for model builders by the pioneering work of Box and Jenkins. The method converts a time series to white noise, i.e., a series of uncorrelated random shocks, and in so doing, extracts the maximum amount of systematic behavior from the data for forecasting.

Most marketing models, however, are structural, i.e., they are built on cause-and-effect mechanisms. The transfer function extends the ARMA model by allowing input variables other than white noise to affect a performance variable such as sales. We have discussed the prewhitening method due to Box and Jenkins as a technique for specifying single-input transfer functions. When there is more than one input variable, as is very common in marketing, this method becomes cumbersome, even unreliable. We follow the proposition of Liu and Hanssens to use least-squares techniques and common filters to specify such models. This method is an example of the combined use of time series and structural (econometric) analysis.

In some cases, marketing models contain several equations, a situation which poses special challenges to lag specification. The vector ARMA model can be used in this case as a direct extension of univariate Box-Jenkins analysis. However, that model is less useful when structural equations are needed. A more relevant approach for marketing modelers is to work with a dynamic econometric model and to specify its dynamic structure by an instrumental variables least-squares technique.

With the exception of the vector ARMA model, all the methods discussed in this chapter assume that the model builder knows the causal ordering of the marketing variables (level 1 prior knowledge). When this is not the case, the model builder may use time series techniques for empirically determining the direction of causality in the marketing system. This is the subject of chapter 5.

Notes

1. Strictly speaking, we do not need to know causal ordering in order to perform a univariate time series analysis. Univariate techniques, however, need to be understood before addressing modeling with causal ordering. Consequently, the examples in the univariate part of chapter 4 all use a general variable, Z, which may be endogenous or exogenous to a system.

2. Many important sample statistics have desirable large-sample properties for 30 observations or more. When complex models are needed to describe the data, this minimum may be higher, for example, in the case of seasonal models.

3. As the section title implies, the discussion is restricted to linear time series models. Non-linearities are typically incorporated by transforming the data. Formal nonlinear time series models exist, but they have not been used in marketing to date. See, for example, Mohler (1988).

4. A new literature on cointegration challenges the need for imposing stationarity on all the data prior to model building. In brief, this literature argues that a long-term equilibrium relation between variables Y and X may exist such that the individual time series are nonstationary but some linear combination $Z = Y + aX$ is stationary. It is too early to assess the value of cointegration in marketing models; the interested reader may consult a special issue of the *Oxford Bulletin of Economics and Statistics* 48 (no. 3, 1986) for an overview.

5 DETERMINING CAUSAL ORDERING

Determining the direction of causality may be straightforward when only two variables are involved, but real-world marketing systems are often so complex that the causal chains cannot be easily established a priori. For example, in competitive markets, causal relations may exist in many directions among the following variables: product sales, industry sales, market share, profits, marketing efforts, competitive marketing efforts, and environmental conditions. Although in this case we would have a good idea of the elements in the information set (level 0), it would be difficult to posit one structural marketing model from prior insight alone.

This chapter discusses ETS model-building techniques for the data-driven assessment of causality in marketing systems. We begin with a brief discussion of the meaning of causality in nonexperimental settings. We then show that time series data may be used to determine the causal ordering of marketing variables without prior knowledge of the underlying structural model. Next, we explain the relation between time series and structural models. Finally, we introduce the concept of Granger causality, discuss empirical testing procedures, and summarize the use of these techniques in marketing models to date.

Causal Relations

One way in which a response model may be complex is when it involves simultaneous relations among variables in the model. For example, sales of a firm may be interdependent with sales of another firm. Or sales of a firm may be interdependent with decision rules of that firm. In either case, the appropriate response model may require a system of equations that are simultaneous in variables or disturbances. This issue is related to marketing theory because it raises questions of *causality*.

In a model of sales and advertising, three mutually exclusive specifications are possible in terms of the causal ordering of the model: (1) advertising determines sales, (2) sales determines advertising, or (3) advertising determines sales, and vice versa. How does the model builder know which specification is correct? The answer depends upon a priori knowledge, empirical evidence, or both. For example, the researcher may have independent reasons for hypothesizing the existence of both a sales response function, $S = f(A)$, and an advertising decision rule, $A = f(S)$. The sales response function may have originated from observation of the market; the advertising decision rule may have originated from interviews with management. The two relations taken together imply that both sales and advertising are contemporaneously correlated and thus both endogenous variables in period t. On the other hand, the researcher may have reason to believe that one relation holds but be uncertain about the other, mainly because there is no theory to explain the presence or absence of the other relation.

ETS research can be very helpful in such cases. ETS techniques can be used to rule out one of the relations, show that the relations are correlated over different time periods, or deal directly with estimation problems associated with simultaneity.[1] Although ETS research is not typically based on experimental data, we can speak of causality in a very legitimate and practical way.

We follow Simon (1953), who argues that causal ordering is (or can best be treated as) a property of the model. Thus, we talk about the causal ordering of the model equations 1.3–1.4. Schultz (1971a) discusses the causal ordering of his model and the *revealed* causal ordering; in both cases, the word *causal* attaches to the model as a characteristic. This view is consistent with Hume's argument that as scientists we can observe (or perceive) events but not the relation (or force) between events. One event can be called a cause and another event an effect as long as it is clearly understood that this means no more or no less than that A is always followed by B (Kemeny 1959). In practice, since the notion of force can never be tested, causality must necessarily be treated in this more limited way. Thus, a functional relation, e.g., between sales and advertising, $S = f(A)$, is treated here at most as the propositional statement

"If A, then B" and typically only as the generalization or association between S and A implied by the function itself. In systems of relations, we employ Simon's framework of causal ordering to suggest the asymmetrical relations in a model. When we do not have strong a priori knowledge about the direction of causality, we use a concept called Granger causality to help determine the causal ordering of a model (Granger 1969).

A final consideration of simultaneous relations involves decision variables other than advertising. Personal selling expenditures, distribution expenditures, sales promotion budgets, prices, and other marketing factors may be set in relation to present or past sales. This means that in marketing mix models the problem of simultaneous relations is also likely to occur.

Modeling When Only the Information Set is Known

Although logically the first task in market response modeling, the causal ordering of variables is a relatively new ETS technique and, in fact, can be performed only with time series data.[2] Traditionally, marketing models have been estimated under the assumption of a simple market response mechanism:

$$\text{market performance} = f(\text{marketing effort}).$$

There are, however, two major marketing phenomena that may invalidate models based on unidirectional causality. First, it has been shown empirically and theoretically that marketing decisions may depend on past, present, or future marketing outcomes. And, second, competitive actions and reactions may occur as a result of marketing outcomes. In both cases, the resulting marketing model may exhibit multidirectional causality:

$$\text{market performance} = f(\text{own and competitive marketing effort}),$$

$$\text{own marketing effort} = g(\text{market performance, competitive marketing effort}),$$

$$\text{competitive effort} = h(\text{market performance, own marketing effort}).$$

The econometrics literature has long offered estimation solutions for these more complex models (see chapter 3). These solution techniques require the a priori specification of a simultaneous-equation model, including endogenous, exogenous, and lagged endogenous variables. More often than not, however, such a priori specification is very difficult in a marketing context, and until recently the model builder was confronted with the following dilemma: one needs a correctly specified structural model in order to make statistical inferences about the parameters, but the parameters must be known in order to validate the structural model. In other words, one cannot test the model without estimating its parameters but cannot use the parameters until the structural model is known to be valid.

Time series analysis has produced an elegant solution to this dilemma: the key contribution is that *the model builder does not need to know the exact structural model in order to make causal inferences.* Every structural model on longitudinal data implies a set of time series processes on the variables, which can be used to establish causal ordering, functional form, and lag structures. When prior knowledge is sparse, some preliminary time series analyses on the data can be performed that advance the researcher to level 1 or level 2 prior knowledge. At that point, the structural model can be estimated and evaluated.

To explain these fundamental ideas, we need to (1) demonstrate the inherent relation between structural and time series models, and (2) introduce a workable definition of causality in nonexperimental data.

The Relation Between Structural and Time Series Models

When the Box-Jenkins method for univariate time series became known for its superior forecasting performance, several researchers viewed this technique as a competitor to the traditional econometric approach to model building. For example, Nelson (1972) compared univariate forecasts of key macroeconomic variables against those obtained from the well-established Wharton model of the the U.S. economy.[3] Such comparisons quickly led to the formation of two opposing schools of model builders: the "structural" approach, favoring hypothetico-deductive and theoretical modeling, and the "time series" method, which advocates more extrapolative statistical model building.

A seminal article by Zellner and Palm (1974) demonstrated that competition between structural and time series modeling is unnecessary and that, in fact, much can be gained from integrated econometric and time series (ETS) analysis. This relation is derived from the general multivariate ARMA model on the $p \times 1$ vector z_t:

$$H(L)z_t = c + F(L)\alpha_t, \qquad (5.1)$$

in which $H(L)$ is a $p \times p$ matrix of autoregressive parameter polynomials of the form

$$H(L) = \{h_{ij}(L)\} = \sum_{l=0}^{r_{ij}} h_{ij}^{(l)}L^l,$$

$F(L)$ is a $p \times p$ matrix of moving average parameter polynomials of the form

$$F(L) = \{f_{ij}(L)\} = \sum_{l=0}^{q_{ij}} f_{ij}^{(l)} L^l,$$

c is a $p \times 1$ vector of constants, and α_t is a $p \times 1$ vector of white noise residuals, generally assumed to be i.i.d. normal with $E(\alpha_t) = 0$, and $E(\alpha_t \alpha_t') = d_{tt} \mathbf{I}_p$, where d_{tt} is the Kronecker delta.

The multivariate ARMA model is the most general linear time series model. As does the vector ARMA model introduced in chapter 4, it allows for within-series and across-series dynamic effects. It is more general than the vector ARMA model because it allows for contemporaneous effects among the elements of $\mathbf{z}_t$ via the parameters h_{ij}^0 and f_{ij}^0. However, the practical value of this model in empirical research is rather limited because there is no distinction between endogenous and exogenous variables.

If the matrix $\mathbf{H}(L)$ is of full rank, the multivariate ARMA model can be written as (ignoring the constants)

$$\mathbf{z}_t = \mathbf{H}^{-1}(L)\mathbf{F}(L)\alpha_t, \tag{5.2}$$

or

$$|\mathbf{H}(L)|\mathbf{z}_t = \mathbf{H}^*(L)\mathbf{F}(L)\alpha_t, \tag{5.3}$$

where $|\mathbf{H}(L)|$ is the determinant and $\mathbf{H}^*(L)$ is the adjoint matrix, i.e., the inverse of the matrix of cofactors, of $\mathbf{H}(L)$. Therefore, for each element i in the data vector,

$$|\mathbf{H}(L)|\mathbf{z}_{it} = a_i' \alpha_t, \tag{5.4}$$

where a_i' is the ith row of the matrix $\mathbf{H}^*(L)\mathbf{F}(L)$. As it turns out, the right-hand side of this equation, which is the sum of moving-average processes, is also moving-average (Granger and Morris 1976). Since the left-hand side is a polynomial in L, which is the same for each element i, we conclude the following:

1. Each element of a multivariate ARMA model follows a univariate ARMA model,
2. The autoregressive components of these ARMA models are the same for each element.

To make the link with dynamic econometric models, suppose the model builder has level 1 prior knowledge, i.e., the vector $\mathbf{z}_t$ can be decomposed into subvectors of endogenous and exogenous variables $\mathbf{y}_t$ and $\mathbf{x}_t$:

$$\begin{bmatrix} \mathbf{H}_{11}(L) & \mathbf{H}_{12}(L) \\ \mathbf{H}_{21}(L) & \mathbf{H}_{22}(L) \end{bmatrix} \begin{bmatrix} \mathbf{y}_t \\ \mathbf{x}_t \end{bmatrix} = \begin{bmatrix} \mathbf{F}_{11}(L) & \mathbf{F}_{12}(L) \\ \mathbf{F}_{21}(L) & \mathbf{F}_{22}(L) \end{bmatrix} \begin{bmatrix} \alpha_{1t} \\ \alpha_{2t} \end{bmatrix}. \tag{5.5}$$

The definition of exogeneity implies that the stochastic process generating $\mathbf{x}$ does not contain elements of $\mathbf{y}$; therefore,

$$\mathbf{H}_{21}(L) = \mathbf{F}_{12}(L) = \mathbf{F}_{21}(L) = \mathbf{0},$$

and thus the model can be rewritten in two blocks of equations:

$$(1) \qquad \mathbf{H}_{11}(L)\mathbf{y}_t + \mathbf{H}_{12}(L)\mathbf{x}_t = \mathbf{F}_{11}(L)\boldsymbol{\alpha}_{1t}, \tag{5.6a}$$

$$(2) \qquad \mathbf{H}_{22}(L)\mathbf{x}_t = \mathbf{F}_{22}(L)\boldsymbol{\alpha}_{2t}. \tag{5.6b}$$

The first block is the familiar dynamic structural form of an econometric model. The second block shows the stochastic structure of the exogenous variables, which is different from traditional econometric analysis in the sense that the exogenous variables are not fixed. Thus, if we are willing to accept that the exogenous variables in a model are generated by a stochastic process not involving past y, a clear relation between the dynamic structural form, the multivariate ARMA form, and even the individual ARMA models of the variables can be made. The existence of such a relation in itself does away with contentions that time series analysis is a pure data-fitting operation void of any substantive content. It also explains why simple ARMA models sometimes outperform complex multiple-equation systems.

Zellner and Palm (1974) further relate structural and time series methods by rewriting block 1 as a set of transfer functions as follows:

$$|\mathbf{H}_{11}(L)|\mathbf{y}_t = -\mathbf{H}_{11}^*(L)\mathbf{H}_{12}(L)\mathbf{x}_t + \mathbf{H}_{11}^*(L)\mathbf{F}_{11}(L)\boldsymbol{\alpha}_{1t}. \tag{5.7}$$

Here again, the denominator polynomials of the transfer functions are the same for each endogenous variable.

As a marketing illustration, consider the following structural model relating unit sales (Q_t), price (P_t), and advertising (A_t):

$$Q_t = a_0 + a_1 A_t + a_2 A_{t-1} + a_3 P_t + \varepsilon_{1t}, \tag{5.8a}$$

$$A_t = b_0 + b_1 Q_{t-1} + b_2 A_{t-1} + \varepsilon_{2t}. \tag{5.8b}$$

Price effects on sales are immediate, and advertising effects are contemporaneous and one-period lagged. Advertising is dynamically adjusted from previous sales levels. Price is strictly exogenous, and the structural disturbances are white noise.

The dynamic econometric form of this model is

$$\begin{bmatrix} 1 & -a_1 - a_2 L & -a_3 \\ -b_1 L & 1 - b_2 L & 0 \\ 0 & 0 & \Phi(L) \end{bmatrix} \begin{bmatrix} Q_t \\ A_t \\ P_t \end{bmatrix} = \begin{bmatrix} a_0 \\ b_0 \\ c_0 \end{bmatrix} + \begin{bmatrix} 1 & 0 & 0 \\ 0 & 1 & 0 \\ 0 & 0 & \Theta(L) \end{bmatrix} \begin{bmatrix} \varepsilon_{1t} \\ \varepsilon_{2t} \\ \alpha_t \end{bmatrix}, \tag{5.9}$$

where $\Phi(L)P_t = c_0 + \Theta(L)\alpha_t$ is the ARMA process on the price series. For example, if price follows the AR(1) process, $P_t = c_0 + \phi P_{t-1} + \alpha_t$, the model simplifies to

$$
\begin{bmatrix}
1 & -a_1 - a_2 L & -a_3 \\
-b_1 L & 1 - b_2 L & 0 \\
0 & 0 & 1 - \phi L
\end{bmatrix}
\begin{bmatrix}
Q_t \\
A_t \\
P_t
\end{bmatrix}
=
\begin{bmatrix}
a_0 \\
b_0 \\
c_0
\end{bmatrix}
+
\begin{bmatrix}
\varepsilon_{1t} \\
\varepsilon_{2t} \\
\alpha_t
\end{bmatrix},
\qquad (5.10a)
$$

so that

$$
\mathbf{H}_{11}(L) =
\begin{bmatrix}
1 & -a_1 - a_2 L \\
-b_1 L & 1 - b_2 L
\end{bmatrix},
\qquad (5.10b)
$$

$$
\mathbf{H}_{12}(L) =
\begin{bmatrix}
-a_3 \\
0
\end{bmatrix},
\qquad (5.10c)
$$

$$
\mathbf{H}_{21}(L) = [0 \quad 0],
\qquad (5.10d)
$$

$$
\mathbf{H}_{22}(L) = 1 - \phi L,
\qquad (5.10e)
$$

$$
\mathbf{F}_{11}(L) =
\begin{bmatrix}
1 & 0 \\
0 & 1
\end{bmatrix},
\qquad (5.10f)
$$

$$
\mathbf{F}_{22}(L) = 1,
\qquad (5.10g)
$$

$$
\mathbf{F}_{12}(L) =
\begin{bmatrix}
0 \\
0
\end{bmatrix},
\qquad (5.10h)
$$

$$
\mathbf{F}_{21}(L) = [0 \quad 0].
\qquad (5.10i)
$$

The dynamic structural model is consistent with the following transfer functions on sales and advertising:

$$
[(1 - b_2 L) - b_1 L(a_1 + a_2 L)]Q_t = a_0' + (1 - b_2 L)a_3 P_t
$$
$$
+ (1 - b_2 L)\varepsilon_{1t} + (a_1 + a_2 L)\varepsilon_{2t}, \quad (5.11)
$$

and

$$
[(1 - b_2 L) - b_1 L(a_1 + a_2 L)]A_t = b_0' + b_1 a_3 L P_t + b_1 L\varepsilon_{1t} + \varepsilon_{2t}, \quad (5.12)
$$

where a_0' and b_0' are new constants.

Furthermore, the model is consistent with the following ARMA processes on its variables:

$$
(1 - \phi L)[(1 - b_2 L) - b_1 L(a_1 + a_2 L)]Q_t
$$
$$
= a_0'' + (1 - \phi L)(1 - b_2 L)\varepsilon_{1t} + (a_1 + a_2 L)(1 - \phi L)\varepsilon_{2t}
$$
$$
+ (1 - b_2 L)a_3 \alpha_t, \qquad (5.13)
$$

and

$$(1 - \phi L)[1 - b_2 L) - b_1 L(a_1 + a_2 L)]A_t = b_0'' + (1 - \phi L)b_1 L\varepsilon_{1t}$$
$$+ (1 - \phi L)\varepsilon_{2t} + b_1 a_3 L\alpha_t, \quad (5.14)$$

where a_0'' and b_0'' are yet a different set of constants. Although many conclusions can be drawn from this exercise, the most prominent are the following:

- The AR orders of sales and advertising are the same and are of order 3 or less. The earliest price effect on sales is contemporaneous; the earliest effect on advertising is of lag 1.
- The univariate process on sales is at most ARMA(3, 2): If all parameters are significant, the highest order in L is 3 on the left-hand side of the ARMA equation and 2 on the right-hand side.

The relation between econometric and time series models makes it possible to test the implications of one model, like a structural model relating market share to relative prices, for another like the ARMA processes governing market shares and relative prices. In a study of competition among domestic airlines, Hanssens (1977) tested various hypotheses about competitive flight scheduling and advertising spending by examining the ARMA processes of the quarterly number of flights and the advertising expenditures for each airline. The major advantage of such an approach is that we can test structural hypotheses without actually knowing the structure of the model. Other examples of the combined use of structural and time series models can be found in Zellner and Palm (1974).

The Concept of Granger Causality

It is difficult to establish a workable definition of causality in nonexperimental research. As far as statistical analysis is concerned, we often hear the remark that "correlation does not imply causation." But when we adopt a stochastic view of time series behavior, temporal ordering of events can be used to make an empirical distinction between leading and lagging variables. That distinction is at the basis of a well-known definition of causality due to Granger (1969).

Suppose a marketing system is defined by a two-variable information set (X, Y). In an attempt to forecast Y, we could build a univariate model, considering the past of Y alone, or we could combine the past of Y and the past of X in a bivariate model. Now, X is said to *Granger cause* Y if the mean squared forecast error (MSFE) of Y using the bivariate model is smaller than the MSFE of the univariate model. Formally:

For the information set containing X and Y, X is said to Granger cause Y if

$$\text{MSFE}(Y_t | Y_{t-1} \ldots Y_{t-k}, X_{t-1} \ldots X_{t-m}) < \text{MSFE}(Y_t | Y_{t-1} \ldots Y_{t-k}),$$

where k and m are positive integers indicating the maximum memory length in Y and X.

There are three distinctive components to Granger's definition:

1. It stresses the importance of an adequately formulated information set.
2. The empirical detection of causality between X and Y is valid only insofar as no major factors Z are missing from the information set. The null model, against which forecasting performance is evaluated, is a powerful rival. For example, univariate time series models have been shown to outperform complex econometric models of the U.S. economy (Nelson 1972).
3. The ultimate test is done out-of-sample. Thus, statistical significance of transfer function parameters alone is not sufficient to establish Granger causality.

Granger causality applies well in a marketing context. For example, monthly time series of the number of airline passengers on a route have often been found to follow an $\text{ARIMA}(0, 1, 1)(0, 1, 1)_{12}$ process—known as the airline model—which predicts future passenger levels remarkably well. The marketing question, Does manipulating the air fares affect demand? might be poorly answered by merely correlating or regressing passenger and air fare series. Granger's definition would assess whether or not air fare information improves the prediction of passenger levels beyond what is achieved by extrapolation. If the airline pricing managers act rationally and forecast demand accurately, the air fares may follow a rigid seasonal pattern with little extra variation. In that case, we may well find that they do not Granger cause passenger demand but instead are caused by (perfectly anticipated) passenger movements. One extension of the definition includes present as well as past values of X in the prediction of Y. This is known as Granger instantaneous causality and is more difficult to measure empirically (Layton 1984).

Test Procedures

Although the concept of Granger causality was developed in economics, it did not achieve recognition until time series methods for its execution became available. Several procedures have been proposed, of which we discuss the three most popular: the double prewhitening technique and two regression-based methods due to Granger and Sims.

The *double prewhitening* method, first proposed by Haugh (1976) and later extended by Haugh and Box (1977), Pierce (1977), and Pierce and Haugh (1977), establishes the direction of causality between two series by cross-correlating the residuals of univariate models fitted to each. Formally, let:

$$\phi_1(L)x_{1t} = \theta_1(L)\alpha_{1t}, \tag{5.15a}$$

$$\phi_2(L)x_{2t} = \theta_2(L)\alpha_{2t}. \tag{5.15b}$$

Then $r_{\alpha_1\alpha_2}(k) \sim N(0, \sigma_r^2)$ under the assumption of independence between the series. Haugh (1976) has shown that this property also holds asymptotically for the estimated ARMA residuals $\hat{\alpha}_1$ and $\hat{\alpha}_2$. Thus, we can construct a chi-square test on the ARMA residuals to test an hypothesis of overall independence of the series:

$$Q = T \sum_{k=-M}^{M} r_{\hat{\alpha}_1\hat{\alpha}_2}(k) \sim \chi^2(2M + 1), \tag{5.16a}$$

where M is the maximum cross-correlation lag under consideration and is set separately by the analyst.

The extension of Haugh's test to the direction of causality is as follows:

X causes Y is tested by the statistic

$$Q_1 = T \sum_{k=1}^{M} r_{\hat{\alpha}_1\hat{\alpha}_2}(k) \sim \chi^2(M). \tag{5.16b}$$

Y causes X:

$$Q_2 = T \sum_{k=-1}^{-M} r_{\hat{\alpha}_1\hat{\alpha}_2}(k) \sim \chi^2(M). \tag{5.16c}$$

X causes Y instantaneously:

$$Q_1' = T \sum_{k=0}^{M} r_{\hat{\alpha}_1\hat{\alpha}_2}(k) \sim \chi^2(M + 1). \tag{5.16d}$$

Y causes X instantaneously:

$$Q_2' = T \sum_{k=0}^{-M} r_{\hat{\alpha}_1\hat{\alpha}_2}(k) \sim \chi^2(M + 1). \tag{5.16e}$$

How does the double prewhitening method relate to the definition of Granger causality? In a first stage, the predictive power of each series' past is removed via the prewhitening operation. Then, by cross-correlating the residuals at various lags, the method scans the data for any additional sources of covariation. If a significant cross-correlation exists at lag $k \neq 0$, it contributes to Granger causality in one direction. If the spike occurs at $k = 0$, it contributes to Granger instantaneous causality, but the direction of the effect cannot be established by itself. The main restriction of double prewhitening, though, lies in the fact that both stages are typically carried out on the same sample, so there is no true forecasting test. That limitation prompted Ashley, Granger, and Schmalensee (1980) to develop a supplementary test for the out-of-sample performance of univariate versus bivariate time series models.

The double prewhitening method has been instrumental in stirring controversial debates of cause and effect in the macroeconomic and financial economics literature. For example, Pierce (1977) reported a lack of relations among several key interest and money indicators previously thought of as highly interrelated. In marketing it was first used to establish primary demand versus market share effects of airline flight scheduling and advertising and to sort out various patterns of competitive reactions among airlines (Hanssens 1977; 1980b). A more comprehensive overview of causality tests in marketing can be found in table 5–1.

The double prewhitening method has been criticized for rejecting the null hypothesis of independence too infrequently, i.e., it may produce spurious independence. It is indeed true that the statistical power of a cross-correlation test is low (e.g., Schwert 1979), but that reflects the fact that the research hypothesis is rather vague, which is consistent with having level 0 prior knowledge. For example, by increasing M in the test (which implies reducing the precision of the research hypothesis), we can sometimes change the outcome with the same Type I error. In conclusion, the test should be carried out with care and its results supplemented by other analyses.

Regression methods have been used as well, in particular one technique attributed to Granger (1969) and a second one due to Sims (1972). The Granger method is based on the following model:

$$Y_t = c + \sum_{i=1}^{\infty} \gamma_i Y_{t-i} + \sum_{j=1}^{\infty} \beta_j X_{t-j} + \varepsilon_t, \qquad (5.17)$$

which establishes Granger causality if $\{\beta_j\} \neq 0$. The Sims method regresses Y against all possible past and future X:

$$Y_t = c + \sum_{i=1}^{\infty} \gamma_i X_{t-i} + \sum_{j=1}^{\infty} \beta_j X_{t+j} + \varepsilon_t, \qquad (5.18)$$

which establishes Granger causality from Y to X if $\{\beta_j\} \neq 0$, and from X to Y if $\{\gamma_i\} \neq 0$. In both cases, we must truncate the parameter polynomials $\{\gamma_i\}$

Table 5–1.   Tests for the Direction of Causality in Marketing

Source	Industry	Method	Findings
Aaker, Carman, and Jacobson (1982)	Ready-to-eat cereals	Double prewhitening and Sims test	Weak or no causality between advertising and sales.
Bass and Pilon (1980)	Catsup	Double prewhitening	Relative price causes market share.
Batra and Vanhonacker (1988)	Liquor	Sims test with forecasting test	High brand awareness, advertising frequency: attitudes predict purchase intentions. Low brand awareness, advertising frequency: ad and brand awareness influence attitudes and purchase intentions.
Doyle and Saunders (1985)	Natural gas	Double prewhitening	Sales lead commission rates, advertising leads sales.
Hanssens (1980a)	Lydia Pinkham (monthly series)	Double prewhitening with forecasting test	Causality in both directions between sales and advertising.
Hanssens (1980b)	Domestic air travel	Double prewhitening	Flights cause primary demand or market share, advertising does not; various competitive reactions.
Jacobson and Nicosia (1981)	N/A	Double prewhitening and Sims test	Causality in both directions between advertising and aggregate consumption.
Leone (1983)	Frequently purchased grocery product	Double prewhitening	Advertising has primary and selective demand effects.

N/A = not applicable.

and $\{\beta_j\}$ in order to carry out the test. If Y_t is an autoregressive series, there is little problem as long as the lags are long enough. To the extent that Y_t contains moving-average elements ($q > 0$ in the ARMA model for Y_t), the autoregressive approximation may not capture all of the predictive power of the series' own past.

It has been shown that these three methods of causality testing are asymptotically identical (Geweke, Meese, and Dent 1983). As far as finite sample performance is concerned, some Monte Carlo simulations suggest that the double prewhitening method has less power than the regression methods and that Sims's method is about as powerful as Granger's when a correction is made for autocorrelated disturbances (Nelson and Schwert 1979). In addition, the Granger method is the easiest to implement on statistical software packages, as it requires neither prewhitening nor regression against future variables.

Regression-based causality tests were first used in marketing to determine the causal ordering of advertising and aggregate consumption. Using the Sims method, Jacobson and Nicosia (1981) established a contemporaneous relation between annual advertising and personal consumption in the U.K., plus one-year lagged effects in both directions. Interestingly, these results were confirmed by a double prewhitening test on the same data.

Summary

Causality among marketing variables can run in many directions, and the model builder is not always clear a priori which variables are exogenous or endogenous to a marketing system (level 0 prior knowledge). If longitudinal data are available, some recent advances in time series analysis may be used to infer the direction of causality empirically. These techniques are based on the definition of Granger causality, which says that X causes Y if, other things being equal, Y can be predicted better from the past of X and Y than from the past of Y alone.

The time series tests that are used to establish Granger causality are not void of marketing content because there exists a unique relation between a fully specified (structural) marketing model and the time series processes of the variables in that model. Thus, the modeler may use these techniques to reach higher levels of knowledge about the marketing system, i.e., levels 1 and 2. ETS research provides a full array of techniques for improving our knowledge of a market or a marketing phenomenon. Part II explores the ways in which marketing researchers have used ETS techniques to advance the state of the art in three important areas: sales and market share response models, models of competition, and marketing dynamics.

Notes

1. We must also allow for the possibility of simultaneity *within* data periods. This means that, in principle, a variable could be both a cause and an effect *at the same time*. Other techniques, more appropriate to the modeling of consumer behavior, include path analysis and causal modeling. See, for example, Bagozzi (1980).

2. Causal direction may also be determined through experimentation, for example, in test markets.

3. The results of an extensive forecasting competition may be found in Makridakis et al. (1982).

III ETS MODELS IN MARKETING

6 SALES AND MARKET SHARE RESPONSE MODELS

The relation between sales response and marketing variables is the core of the theory and practice of marketing management. In making decisions, marketing managers must have some ideas about how their actions will influence sales and profits. Usually these ideas concerning the link between apparent causes (marketing decision variables, the actions of competitors, and certain environmental factors) and measurable market responses (sales or market share) are based on experience—a "feel" for the implications of a firm's marketing decisions. Such casual interpretations of market response may be expedient, serving managers as guides to marketing planning, but they are severely limited in their ability to provide managers with more objective evidence on how to improve the quality of their decisions. Sales response models are formal ways of describing the complex relation between a firm and its market. They are designed to overcome as much uncertainty as possible regarding the nature of sales response and, in addition, to provide the behavioral mechanism in a decision model that allows management to explore optimal policies.

In order for a marketing decision model to be useful, it must embody some mechanism for relating the effects of marketing decisions to sales. This mechanism, usually called a sales response function, is the keystone of the model, and thus the quality of its measurement is an important determinant of the model's eventual success. In earlier chapters, we described a sales response function as a model of the relation between sales and relevant marketing instruments. For example, the dependence of sales on advertising can be estimated from marketing data using econometric methods. The result is a sales response equation that shows the effect of advertising on sales. Of course, sales response equations can be quite complex and often include the effects of marketing mix interactions, lagged responses, competition, and simultaneous relations. The purpose of these more complex models is the same: to link marketing actions to market response.

Company marketing decisions lead to company sales. Two factors mediate this process: industry demand and competitive behavior. A number of variables may influence total industry demand, including price, income, and population; advertising may also influence industry demand. In addition, a company's market share can be considered to be a function of the marketing efforts of competitors. In this chapter, we initially examine the modeling of company sales, industry demand, and market share without taking into account competitive behavior; then we extend the analysis to include the explicit modeling of competition.

Measuring Marketing Effects

We are interested in identifying and measuring the effects of marketing decision variables on brand and industry (or market) demand. When the effect of a brand's marketing activities is to increase its own sales without affecting competitors' sales, it is called a *primary sales effect*. When the effect is to increase its own sales and those of its competitors, it is a *primary demand effect*. And when the effect is to increase its own sales and to decrease those of its competitors, it is a *competitive effect*. To understand the consequences of marketing actions, we must be able to separate these effects in the model.

In any empirical situation, these three pure cases of marketing effects can be confounded; the result is a number of mixed cases. A taxonomy due to Schultz and Wittink (1976) is shown in table 6–1. In their taxonomy, cases I, II, and III represent the pure cases of primary demand effect only, primary sales effect only, and competitive effect only. Cases IV, V, and VI represent the combinations of primary demand effect and primary sales effect, primary demand effect and competitive effect, and primary sales effect and competitive effect. Case IV would seem more likely than case I. If a firm's selective advertising stimulates primary demand, it should benefit more from this new market demand than its competitors. (Recall the discussion of differential-

Table 6–1. A Taxonomy of Marketing Effects

Case	Effect	Industry Sales	Response to an Increase in a Firm's Marketing Effort				
			Brand Sales	Rival Sales	Brand Share	Rival Share
I	Primary demand only	Increase	Increase	Increase	No change	No change
II	Primary sales only	Increase	Increase	No change	Increase	Decrease
III	Competitive only	No change	Increase	Decrease	Increase	Decrease
IV	Primary demand/ primary sales	Increase	Increase	Increase	Increase	Decrease
V	Primary demand/ competitive	Increase	Increase	?	Increase	Decrease
VI	Primary sales/ competitive	Increase	Increase	Decrease	Increase	Decrease

effects models in chapter 2.) If it accrues all the benefits of the new market demand as well as taking sales from competitors, we have case VI.

The existence of case V, in which the way competitors' sales are affected depends on the strength of the primary demand effect relative to that of the competitive effect, creates a discrimination problem. Depending on the net effect, case V cannot be distinguished from case II, case IV, or case VI. Schultz and Wittink argue that the existence of case V is implausible, but consider a new brand of a consumer product. Its marketing activities may stimulate primary demand by drawing less knowledgeable consumers into the market. Some of these might purchase competitive brands. At the same time, more knowledgeable existing consumers might recognize the advantages of the new product and switch do it. We accept Schultz and Wittink's argument only when it is restricted to competition among established brands.

Schultz and Wittink go on to describe the empirical conditions necessary to identify the remaining five cases. Our restatement of these conditions is shown in table 6–2. Three pieces of information are needed: (1) the signs of the brand's market share elasticity, (2) its primary demand elasticity, and (3) its rival sales cross-elasticity. In addition, we note that the firm's sales elasticity can be calculated, since it is equal to the firm's primary demand elasticity plus its market share elasticity. This relation is discussed in more detail later (equation 6.3). The sales elasticity is assumed to be positive in all cases.

The needed information requires that a market share response function be estimated for the brand and that sales response functions be estimated for the industry and for competitors. Thus, a complete understanding of the effects

Table 6–2.   Discriminating among a Brand's Marketing Effects

Case	Effect	Market Share Elasticity	Primary Demand Elasticity	Rival Sales Cross-Elasticity
I	Primary demand only	Zero	Positive	Positive
II	Primary sales only	Positive	Positive	Zero
III	Competitive only	Positive	Zero	Negative
IV	Primary demand/ primary sales	Positive	Positive	Positive
VI	Primary sales/ competitive	Positive	Positive	Negative

of a marketing activity requires decomposing a brand's sales response function into an industry sales response function and its market share response function.

Lancaster (1984) used the Schultz and Wittink framework to assess the effects of advertising in several product categories. He pooled annual data within product categories so that the results represent a prototypical brand. He found a primary demand only effect for shaving cream and ready-to-eat cereal, a competitive effect only for bath and toilet soap and cigars, a combined primary demand and primary sales effect for deodorants and antiperspirants, a combined primary sales and competitive effect for heavy-duty laundry detergents, and no measurable effect for light-duty liquid detergents.[1] These results are shown in table 6–3.

We have just seen that we must be able to decompose the market response function in order to identify certain effects of marketing decision variables. But we know that for planning purposes (cf. chapter 1), we may choose only to estimate a sales response function directly. Thus, if we care where sales are coming from, we decompose; if we don't, we don't. We now turn to a closer

Table 6–3. Empirical Evidence on Advertising Effects

Product Category	Market Share Elasticity	Primary Demand Elasticity	Rival Sales Cross- Elasticity	Conclusion about Effects
Cereals, ready-to-eat	N/S	.029 (.006)	.038 (.006)	Primary demand only
Cigars	.076 (.007)	N/S	−.079 (.012)	Competitive only
Deodorants, anti-perspirants	.177 (.028)	.015 (.005)	.043 (.004)	Primary demand/ primary sales
Detergents, heavy-duty laundry	.191 (.044)	.079 (.026)	−.078 (.006)	Primary sales/ competitive
Detergents, light-duty liquid	N/S	N/S	N/S	None measurable
Shaving cream	N/S	.025 (.010)	.053 (.014)	Primary demand only
Soap, bath and toilet	.258 (.069)	N/S	−.046 (.024)	Competitive only

Note: Lancaster used advertising share as the independent variable in his market share equation. To get the correct market share elasticity, we calculated it from the sales elasticity and the primary demand elasticity. Significance is based on a one-sided (positive) test for the market share elasticity and the primary demand elasticity and a two-sided test for the rival sales cross-elasticity. Asymptotic standard errors are in parentheses.

N/S = not significant.

examination of the response functions for brand sales, industry sales, and brand market share.

The Shape of the Response Function

The shape of response to a particular nonprice marketing instrument, with the remainder of the marketing mix held constant, is generally concave. Sales generally increase with increases in marketing effort, but exhibit diminishing returns to scale.[2] Sometimes the sales response function might be S-shaped with effort. Initially sales may exhibit increasing returns to scale, then diminishing returns to higher levels of marketing effort. Jones (1984) has emphasized that "nowhere is it suggested that increasing returns are anything but limited and temporary." The temporary increasing return phenomenon may be localized in the introductory stage of the product life cycle and related to increasing distribution coverage, i.e., an improvement in the conversion of demand into sales (cf. Steiner 1987). The shape of the response function might be different depending on whether marketing effort is increasing or decreasing, that is, response may be asymmetric. The shape of the response function also might vary with changes in the environment.

Concave Functions

The preponderance of empirical evidence favors the strictly concave sales response to nonprice marketing decision variables. This is especially true for mass media advertising of frequently purchased goods. For instance, Lambin (1976, p. 95), after doing an analysis of 107 individual brands from 16 product classes and eight different countries of Western Europe, concluded that "the shape of the advertising response curve is concave downward, i.e., that there is no S-curve and no increasing returns in advertising a given brand by a given firm." Earlier, Simon (1970, pp. 8–22) had surveyed the evidence then available on the shape of the response function and found that "both sales and psychological [nonsales measures of behavior] suggest that the shape of the advertising-response function is invariably concave downward, i.e., that there is no S-curve. . . ." Reviews by Simon and Arndt (1980) and Aaker and Carman (1982) also indicate diminishing returns to advertising.

There are several reasons to expect diminishing returns to increased advertising expenditures (Jagpal, Sudit, and Vinod 1979). For one, the fraction of unreached prospects is progressively reduced as advertising increases. Consequently, most of the impact of additional advertising messages at high levels of advertising takes place by means of increased frequency. Moreover, after a small number of exposures, perhaps as few as three, increased frequency has very limited marginal effectiveness. Grass and Wallace (1969), among others, have reported on the satiation effects of television commercials. Ottesen (1981) proposed a theory of the individual's purchase response function, and on the basis of this theory, he concluded "as advertising effort is being increased, returns in sales must generally be expected to diminish."

S-Shaped Functions

An S-shaped sales response to advertising has long been conjectured (Zentler and Ryde 1956). However, this proposition has not been tested explicitly. Two studies have explored the proposition that the relation between *market share* and advertising is S-shaped. Johansson (1973) found for a women's hair spray that the advertising effect was concave rather than the proposed S-shape. Rao and Miller (1975) adopted an ad hoc procedure to develop S-shaped response functions for five Lever brands. The work of Miller and Rao seems suspect, however, since they discarded markets that were "out of line." This meant that for the two brands they discussed in detail, 27% and 20%, respectively, of the markets were omitted. Eastlack and Rao (1986) also applied Miller and Rao's methodology. A linear sales response to radio gross ratings points and television gross ratings points was estimated for each Selling Areas Marketing, Inc. (SAMI) market. Gross ratings points (GRPs) refers to the total number of exposures generated by an advertising schedule. It is a measure of delivered advertising. Inspection of per capita estimates of marginal response to radio gross ratings points levels revealed no significant response below 180 GRPs (an indication of a threshold), a sharp increase in response as GRPs increased between 180 and 230 GRPs, a slight (almost flat) decline in response at GRPs increased from 230 to 340 (an indication of saturation), and low response to a few observations with GRPs above 400 (an indication of supersaturation?). These two works, unfortunately (because of their ad hoc nature), are the only published support for an S-shaped response function. Broadbent (1984, p. 310), in a discussion of the adstock model, reported that "the uncertainty in the data also makes it difficult—we would say from our experience impossible—to prove or disprove the reality of an S-shaped or step function."

The lack of evidence for an S-shaped curve has an important implication for the timing of advertising expeditures. An advertiser might want to choose between two alternative policies, a constant spending rate per period or a pulsed expenditure. Rao (1970, p. 55) defined a pulsing policy as a pattern of advertising where periods with high advertising intensity alternate with very little or no advertising. A sufficient condition (Rao 1970, p. 5) for adopting a pulsing policy would be that the sales response function be S-shaped and the budget constraint be binding. The budget constraint has to require that the alternate constant rate policy be in the region of increasing returns to scale. But most empirical evidence says that a typical brand has a concave sales response function; consequently, the S-shape cannot be used justify a pulsing policy.

The relation between market share and share of retail outlets seems to be S-shaped. Cardwell (1968) reported that in marketing gasoline incremental new outlets were substantially below average in gallonage until a certain share of market was achieved. Above this critical market share, performance improved markedly. Lilien and Rao (1976) also postulated an S-shaped relation between share of market and share of outlets. Neither study provides empirical evidence supporting its claims. Naert and Bultez (1973) did an analysis of the effect of market share on the distribution network of a major brand of gasoline in Italy. Their results support the S-shaped hypothesis at the market share level. However, when the hypothesis was tested at the aggregate brand-switching level, it was rejected. In any event, the relation between market share and share of outlets may be simply an expression of the difference between demand and sales.

Threshold

If support for S-shaped sales response is weak, even less support exists for the threshold effect. Although many marketing managers believe that a threshold effect operates within their market (Corkindale and Newall 1978), Simon (1970, p. 22) expressed his opinion that "threshold effects ... constitute a monstrous myth." Even though the argument might be made at the individual level that a prospect might be unaware of a brand or unwilling to buy it until several advertising messages have been received, little evidence of this threshold phenomenon in aggregate sales response functions has been found. Corkindale and Newall (p. 373) have noted that "little generalisable evidence of either phenomena [threshold and wearout levels of expenditure] seems to exist. This is mostly because managers and their agencies avoid operating at or near the supposed limits."

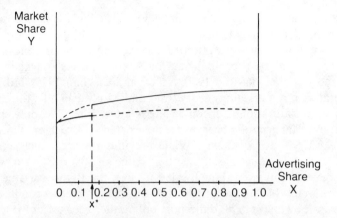

Figure 6-1. Switching Model. *Source*: Bemmaor (1984).

The most serious attempt to identify a threshold effect in an aggregate sales response was by Bemmaor (1984). A market share response function was partitioned into two regimes—above and below the threshold (figure 6-1). A multiplicative function (see equation 2.14) was used to describe each segment. A random shift between these two regimes was postulated. (Recall our discussion of random switching models (see equation 2.66).) For the product studied, the best fit occurred when the estimate of the proportion of observations above the threshold was 73%. The corresponding threshold advertising share was deduced to be about 18. Thus, these results indicate decreasing returns to scale but with a discontinuity.

Saturation and Supersaturation

The existence of a saturation level is universally accepted. Nonetheless, the saturation level is rarely explicitly modeled and measured. The usual procedure is to represent response by a function that allows any given level to be surpassed but requires increasing difficulty to exceed each higher level. This approach is probably adequate for use in decision models focusing on short-run marketing tactics; however, when interest is in long-term strategy, the saturation ceiling should be estimated.

One industry sales response function in which the saturation level was explicitly modeled was Ward's (1975) study of canned, single-strength grapefruit juice. He used a reciprocal model (see equation 2.24). Saturation sales,

Q^o, were estimated to be 69.82 million gallons. The highest sales observed to date were 53.77 million gallons.

The notion of a supersaturation effect, excessive marketing effort causing negative sales, has been promulgated by Ackoff and his colleagues (Waid, Clark, and Ackoff 1956; Rao 1970; Ackoff and Emshoff 1975) and is being incorporated into marketing theory (Enis and Mokwa 1979). Still, the argument for supersaturation is unconvincing in advertising. The only empirical evidence even tangentially bearing on the existence of such an effect comes from Ackoff's Budweiser study. While previous research, such as that of Parsons and Bass (1971) has shown that reducing advertising expenditures may increase profits even though sales are lost, the Budweiser study is the only research in which reducing advertising not only increases profits but also increases sales. Haley (1978) did report on another beer test in which those areas where advertising was stopped showed better results than the remaining areas. However, subsequent investigation revealed that local distributors, upon finding their advertising support dropped, invested their own funds in advertising. Their efforts more than offset the cuts made by the manufacturer. Participants in the Budweiser study have asserted that adequate controls were maintained in their work; consequently, their results remain an anomaly. Even if supersaturation does exist, it is well outside the usual operating ranges for marketing instruments, since management has little incentive to operate, even at saturation. Of course, a firm could operate in this region by mistake.

A more plausible argument for supersaturation might be made for marketing decision variables other than advertising. For example, a reduction in sales force size might lead to more effort, and consequently sales, if territories and hence potential were realigned and salespeople were more highly motivated because of this. Also, it was recently reported in the business press that a major computer manufacturer increased its sales by decreasing the number of retail outlets carrying its personal computers. The explanation was that having fewer dealers resulted in less price competition, higher retail prices and hence increased margins, and thus more funds available to each retailer to support direct sales effort. Still, there have been no empirical studies of supersaturation for sales force or distribution variables.

Although the shape of the sales response function is almost surely concave, we should be alert to the possibility of other shapes. Johansson (1979) has suggested an approach for identifying whether a relation under analysis is S-shaped. In general, because different combinations of phenomena such as threshold, asymmetry, and saturation effects might be present in a particular market, we should not think in terms of a single aggregate response function. A specific response function should be constructed for each product or market situation.

Asymmetry in Response

Asymmetry in response occurs when the magnitude of response to a change in a marketing instrument differs depending on whether the change is an increase or a decrease. This is different from asymmetry in competitive effects, that is, a change in a brand's marketing effort affecting each competitive brand differentially.

Asymmetry can arise in durables because of a saturation effect—the pool of potential customers shrinks as sales are made. Asymmetry can arise in frequently purchased branded goods because of the phenomenon of fast learning and slow foregetting on the part of consumers. Asymmetry in response to advertising has been addressed by Parsons (1976), Haley (1978), Little (1979a), and Somon (1982).

Haley reported on some experiments that showed an immediate sales response to increased advertising. In addition, these experiments indicated that even though the advertising was maintained at the new and higher levels, the magnitude of response gradually became less and less. Little offered two explanations for this. One is that advertising causes prospects to try a product. Only a portion of these new customers become regular purchasers. Consequently, sales taper off from their initial gain to a lower level. The second explanation is that the advertising copy is wearing out. We believe another possible explanation would be competitive reaction.

Asymmetry in response to price has been discussed by Moran (1978). He provided a summary of price research that had been conducted in a variety of consumer product categories. He argued that the only way to analyze a price elasticity is in terms of relative price.[3] Relative price expresses a brand's price relative to the average price for the product category in which it competes. One of his major findings was that a brand's upside demand elasticity and downside elasticity can differ. He conjectured that one reason these elasticities might differ is that consumer segments are not equally informed about what is going on. For instance, an unadvertised price change is more likely to be noticed by current customers.

Systematic Variation

One source of systematic parameter variation is the interaction of the marketing decision variables with each other. Advertising expenditures often influence the magnitude of price elasticity (Moran 1978; Sunoo and Lin 1979). Conventional wisdom is that advertising decreases price sensitivity. Schultz and Vanhonacker (1978) provided some empirical support for this proposition, yet

Wittink (1977a) gave some evidence that relative price becomes more elastic as advertising share increases. The implication is that advertising tends to increase the price competitiveness of the brand investigated. This supports earlier findings (Eskin 1975; Eskin and Baron 1977) that a high advertising effort yields a higher price elasticity than a low advertising effort. Farris and Albion (1980) suggested that the concept of vertical market structures might reconcile what appears to be conflicting evidence. They posited that the relation between advertising and price depends on whether price is measured at the factory level or at the consumer level. Krishnamurthi and Raj (1985) found that, for a well-established brand, increased noninformational advertising of the mood type decreased price sensitivity.

Moreover, many secondary dimensions of marketing variables are only operative when the primary dimension of the variable is present. If no advertising expenditure is made, the advertising copy can have no impact on sales. Samples and handouts are distributed in conjunction with a sales call. Parsons and Vanden Abeele (1981) demonstrated that the effectiveness of the calls made by the sales force of a pharmaceutical manufacturer for an established ethical drug varied systematically as a function of collateral material, such as samples, used. Similarly, Gatignon and Hanssens (1987) found that personal selling effectiveness in U.S. Navy recruiting increases with local advertising support.

Another source of systematic variation in marketing is the product life cycle. Marketing theory states that the demand elasticities of managerial decision variables change over the product life cycle. The theory has been interpreted to say that the advertising elasticity is highest at the growth stage of a product's life because of the need to create increased product awareness, and lowest during maturity, with elasticities increasing slightly through saturation and decline stages of the product life cycle (Mahajan, Bretschneider, and Bradford 1980). The theory supposedly conjectures that the price elasticity increases over the first three stages—introduction, growth, and maturity—and decreases during the decline stage (Mickwitz 1959).

Empirical evidence on changes in the efficiency of various marketing instruments at different stages of the product life cycle is sparse. Indications are that advertising elasticities generally fall as products pass through their life cycles (Arora 1979; Parsons 1975b). Price elasticities seem to decrease markedly during the introduction and growth stages, reaching a minimum in the maturity stage, after which they may experience an increase during the decline stage (Simon 1979). For industrial chemicals, Lilien and Yoon (1988, p. 273) concluded:

The level of price elasticity tends to be lower during the later stages of the product life cycle (maturity and decline) than during the earlier stages (introduction and growth). There is no clear tendency of shift in the level of the price elasticity between the introduction and growth stages. Over the latter two stages of the product life cycle (maturity and decline), price elasticity shows a tendency to be stable.

Although these results may be tentative, because of methodological problems, e.g., Shoemaker's (1986) comment on Simon (1979), nonetheless, the empirical findings do seem inconsistent with current marketing theory.

Systematic variation might occur over individuals or territories rather than over time. Moran (1978) found that the price elasticities for a brand varied from market to market and from segment to segment. Wittink (1977b) tested one brand to evaluate whether demographic variables explained differences in the estimated parameters of the sales response functions for various territories. He found that they did not. Elrod and Winer (1979) had only somewhat better luck in relating household characteristics to the estimated parameters in purchasing response functions for different households. Gatignon and Hanssens (1987) reported that marketing effectiveness is inversely related to environmental conditions, in particular, the civilian employment rate.

Market Share as the Dependent Variable

We have argued that a desirable property of market share models is that they be logically consistent. Attraction models such as equation 2.36 meet this requirement. However, they do so at a cost. They are not very parsimonious and are often overparameterized, that is, they may contain a large number of parameters relative to the size of the sample and variability in the data. As a result, linear or multiplicative market share models are often used in practice despite not being logically consistent in most situations.

This state of affairs has led to a series of studies on the estimation and testing of market share models (Naert and Weverbergh 1981a, 1985; Brodie and de Kluyver 1983; Ghosh, Neslin, and Shoemaker 1984; and Leeflang and Reuyl 1984).[4] These studies are summarized in table 6-4. Most studies emphasized assessing the degree of heterogeneity in the parameters of a model. Hypotheses that some of the parameters are equal were tested, and the descriptive and predictive power of the alternative models were examined. The studies differed on whether the linear, multiplicative, or attraction model was best. This suggests that the answer may well be product-specific. Market share models are discussed further in the section "Models of Competition."

Table 6–4.   Comparative Studies of Functional Forms for Market Share Models

Study	Comparison	Conclusion
Naert and Weverbergh (1981a)	Linear, multiplicative, and attraction models	Attraction model is superior. Better predictions are derived from GLS, but IGLS affords no additional gain. There is a danger of overparameterization.
Brodie and de Kluyver (1984)	Linear, multiplicative, and attraction models	Linear and multiplicative models with brand-specific parameters perform as well as, or better than, the attraction model. OLS and GLS produce similar results.
Ghosh, Neslin, and Shoemaker (1984)	Linear, multiplicative, and attraction models	Linear and multiplicative models with brand-specific parameters perform as well as, or better than, the attraction model. OLS and GLS produce similar results.
Leeflang and Reuyl (1984)	Linear, multiplicative, and attraction models	Neither attraction models nor models with parameter restrictions produce substantially better results than the other model specifications. GLS considerably increases the efficiency of parameter estimates.
Naert and Weverbergh (1985)	The above studies	No cookbook answer as to what functional form with what level of parameterization and what estimation procedure is appropriate when. The attraction model has a number of merits on theoretical grounds. Estimating heterogeneous parameters is difficult if only a few observations are available or if the coefficients of variation for some variables are small. GLS is unlikely to produce better results if the number of brands is large.

Marketing Generalizations

A marketing manager's central concern is how selective marketing activities of a brand affect its sales. One way is through changes in selective demand, the other is through changes in primary demand, and as a consequence, the manager might well want to couple a model of industry demand with a market share model. Whether interested in the brand level or the industry level, the manager would like to know what marketing generalizations have been discovered. This is especially helpful when confronting a new market or product situation.

Brand-Level Generalizations

One of the first marketing generalizations (Leone and Schultz 1980) was that the elasticity of selective advertising on brand sales is positive but low. This is supported by the studies on brand sales elasticities reported in table 6–5 and meta-analyses conducted by Aaker and Carman (1982) and Assmus, Farley, and Lehmann (1984). More evidence is presented in table 6–7. The value for the advertising elasticity with unit sales is probably on the order of 0.10. There is a growing body of information on price elasticities. A meta-analysis conducted by Tellis (1988) found a mean price elasticity of about − 2.5. Broadbent (1980) reported an average advertising elasticity of 0.20 and an average price elasticity of − 1.6 for major British brands. Little information exists on product and distribution elasticities because changes occur rarely, or slowly, for established products. Thus, their effects are usually represented in sales response functions by the constant intercept. Although these effects cannot be identified, this does not mean they are unimportant.

Another marketing generalization identified by Leone and Schultz (1980) is that "increasing store shelf (display) space has a positive impact on sales of nonstaple grocery items." They found support for this statement in the works of Pauli and Hoecker (1952); Mueller, Kline, and Trout (1953); *Progressive Grocer* (1963–1964); Cox (1964); Kotzan and Evanson (1969); Cox (1970); Frank and Massy (1970); Kennedy (1970); and Curhan (1972; 1974a; 1974b). Criticisms of these studies have been made by Peterson and Cagley (1973) and Lynch (1974). They raise the possibility that the relation between sales and shelf space should be expressed in terms of a simultaneous system of (nonlinear) equations.

Another possible marketing generalization might be that "personal selling has a direct and positive influence on sales." Lambert (1968) found that sales volume of medical X-ray film in a district was related to the number of salespeople employed by the company in the district as well as to a product mix measure and a selling price index. However, the direction of causality is not clear. Waid, Clark, and Ackoff (1956), in their analysis of the lamp division of General Electric, indicated that the number of calls was the only variable to influence dollar sales. Turner (1971) refined the concept of calling effort by defining it as the product of the number of calls and the number of people seen per call. Calling effort was shown to have a significant impact on the actual sales to individual customers. Beswick and Cravens (1977) reported that dollar sales of one firm's high-priced consumer goods were determined by the salesperson's percentage of time spent in a geographic area and variables representing potential, workload, company experience, salesperson experience, and sales manager experience. They could not estimate the elasticity

Table 6-5.   Brand Sales Elasticities

Product Class	Price	Advertising	Product	Distribution
Apples[a]				
Belgium	−1.229	0.725		
Automobiles[b]				
Belgium				
A1	−2.223	0.183		
A2	−1.113	0.036		
A3	−2.763	0.059		
A4	−2.549	0.067		
A5	−1.852	0.045		
B1	−2.176	0.126		
B2	−1.399	0.045		
B3	−1.156	0.094		
B4	−1.009	0.071		
Beer[c]				
Australia		0.519[d]		
Cigarettes[c]				
Australia		0.208[d]		
Coffee[a, c]				
Australia		0.372[d]		
Belgium	−5.309	0.035		1.868
Confectionery[a]				
European	−1.982			
Detergent, Laundry[c]				
Australia		0.341[d]		
Frequently Purchased				
Branded Good (FPBG)[e]				
United States				
A	−3.830			
B	−1.860			
C	−2.640			
Motor Oil[c]				
Australia		0.534[d]		
Packaged				
Food Products[f]				
United States				
A	−2.100	0.100		
B	−1.600	0.100		
C	−0.850	0.150		
D	−1.300	0.130		
E	−1.300	0.200		
F	−2.800	0.700		

Table 6–5 (*continued*)

Product Class	Price	Advertising	Product	Distribution
Paint[c]				
Australia		0.434[d]		
Soap, Toilet[c]				
Australia		0.481[d]		
Suntan Lotion[a]				
France		0.328		
Television Sets[a]				
Belgium		0.122		
Toothpaste[c]				
Australia		0.159[d]		
Yogurt[a]				
Belgium				
Plain	−1.206		0.212	
Fruit	−1.135	0.031		

   a. Lambin (1976).
   b. Lambin and Peeters (1982).
   c. Metwally (1980).
   d. Revenue (dollar sales) elasticities.
   e. Urban (1969).
   f. McNiven (1980).

of selling effort precisely. It could be increased by about 50% without changing the reported R^2 because of the flat response surface arising from the high correlations among the independent variables in their nonlinear model. Parsons and Vanden Abeele (1981) found the sales call elasticity of an established Belgian ethical drug to be positive but very small. Having surveyed what is known about brand sales response functions, we now turn to industry sales response functions.

Industry-Level Generalizations

Models of industry demand have also been constructed to assess the impact of trade association or government efforts and to address public policy questions. For example, wool producers might want to determine the effectiveness of advertising the "Wool Mark." In the same vein, public health officials might want to evaluate the relation between cigarette advertising and children's cigarette consumption. These would be examples of primary advertising.

Nerlove and Waugh (1961) discovered that the advertising and promotion expenditures of the two largest organized groups of growers, the Florida Citrus Commission and Sunkist Growers, had a marked impact on the sales of oranges in the United States. Ball and Agarwala (1969) determined that generic advertising for tea in the United Kingdom slowed the downward sales trend but could not reverse the slide. McGuiness and Cowling (1975) decided that advertising had a positive, statistically significant impact on cigarette sales in the United Kingdom, and that this impact was only partly offset by the amount of publicity given and the health effects of smoking. Lambin (1976) found that in only four out of ten product markets did industry advertising increase industry sales. The industry advertising elasticities for these four are shown in table 6–6. Simon and Sebastian (1987), using a model with systematic parameter variation, showed that advertising influenced the diffusion of new

Table 6–6.   Industry Sales Elasticities

Product Class	Price	Advertising	Product	Distribution
Auto-Train[a]				
Belgium	−1.501	0.449	0.675	
Cereal, Ready-to-Eat[b]				
United States				
Total	−0.312			
Presweetened	−1.781			
Cigarettes[c]				
United Kingdom	−0.985	0.085		
Grapefruit[d]				
United States	−0.244	0.054		
Hair Spray[a]				
Belgium	−0.910	0.064		
Oranges[e]				
United States	−0.720	0.170		
Soft Drinks[a]				
Belgium		0.100		
Netherlands	−0.906	0.270		
Telephones[f]				
Germany		0.012		

a. Lambin (1976).
b. Neslin and Shoemaker (1983a).
c. McGuinness and Cowling (1975).
d. Ward (1975).
e. Nerlove and Waugh (1961).
f. Simon and Sebastian (1987).

telephones in West Germany. Their advertising (goodwill) elasticity attained a maximum of 2.14%, then declined nonmonotonically to 0.89% within five years. These and other studies lead to the generalization that primary advertising has a direct and positive influence on total industry (market) sales (cf. Leone and Schultz 1980).

Industry sales are more price-inelastic than individual brand sales. This can be seen by comparing table 6–6 with table 6–5. Industry price elasticities are typically less than 1 in absolute magnitude, whereas brand price elasticities are typically larger than 1 in absolute magnitude. Neslin and Shoemaker (1983a) found that the presweetened segment of the ready-to-eat cereal market in the United States was much more price-sensitive than the market as a whole.

Models of Competition

Marketing managers regularly face the problem of selecting the marketing mix that will optimally accomplish their goals within the constraints in which they operate. This has become known as the marketing programming problem (Kotler 1971). As we have seen, our ability to recommend what a manager should do depends critically on the accuracy of our model of the market mechanism. This model specifies how current marketing actions will produce current or future marketing results. Market mechanisms may involve sales response functions, competitive reaction functions, vertical market structures, cost functions, and other behavioral relations (Parsons 1981). The purpose of this section is to focus on models of market mechanisms that contain a sales response function and competitive reaction functions. Understanding such models can lead to improvement in the marketing productivity of individual firms, as demonstrated by Parsons and Bass (1971). Moreover, this class of market mechanisms may be important in formulating public policy. Lambin (1970a; 1976) and Metwally (1978) have pointed out that a tendency exists in saturated markets for the marketing efforts of competitors to cancel each other out. With competitive reaction, a futile escalation of marketing effort can take place, to the detriment of firms and possibly consumers. Finally, competitive reaction might be a partial explanation for the phenomenon called advertising wearout; Simon (1982), for example, does not take competitive reaction into account.

The following sections look first at empirical research on sales response functions containing competitors' decision variables as well as the firm's own decision variables. Then a brief summary follows of some key work by economists on reaction functions and oligopoly. The use of reaction functions in marketing is covered next. Finally, some research questions and approaches, particularly with respect to reaction functions, are detailed.

Estimated Sales Response Functions

Since each of the instruments in the marketing mix is a multidimensional concept, our ability to make generalizations is facilitated by having one common operational definition of each managerial decision variable across many studies. Fortunately, the studies reviewed in this chapter have similar definitions for all instruments in the marketing mix except product. Advertising refers to advertising expenditures. Price refers to the retail cost to the customer. Distribution refers to the percentage of retail outlets, weighted by volume, selling a product. Product can refer to quality, variety, package sizes, and service. The alternative definitions of product used in the studies surveyed in this review are given in appendix table A6–1.

Meta-analysis has been used to evaluate systematic variations in the estimates of advertising effects reported in the literature (Clarke 1976; Aaker and Carman 1982; Assmus, Farley, and Lehmann 1984).[5] This analysis requires some common measure of advertising effect; an obvious choice is elasticity, a dimensionless variable. If carryover effects are present, a distinction can be made between short-run and long-run elasticity. We report short-run elasticities.[6]

Empirical studies have tended to examine advertising elasticities with respect to market share rather than absolute sales. Naert and Leeflang (1978) provide a summary of the algebra of brand sales models, on which we draw throughout this review. Market share, MS, is defined to equal brand sales, Q, divided by product class sales, Q_T. This relation can be rewritten as

$$Q = Q_T \times MS. \tag{6.1}$$

Then the impact of a change in advertising is

$$\frac{\partial Q}{\partial A} = MS \frac{\partial Q_T}{\partial A} + Q_T \frac{\partial MS}{\partial A}, \tag{6.2}$$

and the corresponding relation between elasticities is

$$\varepsilon_{Q,A} = \varepsilon_{Q_T,A} + \varepsilon_{MS,A}. \tag{6.3}$$

The sales elasticity is equal to the market share elasticity only if the product class elasticity is zero. Clarke (1973) makes this assumption to obtain his "conservative" bounds for sales elasticities for ready-to-eat cereals. The sales elasticity will, in general, be larger in absolute magnitude than the market share elasticity.

The impact of a change in advertising expenditures can be partitioned into direct and indirect effects:

$$\frac{\partial Q}{\partial A} = \frac{\partial Q^*}{\partial A} + \frac{\partial Q^*}{\partial P_c}\frac{\partial P_c}{\partial A} + \frac{\partial Q^*}{\partial A_c}\frac{\partial A_c}{\partial A} + \frac{\partial Q^*}{\partial X_c}\frac{\partial X_c}{\partial A}. \tag{6.4}$$

Indirect effects arise from competitive reaction to a firm's actions. The brand elasticity can be written in terms of an own elasticity, ε, cross-elasticities, η, and reaction elasticities, ρ:

$$\varepsilon_{Q,A} = \varepsilon_{Q^*,A} + \eta_{Q^*,P_c}\rho_{P_c,A} + \eta_{Q^*,A_c}\rho_{A_c,A} + \eta_{Q^*,X_c}\rho_{X_c,A}. \tag{6.5}$$

As shown earlier, these various brand elasticities and cross-elasticities can be partitioned into their product class and market share elasticities.

The estimated own elasticities and cross-elasticities of marketing instruments with sales and market share for various products are shown in tables 6–7 and 6–8, respectively. For comparison, the own elasticities of some additional products were given in table 6–5. One issue is whether a cross-elasticity is equal in magnitude, although opposite in sign, to the corresponding own elasticity under any set of conditions. This issue is important because it is either an implicit or explicit assumption in many sales response functions reported in the literature. For instance, the most common functional form is the multiplicative model:

$$Q = kA^\varepsilon A_c^\eta. \tag{6.6}$$

In models in which the managerial decision variable is expressed in relative share form, this equation becomes

$$Q = k\left(\frac{A}{A_c}\right)^\beta = kA^\beta A_c^{-\beta}. \tag{6.7}$$

The implicit assumption, then, is that

$$\varepsilon = -\eta \quad \text{or} \quad \varepsilon + \eta = 0. \tag{6.8}$$

Bass (1969b) explicitly imposed this last restriction in his model of the market mechanism for cigarettes. Lambin (1976) recognized this property of relative share models. In a similar vein, Simon (1979) expressed sales response to relative price differential, (them − us)/them, as an hyperbolic (sine) function.[7] He had a separate linear term for absolute price effects. He found that absolute price levels had no significant impact on sales of pharmaceuticals or

Table 6–7. Elasticities and Cross-Elasticities with Sales

Product Class	Price		Advertising		Product		Distribution	
	Own	Cross-	Own	Cross-	Own	Cross-	Own	Cross-
Banks[a]								
Belgium			0.003	−0.001				
Cleanser, household[b]								
Germany								
A	−4.480	*						
C	−4.730	*						
D	−1.340	*						
E	−3.490	*						
Cigarettes[a,c]								
Belgium	−1.124		0.154		−0.739			
United States								
Filter		0.305	0.594	*				
Nonfilter	−2.607		0.247	*				
Detergents[d]								
Germany								
A	−2.850	*						
B	−1.220	*						
C	−1.070	*						
D	−2.220	*						
E	−1.920	*						
G	−1.450	*						

Eggs[e]					
United States					
XL	-3.324	0.432			
L	-3.106	1.360			
PL	-2.144	1.996			
M	-2.030	2.756			
20		1.386			
Soft Drinks[a]					
Belgium					
A	-1.751	0.277	-0.034	0.085	0.210
B		0.115	-0.040		3.445
Germany		0.000	-0.040		
Holland					
A		0.010	-0.009		
B		0.057[f]			

*Cross-elasticity same magnitude as own elasticity by functional form.

a. Lambin (1976).
b. Simon (1979).
c. Bass (1969b).
d. Lambin and Peeters (1982).
e. Reibstein and Gatignon (1984).
f. Values displayed between two columns mean that the marketing instruments were expressed in share or relative terms rather than in absolute terms.

Table 6–8. Elasticities and Cross-Elasticities with Market Share

Product Class	Price Own	Price Cross-	Advertising Own	Advertising Cross-	Product Own	Product Cross-	Distribution Own	Distribution Cross-
Beer[a]								
Australia								
A			0.102	−0.110				
B			0.123	−0.140				
Beverage[b]								
United States								
A		−2.000	0.045					
B		−0.974	0.067					
C		−5.650						
F			0.073					
Cereal, Ready-to-Eat[c]								
United States								
A11			0.049	−0.005 −0.015				
B11			0.029	−0.023 −0.002				
C11			0.064	−0.177 −0.064				
Chocolate Biscuits[d]								
New Zealand								
A	−1.780		0.006				0.897	
B	−2.150		0.001				2.608	
C	1.321						−0.231	
Cigarettes[a]								
Australia								
A			0.153	−0.147				
B			0.141	−0.134				

Coffee[a,e]					
Australia					
A			0.147	−0.138	
B			0.188	−0.192	
United States					
Folgers	−4.370	0.590			
Maxwell House	−3.890	1.950			
Deodorants[f]					
France			0.037	−0.059	
Detergents[a,f]					
Australia					
A			0.142	−0.132	
B			0.178	−0.170	
France					
A			0.070		
B			0.037	−0.069	
C			0.055	−0.098	
D			0.129	−0.286	
Detergents, Liquid[d]					
New Zealand					
A1	1.228		0.009		0.377
A2	−0.574		0.017		−0.155
B1	−0.487		0.002		1.128
B2	−1.722		0.007		−0.091
C	−0.823		0.011		0.845
Electric Shavers[f]					
Belgium					
A	−0.446		0.275		
B	−1.261		0.331		
C	−0.036		0.122		

Table 6–8 (*continued*)

Product Class	Price Own	Price Cross-	Advertising Own	Advertising Cross-	Product Own	Product Cross-	Distribution Own	Distribution Cross-
Germany								
A		-1.692	0.140	-0.249	0.303			
B		-5.387	0.180	-0.155	0.534			
Scandinavia								
A			0.482	-0.471				
B				0.217				
C				0.034				
FPBG[g]								
United States	-2.368							
FPBG[h]								
United States								
A				0.006				
C				0.012				
D				0.005				
E				0.011				
Gasoline[f,i]								
Belgium								
A			0.005	-0.049				
B			0.011					
Denmark								
A			0.023					
B			0.023					
C			0.009		0.119			
D			0.005		0.109			
E			0.003					
F			0.020					

Italy					
A					
B		0.028	0.012	−0.035	
C			0.005		
E			0.006		
United States	−1.843				
Grocery item[j]					
United States					
A	−1.116	0.024	−0.027		
B	−0.992	0.032	−0.168	0.034	−0.012
C	−1.588	0.019		0.019	−0.026
Grocery item[k]					
United States					
A	−2.473	0.086			
B	−2.068	0.396			
C	−3.670				
Hair Spray[f]					
Belgium					
A	−1.285	0.027			
B	−1.466	0.021			
C	−2.726				
D	−1.528				
E	−1.316				
I	−1.274				
Insecticides[f]					
France		0.033	−0.119		
Soap, Toilet[a]					
Australia					
A		0.090	−0.090		
B		0.113	−0.111		

Table 6–8 (continued)

Product Class	Price		Advertising		Product		Distribution	
	Own	Cross-	Own	Cross-	Own	Cross-	Own	Cross-
Toothpaste[a,d]								
Australia								
A			0.142	−0.132				
B			0.178	−0.170				
New Zealand								
A1	−1.726		0.062				−0.786	
A2	−1.823						1.720	
B1	−2.506		0.008					
B2	1.199		0.008				1.689	
B3			0.017				0.381	
C			0.091					

Note: Values displayed between two columns mean that the marketing instruments were expressed in share or relative terms rather than in absolute terms.

a. Metwally (1978).
b. Picconi and Olson (1978).
c. Clarke (1973).
d. Brodie and de Kluyver (1983).
e. Cooper (1988).
f. Lambin (1976).
g. Massy and Frank (1965).
h. Beckwith (1972).
i. Claycamp (1966).
j. Wildt (1974).
k. Houston and Weiss (1974).

detergents in West Germany during the period analyzed. As a consequence of his functional form, the direct price elasticity and cross-price elasticity must have the identical magnitude.

Metwally (1978) examined the situation in which firms competed solely to maintain market share equilibrium through advertising. We can write this relation as

$$\varepsilon_{MS^*,A} + \eta_{MS^*,A_c}\rho_{A_c,A} = 0,$$

or (6.9)

$$\frac{-\varepsilon_{MS^*,A}}{\eta_{MS^*,A_c}} = \rho_{A_c,A}.$$

Metwally found this relation to hold in most of the Australian industries he studied (beer, cigarettes, detergents, instant coffee, toilet soap, and toothpaste). In these industries advertising is market-defensive, i.e., done to protect share. The market share elasticities were shown in table 6–8, and the reaction elasticities are presented in table 6–10. In the preceding relation, the elasticity and cross-elasticity will equal each other in magnitude only if the reaction elasticity equals 1. A number of the estimated values of Metwally's reaction coefficients are about 1.

The information we possess on cross-elasticities is sparse. We essentially have no marketing studies on price, product, or distribution cross-elasticities. Wildt (1974) is the sole exception, giving product cross-elasticities as well as advertising cross-elasticities. Advertising cross-elasticities are primarily provided by Lambin (1976). His work suggests that elasticity and cross-elasticity typically are not equal in magnitude. There is an obvious need for more empirical work. Much of the existing work has focused on improving estimation techniques for market share models. Without much careful thought, the managerial decision variables in these market share models have also been expressed in some "share" form. As a result, independent estimates of the cross-elasticities have not been obtained.

Reaction Functions

Construction of the sales response function is just one step in marketing programming. If competitors react to a firm's actions, it must develop competitive reaction functions. For some perspective on this, we briefly review the major relevant thrust in economics, then discuss reaction functions in marketing.

Reaction Functions and Oligopoly.   Economists have used the concept of the reaction function to describe how oligopolists make their decisions. Major critiques of this approach can be found in Fellner (1949), who explicitly mentioned reaction functions and focused on cooperative equilibria, and in Friedman (1977a; 1977b), who focused on noncooperative equilibria. Friedman defined a reaction function as "a function which determines for a firm in a given time period its action (price and/or quantity) as a function of the actions of (all) other firms during the preceding time period."

Cournot (1838) postulated a quantity market model, whose key assumptions are that each firm produces the identical product as every other firm in the industry and does not set price but rather how much of the product it will produce. The market price will then be determined by the total production of the industry. The firms maximize single-period profits and know each others' profit functions. Additional assumptions specify the general shape of the demand and total cost curves. If the firms act simultaneously with single-period time horizons, then market will converge to the Cournot equilibrium, in which no firm, without colluding, can obtain a higher profit by changing its production level. Our interest is in the dynamic version of this model, which was ambiguously specified by Cournot. In this version, the firms remain single-period profit maximizers, but it is unclear whether the firms make their decisions sequentially or simultaneously. In a simultaneous decision model, each firm determines its current production level in order to maximize its current-period profits, assuming its competitors will produce the same amount of product this period as they did last period. This relation between current production and the past production of competitors can be labeled a Cournot reaction function. If these reaction functions are stable, the market will converge to the Cournot equilibrium production levels.

Bertrand (1883) argued that firms set price, not output. In his view, each firm fixes its price on the assumption that its competitors will not change their prices. The assumption that a firm's decisions will have no impact on its rivals' actions seems unrealistic in general, but especially so for pricing decisions. Schmalensee (1976) maintained that Cournot/Bertrand reaction might also apply to nonprice promotion.

Bowley (1924) posited a conjectural variation model to relax Cournot's restrictive assumption that a competitor will produce the same amount this period as last. A firm in a duopoly attempts to take into account two reaction functions. The first function describes how a firm believes its competitor will change output in reaction to its output last period. The second describes how the firm should react to the competitor's output last period if its beliefs about its competitor's behavior is correct.

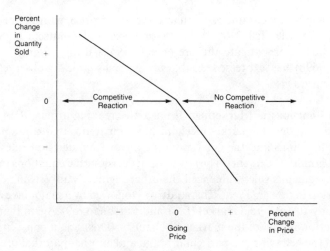

Figure 6–2. Kinked Demand Curve.

Stackelberg (1934) introduced the notion that firms were either leaders or followers. A follower is a company that behaves as if its competitors are going to maintain their production at last period's level. A leader is a company that acts on the assumption that its competitors are followers. This can result in the Stackelberg leader-follower equilibrium.

Sweezy (1939), noting that the traditional demand curve did not apply to oligopolies, investigated the imagined demand curve. In particular, competitors may react differently to a price increase than to a price decrease. If a firm raises its price and its competitors do not, then it is likely to lose market share. Conversely, competitors must meet the firm's price cut to avoid loss of share. As a consequence, the imagined demand curve has a "corner" at the current price, as shown in figure 6–2. The demand curve tends to be elastic when the firm raises price and inelastic when it cuts price. The imagined demand curve has been renamed the kinky, or kinked, demand curve.

Stigler (1947) has elaborated on the theory of kinked demand curves. The difference in the slopes of the demand curve on the two sides of the kink was conjectured to be affected by the number of competitors, the relative size of these competitors, the differences among the competitors' products, and the extent of collusion among the competitors. Stigler presented some ad hoc empirical evidence that generally failed to show the existence of a kinked demand curve. One example supporting the possibility of its existence occurred in the cigarette industry. Lucky Strike increased its price by 25%, and its competitors continued to charge the lower price, with the result that Lucky Strike sales fell 31%. Aykac, Corstjens, and Gautschi (1984) proposed a way to investigate the presence of kinks using dummy variables. Simon (1969b) has expressed doubts about being able to observe kinked demand curves.

Reaction Functions in Marketing. In a path-breaking article, Bass (1969b) presented a model of a market mechanism for cigarettes that contained sales response functions and the corresponding advertising decision rules for the filter and nonfilter segments. The advertising decision rule equations indicated how one segment's sales influenced the other segment's advertising expenditure decision in the same year. This study was followed by a major investigation of the ready-to-eat cereal market (Bass and Parsons 1969). Again there was a four-equation model of the market mechanism. This time a pair of relations described the behavior of a particular brand and another pair that of all other brands combined. A major empirical result was that competitive advertising activities seem to stimulate primary demand in this market. The advertising decision rules were based on marketing actions and results in the previous bimonthly period. Samuels (1970/1971) tested a model very similar to that of Bass and Parsons, with data from three markets: scouring powders, toilet soaps, and household cleansers. Wildt (1974) studied retail price advertising as well as network advertising as a managerial decision rule. Since three firms accounted for the majority of sales in the industry, his market mechanism contained nine equations.

Lambin (1970a) and Lambin, Naert, and Bultez (1975) investigated a small electrical appliance market from the Stackelberg leader-follower perspective. They constructed the followers' reaction functions for advertising, price, and quality. They found that while competitors did react to a change in one marketing instrument by the leader with a change in the same instrument, they also changed other elements in their marketing mix. For instance, the competitors might only partly match a price cut and instead increase their advertising outlays. In their discussion of their results, Lambin, Naert, and Bultez raised the possibility of kinked demand curves coming about if competitors did not react when this would result in increased market share. However, they did not address this in their ordinary least squares estimation of the reaction functions.

Parsons and Schultz (1976) describe the general form of these models, which they call "models with endogenous competition." Our interest is in a typical decision rule for a firm. The level of a particular decision variable for a specific competitor may be affected by the firm's own managerial decision variables, by each of its competitors managerial decision variables, by its own and its competitors' past sales, and by autonomous environmental conditions, including seasonality. What is important to recognize is that the reaction function of the economist can be, and often is, embedded in the more general construct of the decision rule.

Hanssens (1980b) incorporated the phenomenon of the level of one marketing instrument affecting, or being affected by, levels of other marketing instruments within the same firm into a generalized reaction matrix (shown for price and advertising only):

$$
\mathbf{R} = \begin{bmatrix} 1 & \rho_{P_c,P} & \rho_{A,P} & \rho_{A_c,P} \\ \rho_{P,P_c} & 1 & \rho_{A,P_c} & \rho_{A_c,P_c} \\ \hline \rho_{P,A} & \rho_{P_c,A} & 1 & \rho_{A_c,A} \\ \rho_{P,A_c} & \rho_{P_c,A_c} & \rho_{A,A_c} & 1 \end{bmatrix}. \tag{6.10}
$$

This matrix is partitioned so that the main diagonal blocks represent simple competitive reaction. The off-diagonal blocks represent multiple reaction. The diagonal elements represent intrafirm effects, and the off-diagonal ones represent interfirm effects. Hanssens noted that in an oligopoly the interfirm reaction elasticities should be zero if the firm is a follower (Cournot-Bertrand reaction function) and nonzero if the firm is a leader (Stackelberg reaction function).

The empirical evidence on reaction elasticities is given in tables 6–9 to 6–11. Most of what little evidence we have concerns advertising and again is due to Lambin (1976) and Metwally (1978). Whether a recursive or nonrecursive model is necessary to represent the system containing both sales response functions and reaction functions depends largely on the data interval. With a relatively short data interval, at least price movements would be simultaneous. Temporal interrelations might be identified using time series analysis (Hanssens 1980a). The functional form of reaction functions examined has been restricted to either linear or multiplicative. That firms react to either an absolute change or a relative change in competitive behavior seems reasonable; however, no attempt has been made to show which of these is true.

Other phenomena might be present in reaction functions. A firm might react differently to positive or negative changes in a competitor's marketing instrument; that is, the reaction function might have a kink in it. A firm might be nonresponsive to "small" changes in a competitor's marketing instrument, as shown in figure 6–3. Just as Parsons (1975b) and Simon (1979) showed that the parameters in the sales response function can change over time, so might those in a reaction function. Indeed, changes in the parameters in the reaction function are more likely as firms adjust their strategies and learn about

Table 6–9.   Price Reaction Elasticities

	Price Reaction to					
	Price		Advertising		Product	
Product Class	This	Last	This	Last	This	Last
Electric Shavers[a]						
Germany						
A	1.104		−0.005		−0.005	
B	0.664		0.008		0.017	
C	0.879		−0.042		−0.632	
Scandinavia						
B	0.762		−0.004		1.465	
C	0.346		−0.008		0.376	
Hair Spray[a]						
Belgium						
A	1.686					
B	0.771		0.023			
C	0.555					
D	0.743		0.036			
E	0.150					
G	0.514		0.005			
H	0.346		0.031			
I	0.727					

a. Lambin (1976).

Table 6–10.   Advertising Reaction Elasticities

	Advertising Reaction to					
	Advertising		Price		Product	
Product Class	This	Last	This	Last	This	Last
Airlines[a]						
United States						
B	0.900					
Beer[b]						
Australia						
A		1.072				
B		0.979				
Cereals, Ready-to-Eat[c]						
United States						
A		0.036				

Table 6–10 (*continued*)

| | Advertising Reaction to | | | | | |
| | Advertising | | Price | | Product | |
Product Class	This	Last	This	Last	This	Last
Cigarettes[b]						
Australia						
A		0.901				
B		0.887				
Coffee, Instant[b]						
Australia						
A		0.855				
B		0.822				
Detergents[a,b]						
Australia						
A		1.045				
B		1.677				
France						
A	0.415					
B	0.529					
C	0.352					
D	0.134					
Electric Shavers[d]						
Germany						
A		0.504		−9.898		−0.936
B		0.613				−1.704
C		0.022		−1.514		−1.162
Scandinavia						
A		0.239		−0.213		−1.506
C		0.314		−1.447		−2.482
Grocery Item[e]						
United States						
A						0.040
B	0.090					
Hair Spray[d]						
Belgium						
A	0.233		6.926			
B	0.352		5.351			
C	0.386		4.608			
G	0.209		7.747			
H	0.571		2.962			

Table 6–10 (*continued*)

	Advertising Reaction to					
	Advertising		Price		Product	
Product Class	This	Last	This	Last	This	Last
Soap, Toilet[b]						
Australia						
A		0.999				
B		1.016				
Toothpaste[b]						
Australia						
A		1.698				
B		0.950				

a. Gatignon (1984).
b. Metwally (1978).
c. Bass and Parsons (1969).
d. Lambin (1976).
e. Claycamp (1966).

Table 6–11. Product Reaction Elasticities

	Product Reaction to					
	Product		Price		Advertising	
Product Class	This	Last	This	Last	This	Last
Electric Shavers[a]						
Germany						
D		0.901		−0.594		0.023

a. Lambin (1976).

competitive reactions. Wildt and Winer (1983) review the modeling and estimation of this type of model.

Economists have used the reaction function as a hypothetical construct to allow them to determine equilibrium conditions in an oligopoly. Their empirical work has ignored the reaction function and focused on the demand curve in an attempt to see whether it might be kinked. Marketing scientists have examined sales response functions together with decision rules as a system of relations encompassing the market mechanism, but they have been more interested in the sales response function than in the decision rules.

More research is needed to improve the specification and estimation of reaction functions. In order to test for the existence of the kinked demand

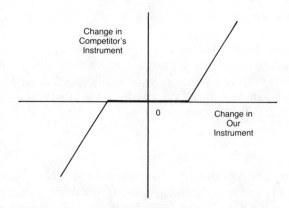

Figure 6-3. Friction.

curve, decision rules must be reducd to the corresponding reaction functions by factoring out the effects of the variables not directly related to competition using experimental or nonexperimental means.

If a competitor does not respond to a firm's actions when it is likely to gain market share, a large number of observations will cluster at zero. The observed value for a managerial decision variable is the actual value for adverse competitive actions and is zero for other competitive actions, that is, values for the dependent variable outside the bound are set equal to the bound itself and the dependent variable is said to be *censored*. This requires that such a reaction function be estimated by Tobit analysis (Tobin 1958).

If competitors are not sensitive to small changes in a firm's marketing mix, the dependent variables in the reaction functions are not related to the independent variables over some finite range. The presence of a mass point anywhere in the distribution of the dependent variable, not just at some upper or lower limiting value of it, can be addressed by a generalization of Tobit analysis due to Rosett (1959), which he called a statistical model of *friction*. DeSarbo et al. (1987) used a friction model for describing and forecasting price changes.

There has been some indication in the popular business press that some managers operate under company guidelines that permit them to change the levels of the company's marketing instruments only up to some prescribed limit. In this case, two-limit Tobit analysis is required. Rosett and Nelson (1975) show how such a two-limit Tobit regression model can be estimated by means of the method of maximum likelihood, and they provide a computer program for implementing their procedure.[8]

To this point, we have been concentrating on the reaction function in isolation. From a managerial point of view, we are also concerned about the impact of better specification of reaction functions on the estimation of the sales response function.[9] Therefore, attention should be given to simultaneous Tobit models. The literature discusses different solutions, depending on the exact structure of the model (Amemiya 1974; 1979; Nelson and Olson 1977; Sickles and Schmidt 1978; Sickles, Schmidt, and White 1979).

Discussion

Our goal is to improve marketing decisions through a better understanding of competitive behavior and its impact on the actions of the firm. We have tried to demonstrate the importance of using a model of the market mechanism for a product that contains not only a sales response function but also reaction functions or more general managerial decision rules. In most functional forms, knowledge of the estimates of the parameters is insufficient to calculate elasticities. In such cases, the average values of these elasticities, and perhaps their range, should be reported.

Knowledge about the nature of market mechanisms has increased appreciably in the last two decades. For example, not long ago managers had little but their own subjective impressions of the effectiveness of their advertising. Today, managers of heavily advertised brands can measure the effect with reasonable accuracy. Even managers of industrial products have at least a benchmark against which to evaluate their advertising effort (Lilien 1979; Lilien and Rudzic 1982). Our task now is to understand the more subtle variations in marketing's impact.

While we know quite a bit about advertising and something about price, our empirical base on other marketing instruments is woefully small. A better grasp of marketing instruments other than advertising is needed. For instance, marketing managers would like to know when and to what degree excessive price promotion changes customers' perceptions of the normal price of a product and of its quality. Also, managers would like to know how to assess the impact of a salesperson's effort, especially since empirical evidence has indicated that territory workload and potential are significant determinants in sales differences among territories, whereas sales effort may have little, if any, effect. Ryans and Weinberg (1979) conjectured that it might be useful to construct a two-stage model of sales force performance. The first part would specify the factors that influence the amount of effort a salesperson puts forth and the second would represent the relation of sales to sales force effort.

Some empirical results, such as those involving the product life cycle, seem to be in conflict with marketing theory. Other empirical results, such as those for the price-advertising interaction, have been contradictory. Consider, for example, the relation between the demand elasticity and relative price. Moran (1978) states that the farther a brand's price is from the category average in either direction, the lower its demand elasticity is, whereas Simon (1979) says that the magnitude of price elasticity increases for increasing positive and negative deviations of a brand's price from the average price of brands competing with it.

There are two ways to resolve these disagreements. One way is to acquire more information. Too many marketing studies focus on the same data bases, such as the Lydia Pinkham data (cf. Pollay 1979). Even worse, some researchers use previously examined data bases without acknowledging their heritage. We know of instances where different theoretical models were each claimed to fit the same data. The question arises whether we are learning something new or merely fitting random noise. The scientific method requires that models be tested on new data and that the data sources, if not the actual data, be made known.

The second approach is to recognize that we may obtain different results in different situations. Basmann (1965) stresses the importance of specifying the background and initial conditions underlying a statistical test of any model. A test cannot be conclusive unless the background and initial conditions allegedly appropriate for application of a model are actually fulfilled for the time period under examination. Also, we have already noted that the different results in the price-advertising interaction literature might be due to different definitions of price. Perhaps the controversy about the shape of the sales response curve is moot. Conceivably the shape of the sales response function is generally concave, and the resultant market share response curves are S-shaped. The bottom line is that we must be very careful about the conditions under which we would expect our model of the market mechanism to hold.

Notes

1. Lancaster misclassified deodorants as primary demand only.

2. We talk about "scale economies of advertising" in the sense of the production function (sales response function) for an individual brand and do not address the purported advantages that large firms derive from advertising. With regard to the latter issue, Boyer and Lancaster (1986, p. 524) found no static relation between advertising costs per dollar of sales and the size of the advertiser.

3. This implies that primary demand for the products studied has not been affected by changes in the absolute price levels. Simon (1979) reports a similar result.

4. These articles build upon earlier work of McGuire et al. (1968), Beckwith (1972; 1973), Bultez and Naert (1975), and McGuire and Weiss (1976).

5. Farley and Lehmann (1986) discuss how to conduct meta-analysis in marketing.

6. If market share is the dependent variable, the estimation method should address the issue of logical consistency. Our interest in this section is in the empirical results rather than in the methodological issues.

7. Modeling relative price by sinh was also done by Albach (1979). Albach displayed figures showing the change in own and cross-elasticities over time.

8. Also see Nelson (1976).

9. The quality of estimated reaction functions is also related to their use in decision analysis or simulation. See the discussion of the Schultz and Dodson model in chapter 8.

Appendix

Table A6–1. Definitions of Product

Product Class	Definition
Auto-train[a]	Frequency of service and variety of destinations: number of trains per week and number of destinations
Cigarettes[a]	Product mix index: number of filter and nonfilter brands
Confectionery[a]	Chocolate content: chocolate weight in product
Electric shavers[a]	Quality index: expert ratings of selected attributes
Grocery item[b]	New variety activity: share of subcategories on market less than one year
Soft drinks[a]	Packages mix index: number of bottle sizes
Yogurt[a]	Product mix index: number of packages and flavors

a. Lambin (1976).
b. Claycamp (1966).

7 MARKETING DYNAMICS

Most managers would agree that their marketing actions are sales- or profit-effective for longer than just the period in which they are taken. This dynamic aspect of marketing is exhibited in two ways: (1) lagged effects, i.e., sales changes, competitive reactions, and other forms of marketing behavior may be noticeable in one or more periods after the original stimulus occurs; and (2) lead effects, i.e., consumers or competitors may anticipate a marketing stimulus and adjust their behavior before the stimulus actually occurs. There has been a great deal of empirical research on lagged effects in marketing and virtually none on lead effects. However, since the methods used in modeling leads and lags are the same, we can discuss them together. Furthermore, as the quality of marketing data continues to increase with advances in management information systems, the accurate modeling of marketing dynamics becomes more important. For example, ignoring lagged advertising effects on sales may be more serious on monthly than on annual data if the true advertising duration is a few months.

An important distinction in marketing dynamics is between *pulse* and *step* actions in marketing. A pulse action is turned on and off by the marketer, e.g., an advertising campaign or a price promotion. A step action is more permanent, for example, the launching of a new product in the line or the tapping

213

of a different distribution channel. Although dynamic effects are expected to occur in both cases, the literature has for all practical purposes only investigated pulse actions. Moreover, these studies have generally focused on two marketing mix elements: advertising and price (in particular, price promotions), although, in principle, all marketing mix variables can have dynamic effects.

This chapter first reviews the dynamic effects of advertising and those of price. Next, it discusses methodological challenges and presents a general model for studying marketing dynamics. This model is also used to discuss the important implications of time aggregation of marketing data.

Advertising Dynamics

There are various reasons why advertising's effect on sales may be distributed over time. The most important ones are the following:

- The advertising may not be noticed by the customer until some time after its expenditure. For example, Montgomery and Silk (1972) found lagged journal advertising effects on prescription drug sales of up to six months. This may have been caused by physicians delaying the reading of their professional journals.
- An advertising-induced purchase may be followed by subsequent purchases *if the product is satisfactory.* Similarly, the positive word-of-mouth resulting from the initial purchase may bring new customers into the market.
- In some instances, competitive reaction to an advertising campaign may be slow. If the advertising is effective, it may affect sales performance until competitive retaliation takes place.
- Advertising may gradually build up customer loyalty and thus be responsible for more than the immediately observable short-term sales fluctuations.

The literature on advertising dynamics has addressed two important questions: (1) What are the cumulative advertising effects, and (2) Does advertising wear out? We address each of these issues in turn.

Cumulative Advertising Effects

It is difficult to specify the advertising dynamics in a market on the basis of marketing or psychological theory alone. Although several approaches are possible, three simple yet intuitively appealing models have been used most frequently. These models all recognize that sales or market share data are typically autocorrelated, but they differ on whether advertising is causing the autocorrelation in sales, i.e., whether an advertising carryover effect exists.

1. *The autoregressive current-effects model (ACE):*

$$Q_t = \beta_0 + \beta_1 A_t + \varepsilon_t, \tag{7.1}$$

where $\varepsilon_t = \rho \varepsilon_{t-1} + \alpha_t$, and α_t is white noise.

This model argues that advertising only has contemporaneous effects on sales. However, other factors such as consumer inertia and habit formation cause sales to fluctuate smoothly over time, which is represented by the autoregressive process of the error term. The implied advertising carryover effect in the ACE model is zero, so that the short- and long-run impact is the same ($= \beta_1$).

2. *The Koyck model:*

$$Q_t = \beta_0(1 - \lambda) + \lambda Q_{t-1} + \beta_1 A_t + \varepsilon_t, \tag{7.2}$$

where $\varepsilon_t = \alpha_t - \lambda \alpha_{t-1}$, and α_t is white noise.

This model arises when advertising has an infinitely long effect on sales, but with an exponentially decaying pattern over time. The short-term effect is β_1, and subsequent-period effects are $\lambda \beta_1$, $\lambda^2 \beta_1$, $\lambda^3 \beta_1$, ..., $\lambda^n \beta_1$, where λ is the carryover effect of advertising and must be less than 1. The implied long-term effect of advertising is $\beta_1/(1 - \lambda)$ and 90% of the long-run impact of advertising occurs in $(-2.3)/\log(\lambda)$ periods (e.g., Russell 1988).

3. *The partial adjustment model:*

$$Q_t = \beta_0(1 - \lambda) + \lambda Q_{t-1} + \beta_1 A_t + \alpha_t, \tag{7.3}$$

where α_t is white noise.

This response pattern occurs when consumers can only partly adjust to advertising or other marketing stimuli. However, they do gradually adjust to the desired consumption level, which causes the advertising effects to be distributed over time. The partial adjustment model is very similar to the Koyck scheme, except for the structure of the error term. The implied long-term advertising effect is also $\beta_1/(1 - \lambda)$.

The Koyck model has been the most frequently used among these three. In an important survey of 70 empirical studies of advertising carryover effects using the Koyck model, Clarke (1976) concluded:

> The published econometric literature indicates that 90% of the cumulative effects of advertising on sales of mature, frequently purchased low-priced products occurs within 3 to 9 months of the advertisement. The conclusion that advertising's effect on sales lasts for months rather than years is strongly supported.

Clarke's conclusion is very interesting, as it gets to the heart of a key advertising management question: How long do the economic effects of advertising last? However, when we try to answer the question with econometric techniques, there is a tendency to find different advertising durations for different data intervals, i.e., there may be a data interval bias problem. In particular, Clarke finds that researchers using annual data tend to discover multiple-year advertising effects, which is in conflict with his empirical generalization. This report has spurred an active interest in the data interval bias problem, which is covered in more detail later in the chapter.

Advertising Wearout

More recent attention has focused on asymmetric patterns in the dynamic sales response to advertising. Little's (1979a) five phenomena of advertising response include three dynamic aspects:

1. Different rise and decay rates.
2. Changing effectiveness over time.
3. Hysteresis, i.e., the response may fall off with constant advertising.

Different rise and decay rates of sales response to advertising are also known as the *wearout* phenomenon (see figure 7–1). Advertising wearout may occur for two reasons. First, for consumer or industrial durables, there may be a fixed number of potential customers actively looking to buy the product at any point in time. As an advertising campaign is launched, the sales rate

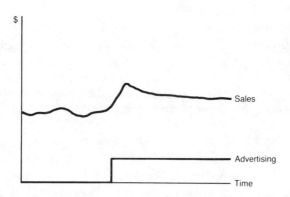

Figure 7–1. Advertising Wearout.

increases immediately but then tapers off because customers leave the market as soon as they purchase the product (i.e., a market depletion effect). Second, for frequently purchased products, we often observe impulse response buying, an immediate reaction to new advertising, which disappears even while the advertising is still running (i.e., an adaptation effect). Either way, the response dynamics may be asymmetric, which must be accommodated by a special function.

Simon (1982) proposes a differential stimulus response model to incorporate the wearout effect. The differential stimulus is the difference between current and previous advertising, or zero, whichever is greater. Formally,

$$Q_t = \beta_0 + \beta_1 A_t + \beta_2 \max(A_t - A_{t-1}, 0), \qquad (7.4)$$

where sales and advertising may be measured in logarithms to incorporate decreasing returns to scale. The wearout hypothesis is tested by a positive coefficient for β_2. This implies that whenever an advertising campaign is new, there will be an extra response effect above and beyond the level stimulus effect (β_1). Simon tested the model successfully on three frequently purchased products. Also, Hanssens and Levien (1983) found differential stimulus effects in print and television advertising for the U.S. Navy recruitment program.

The managerial implications of advertising wearout are interesting. Simon (1982) argues that the advertising budget should be allocated to pulsing and constant-spending budgets and that the share of pulsing increases with the differential stimulus effect. The most profitable advertising strategy is one of alternating pulsation, a pulse in every other period. We do not know, though, what the best length of a pulsing period is.

In conclusion, several empirical studies have demonstrated the existence of dynamic effects of advertising on sales performance. The lag lengths of the effects are several months, although the generalization can only be made for mature, low-priced, frequently purchased products. Furthermore, advertising wearout has been observed in several cases. Both phenomena have important managerial implications for the optimal timing of advertising efforts. Also, it is increasingly important to use good-quality time series data to model advertising dynamics in order to avoid data interval bias.

Price Dynamics

Price setting is complex, involving cost, demand, competitive, and organizational considerations. In many instances, the resulting price is stable over time, perhaps indicating that an equilibrium has been reached. In other cases, there is frequent use of temporary price changes such as price promotions or seasonal price hikes. Empirical research on price dynamics has focused mostly on the latter.[1]

The simplest form of consumer response to a price change is the zero-order model, i.e., sales are a function of the current price only. This situation implies a static response function:

$$Q_t = \beta_0 + \beta_1 P_t + \varepsilon_t. \tag{7.5}$$

Zero-order price response has been observed on several occasions, even when dynamic price effects were specifically tested. For example, price response for 11 brands of an Australian household product was found to be strictly zero-order (Carpenter et al. 1988). An extensive empirical study of coupon usage in various product categories was also done using a static response model (Narasimhan 1984).

Zero-order price response implies that there is no transient component in the sales-price relation. Buyers are reacting to current prices only; they are not taking advantage of temporary price cuts by stocking up on the product, nor are they anticipating future price movements. Thus, competitors are operating along a static demand curve and can only influence the level, not the timing, of their customers' purchases.

If consumers deviate at all from this myopic behavior, dynamic price response should occur. The most common form is *stockpiling*, i.e., moving future purchases to the present to take advantage of a temporary price cut. This leads to an asymmetric response function not unlike Simon's differential stimulus model. For example, if the stockpiling lasts for one period, we could postulate:

$$Q_t = \beta_0 + \beta_1 P_t + \beta_2 \max(P_t - P_{t-1}, 0) + \varepsilon_t, \tag{7.6}$$

where β_2 is predicted to be negative. We are not aware of formal tests of this model. However, several studies have reported positive lagged price coefficients using symmetric response functions (cf. Little 1975b).

A more sophisticated dynamic consumer response is to *anticipate a future price cut* and thus to reduce purchasing levels until the price reduction occurs. This scenario is described by Doyle and Saunders (1985) as regret reduction. Their empirical test on a European supplier of natural gas and gas appliances did reveal such anticipations, not at the customer level but rather at the sales force level. Salespeople were taking advantage of planned promotion campaigns by enticing customers to switch their purchases into the promotion period so that they would receive higher commission rates.

Dynamic price response was studied more formally by Winer (1985), using a vector price model which distinguishes between five price concepts: anticipated price, price uncertainty, unanticipated inflation or deflation, and

reservation price. In an empirical test of seven consumer durables, several of
the price concepts were statistically significantly related to probability of
purchase. Similarly, a price expectations effect was found to exist in an analysis
of coffee buying (Winer 1986). These and other studies highlight the importance of using dynamic models for assessing consumers' price responsiveness.

Price dynamics have also been studied at the firm level. In particular,
DeSarbo et al. (1987) developed a friction model for describing and predicting
price changes. The model posits, first, that in the absence of major frictions,
a company will tend to hold its price constant. However, upward tensions
such as inflation and downward tensions such as competition may build up
in price setting to a point where a threshold is exceeded, which prompts the
firm to adjust its price (upward or downward). The resulting threshold model
of price movements over time is estimated using maximum likelihood. An
application to weekly mortgage interest rate setting revealed that an individual bank will adjust its interest rate in response to the previous weeks' changes
in the cost of money and competitive rates.

Methodological Challenges

The marketing manager has basically only one question about lagged effects:
How long do the effects of marketing actions on sales last? While the question
is straightforward, considerable challenges arise when building the appropriate model to answer it. The most important questions are:

- How do we ensure that the model distinguishes between lagged marketing and lagged sales effects?
- What is the best data interval to use in measuring marketing effects? If
  the grid is too coarse (e.g., annual data), we may not pick up the
  dynamics of the marketing system. If the grid is too fine, we may be lost
  in irrelevant data fluctuations.
- Are the results of a macromodel consistent with those of a micromodel?
  If not, which one should the modeler believe?
- Suppose we only have macrodata but wish to examine a microresponse
  model; can we infer microbehavior from macrodata?

These questions may be clustered in two groups: (1) dynamic model specification, and (2) data interval analysis. They have traditionally been addressed
with econometric techniques. We briefly review this literature and then discuss
a more general approach based on combined econometric and time series
(ETS) techniques.

Specifying Marketing Dynamics

It is often possible to use econometric methods to distinguish between nested rival models, i.e., one model is a special case of the other. For example, Weiss and Windal (1980) set up a generalized test for deciding whether sales are driven by lagged marketing versus lagged sales, or by autoregressive effects, or by both. They start with a general dynamic response model:

$$Q_t = \beta_0 + \frac{\beta_1}{1 - \lambda L} A_t + \frac{1}{1 - \rho L} \varepsilon_t, \qquad (7.7)$$

where

β_1 = short-term effect of advertising,

λ = advertising carryover effect,

ρ = autoregressive effect.

The various combinations of presence and absence of advertising carryover and sales inertia effects allow for a number of dynamic marketing models to be nested in this overall model:

$\lambda = 0$ and $\rho = 0$:   current-effects model,

$\lambda = 0$ and $\rho \neq 0$:   autoregressive current-effects model,

$\lambda > 0$ and $\rho = 0$:   Koyck model,

$\lambda = \rho > 0$:   partial adjustment model.

Weiss and Windal proposed to estimate the various postulated models by maximum likelihood, which involves nonlinear least squares. Then they performed a series of pairwise hypothesis tests by imposing restrictions on one or more key parameters. For example, the current-effects model was tested against the Koyck model by imposing the restriction $\lambda = 0$ on the latter. The common likelihood ratio statistic was used to reach a verdict in each case.

This method is appropriate when the rivalry dynamic model specifications are conveniently nested. There are, however, three practical problems with this approach: (1) all the candidate models have to be estimated separately, which is cumbersome, (2) the tests are pairwise, so it is possible that more than one "winner" emerges, which causes ambiguity for the model builder, and (3) most importantly, the "supermodel" (7.7) may not be sufficiently general. More recent techniques involving time series analysis avoid these problems and open new avenues for specifying marketing dynamics.

Data Interval Analysis

ETS models are built on real-world data, so the model builder seldom has the chance to select a time interval for analysis. Data or time intervals are typically set by accounting or business practice, reflecting the relevant decision interval but not necessarily the best market response interval. Therefore, we must be extremely cautious in making inferences about marketing dynamics from such data.

What constitutes a reasonable data interval? There seems to be an agreement that shorter intervals are better than longer ones. On the other hand, few would attempt to build a marketing model on the minute-by-minute sales transactions offered by scanner equipment. One popular rule is that the data interval should match the purchase cycle of the product (e.g., weekly grocery purchases), although that could not apply to consumer and industrial durables. In most cases, though, the model builder simply must accept the data interval as given and make the best possible use of it.

A well-known survey of the advertising response literature introduced the concept of data interval bias, i.e., that some statistically sound results may be conceptually false because of a wrong (often too long) time interval (Clarke 1976). For example, many advertising response models estimated on annual data reveal advertising carryover effects on sales that are 20 to 50 times as long as those estimated on monthly series. That finding has led to some econometric attempts at recovering microparameters when only macrodata are available. These efforts are summarized in table 7–1. Microparameter recovery procedures start by assuming an underlying microresponse (e.g., a Koyck) model. Next, the shape of the implied macroresponse model is derived, which typically requires an approximation in order to make the function estimable. Finally, the macrofunction's ability to recover microparameters is investigated, usually with simulation methods.

The literature reviewed in table 7–1 presents varied results. For example, Bass and Leone (1983) showed that with increasing aggregation, the short-term response parameter increases and the carryover parameter decreases for Koyck or partial adjustment models. On the other hand, simulation efforts by Weiss, Weinberg, and Windal (1983) failed to uncover a relation between aggregation level (m) and the carryover parameter, λ. The simulation work of Vanhonacker (1983; 1984) suggests that empirical problems in parameter recovery occur for either the ACE or the partial adjustment model. More recent efforts, for example, by Kanetkar, Weinberg, and Weiss (1986a; 1986b), have improved the recovery procedures, but the performance of these methods on actual marketing data rather than simulated data remains unexplored.

Table 7-1. Temporal Aggregation Research in Discrete-Time Marketing
Models

Authors	Micromodel	Contribution	Test
Clarke (1976)	Koyck	λ depends on data interval	Meta-analysis
Windal and Weiss (1980)	ACE	Macro estimation of microparameters	Data
Sasieni (1982)	Koyck or partial adjustment	Derives macroresponse model when advertising is white noise	N/A
Weinberg and Weiss (1982)	Koyck	Estimate of λ appears independent of data interval	Meta-analysis
Bass and Leone (1983)	Koyck or partial adjustment	Recovers bimonthly parameters from annual data	Data
Vanhonacker (1983)	Partial adjustment	Shows specification problems with aggregation	Simulation
Weiss, Weinberg, and Windal (1983)	Partial adjustment	Shows λ independent of m, improves on Bass-Leone method	Simulation
Vanhonacker (1984)	ACE	Shows empirical problems with aggregation methods	Simulation
Russell (1988)	Koyck	Marketing decision behavior affects shape of distributed lag function	Simulation
Kanetkar, Weinberg, and Weiss (1986a)	Koyck or partial adjustment	Extends Weiss-Weinberg-Windal	Simulation
Kanetkar, Weinberg, and Weiss (1986b)	ACE	Improvement of Windal-Weiss method	Simulation
Bass and Leone (1986)	Koyck or partial adjustment	Compares Bass-Leone and Weiss-Weinberg-Windal	Simulation

N/A = not applicable.

A major assumption of the work on data aggregation bias is that the microprocess is known. In practice, however, it is difficult to state with confidence that an ACE or a Koyck advertising response pattern occurs at any level of aggregation. This is a good example of level 1 a priori knowledge: There is little disagreement about the existence of an advertising-to-sales effect, but its duration is essentially unknown. In the following sections, we show how ARMA and transfer function analysis may be used to address the issues of advertising duration and data aggregation, and we discuss continuous-time models as an alternative approach.

The ETS Approach

ETS modeling provides a unifying framework for studying marketing dynamics. This is different from the current research tradition, which has focused on single issues such as data interval bias and recovering microparameters from macroparameters. We start with the overall model and then discuss the specifics.

Without loss of generality, we use a marketing model that is linear in the variables and consists of one equation. Nonlinearities can be incorporated a priori by data transformation, and multiple-equation models would not change the substance of our argument.

The general dynamic marketing model can be written in transfer function form. We use one marketing input variable for simplicity:

$$y_t = c + \frac{\omega(L)}{\delta(L)} L^b x_t + \frac{\Theta(L)}{\Phi(L)} \alpha_t, \tag{7.8}$$

where y is market performance (say, sales) at time t, x is marketing activity (say, advertising), and α_t is a white noise disturbance term. The notation for the transfer function parameters is as in chapter 4, and the time series y_t and x_t may have been transformed to stationarity. This model has the following appealing properties:

- If marketing is absent, or if it has zero effectiveness, sales follow a time path dictated by the ARMA(p, q) model:

$$\Phi(L)y_t = c' + \Theta(L)\alpha_t. \tag{7.9}$$

- Direct measurable effects of marketing are modeled by $\omega(L)$. Notice that the exact lag length is kept implicit, to allow maximum flexibility of the model.

- Smooth decay or carryover patterns such as those often hypothesized to exist in advertising are modeled via $\delta(L)$.
- Possible delays in market reaction are incorporated by the delay parameter b.

A number of well-known marketing hypotheses are special cases of the general marketing dynamics model, a fact that has been recognized by Moriarty (1985a).

The Autoregressive Current-Effects (ACE) Model. As explained earlier for the case of advertising, many marketing actions have significant sales effects only in the period of expenditure (i.e., current effects). For example, temporary and unanticipated price reductions may increase sales only when they are offered. Or competitive reaction to a marketing campaign may quickly erode the marketer's competitive edge. At the same time, however, sales may follow an autoregressive process, reflecting, for example, the influence of brand loyalty and stable interpurchase times. The combination of these two factors may produce the ACE model:

$$y_t = c + \omega_0 x_t + \frac{1}{1 - \rho L} \alpha_t, \tag{7.10}$$

which is a transfer function ($r = 0$, $s = 0$, $b = 0$) with added noise ($p = 1$, $q = 0$). If an ACE model does in fact underlie the data, it will be difficult to detect it with anything other than careful time series techniques. For example, the regression form of the model is

$$y_t = c(1 - \rho) + \rho y_{t-1} + \omega_0 x_t - \omega_0 \rho x_{t-1} + \alpha_t, \tag{7.11}$$

which includes, among others, a spurious lagged effect of marketing on sales. Thus, in general, we need transfer function specification techniques outlined in chapter 4 to discover an ACE process in the data.

Some further insights can be gained by examining the ARMA process on sales implied by an ACE model. For example, if marketing expenditures are white noise around their mean $\bar{x}$, the time series of sales will be AR(1). If marketing efforts are error-correcting, for example MA(1), sales follow at most an ARMA(1, 1) process. These implications add to the identifiability of an ACE model.

The Koyck Model. We have already introduced this popular model, which assumes geometrically declining marketing effects on sales over time plus a white noise error term:

$$y_t = c + \omega_0 x_t + \omega_1 x_{t-1} + \omega_2 x_{t-2} + \cdots + \alpha_t, \tag{7.12}$$

where

$$\omega_k = \phi \omega_{k-1}, \quad 0 < \phi < 1.$$

The Koyck hypothesis is appealing because of the presumed link between marketing effectiveness and consumer memory decay. For example, it seems intuitive that consumers' recall of an advertising campaign peaks immediately and then decays gradually. Under this assumption, the finite form of the model is

$$(1 - \phi L)y_t = c(1 - \phi) + \omega_0 x_t + (1 - \phi L)\alpha_t, \qquad (7.13)$$

or, in transfer function form,

$$y_t = c + \frac{\omega_0}{1 - \phi L} x_t + \alpha_t. \qquad (7.14)$$

Thus identification of a Koyck model would reveal a transfer function ($r = 1$, $s = 0$, $b = 0$) with no added noise parameters. This strict condition has unfortunately been ignored in the literature: usually the mere presence of $\phi > 0$ is used as sufficient evidence of a Koyck response process. It is our speculation that many of the published Koyck models would not survive a careful time series test, especially if the ARMA behavior of the marketing series were taken into consideration.

The ARMA behavior of sales under a Koyck model can again be derived by substituting the ARMA(p, q) of marketing efforts and rearranging terms. The general conclusion is that sales are at most ARMA($p + 1, \max(q, p + 1)$). That pattern is quite different from the one implied by the ACE model.

In conclusion, since marketing dynamics are difficult to model a priori, we propose to use a general dynamic marketing model in which the parameters are implicit functions of the lag operator. For single-equation models, this produces a transfer function that can be parameterized using the methods proposed in chapter 4. A key advantage to this approach is that well-known marketing hypotheses such as current effects or Koyck schemes appear as special cases, i.e., their existence can be inferred or tested by the data. Table 7–2 lists some examples of dynamic marketing models from the recent literature.

Time Aggregation Theory

Consider two stationary series for sales (y_t) and a marketing variable (x_t). We examine the effects of temporally aggregating these variables, first on their individual ARMA behavior, then on the transfer function model connecting the two.

Table 7-2. Examples of Transfer Function Marketing Models

Helmer and Johansson (1977)	Lydia Pinkham Vegetable Compound (annual)	$$\Delta Q_t = \frac{0.52}{1 - 0.36L}\Delta A_t + \frac{1}{1 - 0.25L}\alpha_t$$
Hanssens (1980a)	Lydia Pinkham Vegetable Compound (monthly)	$$\Delta^{12}Q_t = \frac{0.37}{1 - 0.55L}\Delta^{12}A_t + (1 + 0.37L^3)\alpha_{1t}$$ $$\Delta^{12}A_t = 0.42L^{12}\Delta^{12}Q_t + (1 - 0.57L^{12})\alpha_{2t}$$
Bass and Pilon (1980)	Catsup (monthly)	$$M_t = 0.66 + \frac{-0.49 + 0.24L}{1 - 0.21L}P_t + \frac{1}{1 - 0.21L}\alpha_t$$
Aaker, Carman, and Jacobson (1982)	Corn flakes (monthly)	$$Q_t = 2{,}910 + \frac{0.41L^4}{1 - 0.66L^{12}}A_t + \frac{1 + 0.17L - 0.34L}{1 - 0.66L^{12}}\alpha_t$$
Leone (1983)	Grocery product (bimonthly)[a]	$$S_t = \frac{0.14 + 0.10L}{1 - 0.82L}A_t + \frac{1}{1 - 0.82L}\alpha_t$$
Krishnamurthi, Narayan, and Raj (1986)	Frequently purchased product (weekly)[b]	$$QE_t - QC_t = 1{,}186A_t + \frac{1}{1 + 0.52L^2}\alpha_t$$

a. One of several reported models.
b. Experimental setting, where QE = experimental sales, QC = control sales.

If the sales data are collected at, say, a quarterly level, we can write the annual series Y_t as

$$Y_t = y_t + y_{t-1} + y_{t-2} + y_{t-3}, \qquad (7.15a)$$

However, the aggregated series is nonoverlapping, so in examining its behavior we are not using the usual time index $t, t - 1, t - 2, \dots$ but the index t, $t - 4, t - 8, \dots$. This is an important feature in aggregation analysis.

Now, the aggregation can also be written as

$$Y_t = y_t + Ly_t + L^2y_t + L^3y_t, \qquad (7.15b)$$

or

$$Y_t = (1 + L + L^2 + L^3)y_t, \qquad (7.15c)$$

or

$$Y_t = \frac{1 - L^4}{1 - L} y_t. \qquad (7.15d)$$

This equation makes a tight link between microdata and macrodata in such a way that the time series behavior of one can be related to that of the other. We do so first for the univariate case and then for the transfer function.

Univariate Aggregation. Suppose y_t follows an AR(1) process:

$$(1 - \phi L)y_t = \alpha_t, \qquad (7.16)$$

where t is measured at quarterly intervals. Then we can infer the annual time series behavior of y_t by applying the aggregation transformation for

$$(1 - \phi L)\frac{1 - L}{1 - L^4} Y_t = \alpha_t, \qquad (7.17)$$

or

$$Y_t = (1 - \phi L)^{-1}\frac{1 - L^4}{1 - L}\alpha_t. \qquad (7.18)$$

Now multiply both sides by $(1 - \phi^4 L^4)$:

$$(1 - \phi^4 L^4)Y_t = \frac{1 - \phi^4 L^4}{1 - \phi L}\frac{1 - L^4}{1 - L}\alpha_t. \qquad (7.19)$$

This expression reveals an ARMA process on the index set $t, t - 4, t - 8, \dots$. The left-hand side is an AR(1) with parameter ϕ^4. The right-hand side is a moving average of order $(2m - 2)$, or 6 in this case. But since we can only count every mth observation, the aggregate moving-average process is of order 1 at most.

In conclusion, when an AR(1) process is aggregated m times, the macro-model may be ARMA(1, 1), which is certainly not an obvious result. Depending on the aggregation level m, the AR parameter may or may not be significant. For example, a monthly AR(1) parameter of 0.8 would be consistent with an annual parameter of $0.8^{12} \simeq 0.07$, which is practically zero.

The generalization of aggregating a univariate model over m data intervals is as follows (e.g., Amemiya and Wu 1972; Cogger 1981): An ARMA(p, q) process on the microinterval leads to an ARMA(p, q') process on the macro-interval, where q' is the greatest integer less than or equal to $\{(p + 1)(m - 1) + q\}/m$. For large m, this converges to ARMA(p, p) if $q < p + 1$ and to ARMA($p, p + 1$) if $q \geq p + 1$.

These results are useful for marketing models that focus on the time patterns of key marketing constructs. For example, the linear learning model implies an AR(1) model on the purchase probabilities of a certain brand:

$$p_t = \lambda p_{t-1} + \alpha_t. \tag{7.20}$$

Suppose that a customer or a market segment behaves as in the linear learning model on a daily basis. However, the model builder has only weekly sales or market share observations available. Then, aggregation theory would reveal the relation

$$(1 - \lambda^7)p_t = (1 - \theta L)\alpha'_t, \tag{7.21}$$

where p'_t is weekly purchase probability, and α'_t is a new white noise term defined over the index set $(t - 7)$. If the linear learning parameter is 0.5, then the weekly ARMA model may well be white noise, or MA(1). In other words, weekly aggregation is masking the true process, and the researcher should actually infer a microlinear learning model from this seemingly zero-order or error-correcting macromodel.

Transfer Function Aggregation. The effects of time aggregation are considerably more important to marketing modelers when actual cause-and-effect models such as transfer functions are involved. For example, if advertising influences sales over a two-month period, what would be the implied lagged effects on quarterly data or on annual data? Since the literature has reported conflicting empirical results, some formal insights from aggregation theory are in order.

Time aggregation of the simple dynamic relation

$$y_t = v(L)x_t + \varepsilon_t, \tag{7.22}$$

has four essential aspects:

1. The shape of the aggregate model

$$Y_t = V(L)X_t + E_t, \qquad (7.23)$$

   depends on the time series structure of the input variable x_t.
2. Unless x_t is white noise, the aggregate model may well exhibit a feedback relation between Y and X. What started out as a single equation connecting sales and advertising may become a system of equations with both sales and advertising endogenous.
3. The higher the aggregation, the more the effects between Y and X become contemporaneous.
4. Time aggregation always results in information loss, i.e., the signal-to-noise ratio decreases.

The first two properties are seldom recognized in the marketing literature, notable exceptions being the work by Sasieni (1982) and Russell (1988). In particular, the fact that the micro time series pattern of advertising affects the distributed lag function between aggregated sales and advertising is very important. Formally, it is explained by the fact that the cross-covariance function between Y and X contains lagged as well as lead terms. Intuitively, let us represent time aggregation schematically as follows (using $m = 3$):

$$Y_T = y_t + y_{t-1} + y_{t-2}, \qquad (7.24a)$$

$$X_T = x_t + x_{t-1} + x_{t-2}. \qquad (7.24b)$$

If the micromodel is contemporaneous and x is highly autocorrelated, then the macromodel way well contain lags between Y and X in both directions:

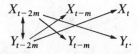

In conclusion, the time aggregation problem in multiple time series settings such as the sales-advertising relation cannot be properly investigated without examining the behavior of the input series, e.g., advertising. The major marketing implication is that *advertising decision rules themselves will affect the dynamic shape of the sales response function.*

Adapting an example by Tiao and Wei (1976), suppose that quarterly advertising effects sales only in the subsequent quarter,

$$q_t = \beta_0 + \beta_1 a_{t-1} + \alpha_t, \qquad (7.25)$$

where α_t is white noise. Assume further that quarterly advertising is spent in a first-order autoregressive pattern,

$$a_t = \rho a_{t-1} + \alpha'_t. \tag{7.26}$$

Then the following distributed leads and lags would be obtained on annual data:

ρ	Lead 3	Lead 2	Lead 1	Current	Lag 1	Lag 2	Lag 3
$-.5$	.001	.011	.153	.360	.442	.030	.002
0	0	0	0	.667	.333	0	0
.5	$-.003$	.015	$-.091$	.767	.363	$-.060$	.010
.9	$-.007$	.026	$-.118$	.787	.378	$-.083$	.018

It can be seen that lead effects (i.e., sales leading advertising) are absent only when the quarterly advertising is white noise ($\rho = 0$). Furthermore, the contemporaneous advertising-to-sales effect dominates the annual relation unless $\rho < 0$. Assessing the duration effects of advertising on sales for annual data, even when a very simple quarterly relation holds, is difficult and, in fact, unlikely to be successful in most cases.

Sasieni (1982) and Russell (1988) shed some further light on time aggregation in marketing when the microresponse model is either Koyck or partial adjustment:

$$q_t = \lambda q_{t-1} + \beta a_t + \varepsilon_t. \tag{7.27}$$

Upon aggregation over m periods, Sasieni derives the macromodel when the advertising series a_t is white noise:

$$Q_t = \lambda^m Q_{t-1} + \beta' A_t + \beta'' A_{t-1} + E_t. \tag{7.28}$$

As is to be expected from transfer function aggregation theory, the structure of the macromodel is different from that of the micromodel. In particular, a lagged advertising term appears in the equation. Sasieni examines the consequences of using a simple Koyck model on the macrodata. If the advertising expenditures are white noise, the misspecified macromodel would still provide a reasonable estimate of the *magnitude* of advertising effect, but the *duration* would be grossly overstated. This is an elegant theoretical explanation for Clarke's (1976) empirical findings, subject only to the white noise assumption in the advertising series.

Russell (1988) takes these results one step further. He posits that meaningful statistical inference of dynamic sales response necessitates two forms of a priori knowledge: the shape of the microresponse function, and the firm's decision behavior with respect to allocating advertising over microperiods. Simulation evidence based on a micro Koyck model shows that the advertising spending pattern has a strong effect on the shape of the macro distributed lag function. The proposed aggregation methods in table 7–1 typically assume a uniform advertising spending pattern. Their performance quickly deteriorates when this assumption is violated, for example when the firm spends heavily in the earlier or the later parts of the macroperiod.

Continuous-Time Approach

A different approach to time aggregation is offered by continuous-time modeling (Blattberg and Jeuland 1981b; Rao 1986). It offers the conceptual advantage that the underlying sales response model can be developed regardless of the microdata interval.

The model by Blattberg and Jeuland (1981b) is based on two behavioral assumptions: (1) the population is homogeneous in that each consumer has a constant probability of being exposed to an ad, and (2) the ad effectiveness decays exponentially due to consumer forgetting. Aggregating this process across consumers and across time reveals a dynamic sales response function where the advertising carryover effect depends on present and past levels of advertising. This finding is consistent with our earlier observation that advertising carryover depends on the advertising spending pattern. The commonly used aggregate-level Koyck model ignores this and is shown to lead to false interpretations of advertising duration.

Rao (1986) developed a continuous-time version of the well-known Nerlove-Arrow (1962) model of advertising response. This model postulates that sales depend on advertising goodwill and that advertising goodwill decays over time but increases with concurrent advertising efforts. The estimating equation, that is, the equivalent model for discrete data, is similar to Sasieni's (1982) macroresponse model in that it includes current and lagged advertising plus lagged sales. Rao proves that the model is equivalent to Blattberg and Jeuland's when the advertising-reach parameter goes to zero.

Continuous-time models are theoretically appealing and deserve further attention in marketing research. They can be used for operationalizing behavioral theories of individual advertising response without the need for specifying a "true" microinterval. They are, however, limited in applicability to ETS modeling because continuous time cannot be measured in empirical applications. If the postulated theoretical response model is simple, however, an estimating equation on discrete time data can usually be derived.

Summary

Marketing modelers have paid increasing attention to the subject of marketing dynamics over the years. These efforts have focused on the lagged relations between sales and marketing pulse actions such as advertising and price promotions. In the case of advertising, there is some agreement that lagged effects are several months in length. For price promotions, there seems to be either a strict zero-order effect or a consumer tendency to stockpile, which creates a short negative lag structure.

The major challenges to correct dynamic model building are methodological in nature. There is evidence that the data interval has an effect on the lag structures obtained. There are solutions to this problem, but they assume that the dynamic nature of the process relating sales and marketing on microdata is known (level 2 prior knowledge). However, this is usually not the case, and thus we must apply level 1 techniques to study the problem. It is possible to specify an overall marketing dynamics model as a transfer function that has the more popular response models as special cases. We can also use time series techniques to examine the macromodel behavior of any empirically obtained micromodel. Applying time aggregation techniques to this model reveals that the time series structure of the input series (the marketing effort) has a major effect on the dynamic shape of the macroresponse function. In fact, not much can be inferred from macrodata unless the marketing efforts are white noise, which is rare.

The methodological issues surrounding distributed lag models cast a new light on this area of marketing modeling. From an academic perspective, there is a clear need for further work in the development of realistic microresponse models whose macroimplications may be studied analytically. Such work could benefit from the continuous-time approach but also from a better use of empirical findings in consumer psychology (see, for example, the insightful review of carryover effects in advertising communication by Sawyer and Ward (1979)). From a marketing planning perspective, we must choose a reasonable data interval and develop the best possible dynamic models, for example, using transfer function analysis. These models will be robust as long as no major inferences are made at a different time interval and the marketing spending pattern does not change significantly. Changes in spending patterns can, of course, be readily assessed using univariate time series analysis.

It is also important to extend the concept of marketing dynamics to include lead effects in addition to lagged effects. When consumers or competitors are smart and opportunistic, they may anticipate marketing actions and respond before the action takes place. The development of realistic lead/lag models is another important area for future research.

Notes

1. Price dynamics are often closely related to cost dynamics, and there is, of course, a large literature on the empirical estimation of learning curves.

8 IMPROVING MARKETING DECISIONS

Response models can be used to improve organizational effectiveness through a process involving three steps: (1) intervention, (2) implementation, and (3) improvement (Schultz and Henry 1981). Intervention takes place when management recognizes a need for change in the way decisions are made and activity to meet that need is initiated. One example would be the development of a marketing decision model to aid in planning and forecasting. If the resulting model actually changes the way decisions are made, we can think of the model as having been implemented. If, in addition, the model improves the decision process, we would call this implemented model successful. Successful implementation is the goal of marketing science.

Issues concerning the implementation of marketing models are discussed in chapter 10. This chapter explores what is meant by improvement in decision making and how that improvement can be obtained: we first look at what managers do in making decisions and then at what they can or want to do.

Decision Rules

Decision rules are ways that managers codify experience, data, and, to a lesser extent, marketing science in their decision making. They use decision rules because the world in which they operate is complex and dynamic, and if every management problem were faced anew, it would severely tax their cognitive abilities. In both a behavioral and normative sense, managers rely on experience and reasoning to do their work.

Experience

Experience is a manager's ability to recognize patterns. A seasoned marketing manager who has seen different competitive responses time and time again is far more able than an inexperienced manager to recognize and interpret a new competitive reaction. Experience is not, however, merely a function of time. Managers exposed to a variety of patterns are better prepared to recognize any one pattern:

> In any field in which we have gained considerable experience, we have acquired a large number of "friends"—a large number of stimuli that we can recognize immediately. We can sort the stimulus in whatever sorting net performs this function in this brain (the physiology of it is not understood), and discriminate it from all other stimuli we might encounter. (Simon 1983, p. 26)[1]

This is why five years of experience can be very useful if they are five years of different experiences, or not so useful if they are five years of the same experience.

Simon goes on to link intuition with recognition, noting Poincaré's dictum that inspiration comes only to the prepared mind. World-class creative performance, it seems, requires about ten years of intensive learning and practice. Although managers are not usually considered creative in the same way as chess masters, composers, painters, and mathematicians (where empirical data support the ten-year rule), the most effective managers do seem to exhibit the kind of inspiration that only comes to the prepared, or practiced, mind.

This is the sense in which management is an art, and this is the undeniable value of experience. Some management experience is formalized in decision rules, or heuristics (cf. Newell and Simon 1972). In marketing, percent-of-sales formulas for advertising, constant markup schemes for pricing, and workload equalization plans for salespeople are all examples of decision rules designed to embody experience. The most complete discussion of descriptive models of marketing management is found in Hulbert (1981).[2]

Reasoning

But in a complex and dynamic world, how do managers make rational decisions that go beyond experience? "We live in what might be called a nearly empty world—one in which there are millions of variables that in principle could affect each other but most of the time don't." (Simon 1983, p. 20) Ehrenberg (1969) has long made the same point in marketing: of many things that could matter, only a few do.

Thus, managers- make choices using what is called *bounded rationality* (March and Simon 1958). The environment is factored into separate problems, emotion focuses us on the most important ones, we search for "good alternatives, or for improvements in alternatives that we already know," and we develop a "capability for acquiring facts about the environment in which we find ourselves, and a modest capability for drawing inferences from these facts." (Simon 1983, p. 22) In marketing we augment our capability for acquiring facts with marketing research. And we augment our capability for drawing inferences with statistical models (such as ETS) and other decision aids.

Simon's argument is compelling: "In a world that is nearly empty, in which not everything is closely connected with everything else, in which problems can be decomposed into their components—in such a world, the kind of rationality I've been describing gets us by." (pp. 22–23)

Models

To go beyond "getting by," or what Simon himself has described as "satisficing" (March and Simon 1958), we often turn to management science models designed to improve decisions by replacing the descriptive decision rules in use with new, normative decision rules. The models work to do this by (1) simplifying the decision situation, (2) representing the decision situation, (3) drawing inferences from facts, (4) maximizing a utility function, and (5) making the overall decision process more consistent and less biased.

Models by definition are simplifications and representations, and we have seen that simplification alone is an important element of the way managers cope with complex and dynamic environments. Models just do this in a formal way—assumptions and premises are laid out for everyone to see.

The *representativeness* of a model, particularly the kind of model that is the subject matter of this book, is very important.[3] The model must be a good representation of the decision situation. A response model that will be used for planning and forecasting must adequately represent the mechanism generating sales. The mere fact that a model represents the situation in a formal manner goes a step beyond implicit representations of reality in a manager's mind.

Models also aid managers in improving inference. Rather than only seeing heuristics as efforts to overcome cognitive limitations of managers (cf.

Kahneman, Slovic, and Tversky 1982), we can view decision rules as adaptive mechanisms for dealing with difficult management problems (Hogarth 1981; Einhorn and Hogarth 1981), particularly decision rules stemming from the application of decision aids (Hogarth 1980).[4]

One of the most significant ways in which models can go beyond intuition is by utilizing the powerful concepts of decision theory to maximize a utility function across a set of alternatives. Expected utility theory (von Neumann and Morgenstern 1947; Savage 1954; Luce and Raiffa 1957; Raiffa and Schlaiffer 1961; Fishburn 1970; Keeney and Raiffa 1976) offers a way for managers to incorporate beliefs (probabilities) and preferences (utilities) into a model that suggests how to make a "best" choice. Howard (1988) discusses how the advantages of decision analysis might be extended to almost everyone interested in using it.

Finally, the use of models can strengthen decision making by helping managers to be more consistent and less biased and also by helping to make the decision *process* more consistent and less biased. A good deal of empirical evidence indicates the superiority of models over the judgments of individual managers in terms of consistency and bias (cf. Hogarth and Makridakis 1981). But even if this were not the case, the overall decision process could be improved by using models to make it more invariant to personalities.[5]

Notice that these particular characteristics of models are close to what managers do or want to do. It turns out that this will be very important when considering if managers will actually use a model as a decision aid (see chapter 10).

Normative Marketing Models

A marketing manager in making a decision must choose among two or more alternatives. This manager would like to select the alternative that will best achieve corporate objectives. What would be helpful is a model that tells a manager what he or she *should* do. We call such a model a *normative model*. Normative models can be classified in various ways. One classification scheme by Zoltners (1981) is shown in figure 8–1.

The first distinction in this classification scheme is between theoretical models and decision models. A theoretical model is built around a mathematical expression for the sales response function, whereas a decision model is built around an empirical expression for the sales response function. The solution of a theoretical model provides a generalizable answer that applies across markets, while the solution of a decision model provides guidance only in the specific market studied.

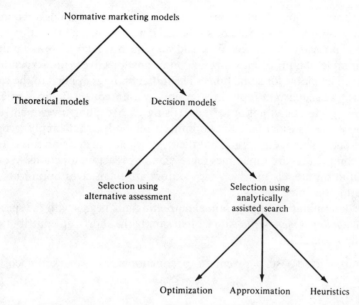

Figure 8–1. A Classification Scheme for Normative Marketing Models. *Source*:
Zoltners (1981, p. 59).

Theoretical Models

Theoretical models identify the conditions under which a single- or multi-
attribute objective function is optimized. If the theoretical conditions can be
evaluated empirically, these results can be used to determine whether or not
a brand is operating at, or near, an optimal point. For example, if profit is
maximized where marginal revenue equals marginal cost, a firm would have
some idea whether it was meeting this *condition* for optimal pricing. Optimality conditions do not tell a firm what adjustments it needs to make in its
marketing mix if it is not currently operating optimally. When marginal
revenue does not equal marginal cost, a firm does not know what price it
should charge. Fortunately, knowledge of optimality conditions frequently
can be used to better understand the way in which a firm can reach an optimal
point in its operations. This usually requires the specification of a concrete
sales response function. The actual optimal values for marketing instruments
in any particular situation will depend on empirical parameter values.

Theoretical models are usually developed by making simplifying assumptions. As a start, preliminary results would be easier to obtain if we ignored

competitors. We might make the assumption that a brand holds a monopoly. Similarly, our problem would be simplified if we assumed a marketing instrument had no lead or lag effects. We could subsequently relax these assumptions. For example, the profit-maximizing conditions for advertising expenditures have been available for some time.[6] The initial findings applied to the case of advertising as a current input in a monopoly. Subsequent findings extended the findings to the situation of advertising as a capital investment in an oligopoly. We consider here only optimization models that simply recognize the presence of competitors and not their explicit actual decision rules. Activities of competitors are sometimes represented by reaction functions. We defer discussion on models in which competitors are themselves optimizers until the section on game theory.

The determination of the optimal marketing mix begins with the specification of a *policy preference function*, often simply the short-run contribution to profit and overhead:

profit − fixed costs = revenue − production costs − marketing costs

$$= PQ - CQ - g(\mathbf{X}), \tag{8.1}$$

where

$\mathbf{X}$ = marketing control variables other than price,

$Q = f(P, \mathbf{X}, \mathbf{EV})$, in which $\mathbf{EV}$ = environmental variables, and

$C = h(Q, E, \mathbf{X})$, in which E = accumulated experience (volume).

If the planning horizon is more than one period, attention turns to the long-run contribution, which is usually discounted to yield a present value. Although we focus on maximizing one of these contribution functions, we recognize that some firms have other objectives. Japanese firms often seek to maximize the present value of sales subject to a minimum level of the present valued profit (Tsurumi and Tsurumi 1971). Firms launching new products usually price for profit maximization subject to distribution, sales, or market share targets (Parsons 1974; Saghafi 1988). Established brands often seek to maintain stable sales or market share levels. Theoretical decision models were first developed for pricing.

Pricing.   When price is the only factor affecting unit sales, and it only affects current unit sales, then the only other phenomenon influencing performance is the nature of the production unit cost function. If unit production costs are fixed, only the current information is relevant and a static pricing policy can be adopted. However, if experience results in unit production costs declining with accumulated volume or if market demand is time dependent, then a dynamic pricing policy is needed to obtain strategic implications. Price differs from other marketing variables in that the cost of a price reduction manifests itself through a reduction in gross margin.

Static Pricing. If unit production costs are fixed, then the optimal price, expressed in terms of the price elasticity, is

$$P^* = \frac{\varepsilon_P}{(\varepsilon_P + 1)} C. \tag{8.2}$$

The firm combines information on its price elasticity obtained from estimating the sales response function with information on its costs obtained from accounting to determine the most profitable price for its product. It follows (Stigler 1952, p. 38) that the optimal markup on cost is

$$MUC^* = -\frac{1}{(\varepsilon_P + 1)}, \tag{8.3a}$$

and the optimal markup on selling price is

$$MUSP^* = -\frac{1}{\varepsilon_P}. \tag{8.3b}$$

An optimal markup is an administratively convenient way for a retailer to delegate future pricing decisions to its various outlets.

Dynamic Pricing Policy. One way to find an optimal pricing policy over time is *optimal control theory* (Kamien and Schwartz 1981). A dynamic market mechanism is modeled using either differential or difference equations. A policy preference function is optimized subject to the model by applying Pontryagin's maximum principle via optimal control theory.

Before applying Pontryagin's maximum principle to pricing, we discuss it in general because we want to use it for setting dynamic advertising policy as well as dynamic pricing policy. A simple version of the optimization problem involves maximizing a measure of performance, $g[Q(t), X(t), t]$, over the planning horizon, T, subject to a system of equations that describes the *state* of the system at any time t, $Q(t)$, given the value of the *control* function, $X(t)$, and the initial state of the system, $Q(0)$:

$$\max_{X(t)} \int_0^T g[Q(t), X(t), t] dt \tag{8.4a}$$

subject to

$$\frac{dQ(t)}{dt} = f[Q(t), X(t), t], \qquad 0 \le t \le T, \quad Q(0) \text{ known}, \quad Q(T) \text{ free}. \quad (8.4b)$$

We have shown the continuous-time version; there is also a discrete-time analog. The problem can be solved by introducing time-varying versions of Lagrangian multipliers, $\gamma(t)$. The augmented performance measure can be expressed as

$$g[Q(t), X(t), t] + \gamma(t)\left(f[Q(t), X(t), t] - \frac{dQ(t)}{dt} \right), \qquad (8.5)$$

where $\gamma(t)$ is the marginal valuation of the associated state variable at time t.

When there are no constraints on either the control or state variables, the necessary conditions for an optimum are the *optimality equation*

$$\frac{\partial}{\partial X} g[Q(t), X(t), t] + \gamma(t)\frac{\partial}{\partial X} f[Q(t), X(t), t] = 0, \qquad (8.6)$$

the *multiplier (or adjoint) equation*

$$\frac{d\gamma(t)}{dt} = -\left(\frac{\partial}{\partial Q} g[Q(t), X(t), t] + \gamma(t)\frac{\partial}{\partial Q} f[Q(t), X(t), t] \right), \qquad \gamma(T) = 0, \quad (8.7)$$

and the *state equation* (8.4b). Since $Q(T)$ is free, the transversality condition $\gamma(T) = 0$ is required. These equations can be generated using the Hamiltonian function:

$$H[Q(t), X(t), \gamma, t] = g[Q(t), X(t), t] + \gamma(t)f[Q(t), X(t), t], \qquad (8.8)$$

and the rules

$$\frac{\partial H}{\partial X} = 0, \qquad (8.9a)$$

$$-\frac{\partial H}{\partial Q} = \frac{d\gamma(t)}{dt}, \qquad (8.9b)$$

$$\frac{\partial H}{\partial \gamma} = \frac{dQ(t)}{dt}. \qquad (8.9c)$$

The integral payoff formulation of performance represented by (8.4) is said to be of the *Lagrange type*. There are alternative formulations that may be equivalent, and we must recognize this to be able to read the optimal control literature. One alternative formulation, the *Mayer type*, involves stating the problem in terms of a terminal payoff. Another alternative formulation, the *Bolza type*, posits both an integral and terminal value term.

Usually, in marketing, the control variables are constrained. Marketing variables such as price and advertising are non-negative. The admissible control set is of the form

$$X_o \leq X \leq X^o, \tag{8.10}$$

and it is now necessary to focus on the Lagrangian formulation:

$$H(Q, X, \gamma, t) + \zeta_1(X^o - X) + \zeta_2(X - X_o). \tag{8.11}$$

Only one of the original rules changes; (8.9a) becomes

$$\frac{\partial H}{\partial X} - \zeta_1 + \zeta_2 = 0. \tag{8.12}$$

And, of course, there are the new constraints

$$\zeta_1(X^o - X) = 0 \quad \text{and} \quad \zeta_2(X - X_o) = 0. \tag{8.13}$$

In addition to constraints on the control variables, there may be constraints on the state variables. For instance, unit sales is usually non-negative. This can add a major increase in complexity. Whenever the trajectory of the system moves along the boundary of the admissible region, additional conditions must be in force. These conditions will affect the associated Langrangian multipliers. An acceptable solution approach is to solve the relaxed problem first by ignoring the constraints.

As an example of the application of optimal control theory to pricing decisions, we can look at the new product growth models for consumer durables that have been popularized by Bass (1969a). These models (see equation 2.59) generally assume that for a given price, current sales rate is influenced by accumulated previous sales. Initially, current sales will grow by new customers interacting with previous buyers. Eventually though, the sales rate will fall as the market becomes saturated. Robinson and Lakhani (1975) extended the Bass market growth model to take into account the impact of price. Two phenomena were considered. First, the sales response function was assumed to be a multiplicative separable function of a price function and a cumulative sales function.[7] The sales rate is assumed to vary inversely with price. Second, the possibility that unit production costs might decline with cumulative experience (volume) was taken into account.[8] Kamien and Schwartz (1981, pp. 119–20) formulated the problem as

$$\max \int_0^T [P - C(E)][f(P)h(E)]dt \tag{8.14a}$$

subject to

$$\frac{dE}{dt} = f(P)h(E), \qquad E(0) \text{ known.} \tag{8.14b}$$

Robinson and Lakhani assumed that the price function was one in which the price elasticity was proportional to price:

$$f(P) = e^{-\beta P(t)}, \tag{8.15}$$

whereas Bass (1980) assumed a constant price elasticity function:

$$f(P) = P(t)^{-\varepsilon_P}. \tag{8.16}$$

Both used the Boston Consulting Group's experience curve for the unit production cost function:

$$C[E(t)] = C[E(0)]\frac{E(t)}{E(0)}. \tag{8.17}$$

The solution to (8.14) can be found by forming the Hamiltonian

$$[P - C(E) + \gamma]f(P)h(E). \tag{8.18}$$

Using the set of rules (8.9), the optimal conditions are

$$f(P)h(E) + \frac{df(P)}{dP}[P - C(E) + \gamma]h(E) = 0, \tag{8.19a}$$

$$f(P)\left(\frac{dC(E)}{dE}h(E) - [P - C(E) + \gamma]\frac{dh(E)}{dE}\right) = \frac{d\gamma}{dt}, \tag{8.19b}$$

$$f(P)h(E) = \frac{dE}{dt} \tag{8.19c}$$

After some additional manipulation, Kamien and Schwartz were able to characterize the solution qualitatively as "the optimal price rises as the market expands and falls as the market matures." Bass assumed that the nonprice portion of the separable sales response function shifted exogenously with time over a durable's life cycle rather than with cumulative experience, i.e., $h(E) = h(t)$ in the preceding formulation. In this case, the optimal price decreases monotonically over time.

Notice that (8.19a) can be solved for the optimal price and expressed as a function of price elasticity:

$$P^*(t) = \frac{\varepsilon_P}{\varepsilon_P + 1}(C[E(t)] - \gamma). \tag{8.20}$$

This can be compared to the classical static monopolist's pricing rule (8.2). If unit production costs decline with cumulative experience, the marginal valuation of additional volume at time t will be positive, reflecting the future marginal benefit of current volume. Thus, the optimal price will be lower in the dynamic formulation than in the *myopic* static formulation (Kalish 1983, p. 139). Jeuland and Dolan (1982) extended the Robinson-Lakhani version of the Bass model to include repeat purchases. Jørgensen (1983) investigated a version of the Bass model in which saturation sales (total market potential) was a linearly decreasing function of price. He determined that the optimal policy was to approach long-run stationary equilibrium sales, the turnpike, as fast as possible followed by a permanent stay on the turnpike.

If the planning horizon is very long, the time value of money should be taken into account. If the discount rate is i, $0 < i < \infty$ ($i = 0$ is nondiscounted behavior, while $i = \infty$ is myopic behavior), then the discounted optimization problem is

$$\max_{X(t)} \int_0^T e^{-it}(g[Q(t), X(t), t])dt \qquad (8.21a)$$

subject to

$$\frac{dQ(t)}{dt} = f[Q(t), X(t), t], \qquad 0 \le t \le T, \quad Q(0) \text{ known}, \quad Q(T) \text{ free.} \quad (8.21b)$$

The Hamiltonian function is now

$$H[Q(t), X(t), t] = e^{-it}g[Q(t), X(t), t] + \gamma(t)f[Q(t), X(t), t], \qquad (8.22)$$

and the rules can be applied as before. The multiplier gives a marginal value of the state variable at time t discounted back to time zero. Most of the pricing studies mentioned have focused on discounted profits.

Rather than work with values that have been discounted back to zero, we may be better off to work with current values. Let us rewrite (8.22) as

$$H[Q(t), X(t), \gamma, t] = e^{-it}(g[Q(t), X(t), t] + e^{-it}\gamma(t)f[Q(t), X(t), t]). \quad (8.23)$$

The *current value multiplier* can be defined as $\phi = e^{it}\gamma$, and the *current value Hamiltonian* as

$$H_c[Q(t), X(t), \phi, t] = g[Q(t), X(t), t] + \phi(t)f[Q(t), X(t), t]. \qquad (8.24)$$

The set of rules (8.9) apply as before, but they are expressed in terms of the current-value definitions:

$$\frac{\partial H_c}{\partial X} = 0, \qquad (8.25a)$$

$$-\frac{\partial H_c}{\partial Q} = \frac{d\phi}{dt} - i\phi, \qquad (8.25b)$$

$$\frac{\partial H_c}{\partial \phi} = \frac{dQ}{dt}. \qquad (8.25c)$$

Clarke, Darrough, and Heineke (1982), among others, used the current-value approach. A summary of theoretical monopolistic marketing decision models based on deterministic sales response to price is given in table A8–1.

Advertising.   Advertising can be treated as a current expense or a capital investment, as discussed in chapter 2. This distinction becomes very important in determining optimal advertising expenditures.

Advertising as a Current Input.   Stigler (1961) argued that advertising is like any other productive resource and thus should be employed to the point where the marginal revenue product of advertising equals its marginal cost. Rasmussen (1952) showed that at this level the advertising elasticity would equal the ratio of advertising expenditures to contribution to profit, overhead, and advertising costs. Dorfman and Steiner (1954) found that if the selection of the levels for various marketing instruments are independent decisions, the conditions for the optimal marketing mix of price, advertising expenditures, distribution expenditures, and product quality expenditures are that the negative of the price elasticity equals the marginal revenue product of advertising equals the marginal product revenue of distribution equals the product quality elasticity times the ratio of price to unit cost, viz.,

$$-\varepsilon_P = P\frac{\partial Q}{\partial A} = P\frac{\partial Q}{\partial D} = \varepsilon_{Q'}\frac{P}{C}. \tag{8.26}$$

While this relation does not directly specify the optimal marketing mix, it can be used to evaluate whether or not a brand is operating efficiently. This assessment may be easier to make if we write the first part of (8.26) as

$$\frac{A^*}{R} = -\frac{\varepsilon_A}{\varepsilon_P}, \tag{8.27}$$

where A/R is the ratio of advertising to sales revenue. We make use of this result later in our review of empirical results, i.e., in table 8–2. The optimal advertising-revenue ratio is a constant.

In the special case where the sales response function is the multiplicative model (see equation 2.14) and unit costs are constant, the optimum price is independent of the level of advertising and is simply (8.2). The optimal level of advertising is

$$A^* = \varepsilon_A(P^* - C)Q^*. \tag{8.28}$$

If price is the only other marketing instrument, this becomes

$$A^* = [\varepsilon_A(P^* - C)K(P^*)^{\varepsilon_P}]^{1/(1-\varepsilon_A)}, \tag{8.29}$$

where K is the scaling constant in the sales response function. Naert (1972) applied the Dorfman-Steiner condition to another functional form, a linear sales response function with advertising expressed in logarithms.

Advertising as a Capital Investment. Nerlove and Arrow (1962) extended this analysis to account for the decay of advertising. They suggested that goodwill represents the effect of past and current outlays on demand. A dollar spent on advertising increases goodwill by a similar amount. Goodwill depreciates over time, perhaps at a constant proportional rate. Thus, the net investment in goodwill over a specified time interval is the difference between current advertising expenditures and the depreciation of the stock of goodwill (see equation 2.56). If the discount rate is fixed, then the optimal policy can be found by applying the calculus of variations to the following problem:

$$\max_{A \geq 0, P \geq 0} \int_0^\infty e^{-it}[(P - C)Q - A]dt \qquad (8.30a)$$

subject to

$$\frac{dG}{dt} = A - \delta G, \qquad G(0) \text{ known.} \qquad (8.30b)$$

The structure of this formulation has some noteworthy characteristics. The planning horizon is infinite. The problem is quasiautonomous. Autonomous means that there is no explicit dependence on time. In this problem, time does explicitly enter through the discount term; however, the discount term is a constant. Given that the problem is an infinite horizon and autonomous one, the solution to $G(t)$ is likely to tend toward a steady, or stationary, state, $G(s)$, in the long run. It is in this same sense that we can talk about an optimal static marketing policy in what is intrinsically a dynamic formulation.

Because price appears only in the integrand, the optimal price can be found first while holding goodwill constant. Then, using this optimal price, optimal advertising can be found. Differentiating the integrand with respect to price and setting the result equal to zero yields

$$Q + (P^* - C)\frac{\partial Q}{\partial P} = 0, \qquad (8.31)$$

which turns out once again to be the classical static monopolist's pricing rule (8.2). Now the problem can be restated as

$$\max \int_0^\infty e^{-it}\left[(P^* - C)Q - \frac{dG}{dt} - \delta G\right]dt. \qquad (8.32)$$

In the calculus of variations, the generalization of the standard first-order necessary condition is the *Euler equation*:

$$\frac{\partial}{\partial G}\left[F\left(t, G^*(t), \frac{dG^*(t)}{dt}\right)\right] = \frac{d}{dt}\left[\frac{\partial}{\partial(dG/dt)}F\left(t, G^*(t), \frac{dG^*(t)}{dt}\right)\right], \quad (8.33)$$

where $F(t, G^*(t), dG^*(t)/dt)$ is the integrand. In the Nerlove-Arrow formulation, the needed derivatives are

$$\frac{\partial F}{\partial G} = e^{-it}\left[(P^* - C)\frac{\partial Q}{\partial G} - \delta\right], \quad (8.34a)$$

$$\frac{\partial F}{\partial(dG/dt)} = e^{-it}(-1), \quad (8.34b)$$

$$\frac{d}{dt}\frac{\partial F}{\partial(dG/dt)} = (-i)e^{-it}(-1) = ie^{-it}. \quad (8.34c)$$

Setting (8.34a) equal to (8.34c) yields

$$[P^* - C]\frac{\partial Q}{\partial G} = i + \delta, \quad (8.35a)$$

$$G^* = \frac{\varepsilon_G(P^* - C)Q^*}{i + \delta} \quad \text{(and } A^* = \delta G^*\text{).} \quad (8.35b)$$

This is a generalization of the Dorfman-Steiner condition. The Dorfman-Steiner condition is the special case in which the discount rate, i, is zero and the depreciation rate, δ, is 1 (and consequently $G = A$). As before (8.27), the efficiency of advertising is often assessed in terms of the ratio of advertising to sales revenue. Using (8.35b) and (8.3b), the optimal advertising-revenue ratio can be shown to be

$$\frac{A^*}{R} = -\frac{\delta}{i + \delta}\frac{\varepsilon_G}{\varepsilon_P}. \quad (8.36)$$

It is still a constant, albeit a different one. Picconi and Olson (1978) used this ratio in determining the optimal proportion of sales dollars spent on advertising in the case of a branded beverage. Lambin, Naert, and Bultez (1975) have generalized the Dorfman-Steiner theorem to the case of an oligopoly with multiple reactions and expandable industry demand.

The steady-state solution to (8.32) can be found by expanding the right-hand side of the Euler equation (8.33) using the chain rule:

$$\frac{d}{dt}\left[\frac{\partial F}{\partial(dG/dt)}\right] = \frac{\partial}{\partial t}\left[\frac{\partial F}{\partial(dG/dt)}\right] + \frac{\partial}{\partial G}\left[\frac{\partial F}{\partial(dG/dt)}\right]\frac{dG}{dt}$$

$$+ \frac{\partial}{\partial dG}\left[\frac{\partial F}{\partial(dG/dt)}\right]\frac{d^2G}{dt^2}. \quad (8.37)$$

At equilibrium, $dG/dt = 0$ and $d^2G/dt^2 = 0$. In the discounted formulation, the first term on the right-hand side is

$$\frac{\partial}{\partial t}\left[\frac{F}{dG/dt}\right] = -i\left[\frac{\partial F}{\partial(dG/dt)}\right]. \tag{8.38}$$

Inserting (8.34b) into (8.38) and setting equal to (8.34a) yields (8.35a). We have an optimal steady-state solution.

Dynamic Advertising Policy. So far, although we have considered dynamic problems, we have not gained any dynamic insight into the *temporal* nature of advertising policy. Thus, we need to address the *timing* of advertising.

Even in situations where an optimal long-run stationary equilibrium advertising level exists, we need to know how best to go from current expenditure levels to the stationary solution. We have seen that the Nerlove-Arrow model could be treated as a static-like (equilibrium) formulated problem. The firm would like to attain the optimal policy (8.35b) as fast as possible. This is accomplished by the *most rapid approach path*. The rate of change is governed by differential equation on 8.30b. If the firm has less than the optimal amount of goodwill, it will adopt its maximum feasible spending rate, A^o, until the goodwill is built up to desired level, whereas if the firm has more than the optimal level, the best it can do is to stop advertising until the stock of goodwill falls to the optimal level.

The Nerlove-Arrow model is amenable to solution by optimal control theory. The state variable is now goodwill rather than unit sales, and the control variable is advertising. Taking the current-value approach (8.25) results in these three equations:

$$\frac{\partial H_c}{\partial A} = (P^* - C)\frac{\partial Q}{\partial A} - 1 + \phi = 0, \tag{8.39a}$$

$$-\frac{\partial H_c}{\partial G} = -\left[(P^* - C)\frac{\partial Q}{\partial G} - \phi\delta\right] = \frac{d\phi}{dt} - i\phi, \tag{8.39b}$$

$$\frac{\partial H_c}{\partial \phi} = A - \delta G = \frac{dG}{dt}. \tag{8.39c}$$

The solution is

$$G^* = \frac{\varepsilon_G(P^* - C)Q^*}{\phi(i + \delta) - d\phi/dt}. \tag{8.40a}$$

This can be compared to Nerlove and Arrow's result (8.35b). [At the optimal long-run stationary equilibrium, $d\phi/dt = 0$ and $\partial Q/\partial A = 0$, which from (8.35a) implies that $\phi = 1$.] The optimal advertising-sales ratio now becomes

$$\frac{A^*}{R} = -\frac{\delta}{\phi(i + \delta) - d\phi/dt}\frac{\varepsilon_G}{\varepsilon_P}. \tag{8.40b}$$

This ratio is no longer a constant.

Gould (1970) considered a version of the Nerlove-Arrow model in which the cost of adding goodwill is nonlinear. His assumption that the marginal cost of adding goodwill is positive and increasing has been controversial. Schmalensee (1972, p. 24), for one, has questioned this assumption. However, Sethi (1977b, p. 693) argued that the cost of advertising function might be considered a production function for converting advertising expenditures into goodwill. If so, increasing costs in the conversion process are not implausible.

Jacquemin (1973) extended the Nerlove-Arrow sales response function to take into account both the current advertising of the brand and the total current advertising of all other competitors. The "all others" advertising was eliminated from the response function by using a general instantaneous reaction function. In this reformulation, if goodwill is initially below the desired stock level, a "bang-bang" instantaneous jump is no longer optimal. Rather it is better to initially advertise heavily and then gradually decrease the level of advertising outlays. Additional details are given in Bensoussan, Hurst, and Näslund (1974, pp. 142–49).

Bensoussan, Bultez, and Naert (1978) generalized Jacquemin's model to take into account the dynamics of competitive reaction. Their model applies to oligopolistic markets in which one firm is the leader and the remaining firms are followers. The leader, in making decisions, will explicitly take into account competitors' expected reactions. Forecasts of expected reactions are provided by behavioral, as opposed to normatively derived, reaction functions. Estimation of these functions from the observation of past reaction patterns was discussed in chapter 6. The leader's sales response function captures the effects of past advertising spending and the time pattern of this spending. Nonmonotonic lag structures are permissible. The optimal control of such models with continuous lags has been addressed by Sethi (1974c).

Sethi (1973; 1974b) and Sweeney, Abad, and Dornoff (1974) found optimal dynamic advertising policies assuming the underlying market mechanism was Vidale-Wolfe (see equation 2.55). Both assume that advertising control is bounded; consequently, impulse control may not be feasible.

Sethi focused on determining the rate of advertising expenditure to achieve a terminal penetration $Q(T)/Q^o$ within specified limits while maximizing the present value of net profit streams over a finite horizon. His policy preference statement was formulated as

$$\max_{0 \le A(t) \le A^o} \int_0^T \left\{ e^{-it}(P - C)Q^o\left[\frac{Q(t)}{Q^o}\right] - A(t) \right\} dt \tag{8.41a}$$

subject to

$$\frac{d[Q(t)/Q^o]}{dt} = \frac{\beta}{Q^o} A(t) \frac{1 - Q(t)}{Q^o} - \frac{\lambda Q(t)}{Q^o}, \qquad 0 \le Q(t) \le Q^o, \quad (8.41b)$$

$$Q(0) \text{ known}, \quad \frac{Q(T)}{Q^o} \in [\text{MinTarget}, \text{MaxTarget}],$$

where $0 \le \text{MinTarget} \le \text{MaxTarget} \le 1$. If MinTarget $= 0$ and MaxTarget $= 1$, the problem is a free-endpoint problem; otherwise, it is treated as a fixed-endpoint problem. The solution strategy is to solve the free-endpoint problem first. If the free-endpoint terminal penetration is found to fall within the terminal target penetration range, use the free-endpoint solution. If it does not, set the fixed-endpoint at the lower or upper end of the target penetration range, depending upon whether the free-endpoint penetration was below or above the desired range, and solve the appropriate fixed-endpoint problem.

Sweeney, Abad, and Dornoff specified a salvage value term rather than an endpoint condition. Their policy preference statement was

$$\max_{0 \le A(t) \le A^o} \left\{ vQ(T) + \int_0^T [(P - C)Q(t) - A(t)]dt \right\} \qquad (8.42a)$$

subject to

$$\frac{dQ(t)}{dt} = \beta A(t) \frac{[Q^o - Q(t)]}{Q^o} - \lambda Q(t), \qquad 0 \le Q(t) \le Q^o, \quad Q(0) \text{ known}, \quad (8.42b)$$

where v is the value a firm attaches to having a certain sales rate at the end of the planning horizon. They do not take into account the time value of money because they believe that the underlying parameters in the sales response function would change over a longer planning horizon.

Sethi noted that the optimal control for the Vidale-Wolfe advertising model has the "turnpike" property, an optimal long-run stationary equilibrium. In situations where it is feasible to ride along the turnpike, the best control is the one that spends the maximum time along the turnpike. This is accomplished by using the fastest entry and exit ramps to and from the turnpike. If the distance is not far or the desired speed cannot be achieved, the best path will not be by means of the turnpike.

If an optimal long-run stationary equilibrium exists and is feasible, a constant advertising policy (after following the most rapid approach path— usually a one-time pulse) is best. If this is not the case, an advertising pulsing policy may be best. An advertising pulsing policy uses an on-and-off pattern of advertising.

One situation that leads to repetitive pulses is an S-shaped advertising response function in combination with a budget constraint (Rao 1970). This can be demonstrated by an example (Simon 1982, pp. 353–54). Suppose the monthly sales response function is log-reciprocal (see equation 2.16):

$$\ln Q = 2.4141565 - \frac{24.141565}{A} \tag{8.43}$$

If the gross margin per unit is \$7.4560204, then the optimal advertising is \$30 per month.[9] The optimal annual expenditure should be \$360. When the annual budget is less than this amount, say \$120, how should it be spent? Compare an advertising schedule of a constant level of \$10 per month with a pulsed strategy of \$30 every three months. The pulsed strategy is superior, yielding annual sales of 20(4 × 5) units versus 12(12 × 1) units for the constant strategy.

Sasieni (1971) conjectured that over time marketing professionals must have found optimal advertising strategies by empirical methods. Moreover, given the widespread belief that circumstances exist in which a cyclical or pulsing strategy is optimal, the discovery of a class of response functions whose coefficients can be chosen to yield a cyclic policy should be possible. Characterization of the optimal policy for a class of optimal control problems that includes the Vidale-Wolfe model was explored by means of dynamic programming. Sasieni's finding was that no response functions will yield a cyclic policy that is optimal in the long run. However, his analysis permitted "chattering control," the mixing of expenditure levels over infinitesimally short intervals. Such mixing is physically impossible. Thus, while a pulsing pattern is not the mathematical optimum, it may be the closest we can come to the optimum in practice.

Ackoff and Emshoff (1975) described experiments with Budweiser beer. Two types of pulsing were evaluated. Under one experimental condition, advertising expenditures in all media were on or off together. Under the other condition, only one medium was used at any one time but the media were alternated. One of their conclusions was that there is no significant difference between time pulsing and media pulsing. They thought media pulsing was easier to administer.

Simon (1982) considered advertising pulsing to be better than constant advertising spending when the phenomenon of advertising wearout is taken into account. Using a specific functional form, a semilogarithmic version of equation 2.31, and assuming pulsing does not affect unit production costs, which it may well, he found a pulsation strategy to be optimal under an unconstrained budget as well as a constrained budget.

Mesak (1985) posited a model in which long-run sales revenue was a function of advertising. The time path to reach this eventual sales revenue was specified as

$$\frac{dR_t}{dt} = [(\alpha + \beta D)][R_\infty(A) - R_t], \tag{8.44}$$

where

$$D = \begin{cases} 1 & \text{if } R_\infty(A) \le R_t \\ 0 & \text{if } R_\infty(A) > R_t \end{cases}.$$

This formulation permits asymmetric growth and decay, as shown in figure 8–2. Given the adjustment process (8.44), Mesak went on to find the duration of the pulse τ^* as well as its intensity A^* that maximized the present value of

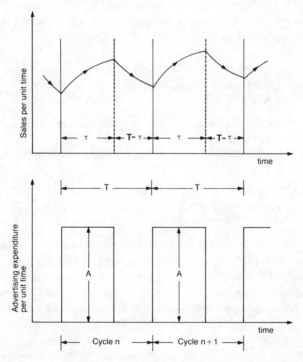

Figure 8–2. Sales Response to an Advertising Pulsing Policy. *Source*: Mesak (1985, p. 29).

Table 8-1.   Questions Related to Advertising Pulsing

How long should the pulsation and nonpulsation phases be?
Should they be equally long?
Should the length of pulses and nonpulses change over time?
How does competitive advertising affect the efficiency of a pulsation strategy?
What happens if a competitor follows a counterpulsation strategy?
Does pulsation lose its effectiveness over time?
Should fresh copy be introduced with new copy?
Is time pulsation or media pulsation superior?

Source: Simon (1982, p. 362).

future profits for a given advertising budget *B* per given period *T*. If the growth rate is greater than the decay rate, if the spread between the growth rate and the decay rate is sufficiently large,[10] and if the shape of the sales response function is convex, then a pulsing advertising policy is superior. In most situations, however, a constant advertising policy will be better. A summary of open questions regarding pulsation is given in table 8–1.

Media Selection.   The Dorfman-Steiner theorem can be extended to cover the multimedia situation. Bultez and Schultz (1979) posited the following theorem and corollary:

> The optimal budget to be spent on advertising in each medium should be equal to the sum of varying proportions of the discounted future sales revenues in which the proportions are determined by the ratio of demand elasticities with respect to advertising and price.

> An optimal steady-state policy requires that the ratio of advertising budgets allocated to any pair of media be equal to the ratio of the corresponding long-run elasticities of sales with respect to advertising.

These decision rules for media allocation should be easily implementable—provided the necessary empirical information is available.

In practice, advertising budgets and media plans are usually determined sequentially: first, an advertising budget is specified based on some sales response function; then a media schedule is selected that maximizes some measure of advertising effectiveness within this budget constraint. Bultez and Schultz offered some support for the validity of such a process.

The Nerlove-Arrow model has been generalized by Srinivasan (1976) to take into account *n* media and *m* markets. If **G** is the vector of exposure levels in each of the *m* markets and **A** is the vector of advertising insertions in each of the *n* media, then the the media scheduling problem can be expressed as

$$\max_{A_t \in \Omega_t} \sum_{t-1}^{T-1} (1 + i)^{-t}[(P_t - C_t)Q_t(\mathbf{G}_t) - c_t(\mathbf{A}_t)] + (1 + i)^{-T}v(\mathbf{G}_T) \quad (8.45a)$$

subject to

$$\mathbf{G}_{t+1} - \mathbf{G}_t = \rho_t(\mathbf{A}_t) - \delta_t\mathbf{G}_t, \qquad \mathbf{G}_0 \text{ given}, \quad (8.45b)$$

where Ω consists of upper and lower bounds as well as a budget constraint $c_t(\mathbf{A}_t) \le \mathbf{B}_t$, if present. He proposed a solution procedure based on the discrete maximum principle of optimal control theory.

A summary of theoretical monopolistic marketing decision models based on deterministic response to advertising is given in table A8–2. These results have been applied in empirical studies.

Stochastic Sales Response. Some inherent randomness may exist in the marketplace. Consequently, sales may not only be affected by the deterministic part of the underlying market mechanism but also by a stochastic element. The state equation for sales (in continuous time) is a stochastic differential equation:

$$\frac{dQ}{dt} = f[Q(t), X(t), t] + \sigma[Q(t), X(t), t]\alpha(t), \quad (8.46)$$

where the random error α satisfies $E[\alpha(t)] = 0$, and $E[\alpha(t)\alpha(s)] = 0$ for all $t \ne s$; i.e., the error process is white noise. The expected rate of change in sales is $f[Q(t), X(t), t]$. Equivalently, (8.46) can be written as

$$dQ = f[Q(t), X(t), t]dt + \sigma[Q(t), X(t), t]dW, \quad (8.47)$$

where $d\dot{W}(t) = \alpha(t)dt$ is the incremental of the Weiner process $W(t)$. In a Weiner process, $W(t) - W(s)$ has a normal distribution with mean zero and variance $\sigma(t - s)$ over the interval $[s, t]$.

If $y = h(Q, t)$, where Q obeys (8.46), then the stochastic differential of this transformed variable y is

$$dy = \frac{\partial h}{\partial t}dt + \frac{\partial h}{\partial Q}dQ + \frac{1}{2}\frac{\partial^2 h}{\partial Q^2}(dQ)^2. \quad (8.48)$$

This is known as *Itô's theorem* (Kamien and Schwartz 1981, p. 244). Using the stochastic differential equation (8.47), it can be rewritten as

$$dy = \left(\frac{\partial h}{\partial t} + \frac{\partial h}{\partial Q}f(Q, X, t) + \frac{1}{2}\frac{\partial^2 h}{\partial Q^2}\sigma^2\right)dt + \frac{\partial h}{\partial Q}\sigma dW \quad (8.49)$$

because under the white noise assumption $(dt)(dW) = (dt)^2 = 0$ and $(dW)^2 = dt$. Itô's theorem can be extended to many variables.

The stochastic optimal control problem is

$$J(Q,t) = \max_{X} E\left(\int_0^T g(Q,X,t)dt + \phi[Q(T),T]\right), \qquad (8.50a)$$

subject to

$$dQ = f(Q,X,t)dt + \sigma(Q,X,t)dW, \qquad Q(0) \text{ known.} \qquad (8.50b)$$

Its solution (Kamien and Schwartz 1981) is found by solving

$$-\frac{\partial J(Q,t)}{\partial t} = \max_{X}\left[g(Q,X,t) + \frac{\partial J(Q,t)}{\partial Q}f(Q,X,t) + \frac{1}{2}\sigma^2\frac{\partial^2 J(Q,t)}{\partial Q^2}\right], \qquad (8.51a)$$

with the boundary condition

$$J[Q(T),T] = \phi[Q(T),T]. \qquad (8.51b)$$

The maximizing X is given by

$$\frac{\partial g}{\partial X} + \frac{\partial J(Q,t)}{\partial Q}\frac{\partial f(Q,X,t)}{\partial X} + \sigma\frac{\partial \sigma}{\partial X}\frac{\partial^2 J(Q,t)}{\partial Q^2} = 0. \qquad (8.52)$$

This rule can be used to find the stochastic version of the deterministic Dorfman-Steiner theorem.

The optimal mix of price, advertising expenditures, distribution expenditures, and product quality expenditures for a monopolist operating in an uncertain environment can be found (Raman 1987a). The problem can be stated as

$$\max_{P\geq 0, A\geq 0, D\geq 0, Q'\geq 0} E\left(\int_0^T e^{-it}\{[P - C(Q,Q')]Q(P,A,D,Q') - A - D\}dt\right)$$
$$(8.53a)$$

subject to

$$dQ = Q(P,A,D,Q')dt + \sigma(P,A,D,Q')dW, \qquad Q(0) \text{ known.} \quad (8.53b)$$

The relation of equation 8.52 applies for each marketing instrument as follows:

$$e^{-it}\left(Q + P\frac{\partial Q}{\partial P} - C\frac{\partial Q}{\partial P} - \frac{\partial C}{\partial Q}\frac{\partial Q}{\partial P}Q\right) + \frac{\partial J}{\partial Q}\frac{\partial Q}{\partial P} + \sigma\frac{\partial \sigma}{\partial P}\frac{\partial^2 J}{\partial Q^2} = 0,$$
$$(8.54a)$$

$$e^{-it}\left(P\frac{\partial Q}{\partial A} - C\frac{\partial Q}{\partial A} - \frac{\partial C}{\partial Q}\frac{\partial Q}{\partial A}Q - 1\right) + \frac{\partial J}{\partial Q}\frac{\partial Q}{\partial A} + \sigma\frac{\partial \sigma}{\partial A}\frac{\partial^2 J}{\partial Q^2} = 0,$$
$$(8.54b)$$

$$e^{-it}\left(P\frac{\partial Q}{\partial D} - C\frac{\partial Q}{\partial D} - \frac{\partial C}{\partial Q}\frac{\partial Q}{\partial D}Q - 1\right) + \frac{\partial J}{\partial Q}\frac{\partial Q}{\partial D} + \sigma\frac{\partial \sigma}{\partial D}\frac{\partial^2 J}{\partial Q^2} = 0,$$

(8.54c)

$$e^{-it}\left(P\frac{\partial Q}{\partial Q'} - C\frac{\partial Q}{\partial Q'} - \frac{\partial C}{\partial Q}\frac{\partial Q}{\partial Q'}Q - \frac{\partial C}{\partial Q'}Q\right) + \frac{\partial J}{\partial Q}\frac{\partial Q}{\partial Q'} + \sigma\frac{\partial \sigma}{\partial Q'}\frac{\partial^2 J}{\partial Q^2} = 0.$$

(8.54d)

These equations can be rearranged to give the optimality condition:

$$-\frac{Q}{\partial Q/\partial P} - K\frac{\partial \sigma/\partial P}{\partial Q/\partial P} = \frac{1}{\partial Q/\partial A} - K\frac{\partial \sigma/\partial A}{\partial Q/\partial A}$$

$$= \frac{1}{\partial Q/\partial D} - K\frac{\partial \sigma/\partial D}{\partial Q/\partial D}$$

$$= \frac{(\partial C/\partial Q')Q}{\partial Q/\partial Q'} - K\frac{\partial \sigma/\partial Q'}{\partial Q/\partial Q'}, \qquad (8.55)$$

where the constant is

$$K = \sigma e^{it}\frac{\partial^2 J}{\partial Q^2}.$$

Additions to goodwill by advertising and depreciation of goodwill by forgetting may be probabilistic effects rather than deterministic effects. Tapiero (1975a; 1975b) has proposed a random walk model of advertising in which Nerlove-Arrow type and Vidale-Wolfe type models are special cases. Farley and Tapiero (1981) have methods of parameter estimation for such a model. Sethi (1979) examined Tapiero's formulation of a deterministic optimal control problem based on his extension of the Nerlove-Arrow model and showed that depending upon the parameters of the problem and initial conditions, the optimal solution may converge monotonically or sinusoidally, or not converge at all, to the optimal stationary equilibrium.

Pekelman and Sethi (1978) went beyond finding the optimal advertising expenditures to determine also the optimal times for copy replacement and the optimal investments in new copy. Two models were involved. The first was a sales-advertising model that reflected the copy effectiveness in its parameters. The second was a copy replacement model that related investment in new copy to the performance of the copy. Solution required a mixed optimization technique involving both dynamic programming and control theory.

A summary of theoretical marketing decision models based on stochastic response to marketing decision variables is given in table A8–3. While these studies took into account uncertainty in the sales response function, they assumed that the marketing manager was risk-neutral. Since managers are generally regarded as being risk-averse, the analysis of optimal advertising under certainty should take this into account (Holthausen and Assmus 1982; Jagpal and Brick 1982; Nguyen 1985). Tapiero, Eliashberg, and Wind (1987) examined a stochastic Vidale-Wolfe type model under the assumption that the firm maximized expected utility of profits, which would reflect the firm's attitude toward risk, and a target market share objective. They concluded that a risk-averse advertiser, facing decreasing advertising effects on sales growth uncertainty, will spend more on advertising than would a risk-neutral advertiser. Similar results can be shown to hold for a parametrically stochastic Bass diffusion model. Moreover, from a prediction standpoint, it appears the Bass model is robust with respect to parametric stochasticity (Eliashberg, Tapiero, and Wind 1987). Hence, if the main objective of the stochastic sales response function is forecasting, the deterministic approximation (i.e., Bass 1969) version of the stochastic diffusion model provides predictions that are quite close to those obtainable from the stochastic formulation.

Empirical Decision Models

Rather than using some abstract sales response function, an empirical decision model uses an estimated sales response function. These empirical studies permit consideration of questions such as, Is your marketing mix optimal? Are you overspending on advertising? Do departures from optimal marketing levels really matter?

Is Your Marketing Mix Optimal?   The Dorfman-Steiner theorem (8.26, especially as 8.27) is often used to evaluate whether a brand is operating efficiently. For example, in the processed grapefruit industry, pricing and advertising are initially set at the processor level. Large processors exercise price leadership. The processors support generic advertising through the Florida Citrus Commission. Although advertising goes directly to consumers, factory prices are converted by the channels of distribution into retail prices. Consumer sales is a function of advertising and retail price. Factory sales are then some function of consumer sales. Ward (1975) specified these relations as

$$Q_c = \beta_0 + \beta_1 P_c + \beta_2 A^{-1}, \tag{8.56a}$$

$$P_c = \alpha_0 + \alpha_1 P_f, \tag{8.56b}$$

$$Q_f = \gamma_0 + \gamma_1 Q_c, \tag{8.56c}$$

where advertising and sales are expressed in millions of dollars and millions of gallons, respectively. From the Dorfman-Steiner theorem, if the marketing mix for the processors is optimal, the negative of the price elasticity should equal the marginal revenue product of advertising. Expressions for these variables can be derived from (8.56a)–(8.56c) using the chain rule:

$$-\varepsilon_P = -\gamma_1 \beta_1 \alpha_1 \frac{P_f}{Q_f} \tag{8.57a}$$

$$P_f \frac{\partial Q_f}{\partial A} = P_f \gamma_1 \frac{-\beta_2}{A^2}. \tag{8.57b}$$

Ward's estimated model of the market mechanism was

$$Q_c = 69.82 - 10.15 P_c - 5.34 A^{-1}, \tag{8.58a}$$

$$P_c = 0.648 + 0.671 P_f, \tag{8.58b}$$

$$Q_f = 1.25 Q_c. \tag{8.58c}$$

In the most recent year available to Ward, the factory price was \$0.953/gallon, factory sales were 66.68 million gallons, and advertising was \$1.837 million. The negative of the price elasticity was then

$$-\varepsilon_P = -(1.25)(-10.15)(0.671)\left(\frac{0.953}{66.68}\right) = 0.128 \tag{8.59a}$$

and the marginal revenue product of advertising was

$$P_f \frac{\partial Q_f}{\partial A} = (0.953)(1.25)\left[-\left(\frac{-5.34}{1.837^2}\right) \right] = 1.885. \tag{8.59b}$$

These values were not anywhere near being equal. Ward attributed this to the grapefruit industry's desire for manageable inventories. Consequently, the industry selected the price that could achieve a target level of sales, a phenomenon also reported by Kohn and Plessner (1973).

Other applications of the Dorfman-Steiner theorem have shown wide variations around optimal spending levels. Some representative results are shown in table 8–2. Naert (1971, p. 64) noted that if the optimality ratio is not optimal, nothing can be said about the optimality of advertising without first being sure that the value of price is either optimal or unchangeable. Moreover, Morey and McCann (1983) have reminded us that the marketing manager must use estimates of these elasticities rather than their precise values. They went on to develop a method for incorporating uncertainties in the point estimates of the elasticities to yield confidence intervals applicable to the ratio of the elasticities.

Table 8-2.　Application of the Dorfman-Steiner Theorem

Product Class	Study	$\dfrac{-\varepsilon_A}{\varepsilon_P}$	$\dfrac{A}{R}$	Performance[a] Index	Conclusion[b]
Apples	Lambin (1976)	.077	.012	0.156	Underspending
Automobiles	Cowling (1972)	.161	.007	23.000	Overspending
Coffee	Cowling (1972)	.678	.162	4.150	Overspending
	Lambin (1976)	.012	.034	2.830	Overspending
Grapefruit juice	Ward (1975)	.442	.029	0.066	Underspending
Hair spray	Lambin (1976)	.021	.013	0.619	Underspending
Margarine	Cowling (1972)	.138	.098	1.410	Overspending
Soft drinks	Lambin (1976)	.033	.092	2.790	Overspending
Toothpaste	Cowling (1972)	.120	.153	0.780	Near optimal
Tractors	Cowling (1972)	.148	.014	10.900	Overspending
Yogurt	Lambin (1976)	.027	.031	1.150	Near optimal

a. A/R divided by $-\varepsilon_A/\varepsilon_P$.
b. Under the assumption that price is optimal, i.e., equation 8.2 is satisfied.

Are You Overspending?　There are at least two reasons why a branded consumer good might be overadvertised (Aaker and Carman 1982). First, organizational considerations favor overspending. Most managers are risk-averse. They are reluctant to reduce advertising because of the potential adverse effects for sales and market share. Moreover, they are aware that once a budget has been cut, it is hard to get it restored. On the other hand, managers often respond to competitive pressure as well as other market factors by increasing advertising. These actions are encouraged by agency personnel, who have a vested interest in increasing advertising billings. Overall, there is a tendency for escalation in advertising, as we discussed in chapter 6. Second, the exact nature of sales response to advertising may, in fact, be unknown. Managers may not have the scientific evidence necessary to determine optimal advertising policy. The thrust of this book has been to encourage managers to adopt the ETS analysis so that they will have the scientific information necessary to offset organizational and personal biases.

Declines in advertising effectiveness over the product life cycle may lead to overspending if a firm unthinkingly maintains original spending levels. Ball and Agarwala (1969) calculated that, in the face of a general shift in tastes, in order to maintain per capita sales of tea, generic advertising would have to double over a five-year period. Parsons and Bass (1971) found that firms were overspending on established brands and underspending on new brands.

Does It Matter? Sensitivity analyses, e.g., Naert (1972), have frequently shown that large percentage changes in advertising expenditures result in only small percentage changes in profit over a wide range of expenditure levels. This has come to be known as the *flat maximum principle*. Profit seems to be somewhat more sensitive to departures of price from its optimal level than it is to departures in advertising expenditures.

Tull et al. (1986) were concerned with the misspecification of the function describing sales response to advertising. After examining models that they believed represented three broad classes of sales response functions (diminishing returns, saturation, and supersaturation), they concluded:

> For a set of function parameters that appear plausible and within the domain of those found in the empirical literature, ...overspending on advertising—in our situation by as much as 25%—may cost very little in terms of profit and may even produce long-term benefits in the form of increased market share.

Thus, there is some indication that overadvertising could cost very little in forgone profit and might lead to appreciable sales gains.

In a similar vein, Bultez and Naert (1979; 1985; 1988b) and Magat, McCann, and Morey (1986; 1988) have explored the issue of whether lag structure matters in optimizing advertising expenditures, and if so, when. Bultez and Naert (1979) found that while misspecifications in the lag structure impacted the optimal advertising budget, profits were not very sensitive to such errors. As a consequence, they asserted that it was sufficient to use a flexible lag structure, the Pascal in their case, and that "the current tendency to build and estimate increasingly sophisticated distributed lag models does not seem totally justified."

Magat, McCann, and Morey (1986) investigated whether Naert and Bultez's result was universally true or whether it depended on the characteristics of the product and market analyzed. In their analysis of a constant elasticity sales response function, they determined that for any given error in "optimal" advertising, profits were less sensitive to misspecification (1) the shorter the duration of advertising effect, (2) the greater the advertising elasticity, (3) the less price-elastic the demand, (4) the lower the unit cost of the product, and (5) the lower the firm's discount rate. They were basically assessing the conditions when the profit function is flat relative to advertising. Bultez and Naert (1988b) showed that higher values of the advertising elasticity caused greater errors in "optimal" advertising and that this could outweigh the effect of the flatter profit function. They also noted that the pattern of prior advertising used to estimate the parameters of the sales response function could affect the sensitivity of profit to lag structure misspecification. A summary of studies involving empirical decision models is shown in table A8-4.

Earlier we considered models in which the competitors were not themselves optimizers. We now relax that assumption.

Game Theory

Insights into the competitive interplay among the marketing decision variables of several firms might be obtained from game theory. Game theory is a collection of mathematical models for the description of conscious, goal-oriented decision-making processes involving more than one brand (Shubik 1975, p. 9). Game-theoretic models may be either descriptive or normative. Marketing review articles include those by Jørgensen (1982), Moorthy (1985), di Benedetto (1986; 1987), and Chatterjee and Lilien (1986).

Basic Concepts

The *rules of the game* state in detail the number of competing firms, their feasible sets of actions at every juncture in the game, their rewards for each combination of moves, the sequence of moves, and the structure of information about moves, specifying who knows what when (Moorthy 1985, p. 263).

Game theory provides three formal descriptions of a game. They are the extensive form, the strategic or normal form, and the coalitional or characteristic-function form. The *extensive form* stresses the details and fine structure of a game. All possible outcomes for all possible actions for each firm are often represented by a decision tree. This form can quickly become unwieldly in practice. As a consequence, it is much more common to use the *strategic form*, which emphasizes strategic considerations. Each firm has a set of possible strategies. Payoffs to each firm will depend on the combination of alternatives chosen across firms. The *coalitional form* concentrates on alliances, bargaining, and group formation.

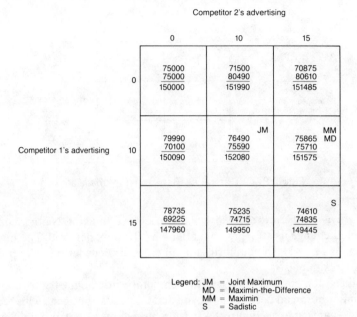

Competitor 2's advertising

Legend: JM = Joint Maximum
        MD = Maximin-the-Difference
        MM = Maximin
        S = Sadistic

Figure 8-3. Two-Competitor Advertising Game.

The strategic form is usually represented by a game matrix. A simple two-competitor pricing game matrix is shown in figure 8–3.[11] The alternative plans of action for the first competitor are shown along the rows of this matrix while those of the second are displayed across the columns. The figures in the cells represent payoffs to the first competitor, the second competitor, and both competitors, respectively. In this example, the payoffs are expressed as contributions to profits and overhead.

The game matrix can indicate the preferred strategy of one brand, given the anticipated strategy of its competitor. For example, suppose each competitor is risk-averse and stresses safety. Consequently, each adopts a strategy that will generate the largest minimum payoff. The largest minimum payoff for the first competitor (70875, 75865, 74610) is achieved when it pursues a moderate advertising strategy; for the second (69225, 74715, 74835), when it engages in a high advertising strategy. This solution to the game is called *maximin*.

The maximin solution happens to be an equilibrium solution. There is no incentive for one competitor to change its strategy, providing its competitor does not change its strategy. Moreover, the solution in this particular instance

Competitor 2's advertising

		0	10	15
	0	0	− 8990	− 9735
Competitor 1's advertising	10	9890	900	155
	15	9510	520	− 225

Figure 8-4. Difference-Between-Payoffs Matrix.

is a *Nash noncooperative equilibrium* because it is dominant. Neither competitor would change its strategy no matter what its opponent did. The maximin solution is not a Nash equilibrium in all cases; di Benedetto (1986) provides a counterexample.

Rather than emphasizing safety, each competitor might try to maximize the minimum spread between its payoff and that of its opponent. This requires that the game matrix (figure 8-3) be replaced by a matrix of differences between payoffs (figure 8-4). The first competitor maximizes its row minima (−9735, 155, −225) by choosing a moderate advertising strategy. The second competitor minimizes its column maxima (9890, 900, 155) by choosing a high advertising strategy. This solution is known as *maximin-the-difference*. For games with more than two competitors, the related beat-the-average solution can be determined (Shubik 1982, p. 327).

Alternatively, each competitor could adopt the strategy that would lead to the worst possible solution for its opponent. The worst payoff for the second competitor is 69225. The first competitor would have to pursue a high advertising strategy for this outcome to be possible. Similarly, the worst payoff for the first competitor is 70875, and the second competitor would use a high advertising strategy. This solution is known as *sadistic*.

Although we expect some form of noncooperative behavioral pattern, a cooperative solution is also possible. If the law permits, the two competitors could jointly choose the solution that maximizes their combined rewards. For our example, figure 8-3 shows that this *joint-maximal* solution occurs when both competitors follow medium advertising strategies. The first competitor would have to provide a kickback to its rival; otherwise, the rival would have no incentive not to pursue its high advertising strategy.

Calatone and di Benedetto (1986) used a game matrix to examine the conduct of two major brands of a routinely purchased consumer good. The two brands accounted for 40% and 12% of the market, respectively, and were premium priced compared to other brands on the market. Their first step was to estimate the sales response function for each firm. Next the estimated sales response functions were used to construct an estimated game matrix expressed in sales dollars. Two price levels and three advertising levels were evaluated. Now the various solution concepts—equilibrium pair, maximin-the-difference, sadistic, and joint maximum—were determined and their implications discussed. The leading brand was found to be following a sadistic strategy of unnecessarily high advertising expenditures. The brand's manufacturer did not follow a product innovation strategy, but rather emphasized protecting its big sellers from competitive attack.

We have assumed for expositional purposes that the competitors have the same objectives and possess similar behavioral intentions toward their rivals. This is unlikely to be the case. Lack of knowledge of the objectives of competitors complicates what we would like to be able to do—infer the behavioral intentions of competitors from information about the payoffs of the game matrix. Indeed, di Benedetto (1986, p. 9) argued that this is difficult if not impossible to do. Identification of behavioral intentions very likely requires that individual managers be surveyed.

Differential Games

In differential game models, two or more brands are optimizers. A game is typically played in continuous time for a fixed interval, T. Competitors may employ open-loop or closed-loop controls. If they use *open-loop controls*, each announces and commits itself to a marketing instrument, $X(t)$, which is a function solely of time. Thus, the time path of a marketing decision variable for each brand must be determined in advance for the entire planning horizon. If they use *closed-loop controls*, each announces and commits itself to a *policy* governing its marketing instrument, $X(t, Q)$. The actual values of each brand's X will be determined as the competition unfolds and the values of the state variables, Q's, become known at each instant in time.

The two control strategies are usually different in nonzero sum differential games. They are often the same in optimal control problems, which is why we did not make the distinction between them earlier. Closed-loop controls are more realistic in that they take into account information on a brand's own performance and its competitors' strategies; unfortunately, they are harder to solve.[12]

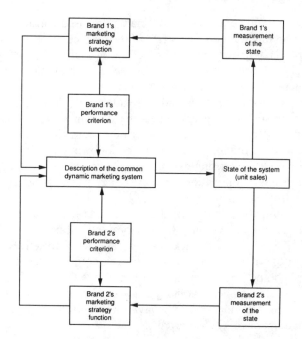

Figure 8–5. Duopoly Game. *Source*: Adapted from Deal (1975, p. 12).

As one might expect from an evolutionary model building point of view, most attention has been focused on the two-player or duopoly game. Other simplifying assumptions include (1) only one control variable for each brand, (2) constant marginal costs, (3) fixed total market potential or maximum attainable sales rate, and (4) ordinary first-order differential state equations for dynamics. The performance indices may be any of the three forms: Lagrange, Mayer, or Bolza. We will continue to emphasize the Lagrange form in our exposition. A diagram of a general duopoly game is given in figure 8–5.

The play of the game may be Pareto-optimal, Cournot-Nash equilibrium, Stackelberg leader-follower. A set of actions by the brands in a game is called *Pareto-optimal* if there does not exist another set of actions that rewards each brand as well and at least one of them better. A *Cournot-Nash strategy* is one in which no competitor, believing that its competitors are committed to their respective strategies, can improve its own performance. A Cournot-Nash equilibrium solution may be Pareto-optimal, but then again it may not. Most of the work in marketing has taken a Cournot-Nash approach.

Given the performance criterion for each brand (g_1, g_2), the Pareto-optimal cooperative solution for a duopoly is found by solving the following optimal control problem for two states (Q_1, Q_2) and two control variables (X_1, X_2):

$$\max_{X_1, X_2} \int_0^T [g_1(Q_1, Q_2, X_1, X_2, t) + g_2(Q_1, Q_2, X_1, X_2, t)] dt \quad (8.60a)$$

subject to the description of the common dynamic marketing system

$$\frac{dQ_1}{dt} = f_1(Q_1, Q_2, X_1, X_2, t), \qquad \frac{dQ_2}{dt} = f_2(Q_1, Q_2, X_1, X_2, t), \quad (8.60b)$$

and the boundary conditions on the state of the system

$$Q_1(0) \quad \text{and} \quad Q_2(0) \text{ known}, \quad Q_1(T) \quad \text{and} \quad Q_2(T) \text{ free}. \quad (8.60c)$$

The time indices have been suppressed. The Hamiltonian now has two Lagrangian multipliers and rules for optimality (8.9a–8.9c) become

$$\frac{\partial H}{\partial X_1} = 0 \quad \text{and} \quad \frac{\partial H}{\partial X_2} = 0, \quad (8.61a)$$

$$-\frac{\partial H}{\partial Q_1} = \frac{d\gamma_1}{dt} \quad \text{and} \quad -\frac{\partial H}{\partial Q_2} = \frac{d\gamma_2}{dt}, \quad (8.61b)$$

$$\frac{\partial H}{\partial \gamma_1} = \frac{dQ_1}{dt} \quad \text{and} \quad \frac{\partial H}{\partial \gamma_2} = \frac{dQ_2}{dt}. \quad (8.61c)$$

At the Cournot-Nash noncooperative equilibrium, competing firms monitor each other's performance indices and announce their strategies at the same instant of time. The problem statement for one brand is

$$\max_{X_1} \int_0^T g_1(Q_1, Q_2, X_1, X_2^*, t) dt \quad (8.62a)$$

subject to

$$\frac{dQ_1}{dt} = f_1(Q_1, Q_2, X_1, X_2, t), \qquad Q_1(0) \text{ known}, Q_1(T) \text{ free}, \quad (8.62b)$$

while that for its competitor is

$$\max_{X_2} \int_0^T g_2(Q_1, Q_2, X_1^*, X_2, t) dt \quad (8.62c)$$

subject to

$$\frac{dQ_2}{dt} = f_2(Q_1, Q_2, X_1, X_2, t), \qquad Q_2(0) \text{ known}, \quad Q_2(T) \text{ free}. \quad (8.62d)$$

Each brand will maximize its Hamiltonian assuming that its competitor is following its own Cournot-Nash strategy. The Cournot-Nash equilibrium solution is given by the following rules:

$$\frac{\partial H_1}{\partial X_1} = 0 \quad \text{and} \quad \frac{\partial H_2}{\partial X_2} = 0, \tag{8.63a}$$

$$\frac{\partial H_1}{\partial Q_1} + \frac{\partial H_1}{\partial X_2^*}\frac{\partial X_2^*}{\partial Q_1} + \frac{\partial H_1}{\partial X_1^*}\frac{\partial X_1^*}{\partial Q_1} = -\frac{d\gamma_{11}}{dt},$$

$$\frac{\partial H_1}{\partial Q_2} + \frac{\partial H_1}{\partial X_2^*}\frac{\partial X_2^*}{\partial Q_2} + \frac{\partial H_1}{\partial X_1^*}\frac{\partial X_1^*}{\partial Q_2} = -\frac{d\gamma_{12}}{dt},$$

$$\frac{\partial H_2}{\partial Q_1} + \frac{\partial H_2}{\partial X_2^*}\frac{\partial X_2^*}{\partial Q_1} + \frac{\partial H_2}{\partial X_1^*}\frac{\partial X_1^*}{\partial Q_1} = -\frac{d\gamma_{21}}{dt},$$

$$\frac{\partial H_2}{\partial Q_2} + \frac{\partial H_2}{\partial X_2^*}\frac{\partial X_2^*}{\partial Q_2} + \frac{\partial H_2}{\partial X_1^*}\frac{\partial X_1^*}{\partial Q_2} = -\frac{d\gamma_{22}}{dt}, \tag{8.63b}$$

$$\frac{\partial H}{\partial \gamma_1} = \frac{dQ_1}{dt} \quad \text{and} \quad \frac{\partial H}{\partial \gamma_2} = \frac{dQ_2}{dt}. \tag{8.63c}$$

If there is more than one Cournot-Nash equilibrium solution, then difficulties may arise. A brand may not know which of several Cournot-Nash strategies its competitor will select, and as a result, it will have trouble in choosing its own strategy. There exist, however, conditions which guarantee uniqueness.

Differential game techniques have been used to solve normative models of pricing and aggregate advertising decisions. Jørgensen (1982; 1986) has reviewed advertising and pricing models. We begin with a discussion of advertising.

Advertising.   Early work using game theoretic concepts (Friedman 1958; Mills 1961; Shakun 1965; 1966) assumed that each competitor's market share was equal to that competitor's share of total marketing expenditures. This work formed the foundation for Bell, Keeney, and Little's (1975) market share theorem.

Olsder (1976) considered a simple advertising model, in which the sales rate was proportional to the difference in advertising pressure between firms, what Jørgensen (1982) called an excess advertising model:

$$\frac{dQ_i}{dt} = \beta_i Q^o (A_i - A_j), \qquad i,j = 1,2, \quad i \neq j. \tag{8.64}$$

Olsder went on to extend this model to the situation involving three competitors:

$$\frac{dQ_i}{dt} = \beta_i Q^o A_i - \gamma_j Q^o \left(\frac{Q_i}{Q_i + Q_j} \right) A_j - \delta_k Q^o \left(\frac{Q_i}{Q_i + Q_k} \right) A_k, \qquad (8.65)$$

where $i, j, k = 1, 2, 3$, $i \neq j \neq k$. Going to a three-player game allowed Olsder to assess the possibility of coalition formation. Olsder also discussed briefly two- and three-player versions of the Lancaster model (see equation 2.61).

Wrather and Yu (1979) emphasized that advertising can be used to increase market share (selective demand) or to enlarge the market (primary demand). When market expansion is possible, the game may involve partial competition and partial cooperation.

Tapiero (1979), Friedman (1983), and Rao (1984) have extended the monopoly model of Nerlove and Arrow to take into account oligopoly competition. Tapiero also took into account uncertainty. One of his conclusions was that his model provided a reconfirmation of the Bell, Keeney, and Little market share theorem. Friedman and Rao proved the existence in an oligopoly of a noncooperative equilibrium under certain conditions.

Deal (1979) extended the monopoly model of Vidale and Wolfe (see equation 2.55) to the case of duopoly conflict (see equation 2.60):

$$\frac{dQ_i}{dt} = \beta_i A_i \left(\frac{Q^o - Q_i - Q_j}{Q^o} \right) - \lambda_i Q_i, \qquad i, j = 1, 2, \quad i \neq j. \qquad (8.66)$$

Having recognized that a manager might desire to attain as dominant a market share as possible while striving to maximize profits over a planning horizon, a *tempered* performance index was proposed for each firm:

$$\max_{x_i} \frac{w_i Q_i}{Q_1 + Q_2} + (1 - w_i) \int_{t_o}^{t_f} (m_i Q_i - A_i^2) dt, \qquad (8.67)$$

where

$\quad i$ refers to one of the firms,

$\quad m_i =$ gross margin per unit,

$\quad w_i =$ weighting factor set by management $(0 \leq w_i \leq 1)$,

$\quad t_o =$ beginning time for the planning horizon,

$\quad t_f =$ corresponding ending time.

The first term in (8.67) represents the relative importance of market share and the second term represents the relative importance of profit.[13]

Deal, Sethi, and Thompson (1979) noted that a major problem with Deal's duopoly version of the Vidale-Wolfe model was the absence of a competitive term in the sales response function. The advertising of one brand had no direct effect on its competitor's sales. To address this problem, they proposed the following bilinear model:

$$\frac{dQ_i}{dt} = \beta_i A_i \left(\frac{Q^o - Q_i - Q_j}{Q^o} \right) + \gamma_i (A_i - A_j) \left(\frac{Q_i + Q_j}{Q^o} \right) - \lambda_i Q_i, \quad (8.68)$$

where $i, j = 1, 2, i \neq j$. The new term in each equation is an approximation of the net gain in sales due to brand switching caused by "excess" advertising by the brand over its competitors. Brand 1, for instance, attracts switchers from brand 2 in proportion to $(A_1 - A_2)Q_2$; meanwhile it is losing switchers to brand 2 in proportion to $(A_2 - A_1)Q_1$. Subtracting those switching out from those switching in yields $(A_1 - A_2)(Q_1 + Q_2)$.

Jones (1983) has obtained a qualitative description of the dynamic system associated with sales in Deal's duopoly advertising model, and a generalization of it. He supposed that advertising policies were steady-state policies, that is, constant expenditures over time, and fixed. He then characterized the dynamics of sales response under such policies. For example, he found the equilibrium set in Deal's model by setting each equation in (8.66) equal to zero and solving. There was a unique equilibrium. He went on to examine what happens in the dynamic system at equilibrium when one of the firms changes its advertising policy while the other holds its own constant.

The concept of hysteresis (Little 1979a) was introduced in chapter 2 during our discussion of asymmetry in response. Deal's model cannot exhibit hysteresis. Under a change in one firm's level of advertising expenditures, the system will move to a new equilibrium value. But when the firm changes its expenditures back to their original level, the system must also return to its original equilibrium value because there is only one possible equilibrium value. However, if a system has multiple equilibrium values, it may exhibit hysteresis. Jones gave an example of how this might occur, as illustrated in figure 8–6. The dynamic system is initially in equilibrium at point A, one of three possible equilibrium values. Firm 1 increases its advertising expenditures, which leads to a new sales equilibrium curve (the dashed curve in figure 8–6). The sales equilibrium curves of the two firms now intersect at a unique equilibrium point, D, and the trajectory of the system under this new regime must converge asymptotically to it. Thus, if the advertising pulse continues for a long enough time, the system will be in the neighborhood of D when advertising is reduced. The system will revert to the old regime but will now be attracted to equilibrium point C rather than A. The impact of the advertising pulse has been to generate a permanent increase in that firm's sales.

Jones proposed an extension of Deal's model that would exhibit hysteresis. The proposed model included terms associated with word-of-mouth advertising:

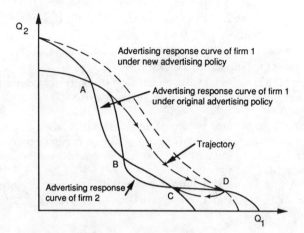

Figure 8–6. An Example of Hysteresis. *Source*: Adapted from Jones (1983, p. 131).

$$\frac{dQ_i}{dt} = \beta_i A_i \left(\frac{Q^o - Q_i - Q_j}{Q^o}\right) + \gamma_i Q_i \left(\frac{Q^o - Q_i - Q_j}{Q^o}\right)$$
$$+ \delta_i (Q_i - Q_j) Q_i Q_j - \lambda_i Q_i, \tag{8.69}$$

where $i, j = 1, 2, i \neq j$. The second term on the right-hand side of the equation represents an increase in the sales rate arising from encounters between customers of firm i and prospects who are currently customers of neither firm. The third term represents the increase (decrease) in sales rate arising from encounters between customers of the two competing firms. Jones gave a numerical example of (8.69) that demonstrated hysteresis.

Earlier in this chapter, in our discussion of dynamic pricing policy, we reviewed how Robinson and Lakhani extended the Bass market growth model to take into account the impact of price. Teng and Tompson (1983) adapted the market growth model for advertising rather than price. Even though they did not permit price to change except with regard to inflation, they allowed production costs to obey a learning curve. Their model was for n firms, where $3 \leq n \leq 10$. Not only was their model too complicated to solve analytically, but with $13n$ parameters, a complete numerical search of the parameter space was impossible—even in the case of a triopoly. Undaunted, Thompson and Teng (1984) went on to add price as a control variable.

Other types of sales response functions have been embedded in differential games. These include the square-root continuous-time version of equation 2.14 with $\beta = \frac{1}{2}$ by Case (1975) and Gasmi and Vuong (1988); the linear

distributed lag equation 2.42 by Schmalensee (1976), the quadratic continuous-
time version of equation 2.23 by Leitmann and Schmitendorf (1978), the
logarithmic equation 2.54 by Jørgensen (1982), and the Lancaster (equation
2.61) with market expansion by Erickson (1985).

Jørgensen (1982, p. 365), at the conclusion of his review, summarized the
optimal structure of optimal advertising strategies:

> 1) When a firm is oriented toward profit maximization, then an optimal policy
> appears to be one of heavy advertising expenditure in the initial part of the period.
> Thereafter, advertising should be decreased. This decrease can be smooth, partly
> smooth, or a bang-bang solution.
> 2) When a firm is oriented toward maximization of terminal market share/
> sales, another type of strategy emerges: increasing advertising expenditures over
> the horizon.

A summary of game-theoretic advertising decision models is given in table
A8–5. We now direct our attention to pricing models.

Price.   One early examination of a duopoly pricing game was conducted by
Osborne (1974). The sales response functions for each brand were linear. Each
brand manager strove to maximize a tempered performance index that indicated the relative importance of profit versus sales revenue. Osborne considered five decision rules or strategies. The Cournot strategy is to choose your
price to maximize your performance on the assumption that your competitor
keeps its price at the same level. The Stackelberg strategy is to choose your
price to maximize your performance on the assumption that your competitor
follows a Cournot strategy. The market share strategy is to choose your price
to hold onto current market share unless your performance can be improved
by lowering price to increase market share. The Nichol strategy is to choose
your price to maximize your profit on the assumption that your competitor
will follow a market share strategy. The Bishop strategy is to behave politely
as long as your competitor does but to react defensively to any aggression
that would drive your market share below a minimally acceptable level.
Osborne found that the Pareto-optimal Nash solution was for both competitors to follow Bishop strategies.

A duopoly game in which one brand competes on the basis of advertising
and the other on the basis of price was studied by Gaugusch (1984). The
structure of the optimal strategies depended on the salvage values for each
firm's sales at the end of the planning horizon.

The Robinson-Lakhani version of a market growth model was extended
to one with duopolistic competition by Dockner (1985). In doing so, he made
a simplifying assumption that the imitation coefficient in the market growth
sales response function is zero. The optimal pricing policies for both brands

are decreasing prices over time. Many of the results obtained from this duopolistic competition model were the same as those found by Dolan and Jeuland (1981) in their optimal control model for a monopoly. Jørgensen (1986) did not find this surprising, as the competitive interaction posited between the two brands were weak.

The implications of experience curves and brand loyalty for optimal dynamic pricing policies were examined by Wernerfelt (1986). He found that the effects of experience curves on variable costs were ambiguous but that the effects of discounting and exogenous declines in variable costs led to prices declining over time, whereas the effects of experience curves on fixed costs and brand loyalty led to increasing prices over time. Whether prices increase or decrease depends on which effects are dominant in a particular market.

Gasmi and Vuong (1988) derived alternative econometric models under the assumption that the data were the equilibrium outcomes of various games in price and advertising, and then identified the game that was most adequate using model selection techniques. The games that they considered were M1, firms set price and advertising levels simultaneously; M2, firms choose price in the first stage and advertising in the second stage; M3, firms choose advertising in the first stage and price in the second stage; M4, one firm sets price in the first stage, while its advertising and the other firm's price and advertising levels are chosen in the second stage; M5, one firm sets advertising in the first stage, while its price and the other firm's price and advertising levels are chosen in the second stage; and M6, one firm acts as a leader in choosing price and advertising levels. Three additional games (M7, M8, M9) were considered. They were variants of the last three games in which the roles of the two firms were interchanged. An appropriate equilibrium concept was used to solve each game. The econometric model associated with each game was a simultaneous-equations one with a specific set of nonlinear constraints on the parameters. Gasmi and Vuong discussed identification and full maximum likelihood estimation of the models. Models M1 and M2 turned out to be represented by the same econometric model.

The battle between Coca Cola and Pepsi Cola in the regular cola drink market was investigated. Using a model selection procedure based on Vuong (1988), Gasmi and Vuong found the following ordering of the models (at the 5% significant level):

$$M6 \approx M7 \approx M8 > M1/2 > M5 > M3 > M9 > M4. \qquad (8.70)$$

Marketing theory would rule out models where the firm's own price does not have a negative effect on sales and its competitor's price does not have a positive effect. Under the first criterion, models M1/2, M4, M5, and M9 were rejected, and under the second criterion, models M1/2, M3, M8, M9 were rejected. Gasmi and Vuong concluded that the best models were M6 (Coca

Cola is the Stackelberg leader in both price and advertising) and M7 (Pepsi Cola is the leader in price only) and that they could not distinguish between them. Perhaps further analysis using Box-Jenkins techniques to implement a test of the Granger concept of causality (e.g., Sturgess and Wheale 1985) might resolve this remaining ambiguity. In any event, Gasmi and Vuong have proposed an interesting methodology for combining game-theoretic considerations and econometric tools.

A summary of game-theoretic pricing decision models is given in table A8–6. Jørgensen (1986, p. 225) concluded:

> The amount of additional knowledge, relative [to] what we already know about the monopoly case, does not seem to be substantial. We are inclined to maintain the hypothesis that oligopolistic pricing *does differ* from monopolistic pricing but the models applied so far have not been sophisticated enough in their modelling of strategic interrelations of the competing firms to detect these differences.

We now discuss the role of simulation in improving decisions.

Simulation

Simulation has been defined as "the use of a process to model a process" (Schultz and Sullivan 1972). Since we have been dealing with such processes as sales response, competitive behavior, and managerial decision making, it should be apparent that any technique that allows systems to be analyzed without oversimplification can complement ETS in building models to improve marketing decisions. In fact, the major appeal of simulation as an aid to practical decision making is basically the same as its appeal to researchers, namely its capacity to deal with considerable complexity in systems and its ability to explore "what if?" type questions (Schultz 1974). There are many applications of simulation in marketing (cf. Kotler and Schultz 1970), but the ones of concern here are those simulations that utilize models of some response process. This includes the work of Balderston and Hoggatt (1962), Preston and Collins (1966), Kuehn and Weiss (1965), Herniter and Cook (1970), Amstutz (1967), Parasuraman and Day (1977), and Neslin and Shoemaker (1983b).

Simulation models provide a means for evaluating alternative marketing strategies in cases where analytical models are not appropriate or cannot be solved. In addition, this class of models permits a great deal of interplay between empirical and subjective inputs, such as combining managerial judgment on competitive behavior with estimated parameters of sales response. An example of an advertising simulation based on econometric measurement of sales response is provided by Lambin (1972a).

Lambin Model

Lambin suggests that the econometric models can be made more flexible by treating the regression coefficients as prior estimates to be adjusted on the basis of the manager's own judgment. In this way, new factors such as the entry of new competition and qualitative factors such as new advertising themes can be incorporated. Computers facilitate this integration. His planning model requires as input estimates of advertising elasticity and the decay rate, estimates of competitive advertising, estimates of total market demand, and planned advertising. He asks the decision maker to give expected (mean), pessimistic (0.10), and optimistic (0.90) values for the firm's decision variables and those of the competition. Various advertising appropriations strategies are evaluated in the simulation and response parameters are updated as desired. The output is expected sales for the company. Another version of his model considers rate of return as the criterion variable (Lambin 1970b).

Lambin argues that the simulation approach reduces risk, since "changes in the current program can be adopted more rapidly in response to an anticipated event or market reactions" (Lambin 1972a, p. 124). Lambin's work is only representative of the potential of marketing simulation models. These models can be extended in a number of directions, including the evaluation of current or discounted profit, the estimation of total market demand, and the treatment of competition, as in the simulation model developed by Schultz and Dodson (1974; 1978).

Schultz and Dodson Model

Schultz and Dodson report on a model designed to overcome some of the problems associated with "fully" empirical models, especially the fact that the manager must essentially either accept or reject them. The development of an endogenous competition model depends to a large extent on the availability of data on competitive sales and marketing actions (Schultz 1973). In many cases, these data are not available or cannot readily be obtained. In these cases, the model builder must rely on subjective estimates by management of competitors' marketing actions if competition is to be included in the model.

When competitive data are available, it is possible in principle to obtain explanatory or predictive competitive decision rules. The ability of the model builder to specify such rules depends upon the extent to which these rules are known and the extent to which they are stable. Where advertising is set as a constant percentage of sales, competitive advertising expenditures can be estimated fairly well. Constant markup pricing, price leadership, regulated pricing, and going rate pricing can lead to good price estimates for competition. In airline markets, flights may be set according to trend or seasonality. In these and other situations, it may be rather straightforward to obtain predictive equations that can be used to estimate competitors' marketing mix variable levels. Then planned firm marketing mix levels and estimated competitive mix levels can be used to forecast company sales or market share. In practice, the search for competitive decision rules may be more difficult. It may be only possible to identify a set of *possible* decision rules for competitors. This is the approach taken by Schultz and Dodson (1974; 1978). These models utilize a combination of empirical estimation and managerial judgment within the framework of decision theory.

The argument of Schultz and Dodson proceeds from the question, What kind of information does a firm have about its competition? The answer, it is assumed, is that the firm is uncertain about competitive decisions but has some knowledge about possible competitive decision rules. In contrast to an exogenous competition approach, where the actual decision is sought, and an endogenous competition (or fully empirical) approach, where the actual decision rule is sought (cf. Parsons and Schultz 1976, pp. 206–13), Schultz and Dodson explore the consequences of competitive reaction by recognizing the uncertainty of both the decisions and the process.

There are two major aspects to their model, which is a simulation of competitive behavior. First, it is a conditional optimization. The firm makes an assumption about the decision process of its competitors and then optimizes its marketing mix variables as if the competition will react in one of several ways with certainty. The optimization is conditional because it depends upon whether the assumed competitive response actually occurs. The payoffs (in profit) to the firm thus result from some combination of assumed and actual behavior. Second, it is an optimization accommodating uncertainty, since the payoff matrix can be examined for optimal assumptions about competitive behavior. In this case, optimal assumptions are equivalent to optimal strategies because they dictate the nature of competitive interaction and consequent market performance.

The model utilizes a sales response equation and a set of equations representing decision rules for the firm and for competitors. Instead of attempting to find one "true" decision rule for each competitor, however, the procedure estimates a set of plausible decision rules on the assumption that each is true. In Schultz and Dodson's model, management experience is employed first to identify the set of competitive decision rules and later to provide a criterion for evaluating the payoff matrix.

The model was tested on airline passenger data, where the control variable was number of flights. The simulation utilizes a market share equation, the competitive decision rules, and such inputs as price, industry demand, and unit cost of a flight. Given the inputs and an estimate of competitors' flights for the next planning period, the firm can compute analytically the number of flights that will maximize its profit. The output generated for each run is based on an assumed and an actual set of decision rules for competitors.

The model is used in planning by presenting managers with the payoff matrix of assumed and actual competitive behavior. Schultz and Dodson report that, for the airline data, if competitors set their flights based on time-dependent or flight-dependent (both nonreactive) decision rules, the best the firm can do is to have as good an estimate of competitors' flights as possible. If, on the other hand, competitors set their flights based on a competitively adaptive policy, then an aggressive marketing strategy on the part of the firm (induced by assuming competitive aggressiveness) will result in higher levels of competition, lower load factors, and reduced firm profit. Managers can also explore the consequences of other criteria such as maximin and Bayesian strategies. Extensions of this work to include optimal strategies for competitors are reported by Schultz and Hanssens (1976).

Developing Plans

We have seen how plans can be developed informally through the use of decision rules. Plans can also be developed and evaluated through the use of such formal methods as decision theory, optimization, game theory, and simulation. The objective of formal analysis is to find out what plans are best in meeting corporate goals. Having already discussed the methods, we need to explore how their use would fit with the model-based approach to planning and forecasting shown in figure 1–4.

Suppose a company has set a certain sales goal, say $\tilde{Q}$. Further, suppose that industry demand can be represented by the response function

$$Q_T = f(P, \text{GNP}), \tag{8.66}$$

and that company market share can be represented by the response function

$$MS_i = f(D_1, \ldots, D_i, \ldots, D_N, S_1, \ldots, S_i, \ldots, S_N),$$

where Q_T, P, GNP, MS, D, and S are industry sales, average industry price, gross national product, company market share, company distribution expenditures, and company sales force expenditures, respectively. The forecasting problem in this simple example is to forecast company sales, $\hat{Q}$, as the product of an industry sales forecast, $\hat{Q}_T$, and a company market share forecast, $\hat{MS}$. To do this, the company must combine certain anticipations about future events with certain plans contingent on those anticipations.

The company may, for example, purchase a macroeconomic forecast of GNP, which may itself be a product of ETS research. In addition, the company may utilize management judgment to come up with forecasts of average industry price and total industry advertising. Alternatively, these forecasts could be based on time series models that the company developed on its own.

If management judgments are sought, they would usually be obtained in the context of a scenario, or set of scenarios, giving the expected economic and competitive environment. For example, managers in the company would be asked what they expected average industry price to be in the face of alternative projections of GNP. Similarly, they would be asked for estimates of competitive distribution and sales force expenditures for various levels of company distribution and sales force effort. Since the latter constitute the company's plans, the final company sales forecast in this case depends on plans, not the reverse.

As an alternative to direct management judgment, company plans could originate from decision rules. Of course, in this informal approach to developing plans, the company can never be sure that its plans are the best in the sense of maximizing (as opposed to merely meeting) a sales or profit goal. Whatever the source of the plans, however, they can still be evaluated through the mechanism of an empirical response model. This is another reason that the model-based approach is so robust.

If $\hat{Q} \geq \tilde{Q}$, the company's plans can be implemented. They are already based on empirical response models, management experience, and a loose but nevertheless real process of making plans contingent on different possible futures. If $\hat{Q} < \tilde{Q}$, the company's plans can be revised using formal analysis. Formal analysis can also be used when the sales goal is met to check for sensitivity of the plans to estimates and assumptions. Finally, in principle, the original plans could have been developed using formal analysis.

For example, decision theory could be used to find the set of plans D', S' that leads to the highest expected sales or profit across different future environments. Or a maximin criterion might be used to ensure that the (minimum) sales goal is met. Optimization could be employed to find, for a given future environment, profit-maximizing plans D^*, S^*. Differential games and simulation offer modeling alternatives that may be more able to capture the complexity of potential competitive response. Each of these techniques can utilize sensitivity analysis to see how much the environment would have to change before the company's plans and decisions would need to change. This type of tactical planning meshes well with the needs of strategic planning, where sensitivity analysis, not perfect forecasts, may be preferred (Naylor 1983).

In the final analysis, we are seeking to improve marketing decisions by using models based on empirical data. One of the reasons that some models seem to be so good is that *any* rational intervention would help the situation.

Profit increases or cost reductions can sometimes arise merely through focusing management attention on simple insights, a kind of Hawthorne effect. The analogy suggests, however that improvement must be carefully defined and the causes for it identified. The effectiveness of a model in producing improvement is a scientific issue in itself (Schultz 1975). It would be better if more model builders and users understood this simple truth.

Notes

1. *Reason in Human Affairs* serves as an antidote to the popular "excellence" books that doubt the power of rational thinking.

2. For other views on learning from experience, see Einhorn (1982) Fischoff (1982), and Chi and Glaser (1985).

3. This concept in marketing is from Parsons and Schultz (1976); it should not be confused with "representativeness" as used in the decision analysis literature (cf. Tversky and Kahneman 1981).

4. Also see Nisbitt et al. (1982) and Pitz and Sachs (1984).

5. This argument applies with particular force to a well-defined task such as planning and forecasting; however, other aspects of decision making may require innovation and hence "inconsistency." See Hogarth (1982).

6. When we speak of optimization, it is in the sense of bounded optimization, i.e., optimization of a model, which itself is a representation and simplification of the real problem. So we are always cautious about Type III errors.

7. The Bass growth model contains two coefficients representing external and internal influences, respectively (Lekvall and Wahlbin 1973). When a multiplicative response term for a marketing decision variable is introduced into the Bass model, the implication is that the decision variable affects both coefficients identically. Simon and Sebastian (1987, pp. 453–54) argued that there is no behavioral substantiation for this hypothesis.

8. Devinney (1987) pointed out that the fact that costs have declined may have nothing to do with learning but may be driven by their reaction to competitive pressure, especially competitive entry. Since entry and learning yield similar observable effects, an identification problem exists that precludes single-equation estimation of learning effects.

9. The profit function is $m(\exp[\beta_0 - \beta_1/A]) - A$, and the optimality condition is $\beta_0 - \beta_1/A = \ln[A^2/m\beta_1]$.

10. Sufficiently large means $-\beta > i(1 - \alpha T)$.

11. The game matrix was constructed using the following two sales response functions:

$$Q_1 = 1500 + 20A_1 - 1.00A_1^2 - 10A_2 + 0.3A_2^2$$
$$Q_2 = 1500 - 14A_1 + 0.42A_1^2 - 18A_2 - 0.7A_2^2.$$

In calculating profits, the gross margin per unit exclusive of advertising costs for each brand was assumed to be 50 monetary units.

12. Open-loop controls are easier to solve because they involve ordinary differential equations rather than partial differential equations. Thus, $\partial X/\partial Q$ terms in (8.63b) disappear.

13. Deal squares advertising in the performance index as a way of capturing the diminishing returns to scale of advertising expenditures. It would seem more appropriate to modify the sales response functions. Case (1979, pp. 171, 200) gets a squared advertising term as a result of the normalization of a specific sales response function.

Appendix

Table A8–1. Theoretical Monopolistic Marketing Decision Models: Deterministic Sales Response to Price

Model	Criterion Variable	Information Output: Optimal Marketing	Method of Solution	Information Input
Evans (1924)/ Miller (1979)	Total profit	Price path	Calculus of variations	Linear s.r.f., quadratic unit cost function, planning horizon, initial and ending prices
Amoroso (1954)	Current profit	Price	Calculus	General s.r.f., unit production cost
Robinson and Lakhani (1975)	Discounted profit	Price path	Dynamic programming	Market growth s.r.f., BCG unit cost function, initial cumulative volume, discount rate
Bass (1980)	Current profit	Price	Calculus	Market growth s.r.f., BCG unit cost function, initial cumulative volume
Dolan and Jeuland (1981)	Discounted profit	Price path	Optimal control theory	Diffusion with repeat buying s.r.f., general unit cost function, discount rate
Bass and Bultez (1982)	Discounted profit	Price path	Dynamic programming	Market growth s.r.f., BCG unit cost function, discount rate
Jeuland and Dolan (1982)	Discounted profit	Price path	Optimal control theory	Diffusion with repeat buying s.r.f., general unit cost function, discount rate
Clarke, Darrough, and Heineke (1982)	Discounted profit	Price path	Optimal control theory	General s.r.f., general unit cost function, discount rate
Jørgensen (1983)	Discounted profit	Price path	Optimal control theory	Market growth s.r.f., unit production cost, discount rate

Kalish (1983)	Discounted profit	Price path	Optimal control theory	General s.r.f., general unit cost function, discount rate
Feichtinger, Luhmer and Sorger (1988)	Discounted profit	Store prices, store advertising	Optimal control theory	Multiplicative s.r.f., vector of direct unit costs, discount rate
Nascimento and Vanhonacker (1988)	Discounted profit	Price path	Optimal control theory	Modified (for copy piracy) market growth s.r.f., unit production cost, discount rate

Table A8–2.   Theoretical Monopolistic Marketing Decision Models: Deterministic Sales Response to Advertising

Model	Criterion Variable	Information Output: Optimal Marketing	Method of Solution	Information Input
Rasmussen (1952)	Current profit	Advertising	Calculus	General s.r.f., gross margin per unit
Dorfman and Steiner (1954)	Current profit	Price, advertising, distribution, product quality	Calculus	General s.r.f., unit production cost
Nerlove and Arrow (1962)	Discounted profit	Advertising	Calculus of variations	Special s.r.f., unit cost function, goodwill depreciation rate, discount rate
Dhyrmes (1962)	Discounted profit	Advertising, capital stock, R&D	Calculus of variations	Nerlove-Arrow s.r.f., unit cost function, goodwill depreciation rate, discount rate
Gould (1970)	Discounted profit	Advertising	Optimal control theory	Nerlove-Arrow s.r.f., unit cost function, advertising cost function, goodwill depreciation rate, discount rate
Sasieni (1971)	Discounted profit	Advertising schedule	Dynamic programming	Concave s.r.f., gross margin per unit, discount rate, planning horizon
Tsurumi and Tsurumi (1971)[a]	Discounted revenue subject to minimum discounted profit	Advertising	Discrete optimal control theory	Nerlove-Arrow s.r.f., unit cost function, goodwill depreciation rate, discount rate, planning horizon
Ireland and Jones (1973)[a]	Discounted profit	Advertising	Optimal control theory	Linear (in advertising share) s.r.f., markup rate, discount rate, planning horizon
Jacquemin (1973)	Discounted profit	Advertising	Optimal control theory	Nerlove-Arrow s.r.f., general reaction function, unit cost function, goodwill depreciation rate, discount rate

Study	Objective	Decision variable(s)	Method	Model/assumptions
Kohn and Plessner (1973)[a]	Total revenue	Advertising	Discrete optimal control theory	Linear s.r.f., minimum target sales, maximum shipping capacity, planning horizon
Sethi (1973; 1974b)	Discounted profit subject to terminal market share	Advertising schedule	Optimal control theory	Vidale-Wolfe s.r.f, gross margin per unit, initial sales rate, discount rate, planning horizon
Tsurumi (1973)[a]	Discounted profit	Advertising	Calculus of variations, discrete optimal control theory	Nerlove-Arrow s.r.f., unit cost function, goodwill depreciation rate, discount rate
Sweeney, Abad, and Dornoff (1974)	Undiscounted profit	Advertising schedule	Optimal control theory	Vidale-Wolfe s.r.f., initial sales rate, value of ending sales rate, gross margin per unit, planning horizon
Lambin, Naert, and Bultez (1975)[a]	Undiscounted profit	Price, advertising, product quality	Calculus	Various s.r.f.'s, unit cost function
Mann (1975)[a]	Discounted profit	Advertising	Calculus	Modal-delayed carryover effects s.r.f., gross margin per unit, discount rate
Sethi (1975)	Discounted profit	Advertising	Optimal control theory	Logarithmic s.r.f., gross margin per unit, discount rate
Turner and Neuman (1976)	Discounted profit	Advertising	Optimal control theory	Modified Vidale-Wolfe s.r.f., gross margin per unit, discount rate, initial market share
Srinivasan (1976)	Discounted profit	Advertising media plan	Discrete optimal control theory	General s.r.f., gross margin per unit, discount rate
Sethi (1977b)	Discounted profit	Advertising	Optimal control theory	Nerlove-Arrow s.r.f., unit cost function, goodwill depreciation rate, discount rate, planning horizon

Table A8–2 (continued)

Model	Criterion Variable	Information Output: Optimal Marketing	Method of Solution	Information Input
Bensoussan, Bultez, and Naert (1978)	Discounted profit	Price, advertising	Optimal control theory	Carryover effects s.r.f., competitive reaction functions, unit production cost, discount rate, planning horizon
Bultez and Schultz (1979)[a]	Discounted profit	Price, advertising	Calculus	General s.r.f., unit production cost, discount rate
Freeland and Weinberg (1980)	Sales subject to budget constraint	Advertising	Marginal analysis of concave approximation	Nondecreasing S-shaped s.r.f., planning horizon
Simon (1982)[a]	Discounted profit	Advertising schedule	Calculus	Semilogarithmic s.r.f with partial adjustment and asymmetric response, gross margin per unit, planning horizon, discount rate, advertising budget
Welam (1982)	Discounted profit	Advertising, price	Calculus	Geometric lag carryover effects/multiplicative s.r.f., unit production cost, discount rate
Horsky and Simon (1983)[a]	Discounted profit	Advertising	Optimal control theory	Market growth s.r.f., gross margin per unit, discount rate
Sethi (1983)	Discounted profit	Number of advertising insertions	Discrete optimal control theory	Blattberg-Jeuland s.r.f., gross margin per unit, cost per advertising insertion, discount rate

Gijbrechts and Naert (1984)	Total profit across product groups subject to budget constraint	Product group marketing expenditures, prices, values[b]	Inspection of graphical representation	Special s.r.f.'s, unit production costs, bounds on market shares, budget constraint
Kalish (1985)	Discounted profit	Advertising, prices	Optimal control theory	Market growth s.r.f., market potential, unit production costs, discount rate
Mesak (1985)	Discounted profit subject to budget constraint	Advertising	Langrangian multiplier	Special s.r.f., growth rate, decay rate, budget cycle duration, marginal profit of dollar sales, discount rate
Dockner and Jørgensen (1988)	Discounted profit	Advertising	Optimal control theory	Market growth s.r.f., BCG unit cost function, discount rate, planning horizon
Jedidi, Eliashberg, and DeSarbo (1989)	Discounted profit	Advertising, price	Optimal control theory	Market growth s.r.f., BCG unit cost function, planning horizon

a. These studies also provide empirical results.
b. Value is a measure of product quality weighted by breadth of product line.

Table A8–3.   Theoretical Marketing Decision Models: Stochastic Sales Response Functions

Model	Criterion Variable	Information Output: Optimal Marketing	Method of Solution	Information Input
Little (1966)	Expected profit	Advertising	Adaptive control	Quadratic s.r.f., gross margin per unit
Anderson and Amato (1974)	Expected profit	Brand assortment and number of facings	Special algorithm	Linear s.r.f. with stochastic parameter variation, product display area, sizes of each brand, market potential, gross margin per unit
Tapiero (1975a)	Expected discounted profit	Advertising schedule	Stochastic optimal control theory	Stochastic (random-walk) version of Nerlove-Arrow s.r.f., unit cost function, goodwill depreciation rate, discount rate
Tapiero (1975b)	Expected discounted profit	Advertising schedule	Stochastic optimal control theory	Stochastic (random-walk) version of Vidale-Wolfe s.r.f., unit cost function, discount rate
Pekelman and Sethi (1978)	Expected discounted profit	Advertising schedule, copy replacement	Dynamic programming, optimal control theory	Stochastic version of Vidale-Wolfe s.r.f., gross margin per unit, discount rate
Pekelman and Tse (1980)[a]	Expected discounted profit	Advertising schedule	Adaptive control	Stochastic linear s.r.f., profit margin per unit, discount rate
Monahan (1983)	Expected discounted profit	Advertising	Dynamic programming (Markov decision process)	Stochastic concave s.r.f., gross margin per unit, discount rate, planning horizon

Monahan (1984)	Expected discounted profit	Advertising	Dynamic programming (Markov decision process)	Market growth s.r.f., gross margin per unit, discount rate
Raman (1987a)	Expected discounted profit	Price, advertising, distribution, product quality	Dynamic programming	General s.r.f., unit product cost, discount rate
Tapiero, Eliashberg, and Wind (1987)	Expected utility of discounted profit and target market share	Advertising	Stochastic optimal control theory	Stochastic (random-walk) version of Vidale-Wolfe s.r.f., gross margin per unit, discount rate, planning horizon
Eliashberg, Tapiero, and Wind (1987)	Expected utility for profit	Advertising	Stochastic optimal control theory	Bass s.r.f. with stochastic parameters, and advertising influencing linearly the external source of communication parameter, budget constraint, planning horizon
Horsky and Mate (1988)	Expected discounted profit	Advertising	Dynamic programming (Markov decision process)	Market growth s.r.f., gross margin per unit, discount rate

a. This study also provides empirical results.

Table A8–4. Empirical Marketing Decision Models

Model	Criterion Variable	Information Output: Optimal Marketing	Method of Solution	Information Input
Ball and Agarwala (1969)	Maintenance of sales	Advertising	Algebra	Linear geometric distributed lag s.r.f.
Urban (1969)	Current profit	Price and number of facings	Iterative search routine	Multiplicative s.r.f., cost function
Parsons and Bass (1971)	Discounted profit	Advertising schedule	Nonlinear programming	Multiplicative s.r.f.'s with partial adjustment, competitive advertising, gross margin per unit, discount rate
Schultz (1971a)	Discounted profit	Advertising schedule and number of flights	Calculus	Linear market share s.r.f.'s with partial adjustment, competitive advertising, total market demand, planned prices
Clarke (1973)	Current profit	Advertising	Calculus	Linear market share s.r.f.'s with partial adjustment, competitive advertising, total market demand, planned gross margin per unit
Parsons (1974)	Total profit	Advertising and distribution schedules	Nonlinear programming	Multiplicative s.r.f. with partial adjustment, gross margin per unit
Wildt (1974)	Current profit	Price path and advertising schedule	Calculus	Multiplicative market share s.r.f.'s, competitive advertising and price, total market demand, unit production costs

Reference	Objective	Decision variable	Method	Model
Parsons (1975a)	Total profit	Advertising schedule	Nonlinear programming	Multiplicative s.r.f. with a time-varying elasticity, gross margin per unit
Turner and Wiginton (1976)	Discounted profit	Advertising schedule	Optimal control theory	Vidale-Wolfe s.r.f., gross margin per unit, initial sales rate, discount rate, planning horizon
Horsky (1977b)	Discounted profit	Advertising schedule	Optimal control theory	Lancaster s.r.f., gross margin per unit, industry sales rate, competitive goodwill, discount rate
Picconi and Olson (1978)	Discounted profit	Advertising schedule	Optimal control theory	Multiplicative s.r.f. with geometric distributed lag, discount rate
Wierenga (1981)	Number of visitors	Advertising media schedule	Heuristic	Multiplicative s.r.f.
Reibstein and Gatignon (1984)	Total profit	Product line prices	Calculus	Multiplicative s.r.f.'s (with disturbances correlated across items), unit production costs

Table A8–5.   Competitive Advertising Decision Models

Model	Criterion Variable	Information Output: Optimal Marketing	Method of Solution or Solution Concept	Information Input
Friedman (1958)	Current profit	Advertising	Calculus	Linear s.r.f., contribution margin per unit, total unit volume
Mills (1961)	Current profit	Promotion	Algorithm	Linear s.r.f., contribution margin per unit, total unit volume
Shakun (1965)	Current profit	Product line advertising	Calculus	Modified exponential s.r.f.'s, contribution margins per unit, saturation level
Shakun (1966)	Discounted profit	Product line advertising	Calculus	Modified exponential s.r.f.'s, contribution margins per unit, saturation level, discount rate
Case (1975)	Discounted profit	Advertising	Cournot-Nash equilibrium	Square root s.r.f.'s, contribution potentials, initial market shares, discount rate
Olsder (1976)	Total profit	Advertising	Cournot-Nash equilibrium	Linear s.r.f.'s, contribution margins per unit, industry sales, initial sales, planning horizon
Schmalensee (1976)	Discounted profit	Advertising	Cournot-Nash equilibrium	Linear distributed lag carryover effects s.r.f.'s, contribution margins per unit, discount rate
Leitmann and Schmitendorf (1978)	Total profit	Advertising	Cournot-Nash equilibrium	Quadratic s.r.f.'s, contribution potentials, initial market shares, planning horizon
Deal (1979)	Multiobjective performance index	Advertising	Cournot-Nash equilibrium	Vidale-Wolfe s.r.f.'s contribution margins per unit, performance weighting factors for brand

Deal, Sethi, and Thompson (1979)	Discounted profit	Advertising	Cournot-Nash equilibrium	Modified Vidale-Wolfe s.r.f.'s, contribution margins per unit, discount rates
Tapiero (1979)	Sales, discounted profit	Advertising	Cournot-Nash equilibrium	Stochastic version of Nerlove-Arrow s.r.f., unit cost function, goodwill depreciation rate, discount rate, total industry sales (or its probability distribution)
Wrather and Yu (1979)	Sales	Selective advertising, primary demand advertising	Cournot-Nash equilibrium	Quadratic s.r.f.'s, budget constraints
Jorgensen (1982)	Discounted profit	Advertising	Cournot-Nash equilibrium	Logarithmic s.r.f.'s, contribution margins per unit, discount rates, planning horizon
Friedman (1983)	Discounted profit	Advertising	Cournot-Nash equilibrium	Nerlove-Arrow type s.r.f.'s, unit cost function, goodwill depreciation function, discount rate
Jones (1983)	Sales	Equilibrium sales	Calculus	Vidale-Wolfe and modified Vidale-Wolfe s.r.f.'s
Teng and Thompson (1983)	Discounted profit	Advertising	Cournot-Nash equilibrium	Vidale-Wolfe/market growth s.r.f.'s, unit cost functions, advertising cost functions, prices, discount rates, planning horizon
Rao (1984)	Discounted profit	Advertising	Cournot-Nash equilibrium	Nerlove-Arrow s.r.f.'s initial sales rates, contribution margins per unit, discount rates
Thompson and Teng (1984)	Discounted profit	Advertising prices	Cournot-Nash equilibrium	Vidale-Wolfe/market growth s.r.f.'s, unit cost functions, advertising cost functions, prices, discount rates, planning horizon

Table A8–5 (continued)

Model	Criterion Variable	Information Output: Optimal Marketing	Method of Solution or Solution Concept	Information Input
Erickson (1985)	Discounted profit	Advertising	Cournot-Nash equilibrium	Lancaster s.r.f.'s with market expansion, contribution margins per unit, discount rates, planning horizon
Calantone and di Benedetto (1986)[a]	Sales dollars	Advertising, prices	Game matrix	Carryover effects s.r.f.'s
Dockner and Feichtinger (1986)	Discounted profit	Advertising, prices	Cournot-Nash equilibrium	Concave s.r.f.'s, unit production costs, discount rates

a. This study also reports empirical results.

Table A8–6. Competitive Pricing Decision Models

Model	Criterion Variable	Information Output: Optimal Marketing	Method of Solution or Solution Concept	Information Input
Osborne (1984)	Multiobjective performance index	Prices	Cournot-Nash equilibrium, Pareto optimal	Linear s.r.f.'s, unit production costs
Gaugusch (1984)	Discounted profit	Prices, advertising	Cournot-Nash equilibrium	Special s.r.f.'s unit production costs, discount rates, planning horizon, salvage values
Dockner (1985)	Discounted profit	Prices	Cournot-Nash equilibrium	Market growth s.r.f.'s, unit production costs, discount rates, planning horizon, initial unit sales
Feichtinger and Dockner (1985)	Discounted profit	Prices	Cournot-Nash equilibrium	Diffusion with repeat buying s.r.f.'s, unit production costs, planning horizon, initial market shares
Eliashberg and Jeuland (1986)	Total profit	Prices	Cournot-Nash equilibrium	Linear (in prices) s.r.f., diffusion with no internal communication, constant marginal unit cost
Wernerfelt (1986)	Discounted profit	Prices	Cournot-Nash equilibrium	Concave s.r.f., unit cost function, initial costs and market shares, discount rate
Gasmi and Vuong (1988)[a]	Current profit	Advertising, prices	Cournot-Nash equilibrium	Square root s.r.f.'s, unit production costs
Dockner and Jørgensen (1988)	Discounted profits	Pricing	Cournot-Nash equilibrium	Diffusion s.r.f.'s, unit production functions, discount rates, planning horizon

a. This study also provides empirical results.

9 AN APPLICATION OF ETS MODELING

The previous chapters have developed a combined econometric-time series analytic approach to market response modeling. Since the integration of these techniques is fairly new, few published market response models have been built using ETS. Instead, we typically find applications of either econometric or time series techniques in market response models, as evidenced by the articles on sales response and competition surveyed in chapter 6.

The purpose of this chapter is to illustrate the use and the advantages of ETS using a completely worked-out example. We focus on (1) the specification of an ETS model in a real-world competitive market using different levels of prior knowledge, and (2) the implications of the model for marketing diagnostics and improved marketing decision making.

The chosen setting involves estimating marketing effectiveness for several competitors in a stable market of Australian household products.[1] The market consists of eight major brands belonging to conglomerates, 1 and 2, and one independent producer, 3. For completeness, we also consider three "all other" (A) or catchall brands, mainly of the regional and store variety. Competition in this market occurs mainly on the basis of price, advertising, and product forms, dry (D) and wet (W). Some brands have physical characteristics that offer tangential (T) benefits to the consumer (brands TD1, TD2, and TW2),

Table 9–1. Average Market Shares, Advertising, and Prices*

Brand	Description	Average Market Share	Average Price	Average Advertising
ED1	Economy Dry	5.4	$1.48	$ 8,100
ED2	Economy Dry	2.6	1.51	0
ED3	Economy Dry	7.1	1.59	14,300
ID1	Image Dry	10.0	1.79	34,800
ID2	Image Dry	4.9	1.87	42,400
TD1	Tangible Dry	4.5	2.14	25,600
TD2	Tangible Dry	4.5	1.87	29,400
TW2	Tangible Wet	7.8	1.81	50,000
AO1	All Other Co. 1	9.5	1.82	37,300
AD4	All Other Dry	26.2	1.34	2,300
AW4	All Other Wet	17.5	1.00	39,500

* Reprinted by permission. "Modeling Asymmetric Competition," Gregory S. Carpenter, Lee G. Cooper, Dominique M. Hanssens, and David F. Midgley, *Marketing Science*, vol. 7, no. 4, Fall 1988. © 1988, The Institute of Management Sciences and the Operations Research Society of America.

others position themselves as premium image (I) brands (ID1 and ID2), and still others offer lower prices, which qualifies them as economy (E) brands (ED1, ED2, and ED3). An overview of the brands and their average performance levels for a 26-month time sample in the 1980s is given in table 9–1. The market share and price data are collected from a national panel of several thousand consumers, and the advertising data (mainly television) come from a separate agency.

Since industry demand is stable over the sample period, we wish to investigate marketing effectiveness using market share as the criterion variable. In particular, the following research and planning questions are of interest:

1. How does each brand's market share respond to changes in price and advertising support?
2. Are there interbrand differences in the magnitude and the duration of that response?
3. Are there market asymmetries, i.e., pairs of brands that are particularly vulnerable to each other's actions?
4. What are the patterns of competitive behavior in pricing and advertising, if any?
5. How can the answers to the previous questions be used to improve pricing and advertising allocations for a brand?

We know a priori that simultaneous causality between marketing effort and market performance cannot occur; brand managers do not receive market intelligence reports until four months after the fact, so they cannot react instantaneously to monthly market share changes. We therefore have level 1 prior knowledge about market response: market share is hypothesized to be influenced by brand and competitive price and advertising movements, but the magnitude and the duration of these effects remain to be determined. On the other hand, studying competitive reactions must be done at level 0 prior knowledge: in this oligopolistic market it is unclear a priori if any brand acts as a price or advertising leader or if the brand managers make marketing decisions independently of one another. The ETS techniques developed in chapter 5 may be used to establish empirically temporal sequences in competitive actions. Finally, we use the framework of chapter 8 to offer some recommendations for improved decision making for the various brands.

Market Share Response Model

The functional form for market response modeling is chosen on theoretical as well as practical grounds. Because information is available on all relevant brands (including three aggregate brands), we wish to model the market in its entirety rather than selecting a particular brand's market share as the criterion variable. Modeling the market in its entirety also allows the study of competitive asymmetry, i.e., the phenomenon that some brands may be more affected by competitive actions than others. Following up on the discussion in chapter 2, we select the attraction or multiplicative competitive interaction (MCI) model, as a basis for measuring market share response to price and advertising. The MCI model is intuitively appealing in that it relates competitive market shares to the relative attractiveness of the brands to consumers. Although its functional form is complex, the model is linearizable and therefore easily estimable, and it generates market share predictions that are range- and sum-constrained (e.g., Nakanishi and Cooper 1974; 1982). A general form of the MCI model, known as the differential-effects model (see equation 2.37), applied to the Australian product data is

$$MS_{it} = \frac{MS_{io} A_{it}^{\beta_{1i}} P_{it}^{\beta_{2i}} e^{u_{it}}}{\sum_{j=1}^{I} A_{jt}^{\beta_{1j}} P_{jt}^{\beta_{2j}} e^{u_{jt}}}, \tag{9.1}$$

where MS denotes market share, A is advertising, P is price, i refers to brand i ($i = 1, \ldots, 11$), and t refers to period t ($t = 1, \ldots, 26$).

This version (9.1) of the attraction model is flexible in that it allows for the brands to have their own advertising and price sensitivities (β_{1i} and β_{2i}) and their own market share constants (MS_{io}). As we shall see, simple empirical tests will reveal whether this much flexibility is needed. However, model 9.1 does not incorporate the dynamics of market share response nor does it allow for market asymmetries to exist. We discuss how ETS techniques may be used to answer the key questions about the market by expanding or simplifying the structure of (9.1).

As mentioned, the attraction model is linearizable and therefore can be estimated with ordinary or generalized least squares. This is done either by log-centering the data or by taking logarithms and adding brand-specific and time-specific intercepts in the equation. The second technique, proposed by Nakanishi and Cooper (1982), is easily implementable and produces the following estimation equation:

$$\log MS_{it} = \beta_0 + \beta_{1i} \log A_{it} + \beta_{2i} \log P_{it} + \sum_{i'=1}^{I-1} \alpha_i D_{1i'} + \sum_{t'=1}^{T-1} \gamma_t D_{2t'} + u_{it},$$

$$(9.2)$$

where the dummy variables are defined as

$$D_{1i'} = \begin{cases} 1 & \text{if } i = i' \\ 0 & \text{otherwise} \end{cases}$$

$$D_{2t'} = \begin{cases} 1 & \text{if } t = t' \\ 0 & \text{otherwise} \end{cases}$$

In what follows we develop the ETS specification methods on the estimation form (9.2) of the attraction model.

Specifying Attraction Dynamics

As discussed in chapter 7, the dynamics of advertising and price response often need to be identified from empirical analysis, a typical case of level 1 prior knowledge. What complicates the problem in this case is that the inclusion of several lagged terms in the MCI model will create severe collinearity problems (cf. Cooper and Nakanishi 1988). Remember that we must already estimate $(I - 1) + (T - 1) = 35$ dummy variables in addition to the response parameters. Then, if the price and advertising variables are autocorrelated, collinearity problems will become serious. It is preferable from an estimation perspective to summarize the lag structure for each marketing variable in a dynamic attraction variable. Such a dynamic attraction variable is then entered as a single explanatory variable in the market share model.

Suppose we find the effects of advertising on market share die out gradually over three periods. The dynamic advertising attraction component, or "effective advertising" (EA), might be

$$EA_t = .6A_t + .3A_{t-1} + .1A_{t-2}, \tag{9.3}$$

where the weights are determined empirically.

The general marketing dynamics model we formulated in chapter 7 lends itself particularly well to this task. Applying the transfer function specification we formulated in that chapter to a single-equation dynamic response model in price and advertising, we may write for each brand

$$\log MS_{it} = c_i + \frac{\omega_{1i}(L)}{\delta_{1i}(L)} \log A_{it} + \frac{\omega_{2i}(L)}{\delta_{2i}(L)} \log P_{it} + v_{it}, \tag{9.4}$$

where ω_{1i}, δ_{1i} are the advertising transfer function parameters, and ω_{2i}, δ_{2i} are the price transfer function parameters for brand i.

By writing a separate transfer function for each brand we recognize that lag structures in price and advertising response need not be identical for each brand. For example, brands may use different advertising media, which may result in varying response patterns. Therefore, a separate two-input transfer function should be identified for each brand. This is done on the logarithms of the data in order to be consistent with the multiplicative specification of the market share response model. Using the Liu-Hanssens (1982) method we estimate for each brand i:

$$\log MS_{it} = c_i + V_{1i}(L) \log A_{it} + V_{2i}(L) \log P_{it} + w_{it}, \tag{9.5}$$

where the maximum lag lengths were set at 6 for price and advertising. Preliminary investigation revealed the price data to be autoregressive, with an average first-order autocorrelation of 0.7 (see also table 9.6). Thus, we applied the filter $(1 - .7L)$ to the data, following the recommendation of Liu and Hanssens (1982).

The least-squares specification method revealed contemporaneous effects of price and zero- and first-order effects of advertising. The pricing result suggests that consumers are opportunistic and short-sighted about prices, i.e., they make brand choice decisions based on current price only. The current and one-month delayed advertising effects are not uncommon in the frequently purchased branded goods sector; the interbrand differences in the lag weights are strong, ranging from 100% current effects to 100% lagged effects, suggesting that it was a worthwhile idea to investigate brand-specific dynamic response to advertising. Consequently, we must construct brand-specific effective advertising variables. These are listed in table 9–2.

Table 9–2. Dynamic Advertising Components

Brand	LAG 0	LAG 1
ED1	.33[a]	.67
ED2[b]		
ED3	.90	.10
ID1	.25	.75
ID2	1.00	0
TD1	.10	.90
TD2	.60	.40
TW2	0	1.00
AO1	.50	.50
AD4	1.00	0
AW4	.60	.40

a. Weights are normalized to sum to 1.
b. This brand does not advertise.

Assessing Interbrand Differences in Market Response

Once the functional form and the dynamics of market response are specified, there are two more ways in which brands may be either unique or homogeneous in their market share sensitivity to advertising and pricing. The constant portion of market share (base share) may be brand-specific, or the advertising and price slope coefficients may be brand-specific.

If the base share and slope vectors are the same for each brand, a simplified version of the attraction model would result:

$$MS_{it} = \frac{MS_o A_{it}^{\beta_1} P_{it}^{\beta_2} e^{u_{it}}}{\sum\limits_{j=1}^{I} A_{jt}^{\beta_1} P_{jt}^{\beta_2} e^{u_{jt}}}. \tag{9.6}$$

Since the simple-effects model is nested in the differential-effects model, a straightforward test consists of restricting the set of brand-specific intercepts MS_{oi} and slopes β_{1i} and β_{2i} to be common and computing the F-statistic on the restriction. It is easy to do this in the context of an MCI model by using the linear form of the model (9.2). This model may be tested against the restricted model:

$$\log MS_{it} = \beta_o + \beta_1 \log A_{it} + \beta_2 \log P_{it} + \sum_{t'=1}^{T-1} \gamma_t D_{2t'} + u_{it}. \tag{9.7}$$

The results of these tests for common base shares and common response to

Table 9–3. Testing for Differences in Market Share Response

	Model				
Base Share	Advertising	Price	RSS	DF	Test
Specific	Specific	Specific	13.932	219	
Specific	Common	Specific	15.082	228	$p < .05$
Specific	Specific	Common	16.809	229	$p < .01$
Specific	Common	Common	17.984	238	$p < .01$
Common	Specific	Specific	16.307	229	$p < .01$
Common	Common	Specific	17.578	238	$p < .01$
Common	Specific	Common	89.398	239	$p < .01$
Common	Common	Common	87.880	248	$p < .01$

RSS = Residual sums of squares.
DF = Degrees of freedom.
Test = Type I error probability of the restriction against the first model.

price and advertising are shown in table 9–3. They are overwhelmingly in favor of a differential response structure, i.e., brands have different base shares and exhibit different responses to advertising and prices. Though this result implies that a fairly complex response model is needed to represent the market, it also offers a special opportunity to investigate the advertising and pricing implications for each brand and how they differ.

Testing for Marketing Asymmetries

So far, we have established that consumers in this Australian household product market react instantaneously to monthly prices, that they respond to advertising with up to one month lag, and that the market shares of the competing brands have unique base shares and price-advertising sensitivities. One critical question remains unanswered before a complete market share model can be estimated: Are there pairs of brands that are particularly vulnerable to each other's actions? A positive answer implies the market is asymmetric in its response to competitive marketing actions.

Since the data base is restricted to movements in market shares, prices, and advertising efforts, such qualitative factors as product positioning are not formally recognized. For example, if brands A and B are perceived by consumers as being close substitutes of one another, a price cut initiated by A may well affect the share of B more negatively than the shares of other competitors. This is a simple example of an asymmetric response to prices,

which our model has not yet accounted for. Its immediate managerial implication is that B's manager should be more alert to price moves by brand A than
to price changes by other competitors.

The attraction model may be extended to include market asymmetries by
adding special attraction components. In our example, A's attraction and
therefore market share would be directly determined by the price of B in
addition to brand A's own attraction components. With 11 brands and 2
marketing variables there could be up to 220 sources of asymmetry in the
general asymmetric model

$$MS_{it} = \frac{MS_{io} \prod\limits_{j=1}^{I} A_{jt}^{\beta_{1ij}} P_{jt}^{\beta_{2ij}} e^{u_{it}}}{\sum\limits_{k=1}^{I} \prod\limits_{j=1}^{I} A_{jt}^{\beta_{1kj}} P_{jt}^{\beta_{2kj}} e^{u_{kt}}}. \qquad (9.8)$$

Such a model clearly puts too many demands on the data, and so the critical
question is how to distinguish between fundamental or systematic asymmetries
and those that are small enough so that they can safely be set to zero.

The principles of transfer function specification may be used to identify
nonzero marketing asymmetries. For example, consider the market share
response of brand 1. We have at this point made preliminary estimates of
advertising and price sensitivity. Using lowercase notation for the variables
to indicate a log-centered form of the response model, and omitting the time
subscript t, we may write

$$ms_1 = b_1 a_1 + b_2 p_1 + u_1. \qquad (9.9)$$

If brand 2's advertising has a direct impact on brand 1's share beyond the
symmetric effect due to the sum constraint on market shares, then the true
log-centered model for brand 1 is

$$ms_1 = c_1 a_1 + c_2 p_1 + c_3 a_2 + v_1, \qquad (9.10)$$

where c_3 is expected to be negative. Now compute the cross-covariance
function between the omitted competitive variable a_2 and the residuals u_1 (9.9):

$$E(u_1 a_2) = E(ms_1 - b_1 a_1 - b_2 p_1)a_2$$
$$= E(c_1 a_1 + c_2 p_1 + c_3 a_2 + v_1 - b_1 a_1 - b_2 p_1)a_2$$
$$= (c_1 - b_1)E(a_1 a_2) + (c_2 - b_2)E(p_1 a_2) + c_3 E a_2^2, \qquad (9.11)$$

since $E(v_1 a_2) = 0$ by definition. The main contributor to this cross-covariance
is the cross-effect c_3 and the variance of brand 2's advertising. Therefore, the
cross-covariance or cross-correlation between the residuals of the differential-
effects models and the competitive marketing variables can be used to detect

market asymmetries. A significant cross-covariance or cross-correlation would be an indicator of a market asymmetry between the share of brand 1 and the advertising of brand 2.[2] Although the analysis could be performed at various lags of the cross-correlation function, it seems reasonable to assume that any dynamic effects are already included in the dynamically weighted attraction components; therefore the cross-correlations are computed only at lag zero. As a result of this specification test, the differential-effects model (9.1) may be augmented by a subset of cross-effects of the fully asymmetric model (9.8).

Table 9-4 shows the results for the named brands. In order to avoid capitalizing on chance, the results are cross-validated on another market in Australia. While one cross-correlation is significant at $p < .01$ and ten others at $p < .10$, they do not hold up in cross-validation on market 2. We therefore conclude that there is no hard evidence of systematic market asymmetries in this case and proceed to estimate the differential-effects model (9.1) on the data.

Table 9-4a. Testing for Marketing Asymmetries: Advertising

	ED1	ED3	ID1	ID2	TD1	TD2	TW2
ED1		−.02	.30	.02	.24	.20	−.18
ED3	.00		−.12	.09	.33	.09	.14
ID1	−.33	−.20		−.20	.31	.34	.08
ID2	−.11	−.02	−.07		−.08	.06	−.07
TD1	−.34	−.16	−.13	−.28		.15	.23
TD2	.23	.10	−.15	−.26	.36		.06
TW2	−.22	−.14	−.02	−.11	.35	.12	

Note: Correlations for the named brands only.

Table 9-4b. Testing for Marketing Asymmetries: Pricing

	ED1	ED2	ED3	ID1	ID2	TD1	TD2	TW2
ED1		.01	−.30	.36	−.07	.06	.30	.16
ED2	−.02		−.02	.23	−.03	−.01	.35	−.09
ED3	.39	−.14		.20	.11	.03	.20	−.03
ID1	.26	.02	−.16		.04	.19	.12	.00
ID2	.51[a]	−.06	.17	.09		.08	−.20	−.39
TD1	.24	−.09	−.05	.35	.25		.31	.05
TD2	.22	.15	−.09	.05	.14	.20		−.07
TW2	.33	−.18	.13	.14	.29	−.08	.33	

Note: Correlations for the named brands only.
a. Significant at $p < .01$.

Estimation Results

The MCI model is complex relative to more standard market response models, yet easy to estimate. As noted before, Nakanishi and Cooper (1974; 1982) have shown that the model is linearizable in two ways:

1. Log-center the dependent and independent variables and use OLS or GLS estimation on the transformed data (Nakanishi and Cooper 1974).
2. Use OLS or GLS on the logarithms of the data while including dummy variables for each brand and each time period (Nakanishi and Cooper 1982).

Either method is likely to suffer from collinearity in the differential-effects case when the number of brands and marketing variables gets larger. An extensive treatment of the sources of, and remedies for, collinearity may be found in Cooper and Nakanishi (1988).

Table 9–5 shows the parameter estimates obtained with generalized least squares along with the implied elasticities of these parameters for an average scenario. These elasticities are related to the attraction parameters as follows:

$$\varepsilon_{MS_i, A_i} = \beta_{1i}(1 - MS_i),$$

$$\eta_{MS_i, A_j} = -\beta_{1i}MS_j, \quad j \neq i, \tag{9.12}$$

Table 9–5. Attraction Parameters and Implied Elasticities

Brand	Advertising Parameter	Price Parameter	Advertising Elasticity[a]	Price Elasticity[a]
ED1	.22(.04)[b]	−2.70(.58)[b]	.21	−2.55
ED2		−3.60(.48)[b]		−3.51
ED3	.07(.02)[b]	−2.59(.46)[b]	.07	−2.41
ID1	.07(.03)[c]	−1.49(.50)[b]	.06	−1.34
ID2	.02(.03)	−2.21(.64)[b]	.02	−2.10
TD1	.07(.04)	−1.35(.74)[c]	.07	−1.29
TD2	.11(.06)[c]	−1.08(.57)[c]	.11	−1.03
TW2	.00(.04)	−1.43(.32)[b]	.00	−1.39
AO1	.06(.03)[c]	−1.31(.51)[b]	.05	−1.19
AD4	.03(.06)	−0.74(.44)[c]	.02	−0.55
AW4	−.12(.07)	−0.22(.56)	−.10	−0.18

a. At the mean market share for each brand.
b. Significant at $p < .01$.
c. Significant at $p < .05$.

where ε_{MS_i, A_i} is the advertising elasticity of brand i, and η_{MS_i, A_j} is its advertising cross-elasticity which brand j, and β_{1i} is the advertising response parameter. A similar result holds for price elasticities. The main implication is that the elasticities vary with market shares. The implied elasticities in table 9–5 are based on the average market share for each brand.

We may draw the following marketing inferences from these results:

1. The economy brands (ED1, ED2, and ED3) have the highest price sensitivity, followed by the premium image brands (ID1 and ID2) and the premium tangible brands (TD1, TD2, and TW2). This is an intuitively appealing and managerially very important result. Offering tangible benefits in the product lowers price elasticity more than merely positioning a brand as premium. Offering bargains attracts the price-sensitive customer but makes the brand more vulnerable to price changes.

2. The advertising effectiveness varies significantly across the brands, with the two advertising economy brands having the highest parameters. Interestingly, there is a virtually perfect match between the rank orders of advertising effectiveness and the coefficients of variation in advertising. This finding supports the notion that high-variance advertising allocation schemes such as pulsing may be more effective than low-variance allocations.

The insights provided by the MCI model so far contain valuable diagnostic information about the market and may be used to make certain strategic recommendations about pricing or advertising for each brand. For example, some brands could be advised that their advertising is ineffective in generating market share, while others might be made aware of unusually high or low consumer sensitivity to their retail prices. Although many ETS projects might be concluded right here, it would also be possible to investigate important issues beyond descriptive market response, in particular the behavior of competitors in the market, and the implications of both for optimal pricing and advertising allocations.

Examining Competitive Behavior

When empirically examining patterns of competitive behavior, we are typically operating at a level 0 prior knowledge: we know who the competitors are and what they are competing with (in this case, prices and advertising), but we do not know a priori whose actions would lead to counteractions, i.e., who if anybody, behaves as leader and follower. Furthermore, we do not know whether competitive reactions are pure (e.g., matching a competitive price cut) or mixed (e.g., launching an advertising campaign in retaliation for a competitive price cut).

This situation calls for the modeling techniques developed in chapter 5, namely, removing the systematic time series behavior of each competitive variable and searching for patterns in the residuals. We do so for 18 of the 22 competitive variables, excluding prices of the three catchall brands and the advertising of ED2, which is always zero. Since the over-time sample size in this application is only 26, we cannot perform a full-scale ARIMA analysis on the 18 time series of competitive prices and advertising. We may, however, compute the autocorrelation functions of the various series and make some simple inferences. The results of this autocorrelation analysis are summarized in table 9–6.

There is a remarkable similarity in the longitudinal behavior of prices and advertising. With one exception (ED1), prices are autoregressive, i.e., they exhibit a smooth pattern such that the current price is a strong predictor of next month's price. Advertising, on the other hand, generally behaves as a white noise process around a mean, with two exceptions (ID1 and ED3). In order to make robust inferences about cross-competitive influences of price

Table 9–6. Autocorrelation Analysis of Prices and Advertising

	Ljung-Box Q-Statistic				Conclusion	
Brand	*Advertising*		*Price*		*Advertising*	*Price*
	$Q(6)$	$Q(12)$	$Q(6)$	$Q(12)$		
ED1	7.54	8.27	8.75	11.78	White noise	White noise
ED2			17.94[a]	19.94[b]		AR(1)
ED3	23.09[a]	38.28[a]	60.04[a]	68.75[a]	MA(6)	AR(1)
ID1	12.22[b]	18.41[b]	50.72[a]	51.95[a]	AR(1)	AR(1)
ID2	8.84	13.45	26.68[a]	27.59[a]	White noise	AR(1)
TD1	2.11	12.70	47.55[a]	50.72[a]	White noise	AR(1)
TD2	1.71	4.48	28.25[a]	28.87[a]	White noise	AR(1)
TW2	5.46	13.44	76.35[a]	87.94[a]	White noise	AR(1)
AO1	5.51	18.19			White noise	
AD1	4.21	13.08			White noise	
AW4	5.98	12.69			White noise	

a. Significant at $p < .01$.
b. Significant at $p < .10$.

and advertising, we filter the eight autoregressive variables in table 9–6 as follows:

$$FX_{i,t} = X_{i,t} - .7X_{i,t-1}$$

and leave the ten other variables at their raw levels. Then, we compute cross-correlations among these series at lags -4 to $+4$. Higher lags are precluded because of the small longitudinal sample.

The cross-correlation results are summarized in table 9–7. To facilitate their interpretation, we replace the actual values by sign markers $(+, 0, -)$, a practice also used by Tiao and Box (1981) in their proposed method for estimating vector ARMA models. The markers are tabulated as follows for each cross-correlation between variables i and j at lag k:

$$\text{if } r_{ij}(k) > 2/\sqrt{T} \text{ then enter '} + \text{'}$$

$$\text{if } r_{ij}(k) < -2/\sqrt{T} \text{ then enter '} - \text{'}$$

otherwise enter '.'

We discuss the results separately for rivalries in price, advertising, and mixed price and advertising.

Price Competition

Of the total possible 256 reaction effects, only 17 are significantly different from zero using $p < .05$. Such a low incidence rate suggests that competitive price reactions are not very prevalent in this industry. One possible exception is the set of reactions to TW2, which accounts for 8 of the 17 observed effects. TW2 is the only named and premium-priced brand in the "wet" category that offers a tangible benefit to consumers. It may be that competitors perceive TW2 as a "strong" brand and are fearful of price disparities with their own offerings. However, the statistical evidence is not overwhelming even in this case.

Advertising Competition

Of the total possible 196 reactions, only 11 are statistically significant. There is no concentration of effects around one or two brands, so we conclude that for all practical purposes competitive reaction in advertising does not occur in this market.

Table 9–7.   Competitive Cross-Correlations*

	PRICE ED1	PRICE ID1	PRICE TD1	PRICE ID2	PRICE ED2	PRICE TD2	PRICE TW2	PRICE ED3
PRICE ED1	·	·	·	·	·	·	·	·
PRICE ID1	·	·	·	·	·	·	·	·
PRICE TD1	·	+	·	·	·	·	+	·
PRICE ID2	·	·	+	+	·	·	·	·
PRICE ED2	·	·	·	·	+	·	·	+
PRICE TD2	·	·	+	·	·	+	+	·
PRICE TW2	+	+	+	·	·	·	+	·
PRICE ED3	+	·	+	·	·	+	·	·
ADV ED1	·	·	·	·	·	·	·	·
ADV ID1	·	·	·	·	·	·	·	·
ADV TD1	·	·	·	+	·	·	·	·
ADV ID2	·	·	+	·	·	·	·	·
ADV TD2	·	·	·	·	·	−	·	·
ADV TW2	·	·	·	·	·	·	−	·
ADV ED3	·	·	·	·	·	−	·	·

	ADV ED1	ADV ID1	ADV TD1	ADV ID2	ADV TD2	ADV TW2	ADV ED3
PRICE ED1	·	·	·	·	·	·	·
PRICE ID1	+	·	·	·	·	·	·
PRICE TD1	+	·	−	·	·	·	·
PRICE ID2	+	·	·	·	·	·	·
PRICE ED2	+	·	−	·	·	·	·
PRICE TD2	·	·	·	·	·	·	·
PRICE TW2	·	·	·	·	·	+	·
PRICE ED3	+	·	·	+	·	·	+
ADV ED1	·	·	·	·	·	·	·
ADV ID1	·	·	+	·	·	−	·
ADV TD1	−	·	·	·	·	·	·
ADV ID2	·	+	+	·	+	·	+
ADV TD2	+	+	·	+	+	−	·
ADV TW2	·	·	·	·	·	·	·
ADV ED3	·	·	·	·	·	−	·

* Reprinted by permission. "Modeling Asymmetric Competition," Gregory S. Carpenter, Lee G. Cooper, Dominique M. Hanssens, and David F. Midgley, *Marketing Science*, vol. 7, no. 4, Fall 1988. © 1988, The Institute of Management Sciences and the Operations Research Society of America.

Mixed Price-Advertising Competition

Of the total 224 possible effects, only 9 are statistically significant. Again we must conclude that competitive reaction of this type is weak in this market, if present at all.

Taken as a whole, the results suggest that managers allocate advertising dollars and set price levels without much regard for the actions of other managers within their firm or for the actions of their counterparts in other firms. Competitive reaction is the exception, not the rule. It may be that the delay with which marketing managers receive marketing information updates makes competitive reaction difficult or that monitoring as many as ten competitors is in itself too time-consuming. However, regardless of patterns in competitive marketing, the fact remains that all brands are affected by all competitors' actions.

Making Inferences about Optimal Marketing Behavior

The previous competitive analysis revealed that no brand may be identified as a systematic leader or follower in either prices or advertising. In the absence of systematic competitive reactions it may prove useful to investigate how individual brands are priced and how their advertising outlays compare to optimal prices and advertising levels derived from the MCI response model.

Making inferences about optimal marketing behavior depends on the competitive context. For example, the optimal price rule for a brand may be quite sensitive to the assumption that a key competitor would or would not match a price cut. The pricing and advertising rules derived here use two extremes of competitive scenarios:

1. *Myopic profit maximization.* Each brand maximizes its profit function independently of competitive considerations. In other words, each brand solves its profit function with respect to advertising and price:

$$\max_i \prod = QMS_i(P_i - VC_i) - FC_i - A_i, \qquad (9.13)$$

   where Q is industry demand, VC is variable cost and FC is fixed cost. The solution is found by setting the first derivatives with respect to advertising and price to zero for each brand separately; it results in the typical marginal-cost-equals-marginal-revenue condition covered in chapter 8. Competitive behavior does not explicitly enter into these optimal values.

2. *Nash profit maximization.* Each brand maximizes profits under the condition that all other brands do the same. This is an application of a noncooperative solution to a game in prices and advertising, also discussed in chapter 8. The mathematical solution is again based on the maximization of (9.13), except here it is done simultaneously for all brands' prices and advertising. It is considerably more difficult to find the optimum in this case because it involves solving a set of 22 nonlinear equations. A solution is guaranteed only if the profit functions for brands are strictly quasiconcave in prices and advertising. Fortunately, this quasiconcavity holds under a fairly general set of conditions.

In the absence of any prior information on how prices and advertising levels are set, these two scenarios should be interpreted as extreme. Myopic profit maximization is a best-case scenario for each firm in that it assumes that the firm could pursue its profit goals without competitive retaliation. The Nash solution is a worst-case scenario because we assume that each competitor acts optimally and so the firm cannot enjoy a free ride owing to competitive inertia. Though these extremes may be unrealistic, they provide an interesting optimal range of prices and advertising outlays against which the brand can gauge its current or planned marketing activity.

The two different solutions to (9.13) are cast in terms of price and advertising elasticities, which are not constant in the MCI model. We must therefore fix the elasticities derived from the response model at some reasonable level. Since we are working in a single-period framework, we choose the levels of market shares, prices, and advertising that come closest to an average period.

Table 9–8 shows the results in terms of the following:

1. The optimal single-period prices and advertising under the myopic condition. For brands for which no meaningful optimum can be calculated (e.g., the catchall brands), the actual average values are substituted and held constant in optimization.
2. The optimal single-period prices and advertising under the Nash condition, using the same restriction as in (1).
3. A comparison of the market shares and profits that would result from (1) and (2).

The results are revealing from several perspectives. Looking at the market in the aggregate, we would conclude that current prices and advertising levels approximate the optimal competitive levels on average. These prices and advertising levels are well below the myopic levels, suggesting that competitive considerations are not totally absent from marketing decision making in this

Table 9–8. Current and Optimal Prices, Advertising Expenditures, Market Shares, and Profits By Brand

Brand	Prices[a]			Advertising[b]			Market Share			Profit[b]		
	Actual	Optimal Response	Nash Equilibrium	Actual	Optimal Response	Nash Equilibrium	Actual	Optimal Response	Nash Equilibrium	Actual	Optimal Response	Nash Equilibrium
ED1	$1.53	$1.47	$1.47	$ 0.00	$35.70	$35.60	1.0	10.3	10.2	$ 82.85	$ 146.00	$146.00
ID1	1.89	2.73	2.71	0.00	19.80	18.06	5.2	5.7	5.2	203.00	268.00	242.00
TD1	2.22	3.20	3.17	41.20	14.10	12.40	5.4	2.9	2.5	143.93	167.00	145.00
AO1	1.88	4.83	1.88[c]	50.90	70.84	50.90[c]	10.9		9.7	220.51	1,019.05	220.51[c]
ID2	2.02	1.65	1.64	55.40	2.80	2.66	4.7	7.3	6.8	87.16	151.00	140.00
ED2	1.65	1.19	1.20	0.00	0.00[c]	0.00[c]	1.9		5.8	41.58	16.58	57.35
TD2	1.90	4.62	4.58	21.20	19.80	17.00	5.1	1.6	1.4	125.49	157.00	135.00
TW2	1.98	3.03	2.81	67.70	67.70[c]	67.70[c]	7.8		4.1	230.88	426.65	162.00
ED3	1.67	1.70	1.70	0.10	9.30	8.50	5.4	7.0	6.5	94.76	129.00	118.05
AD4	1.38	1.38[c]	1.38[c]	1.90	1.90[c]	1.90[c]	31.3		28.5	516.50	516.50[c]	455.30[d]
AW4	1.02	1.02[c]	1.02[c]	29.80	29.80[c]	29.80[c]	21.3		19.3	234.80	234.80[c]	206.45[d]

a. Prices in dollars (Australian).
b. In thousands of dollars (Australian).
c. Constrained to be the same as the actual value.
d. Estimated using actual prices and advertising expenditures and competitive market shares.

industry. However, individual brands are not necessarily operating at a competitive optimum in the selected period. There is ample evidence of over- or underpricing as well as over- or underadvertising. Using the Nash or worst-case competitive scenario as a benchmark, we may distinguish two groups of brands:

1. Suboptimal competitors, or those who are currently making less profit than they could with different price-advertising combinations. This group includes brands ED1, ID1, ID2, ED2, and ED3.
2. Supraoptimal competitors, or these who are deriving extra profits from the fact that others are pricing or advertising at suboptimal levels. This group includes brands TD1, TD2, and TW2.

It may not be coincidental that the economy and premium image brands are all suboptimal and that the tangible benefit brands are supraoptimal. For example, there is substantial price pressure on the economy brands because of their high price sensitivities. Even slight deviations from the optimal price level (as with ED1 and ED2) are very costly to an economy brand in terms of profits. On the other hand, the fact that the tangible-benefit brands are either overpriced (TD1) or underpriced (TD2 and TW2) in this period hurts them significantly less under the Nash scenario. Similar conclusions may be drawn for advertising on a brand-by-brand basis.

These conclusions are only an illustration of the power of ETS modeling in diagnosing markets and offering guidelines for improved brand performance. We have chosen one typical period, we have drawn inferences from static as opposed to dynamic optimization, and we have used as benchmarks two rather extreme scenarios of assumed competitive behavior. Other assumptions and scenarios may be introduced depending on the needs of the researcher or the marketing planner.

Notes

1. These data are also used in a paper on asymmetric market-share model building by Carpenter et al. (1988). We are grateful to the authors for giving us permission to use some of their findings in this chapter.

2. The interaction between coefficient bias and instantaneous competitive reaction may mask the asymmetry. However, this seems unlikely to happen.

IV CONCLUSION

10 ETS IN MARKETING SCIENCE AND PRACTICE

The main use of ETS in marketing, as we have seen, is to establish relations among variables—response functions—that serve as generalizations of marketing behavior. These relations, in turn, provide the mechanism for making decision models useful tools for marketing planning and forecasting. Most of this book has been concerned with how this can be done. In this chapter, we look at three questions that bear on the *impact* of this work: (1) How is knowledge generated? (2) How are models implemented? and (3) How can decisions be supported with ETS?

We begin by looking back at the scientific antecedents of ETS research. Next, we look forward to the conditions surrounding its use. Finally, we look more closely at ETS itself—how it is related to information systems and marketing technology.

Knowledge Generation

Marketing theory is made up of explanations of marketing phenomena that have been summarized as marketing generalizations. The explanations themselves are often made up of premises about the nature of relations. Although there is no cohesive body of theory like microeconomic theory or quantum theory in marketing, there are certain hypotheses that have received support and that can be considered to hold under specified conditions, thus serving as generalizations of marketing behavior. Let us see how ETS research leads to such generalizations and to emerging theory.

Marketing Generalizations and Theory

Marketing theories are constructs capable of being falsified, or tested, by empirical data. The proposition that sales is a function of advertising can be regarded as a marketing theory when the terms *sales* and *advertising* are precisely defined, variables are chosen to represent these terms, the causal ordering, functional form, and lag structure are specified, and the conditions under which the relation is expected to hold are elaborated. In addition, we may require that premises be made about the parameters of the model, e.g., their sign. Marketing propositions that fall short of these requirements should not be regarded as theories because they are not capable of being tested.

The sources of maketing theories are marketing generalizations. A generalization about some phenomena can be viewed as an approximate summary of the data describing the phenomena. This view holds that the origin of generalization, and hence of theory, is data, and thus observation of the phenomena is a precondition to theory development. Simon (1968) describes this process as one involving three stages: (1) "finding simple generalizations that describe the facts to some degree of approximation;" (2) "finding limiting conditions under which the deviations of facts from generalization might be expected to decrease;" and (3) "explaining why the generalization 'should' fit the facts." This third stage, in which the notion of explanation appears, is crucial in defining the purpose of theory: marketing theory seeks to explain marketing phenomena.

Not all generalizations, however, originate from data. Another source of generalizations is from deductive reasoning. This view holds that the origin of generalization is from a priori logic. A priori ideas about the phenomena are employed to make generalizations, and thus reason rather than data plays the central role. Both the empirical and a priori bases for generalizations are used in scientific research.

Theory Development and Testing

Premises are the building blocks of a marketing theory. Consider the preceding proposition about advertising and sales. To qualify as a theory, a number of specific assertions or premises about the world must be embodied in the statement. One premise could be that advertising determines sales (where both terms are defined) and not the reverse, and this assertion would be one of causality. Another premise could be that the functional relation is linear in logarithms of the variables. A premise could be made about the parameter— an elasticity, in this case—of advertising, specifying, for example, that it should fall in the interval 0 to +0.5, which implies that the effect of advertising on sales is positive but small (inelastic). Finally, a premise could be made about the conditions under which the relation is expected to hold. These conditions might be for a class of durable goods sold predominantly in department stores. These premises taken together define a rather specific marketing theory, which can be tested by examining its conformity with marketing data. If the theory survives this test, we continue to entertain it until further tests show it to be inconsistent with the evidence.

The rigor of the test, at least from a theoretical point of view, is defined by the degree to which the premises imply that a model representing the theory, on the condition that the theory is true, belongs to a small subset of all possible models. This concept is essentially what Popper (1961) calls the "degree of falsifiability" of theories, which he equates with the simplicity of a theory. The simplicity of generalizations is an important point to be considered by marketing and other researchers. Simon (1968) makes a useful distinction between the concepts of simplicity and plausibility of theories. Popper desires hypotheses "to be simple so that, if they are false, they can be disconfirmed by empirical data as readily as possible." Simon argues that "a simple hypothesis that fits data to a reasonable approximation should be entertained, for it probably reveals an underlying law of nature." According to Popper, a simple hypothesis describes a highly particular state of the world, which is easily falsified because it is improbable. According to Simon, a simple hypothesis summarizes a highly unique (but actual) state of the world, and thus it is highly plausible. These positions appear to be incompatible, but they are not. Simon seems to follow Hanson (1961) who argued for a logic of discovery (of hypotheses) that would result in *plausible conjectures*. Hanson felt that, while discovery was in part psychological, it was also partly logical in that some generalizations are more likely to succeed than others. The ideas of plausibility, falsifiability, and the confirmation of hypotheses are integrated in a Bayesian framework by Salmon (1967).

Two examples can serve to illustrate these different processes of model development and specification. The deductive approach to marketing generalization is rare; however, Bell, Keeney, and Little (1975) show, using such logic, that for certain assumptions market share is a simple linear normalization of attraction, i.e., a model like that discussed in chapter 2 (see equation 2.36) and employed in chapter 9 can be logically derived from the definition of a set of attractions and several assumptions about the nature of the attractions. Together with other premises, this model can express a theory of sales response, where at least part of the theory (the premise that market share is a linear function of advertising share) was the result of a priori reasoning. Another example of the deductive approach is the derivation of an aggregate sales response model from the microspecification of individual consumer behavior by Blattberg and Jeuland (1981b).

Empirical observation of marketing phenomena can also lead to marketing generalizations and hence to premises for marketing theories. The leading example of such a process is in the work of Ehrenberg (1972). This work begins with an empirical search for regularities in the data. If regularities are found, they can be compared with other sets of data to establish their generality. Only then does the analysis proceed to the search for interrelations (how the regularities occur) and for explanations (why they occur). This research paradigm, which is identical with the approach discussed in connection with Simon, was used by Ehrenberg to develop the NBD-LSD theory of repeat buying. Empirical regularities were used to build the theory, and the theory was employed to predict further conclusions to be checked against different data. Ehrenberg's description of the process as "from facts to theory, and back again" is quite apt.

The relations described in this section are summarized in figure 10-1. Observation or reasoning about marketing phenomena (such as market response) can lead to marketing generalizations. Such marketing generalizations, expressed as a set of premises, are sharpened into marketing theories when they are made more precise and when they carry with them *explanations* of the phenomena. A simple parallel can be drawn with the physical sciences. Boyle's law states that at constant temperature a fixed weight of gas occupies a volume inversely proportional to the pressure exerted on it. This statement is a generalization—a description of a physical relation. It is not, by itself, an explanation (i.e., a theory) but can lead to a theory if certain premises are offered regarding molecular structure. Marketing generalizations and theories have just the same relation.

The purpose of a marketing model is to *represent* a marketing theory. Models in this scheme are tools for implementing research; they have long been regarded as "the central necessity of scientific procedure" (Rosenbleuth and Wiener 1945).

We have seen that knowledge accumulates when facts are related together in generalizations, that this process comes before theory building, and that the generalizations themselves are the basis for theory. This insight was obtained without reference to a "marketing philosophy of science." To be sure, we are indebted to major ideas from the philosophy of science: ideas about

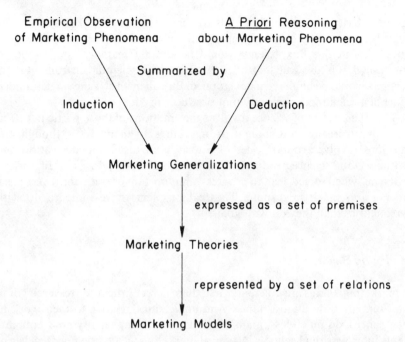

Figure 10–1. Theory Development in Marketing. *Source*: Parsons and Schultz (1976, p. 129).

causality due to Hume or Simon would be examples. But what we borrow from this tradition is not so much the ideas as the activities of science. We learn more from what scientists do than from endless speculation on how they do it.

Scientific Work

Scientific work requires patience and commitment by people who are talented and well trained. Books such as *The Double Helix, Disturbing the Universe, The Eighth Day of Creation*, and *In the Name of Eugenics* tell us much about the life of scientists and the process of discovery.[1] We learn that world-class science comes from dedication to a single, focused question, e.g., what is the molecular structure of DNA? We also learn that the process is as much emotional as objective.

Many bright researchers working on an important scientific problem over a long period of time—this description, more than any other, seems to sum up the activity of science that leads to generalizations and knowledge. The interplay between generalizations and theory is also important, of course, since without this flux, science would be static. Creativity, too, would be diminished. It is also true that without advances in scientific instrumentation, progress would be hindered if not stopped. But, all in all, it is the single-minded effort of a scientific community that produces results.

That the process of science involves the emotions of those participating in it is not surprising to a student of marketing. In many ways, though, the emotions revolve around issues of priority and taste, not motivation and attitude. Good science produces discoveries; bad science does not. Important problems, when solved, lead to progress; unimportant ones do not. These ideas are not too much in dispute. The real problems have more to do with personalities than they do with goals.

Marketing Science

In marketing, things are different. First, there is very little basic research going on. Companies do almost none.[2] And universities, relative to their work in the sciences, do much less, mainly because marketing faculty hold appointments in professional schools. A typical marketing faculty member teaches in one or more professional programs, consults with the business community, and does research that is evaluated as much by its professional relevance as by its scientific merit. There are only a small number of schools—and these are also professional schools—that support basic research in a meaningful way. Since these are the same schools that train research-capable doctoral candidates, it follows that there are only a small number of highly qualified individuals to do such research. So whatever the content of marketing research, very few resources are put behind basic research and hence behind the search for marketing generalizations.

Marketing research is also different from work in the sciences in terms of process. Whereas most scientific discoveries come only after protracted studies by the *same* individuals, research in marketing is usually a one-time affair, mostly by *different* individuals. Other than long-term methodological preoccupation by certain marketing scholars, very few of the major researchers in marketing have devoted anything like the single-minded effort of scientists who ultimately come to understand a specific phenomenon. Of course, some researchers have published many papers on a single topic, but in the sense of "solving" a scientific problem, the results are poor.[3] This is why it has been said that there is very little knowledge in marketing (Leone and Schultz 1980).

Finally, until recently, there has not been a real understanding in marketing of the role of generalizations in knowledge generation. Although the principle of investigating how something happens before inquiring why it happens has governed scientific research since Galileo, there are still too many people in marketing attempting to explain why before knowing how. Ehrenberg's (1972) research, on the other hand, is exemplary; he obtained solid results by finding out how consumers make choices among brands and then explaining why. Leone and Schultz (1980) show how such generalizations can be obtained in the area of sales response. In addition, Fareley, Lehmann, and Ryan (1981) and Assmus, Farley, and Lehmann (1984) use a related technique known as meta-analysis to find generalizations on behavioral intentions and advertising effectiveness.

The comparison between marketing and science should not be pushed too far. Marketing is first and foremost a professional activity. In broader terms, it can even be considered a social process. But the fact that there *are* phenomena unique to marketing suggests that such behavior, e.g., sales response, can legitimately be studied *as a science* (Parsons and Schultz 1976). And, since science progresses in much the same way from field to field, generalization is as important to marketing as it is to physics.

Implementation

Implementation refers to the actual use by managers of a model or system that influences their decision processes. Part of the decision-making process in any organization involves planning and forecasting. If a model is developed to improve this process, then we can describe the possible outcomes of such intervention in the following way. A *successful model* is one that adequately represents the phenomena being modeled and is used for the purpose for which it was designed—this implies that the model has technical validity, capability of solving the problem, and organizational validity, compatibility with the user organization. *Implementation* can be thought of as changed decision making, and *successful implementation* as improved decision making resulting from the building or use of a model. Finally, *organizational success* is the objective improvement in organizational performance resulting from all management actions and interventions—strategic and tactical plans, changes in decision rules and decision processes, and so on. Thus, model success is a narrower concept than implementation success, which in turn is a narrower concept than organizational success.

Two other possible outcomes are change without use and use without improvement. The attempt to implement a planning and forecasting model, for example, could result in the decision process being changed and even improved without actual use of the model. In such a case, however, the change would come about from the model-building process, not from the model per se. Finally, a planning and forecasting model (or any model) could merely change but not improve the decision process. This suggests that not all models *should* be implemented.

The implementation of marketing decision models is discussed by Schultz and Slevin (1972), Larréché (1979), and Schultz and Henry (1981). More general discussions include the implementation of forecasting models (Schultz 1984) and management information systems (Schultz, Ginzberg, and Lucas 1984; Lucas, Ginzberg, and Schultz 1989).[4] This empirical research identifies certain factors relevant to the implementation of model-based planning and forecasting systems. It also links these factors to adoption and postadoption evaluation.

Implementation Factors

The main factors related to the success of a planning and forecasting system are management support, user involvement, personal stake, system characteristics, and implementation strategy. Some empirical evidence in support of these factors is summarized in table 10–1. Also shown in the table are some of the variables that make up the factors. The relations among the factors are discussed elsewhere.[5]

Management Support.   Management support refers to top or divisional management support, or lack of resistance, for the system. Such support is required before, during, and after system development. In a one-stage implementation, where the manager who commissions the system is also the user (as would be the case in most corporate planning and forecasting systems), the support must come from above the manager-user. In a two-stage implementation, where a manager commissions a system for other users, the manager's own acceptance of the system becomes the perceived management support for the set of users. Support can also be interpreted as lack of resistance to change in general and to a system in particular. The evidence for the need for management support is so strong that any attempt to implement a system without it, and without the related conditions of commitment and authority to implement, will probably result in failure.

Three additional variables that may affect implementation through management support are belief in system concept, power, and leadership. Belief in system concept refers to the extent to which a manager believes in the underlying concept or approach behind a system. Planning and forecasting systems

Table 10–1. Factors Affecting Implementation

Management Support	User Involvement	Personal Stake	System Characteristics	Implementation Strategy
Top Management Support Radnor and Bean (1974) Bean et al. (1975) Narasimhan and Schroeder (1979) Ginzberg (1981a)	*Client-Researcher Relationship* Schultz and Slevin (1975) Narasimhan and Schroeder (1979)	*Performance/Goal Congruence/Problem Urgency* Schultz and Slevin (1975) Keim (1976) Robey and Bakr (1978) Robey and Zellner (1978) Rodriguez (1977) King and Rodriguez (1978) Robey (1979) Narasimhan and Schroeder (1979) Franz, Robey, and Koeblitz (1986)	*System Format* Manley (1975) Souder et al. (1975) Ginzberg (1979b)	*Stages* Sorensen and Zand (1975) Ginzberg (1979a)
Support/Resistance Manley (1975) Schultz and Slevin (1975)	*Involvement* Swanson (1974) Manley (1975) Ginzberg (1981a) King and Rodriguez (1981) Adelman (1982) IVES AND OLSON (1984)	*Organizational Change* Schultz and Slevin (1975) Ginzberg (1981b)	*System Quality* Lucas (1975) Narasimhan and Schroeder (1979) Schultz and Slevin (1983)	*Strategy/Resources/Environmental Events* Narasimhan and Schroeder (1979) Ginzberg (1981b) Schultz and Slevin (1983) SCHULTZ (1984)
Commitment/Authority Ginzberg (1981b) Schultz and Slevin (1983)	*Confidence/Communication* Schultz and Slevin (1983)	*Individual Differences* Lucas (1975) Lucas (1979) ZMUD (1979)	*Accuracy* ARMSTRONG (1985)	*Binding[a]* Apple and Zmud (1984)
Belief in System Concept[a] Schultz, Ginzberg, and Lucas (1984)	*Knowledge[a]/Assessment[a]* Souder et al. (1975) Lucas, Ginzberg, and Schultz (1989)		*Organizational Support* EIN-DOR AND SEGEV (1981) Schultz, Ginzberg, and Lucas (1984) Lucas (1984)	*Technology[b]/Structure[b]*
Power[a] Marcus (1983) Robey (1984)	*Conflict[a]* Robey (1984)			

Table 10–1 (continued)

Management Support	User Involvement	Personal Stake	System Characteristics	Implementation Strategy
Leadership[b]		*Attitudes/* *Expectations* DeSanctis (1984) Ginzberg (1981a) SWANSON (1982)		
		Decision Style Huysmans (1970) Doktor and Hamilton (1973) Larréché (1979) Lusk and Kersnick (1979) Robey and Taggert (1981) Huber (1983) Robey (1983)		
		Interpersonal Relations Schultz and Slevin (1975)		

Note: Review articles or books are in capital letters; papers are listed only once in each column even though they may involve contributions in more than one area.

a. New theoretical variables.
b. Neglected variables.

based on ETS, for example, require that managers believe in the concept of measuring response with statistical models and historical data. This implies that a manager will have more involvement in system development and more understanding of the system if the concept on which it is based is accepted first. Power and leadership have to do with achieving support from the "right" top managers and applying the support in the "right" way. There is little doubt in the minds of those with experience in implementing systems of the importance of a "champion" for the system.

User Involvement.   User involvement indicates the degree of interaction between a manager (user) and a system designer. On one side of the system development process is the system designer or researcher, and on the other side is the user or client. The more involvement between the two sides in terms of quantity and quality of interaction, the more likely it will be that there is mutual confidence. This mutual trust, in turn, may lead to acceptance and use of the system. Involvement also includes communication between the system designer and user, in particular, communication to ensure that the designer understands the user's needs—to avoid a Type III error, solving the wrong problem—and that the user understands the designer's approach.

Other variables that may be related to user involvement are knowledge of the system, assessment of the system and support, and conflict between participants in system development. Knowledge of the system means how well a manager understands a particular system. For an ETS model, such knowledge has more to do with how plans and forecasts are integrated into the system than it does with details of estimation or testing. Assessment of the system and support refers to a user's evaluation of the quality of a system and its supporting mechanisms (e.g., people, hardware, data). Both knowledge and assessment would be expected to directly affect acceptance of the system. Finally, since systems are implemented in organizations made up of different departments and divisions, conflicts will arise, and so techniques of conflict resolution involving negotiation or influence can be important in managing user involvement.

Personal Stake.   Personal stake is the extent to which a system user's future performance depends on the system and its use. There is a great deal of evidence showing that the impact of a system on a user's job performance overshadows all other variables in predicting system success. If a planning and forecasting system can improve the quality of a manager's decisions, and if improved decision making leads to better performance and more rewards, then the manager is likely to use the system. Two other aspects of personal stake are goal congruence and problem urgency. Goal congruence refers to the fit between the user's goals and those of the organization; a system that makes them more similar will be one that increases acceptance.[6] Problem urgency reflects the urgency of the problems to which a particular system is addressed. A system that deals with an urgent forecasting need, for example, will increase the stake of the manager with that need.

Although not defined as "personal stake," there are other personal variables that affect implementation success. Individual differences such as age, time with company and in job, and educational background affect an individual's willingness to accept a system. In addition to demographics, an individual's attitudes are important to the implementation process; in fact, many of the variables that we have been discussing are measured as attitudes. Decision style, i.e., an individual's characteristic way of solving a problem or making a decision, can also be a factor in implementation. An analytic decision maker with a fondness for data and analysis should be more predisposed to use ETS in planning and forecasting than a heuristic decision maker who places more value on intuition and experience. Finally, interpersonal relations have been shown to be important to implementation. Individuals will resist changes in interpersonal relations and communication patterns that may be brought about by a new system; such changes may affect their personal stake in the system and consequently acceptance and use.

System Characteristics. System characteristics include the features and capabilities of a system. The leading variables that make up this factor are system format, system quality, accuracy, and organization support. System format refers to the extent to which a system can be easily understood and used, i.e., the "friendliness" of the system. The use of certain optimization procedures in conjunction with model-based planning and forecasting, for example, results in optimal decision rules that very much resemble in form a company's existing decision rules; such a situation greatly facilitates implementation (Bultez and Schultz 1979). System quality refers to the extent to which a system solves the user's problem. An important aspect of system quality for forecasting models is accuracy. Implementation success, defined as improved decision making, requires system quality (accuracy) and an appropriate format. We shall have more to say about what this format should be for model-based planning and forecasting in the final part of this chapter.

Organizational support, although not strictly a characteristic of the system, also provides a measure of ease of use. A planning and forecasting system does not stand alone; it requires computer access, software availability, data base maintenance, and budgetary support to update the model over time. System characteristics are not motivating factors like management support, user involvement, and personal stake, but research has shown conclusively that they cannot be ignored.

Implementation Strategy.   A final set of variables that influences implementation can be categorized as implementation strategy. This factor incorporates the ideas that implementation is a time-dependent process, that implementation can be managed with an appropriate strategy and adequate resources, and that environmental events can and will affect implementation results. First, by recognizing that implementation involves stages—from initial need assessment to final behavior change—the groundwork is laid for considering what implementation strategy should be employed over the stages. The amount of user education and persuasion needed varies for different types of systems and different organizations. As a general principle, however, there is much to be said for a policy of phased implementation, say from simple models to complex, and virtually nothing good about a rushed installation. In fact, time has been shown to be one of the more important resources necessary to achieve implementation, along with funds and the quantity and quality of human resources. Overall, success depends on the availability of resources to get the implementation job done.

Even the best strategy can fail because of environmental events. The most common event that threatens the implementation of a new system is probably a decline in company sales or earnings. If advertising and promotion are the first things to be cut in a budget crisis, research is usually next, particularly research not directly tied to product development. Planning and forecasting systems are particularly vulnerable—today's problems always come before tomorrow's. Other threats to implementation include personnel changes, departmental reorganizations, personal clashes, turbulent environments, even sabotage. The best way to cope with such events seems to be to *anticipate* them, in the sense of planning for the worst and then getting on with the implementation. Many times, however, this simply does not work.

Other variables that may be related to implementation strategy are binding, technology, and structure. Binding, a term borrowed from pharmacokinetics, concerns the process by which new technology replaces existing technology in an organization. A better understanding of the *rate* of implementation and the *potential* for change would help in the management of implementation. Finally, implementation takes place in organizations characterized by certain technologies and certain structures. As technology changes— for example, information technology—an organization's structure changes. The relations between strategy, technology, and structure will be an important area for future implementation research.

Table 10-2. Outcomes of Implementation

Adoption	Postadoption Evaluation
Acceptance	*Performance*
Narasimhan and Schroeder (1979)	Vertinsky, Barth, and Mitchell (1975)
Welsch (1981)	Schultz and Slevin (1975)
Lucas, Ginzberg, and Schultz (1989)	King and Rodriguez (1978)
	Lucas (1979)
Use	Welsch (1981)
Lucas (1979)	Schultz, Ginzberg, and Lucas (1984)
Ginzberg (1981a)	
Welsch (1981)	*Satisfaction*
Ginzberg (1983)	Ginzberg (1979a)
Lucas, Ginzberg, and Schultz (1989)	Ginzberg (1981a)
	Welsch (1981)
	Bailey and Pearson (1983)
	Ginzberg (1983)
	Sanders (1984)
	Lucas, Ginzberg, and Schultz (1989)

Adoption and Evaluation

The key indicators of success for a planning and forecasting system are acceptance, use, performance, and satisfaction. Acceptance and use are measures of change in decision making (implementation), and performance and satisfaction are measures of improvement in decision making. In other words, they are ways of operationalizing our definition of implementation. They also represent the notions of adoption of an innovation and the postadoption evaluation of its impact. Some empirical evidence in support of these measures is summarized in table 10-2.

Acceptance.   Acceptance is a predisposition to use a system. For a planning and forecasting system, it would be an intention to incorporate the system into a manager's repertoire of behavior. Thus, acceptance signals that implementation is likely. Other things being equal, the manager intends to adopt the system, replacing the existing planning and forecasting process with the new one that results from using the new decision-making technology. Recall that it would be possible for implementation, or change, to take place without use, although in such a case the system qua system might be termed a failure.[7]

Acceptance is usually measured by an attitude scale not unlike the scales used to measure consumer preference or intention. In terms of managing the implementation of a system, there is much to be learned from knowing the level of acceptance of a potential user or group of users.

Use. Use is the actual experience of applying a system and implies that a change has taken place. It represents experience over a period of time, i.e., repeat use. Although use is a sufficient condition for identifying change, it is not a necessary condition. Still, when most people think of the implementation of a system, they think of actual use in a specific task environment.

Use can be measured directly or from self-reports of actual experience. Direct measures of the use of a computer-based forecasting system, for example, could include number of times used, time per use session, type of use, balance of use across time or type, and so forth. Since we separate performance from use, such direct measures will almost always be preferred. With the advent of personal computers, however, there may be more need to rely on reports of use, since there is usually no record of system access.[8]

Performance. Performance is the quality of decision making, e.g., planning and forecasting, resulting from the use of a system. It is an objective outcome of system use independent from the user's evaluation of the system. It also captures the idea of successful implementation as improved decision making and, together with other management actions and interventions, can lead to improved organizational performance. For many types of systems, performance is difficult to measure, particularly performance of an individual manager. Planning and forecasting systems, however, are typically used for corporate, divisional, or product planning where the focus is on specific operating results. This permits performance to be measured in terms of profit, cost, and forecast accuracy. Thus, improvements in decision making can be tied to the use of a new model or system.

Satisfaction. Satisfaction is the user's overall attitude toward the system, its use, and its impact on performance. If performance is the objective postadoption evaluation of a new system, satisfaction is the subjective evaluation by the managers who use it. Since use and satisfaction are interdependent, continued satisfaction with a system should lead to continued use of the system.[9]

Satisfaction, like acceptance, is usually measured with an attitude scale. Although the problems associated with attitude-intention-behavior sequences are well known to marketing researchers, the practical advantages to system developers of understanding the factors that determine implementation outcomes cannot be overstated.

A system that is developed without recognition of the behavioral and political milieu in which it is to be used will probably fail to accomplish its purpose. The findings of implementation research provide model builders and managers with insight that helps them to avoid such failure and, indeed, to achieve success.

Models and Decision Support

In chapter 8, we examined the role of management science in improving marketing decisions. In this chapter, we have already looked at the key links between marketing decision models and science (knowledge generation) and marketing decision models and practice (implementation). What remains to be seen is how ETS models relate to the development of information systems technology. If we understand this, we will have some idea about the future of marketing information technology.

Information Systems

An information system is "a set of organized procedures that, when executed, provides information to support decision making and control in the organization." (Lucas 1982, p. 8) Although nothing in the definition requires an information system to be computer-based, it was the explosive development of computer technology over the past several decades that motivated research into management information and decision support systems. Thus, for the most part, when we speak of MIS, DSS, or decision models in marketing, we imply computer-based information systems.

Developments in decision-making technology are summarized in table 10–3. It shows the close connection between certain management needs and evolving (computer) information technology. It also shows the parallel development of marketing technology, including the technology that is the subject matter of this book.

The first management need to be met with information technology was data handling.[10] The advent of electronic data processing (EDP) brought considerable operating efficiencies to organizations for handling data and transactions such as orders, billing, and payrolls. A parallel development in marketing was the application of computers to marketing research. New and more powerful statistical techniques also emerged to process this growing body of data.

Table 10-3. Developments in Decision-Making Technology

Time Period	Management Need	Information Technology	Marketing Technology
1960s	Data handling	EDP	Marketing research
1970s	Information analysis	MIS	Marketing models
1980s	Decision support	DSS	Model-based decision making (e.g., model-based planning and forecasting)
1990s	Decision making	ES	

The next management need to receive the attention of information technology was information analysis. Information was conceived to be something more than data: "data that has been processed into a form that is meaningful to the recipient, and is of real perceived value in current or prospective decisions." (Davis and Olson 1985, p. 200) Within this broadened perspective, the field of management information systems (MIS) arose. At the same time, marketing technology was evolving from marketing research with its somewhat narrow focus on data to marketing models with an emphasis on information and decision making. Most of these systems and models were confined to what could be called programmed or structured tasks, i.e., decisions so routine and repetitive that some specified procedure could be used to make the decision. Advertising budgeting, media allocation, and sales call planning would be examples in marketing.

The most recent advance in information technology is decision support systems (DSS). Here the focus is on less programmed, less structured tasks and the consequent management need for decision support. The analog of DSS in marketing is model-based decision making. Models are not used "off-the-shelf" but rather to help structure the decision task itself. For example, in model-based planning and forecasting, the management situation is initially only loosely structured; it is the process of building a model that defines relations among the variables and ultimately suggests how to reach organizational goals.

Another way to think about these forms of information technology is shown in figure 10-2. Procedural systems are designed to enhance control over the performance of tasks that can be specified unambiguously in advance, whereas decisional systems are designed to enhance decision making where the task cannot be prespecified (Ginzberg 1980). This distinction is very close to what Simon (1965) originally called programmed versus unprogrammed

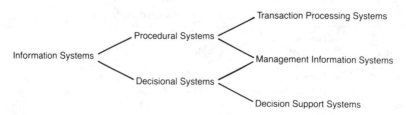

Figure 10-2. Classification of Computer-Based Information Systems.

decisions and to the structured versus unstructured nomenclature more common to DSS (Gorry and Morton 1971). The three kind of computer-based information systems discussed by Moore and Chang (1980) can be related to procedural and decisional systems in the following way. By definition, all transaction processing systems are procedural and all decision support systems are decisional; some management information systems are more procedural and some more decisional. In each case, these systems are technological responses to clear management needs for data handling, information analysis, and decision support.

The most general need of management is decision making, particularly decision making in highly unstructured situations such as strategic decisions in marketing.[11] This need may be met through the future development of expert systems (ES). These systems are designed to represent and apply factual knowledge of specific areas of expertise to solve problems (Hayes-Roth, Waterman, and Lenat 1983). They combine facts, beliefs, and heuristics in computer programs that look for "good enough" answers with the resources available. Expert systems can *make* decisions and have been shown to outperform human experts in areas ranging from geology to internal medicine. It seems clear that both information technology and marketing technology will move toward artificial intelligence applications in the years ahead.

Using ETS

Since ETS is the method behind model-based planning and forecasting, and since model-based decision making is a form of decision support, we can see that there must be some way of integrating the technique with the support if the approach is to be effectively used. An overview of how this can be done is shown in table 10-4. The table compares three types of integration with the design components of a specific DSS—in this case, a DSS designed to embody the elements of model-based planning and forecasting (and hence ETS).

Table 10-4.   Integrating ETS with DSS

Design Components	Types of Integration		
	Separate	Partial	Full
Dialog Management			
User interface	X	X	X
Dialog-control function		X	X
Request transformer			X
Data Management			
Data base	X	X	X
Data base management system		X	X
Data directory		X	X
Query facility			X
Staging and extraction function			X
Model Management			
Model management system			X
Modeling execution	X	X	X
Modeling command processor			X
Data base interface		X	X

The major functions necessary for a DSS are dialog management, data management, and model management (Sprague and Carlson 1982; Ariav and Ginzberg 1985).[12] In a fully integrated DSS, dialog management would include a user interface, a dialog-control function to determine the basic semantics of interactions and the extent to which the interactions are system or user controlled, and a request transformer to translate the user's vocabulary and the system's internal modeling and data access vocabulary. Data management would include a data base, a data base management system, a data directory, a query facility to interpret and respond to data requests, and a staging and extraction function to connect the data base with other data sources or other DSS. Model management, in a fully integrated DSS, would include a model management system to create and revise models, a model execution function to control the running of a model or set of models, a modeling command processor to link modeling-related dialog to model execution, and a data base interface.

The first way of integrating ETS with DSS is simply to build and run models using a separate data base, an independent model execution program, and informal (i.e., not computerized) interaction between a model designer and model user. This approach is sometimes accompanied by a two-step presentation of results by the model designer to the model user. First, a conceptual model, called the *management model*, is used to show management that all relevant variables have been considered in the analysis, although some may not have been measured owing to lack of data or lack of variability. This is usually presented to management in the form of a diagram showing expected cause-and-effect relations. The management model has high credibility because it reflects management's own views about the nature of market response. Second, an empirical model, called the *statistical model*, is used to convey to management how much of the overall response process has been captured in the model. Assuming that this model is good, i.e., its planning and forecasting properties are good, it will also tend to have high credibility even if it includes only a subset of all relevant management variables. This two-step presentation of results allows managers to see models for what they are— useful approximations to reality.

A second type of integration is to combine a data base with model execution using a partly computerized interface. For example, a spreadsheet program on a personal computer could be used as the host for a completed ETS model. This approach adds dialog control, data base management, a data directory, and a data base interface to the three features of a separate-function DSS. The use of spreadsheet software for presenting model results to management permits sensitivity analysis and other scenario alterations to be done easily and quickly. It also allows the analysis of results to focus on a manager's relevant range of decision making and to seek answers to "what if?" questions. In addition, it is possible to include simple optimization within the framework of a spreadsheet. Generalized spreadsheet software, however, is not well suited to presenting conceptual models to management or to doing complex optimization involving, say, decision or game theory.

These limitations can be overcome by fully integrating ETS with DSS. The architecture of such a system would be based on all the subfunctions of a complete DSS as well as the features of the separate- and partial-integration approaches that have been proven to contribute to successful implementation. This is the environment in which ETS research aimed at planning and forecasting would reach its highest potential.

Notes

1. See Watson (1968), Dyson (1979), Judson (1979), and Kevles (1984), respectively.
2. Most company research in the sciences is also applied research, but there are notable exceptions, e.g., Bell Laboratories does basic research.
3. The reward structure in academic marketing encourages publication. It is interesting to note that major awards are given for papers, not for "work."

4. See also Schultz and Slevin (1975), Doktor, Schultz, and Slevin (1979), and Schultz and Ginzberg (1984) on implementing operations research and management science.

5. The most complete discussion is in Schultz, Ginzberg, and Lucas (1984).

6. Depending on how it is measured, goal congruence could influence acceptance directly or be thought of as an aspect of personal stake. See Schultz, Ginzberg, and Lucas (1984).

7. We are reluctant to attribute the educational benefits of model building to a specific model if that model is not used; it would be better to say that such benefits are due to the management science (intervention) process in general.

8. Personal computers used in networks, on the other hand, offer an opportunity to measure access to a central data base directly.

9. Acceptance and use, and use and performance, are also thought to be interdependent, although satisfaction would be expected to influence performance only through use. See Schultz, Ginzberg, and Lucas (1984).

10. All four of these mangement needs have always existed; this is just the sequence of their being met.

11. Recall that model-based planning and forecasting—and hence this book—is primarily concerned with tactical decision making.

12. In the marketing literature, see Montgomery and Urban (1970), Little (1979b), and Montgomery and Weinberg (1979).

BIBLIOGRAPHY

Aaker, David A. and James M. Carman (1982), "Are You Overadvertising?" *Journal of Advertising Research*, 22 (August/September), 57–70.

—— and George S. Day (1971), "A Recursive Model of Communication Processes," in *Multivariate Analysis in Marketing: Theory and Application*. Belmont, CA: Wadsworth, 101–14.

——, James M. Carman, and Robert Jacobson (1982), "Modeling Advertising-Sales Relationships Involving Feedback: A Time Series Analysis of Six Cereal Brands," *Journal of Marketing Research*, 19 (February), 116–25.

Abraham, Bovas and George E. P. Box (1978), "Deterministic and Forecast-Adaptive Time-Dependent Models," *Applied Statistics*, 27 (2), 120–30.

Abraham, Magid M. and Leonard M. Lodish (1987), "PROMOTER: An Automated Promotion Evaluation System," *Marketing Science*, 6 (Spring), 101–23.

Ackoff, Russell L. and James R. Emshoff (1975), "Advertising Research at Anheuser-Busch, Inc. (1963–68)," *Sloan Management Review*, 16 (Winter), 1–15.

Adams, Arthur J. and Mark M. Moriarty (1981), "The Advertising-Sales Relationship: Insights from Transfer-Function Modeling," *Journal of Advertising Research*, 21 (June), 41–46.

Adelman, L. (1982), "Involving Users in the Development of Decision-Analytic Aids: The Principal Factor in Successful Implementation," *Journal of the Operational Research Society*, 33 (April), 333–42.

Albach, Horst (1979), "Market Organization and Pricing Behavior of Oligopolistic Firms in the Ethical Drugs Industry," *KYKLOS*, 32 (3), 523–40.

Alemson, M. A. (1970), "Advertising and the Nature of Competition in Oligopoly over Time: A Case Study," *Economic Journal*, 80 (June), 282–306.

Amemiya, Takeshi (1974), "Multivariate Regression and Simultaneous Equation Models When the Dependent Variables Are Truncated Normal," *Econometrica*, 42 (November), 999–1012.

———— (1979), "The Estimation of a Simultaneous-Equation Tobit Model," *International Economic Review*, 20 (February), 169–81.

———— (1985), *Advanced Econometrics*. Cambridge, MA: Harvard University Press.

———— and Roland Y. Wu (1972), "The Effects of Aggregation on Prediction in the Autoregressive Model," *Journal of the American Statistical Association*, 67 (September), 628–32.

Amoroso, Luigi (1954), "The Static Supply Curve," *International Economic Papers*, 4, 39–65.

Amstutz, Arnold E. (1967), *Computer Simulation of Competitive Market Response*. Cambridge, MA: MIT Press.

Anderson, Evan E. and Henry N. Amato (1974), "A Mathematical Model for Simultaneously Determining the Optimal Brand-Collection and Display-Area Allocation," *Operations Research*, 22 (January–February), 13–21.

Andrews, Donald W. K. and Ray C. Fair (1988), "Inference in Nonlinear Econometric Models with Structural Change," *Review of Economic Studies*, LV (October), 615–639.

Aneuryn-Evans, Gwyn and Angus Deaton (1980), "Testing Linear Versus Logarithmic Regression Models," *Review of Economic Studies*, 48, 275–91.

Apple, Loyal and Robert Zmud (1984), "A Pharmacokinetics Approach to Technology Transfer: Implications for OR/MS/MIS Implementation," in *Applications of Management Science, Supplement 1, Management Science Implementation*, Randall L. Schultz and Michael J. Ginzberg, eds. Greenwich, CT: JAI Press, 29–53.

Arabmazar, Abbas and Peter Schmidt (1981), "Further Evidence on the Robustness of the Tobit Estimator to Heteroscedasticity," *Journal of Econometrics*, 17 (November), 253–58.

———— and Peter Schmidt (1982), "An Investigation of the Robustness of the Tobit Estimator to Non-Normality," *Econometrica*, 50 (July), 1055–63.

Ariav, Gad and Michael J. Ginzberg (1985), "DDS Design: A Systematic View of Decision Support," *Communications of the ACM*, 28 (October), 1045–52.

Armstrong, J. Scott (1985), *Longe-Range Forecasting: From Crystal Ball to Computer*, 2nd Edition. New York: John Wiley.

————, Roderick J. Brodie, and Shelby H. McIntyre (1987), "Forecasting Methods for Marketing: Review of Empirical Research," *International Journal of Forecasting*, 3 (3/4), 355–76.

Arnold, Stephen J., Tae H. Oum, Bohumir Pazderka, and Douglas J. Snetsinger (1987), "Advertising Quality in Sales Response Models," *Journal of Marketing Research*, 24 (February), 106–113.

Arora, Rajinder (1979), "How Promotion Elasticities Change," *Journal of Advertising Research*, 19 (June), 57–62.

Ashley, R., C.W.J. Granger, and Richard Schmalensee (1980), "Advertising and Aggregate Consumption: An Analysis of Causality," *Econometrica*, 48 (July), 1149–67.

Assmus, Gert (1981), "New Product Models," in *Marketing Decision Models*, Randall L. Schultz and Andris A. Zoltners, eds. New York: Elsevier North-Holland, 125–43.

———, John U. Farley, and Donald R. Lehmann (1984), "How Advertising Affects Sales: A Meta Analysis of Econometric Results," *Journal of Marketing Research*, 21 (February), 65–74.

Atkinson, Anthony C. (1969), "A Test for Discriminating Between Models," *Biometrika*, 56 (2), 337–47.

——— (1970), "A Method for Discriminating Between Models," *Journal of the Royal Statistical Society, Series B*, 32 (3), 323–45.

——— (1978), "Posterior Probabilities for Choosing a Regression Model," *Biometrika*, 65 (1), 39–48.

Aykaç, Ahmet, Marcel Corstjens, and David Gautschi (1984), "Is There a Kink in Your Advertising?" *Journal of Advertising Research*, 24 (June–July), 27–36.

Bagozzi, Richard P. (1980), *Causal Modeling in Marketing*. New York: John Wiley.

Bailey, J. E. and S. W. Pearson (1983), "Development of a Tool for Measuring and Analyzing Computer User Satisfaction," *Management Science*, 29 (May), 530–45.

Balderston, F. E. and A. C. Hoggatt (1962), *Simulation of Market Processes*. Berkeley, CA: Institute of Business and Economic Research, University of California.

Ball, R. J. and R. Agarwala (1969), "An Econometric Analysis of the Effects of Generic Advertising on the Demand for Tea in the U.K.," *British Journal of Marketing*, 4 (Winter), 202–17.

Banks, Seymour (1961), "Some Correlates of Coffee and Cleanser Brand Share," *Journal of Advertising Research*, 1 (June), 22–28.

Barnard, Neil (1978), "On Advertising Effectiveness Measurement: An Idiosyncratic View," *ADMAP*, (July), 361–69.

Bartlett, M. S. (1946), "On the Theoretical Specification and Sampling Properties of Autocorrelated Time-Series," *Journal of the Royal Statistical Socitey, Series B*, 8 (April), 27–41, 85–97.

Basmann, Robert L. (1964), "On Predictive Testing a Simultaneous Equation Regression Model: The Retail Market for Food in the U.S." Institute Paper No. 78, Krannert Graduate School of Industrial Administration, Purdue University.

——— (1965) "On the Application of Identifiability Test Statistic in Predictive Testing of Explanatory Economic Models," *Indian Economic Journal*, 13, 387–423.

——— (1968), "Hypothesis Formulation in Quantitative Economics: A Contribution to Demand Analysis," in *Papers in Quantitative Economics*, James P. Quirk and Arvid M. Zarley, eds. Lawrence, Kansas: University Press of Kansas, 143–98.

——— (1988), "Causality Tests and Obervationally Equivalent Representations of Econometric Models," *Journal of Econometrics*, 39 (September/October), 69–104.

Bass, Frank M. (1969a), "A New Product Growth Model for Consumer Durables," *Management Science*, 15 (January), 215–27.

——— (1969b), "A Simultaneous Equation Regression Study of Advertising and Sales of Cigarettes," *Journal of Marketing Research*, 6 (August), 291–300.

———— (1971), "Decomposition Regression Models in Analysis of Market Potentials," *Management Science*, 17 (April), 485–94.

———— (1980), "The Relationship Between Diffusion Rates, Experience Curves, and Demand Elasticities for Consumer Durable Technological Innovations," *Journal of Business*, 53 (July), S51–67.

———— and Alain V. Bultez (1982), "A Note on Optimal Strategic Pricing of Technological Innovations," *Marketing Science*, 1 (Fall), 371–78.

———— and Darral G. Clarke (1972), "Testing Distributed Lag Models of Advertising Effect," *Journal of Marketing Research*, 9 (August), 298–308.

———— and Robert P. Leone (1983), "Estimation of Bimonthly Relations from Annual Data," *Management Science*, 29 (January), 1–11.

———— and ———— (1986), "Estimatimg Micro Relationships from Macro Data: A Comparative Study of Two Approximations of the Brand Loyal Model under Temporal Aggregation," *Journal of Marketing Research*, 23 (August), 291–79.

———— and Leonard J. Parsons (1969), "A Simultaneous Equation Regression Analysis of Sales and Advertising," *Applied Economics*, 1 (May), 103–24.

———— and Thomas L. Pilon (1980), "A Stochastic Brand Choice Framework for Econometric Modeling of Time Series Market Share Behavior," *Journal of Marketing Research*, 17 (November), 486–97.

———— and Dick R. Wittink (1975), "Pooling Issues and Methods in Regression Analysis with Examples in Marketing Research," *Journal of Marketing Research*, 12 (November), 414–25.

———— and ———— (1978), "Pooling Issues and Methods in Regression Analysis: Some Further Reflections," *Journal of Marketing Research*, 15 (May), 277–79.

Batra, Rajeev and Wilfried R. Vanhonacker (1988), "Falsifying Laboratory Results Through Field Tests: A Time-Series Methodology and Some Results," *Journal of Business Research*, 16 (June), 281–300.

Bean, A. S., R. D. Neal, M. Radnor, and D. A. Tansik (1975), "Structure and Behavioral Correlates of Implementation in U.S. Business Organizations," in *Implementing Operations Research/Management Science*, Randall L. Schultz and Dennis P. Slevin, eds. New York: American Elsevier, 77–132.

Beckwith, Neil E. (1972), "Multivariate Analysis of Sales Responses of Competing Brands to Advertising," *Journal of Marketing Research*, 9 (May), 168–76.

———— (1973), "Concerning Logical Consistency of Multivariate Market Share Models," *Journal of Marketing Research*, 10 (August), 341–44.

Beguin, Jean-Marc, Christian Gourieroux, and Alain Monfort (1980), "Identification of a Mixed Autoregressive-Moving Average Process: The Corner Method," in *Time Series*, O. D. Anderson, ed. Amsterdam: North-Holland, 423–36.

Bell, David E., Ralph E. Keeney, and John D. C. Little (1975), "A Market Share Theorem," *Journal of Marketing Research*, 12 (May), 136–41.

Belsley, David A. (1988), "Conditioning in Models with Logs," *Journal of Econometrics*, 38 (May–June), 127–43.

————, Edwin Kuh, and Roy E. Welsch (1980), *Regression Diagnostics: Identifying Influential Data and Sources of Collinearity*. New York: John Wiley.

Bemmaor, Albert C. (1984), "Testing Alternative Econometric Models on the Existence of Advertising Threshold Effect," *Journal of Marketing Research* 21 (August), 298–308.

Benjamin, B. and J. Maitland (1958), "Operational Research and Advertising: Some Experiments in the Use of Analogies," *Operational Research Quarterly*, 9 (September), 207–17.

Bensoussan, Alain, Alain Bultez, and Philippe Naert (1978), "Leader's Dynamic Behavior in Oligopoly," *TIMS Studies in the Management Sciences*, 9, 123–45.

———, E. Gerald Hurst, Jr., and B. Naslund (1974), *Management Applications of Modern Control Theory*. Amsterdam: North-Holland.

Bertrand, Joseph (1883), "Review of Cournot's Recherches sur les Principes Mathématiques de la Théorie des Richesses," *Journal des Savants*, 499–508.

Beswick, Charles A. and David A. Cravens (1977), "A Multistage Decision Model for Salesforce Management," *Journal of Marketing Research*, 14 (May), 135–44.

Blattberg, Robert and John Golanty (1978), "Tracker: An Early Test Market Forecasting and Diagnostic Model for New Product Planning." *Journal of Marketing Research*, 15 (May), 192–202.

——— and Abel Jeuland (1981a), "An Assessment of the Contribution of Log-Linear Models to Marketing Research," *Journal of Marketing*, 45 (Spring), 89–97.

——— and ——— (1981b), "A Micromodeling Approach to Investigate the Advertising-Sales Relationship," *Management Science*, 9 (September), 988–1005.

——— and Alan Levin (1987), "Modelling the Effectiveness and Profitability of Trade Promotions," *Marketing Science*, 6 (Spring), 124–46.

Bowley, A. L. (1924), *The Mathematical Groundwork of Economics*. Oxford: Oxford University Press.

Bowman, E. H. (1963), "Consistency and Optimality in Management Decision Making," *Management Science*, 9 (January), 310–21.

Box, George E. P. and D. R. Cox (1964), "An Analysis of Transformations," *Journal of the Royal Statistical Society, Series B*, 26 (2), 211–52.

——— and G. M. Jenkins (1976), *Time Series Analysis: Forecasting and Control*, second edition. San Francisco: Holden-Day.

——— and D. A. Pierce (1970), "Distribution of Residual Autocorrelations in Autoregressive-Integrated Moving Average Time Series Models," *Journal of the American Statistical Association*, 65 (December), 1509–26.

——— and George C. Tiao (1975), "Intervention Analysis with Applications to Economic and Enviromental Problems," *Journal of the American Statistical Association*, 70 (March), 70–79.

——— and George C. Tiao (1976), "Comparison of Forecast and Actuality," *Applied Statistics*, 25 (3), 195–200.

Boyer, Kenneth D. and Kent M. Lancaster (1986), "Are There Scale Economies in Advertising?" *Journal of Business*, 59 (July) 509–526.

Brewer, K.R.W. (1973), "Some Consequences of Temporal Aggregation and Systematic Sampling for ARMA and ARMAX Models," *Journal of Econometrics*, 1, 133–54.

Broadbent, Simon (1979), "One-Way TV Advertisements Work," *Journal of the Market Research Society*, 21 (3), 139–65.

—— (1980), "Price and Advertising: Volume and Profit," *ADMAP*, 16 (11), 532–40.

—— (1984), "Modelling with Adstock," *Journal of the Market Research Society*, 26 (October), 295–312.

—— (1988), "Advertising Effects—More Methodological Issues," *Journal of the Market Research Society*, 30 (April), 225–27.

—— and Stephen Colman (1986), "Advertising Effectiveness: Across Brands," *Journal of the Market Research Society*, 28 (January), 15–24.

Brobst, Robert and Roger Gates (1977), "Comments on Pooling Issues and Methods in Regression Analysis," *Journal of Marketing Ressearch*, 14 (November), 598–600.

Brodie, Roderick and Cornelius A. de Kluyver (1983), "Attraction Versus Linear and Multiplicative Market Share Models: A Empirical Evaluation," Krannert Graduate School of Management, Purdue University, January. A shorter version appears in *Journal of Marketing Research*, 21 (May 1984), 194–201.

—— and —— (1987), "A Comparison of the Short-Term Forecasting Accuracy of Econometric and Naive Extrapolation Models of Market Share," *International Journal of Forecasting*, 3 (3/4), 423–37.

Brown, G. (1986), "The Link Between Ad Content and Sales Effects," *ADMAP*, March, 151–53.

Brown, R. J., J. Durbin, and J. Evans (1975), "Techniques for Estimating the Constancy of Regression Relationships over Time," *Journal of the Royal Statistical Society, Series B*, 37, 149–63.

Brunner, Karl (1973), "Review of *Econometric Models of Cyclical Behavior*," *Journal of Economic Literature*, 11 (September), 926–33.

Bultez, Alain V. (1978), "Econometric Specification and Estimation of Market Share Models: The State of the Art," in *Marketing: Neue Ergebnisse Aus forschung Und Praxis*, E. Topritzhofer, ed. Weisbaden: Betriebswirschaftlicher Verlag Dr. Th. Gaber K. G., 239–63.

—— and Philippe A. Naert (1975), "Consistent Sum-Constrained Models," *Journal of the American Statistical Association*, 70 (September), 529–35.

—— and —— (1979), "Does Lag Structure Really Matter in Optimizing Advertising Expenditures?" *Management Science*, 25 (May), 454–65.

—— and —— (1985), "Control of Advertising Expenditures Based on Aggregate Models of Carryover Effects," in *New Challenges for Management Research*, A. H. G. Rinnooy Kan, ed. New York: Elsevier Science, 31–43.

—— and —— (1988a), "SH.A.R.P.: Shelf Allocation for Retailers' Profit," *Marketing Science*, 7 (Summer), 211–31.

—— and —— (1988b), "When Does Lag Structure Really Matter ... Indeed?" *Management Science*, 34 (July), 909–16.

—— and Randall L. Schultz (1979), "Decision Rules for Advertising Budgeting and Media Allocation," Krannert Graduate School of Management, Purdue University, Institute Paper No. 694, May.

Bustos, Oscar H. and Victor J. Yohai (1986), "Robust Estimates for ARMA Models," *Journal of the American Statistical Association*, 81 (March), 155–68.

Buzzell, Robert D. (1964a), *Mathematical Models and Marketing Management*. Boston: Harvard University, Division of Research, 136–56.

―――― (1964b), "Predicting Short-Term Changes in Market Share as a Function of Advertising Strategy," *Journal of Marketing Research*, 1 (August), 27–31.

――――, Marshall Kolin, and Malcolm P. Murphy (1965), "Television Commercial Test Scores and Short-Term Changes in Market Shares," *Journal of Marketing Research*, 2 (August), 307–3.

Caines, P. E., S. P. Sethi, and T. W. Brotherton (1977), "Impulse Response Identification and Causality Detection For the Lydia-Pinkham Data," *Annals of Economic and Social Measurement*, 6 (2), 147–63.

Calantone, R. and C. Anthony di Benedetto (1986), "Examining the Conduct of Competitors in a Consumer-Goods Industry Using a Game-Theoretic Framework," Working Paper, Department of Marketing, University of Kentucky, May.

Cardwell, John J. (1968), "Marketing and Management Science―A Marriage on the Rocks?" *California Management Review*, 10 (Summer), 3–12.

Carpenter, Gregory S. (1987), "Modeling Competitive Marketing Strategies: The Impact of Marketing-Mix Relationships and Industry Structure," *Marketing Science*, 6 (Spring), 208–21.

――――, Lee G. Cooper, Dominique M. Hanssens, and David F. Midgley (1988), "Modeling Asymmetric Competition," *Marketing Science*, 7 (Fall), 393–412.

―――― and Dominique M. Hanssens (1987), "Market Expansion, Cannibalization, and Optimal Product-Line Pricing," University of California, Los Angeles, Working Paper Series, Center for Marketing Studies, Paper No. 160, October.

Case, James H. (1974), "On the Form of Market Demand Models," *Econometrica*, 42 (January), 207–13.

―――― (1975), "A Game of Advertising Strategy," in *Proceedings of the IFAC 6th World Congress, Boston: Part 1*. International Federation of Automatic Control, 16.3.1–16.3.3.

―――― (1979), *Economics and the Competitive Process*. New York: New York University Press.

Case, Kenneth E. and James E. Shamblin (1972), "The Effects of Advertising Carry-over," *Journal of Advertising Research*, 12 (June), 37–44.

Chakravarti, Dipankar, Andrew Mitchell, and Richard Staelin (1979), "Judgment-Based Marketing Decision Models: An Experimental Investigation of the Decision Calculus Approach," *Management Science*, 25 (March), 251–63.

Chatfield, C. (1979), "Inverse Autocorrelations," *Journal of the Royal Statistical Society, Series A*, 142 (3), 363–77.

―――― and D. L. Prothero (1973), "Box-Jenkins Seasonal Forecasting: Problems and a Case Study," *Journal of the Royal Statistical Society, Series A*, 136 (3), 295–352.

Chatterjee, Kalyan and Gary L. Lilien (1986), "Game Theory in Marketing Science: Uses and Limitations," *International Journal of Research in Marketing*, 3 (2), 79–93.

Chevalier, Michel (1975), "Increase in Sales Due to In-Store Display," *Journal of Marketing Research*, 12 (November), 426–31.

―――― and Ronald Curhan (1976), "Retailer Promotions as a Function of Trade Promotions: A Descriptive Analysis," *Sloan Management Review*, 18 (Fall), 19–32.

Chi, Michelene T. H. and Robert Glaser (1985), "Problem-Solving Ability," in *Human Abilities*, R. Sternberg, ed. New York: W. H. Freeman, 227–50.

Chow, Gregory C. (1983), *Econometrics*. New York: McGraw-Hill.

Clarke, Darral G. (1973), "Sales-Advertising Cross-Elasticities and Advertising Competition," *Journal of Marketing Research*, 10 (August), 250–61.

——— (1976), "Econometric Measurement of the Duration of Advertising Effect on Sales," *Journal of Marketing Research*, 13 (November), 345–57.

——— (1979), "Measuring the Cumulative Effects of Advertising on Sales: A Response to Peles," *Journal of Marketing Research*, 16 (May), 286–89.

——— and John M. McCann (1977), "Cumulative Advertising Effects: The Role of Serial Correlation: A Reply," *Decision Sciences*, 8, 336–43.

Clarke, Frank H., Masako N. Darrough, and John M. Heineke (1982), "Optimal Pricing Policy in the Presence of Experience Effects," *Journal of Business*, 55 (July), 517–30.

Claycamp, Henry J. (1966), "Dynamic Effects of Short Duration Price Differentials on Retail Gasoline Sales," *Journal of Marketing Research*, 3 (May), 175–78.

Clements, Kenneth W. and E. Antony Selvanathan (1988), "The Rotterdam Demand Model and Its Application in Marketing," *Marketing Science*, 7 (Winter), 60–75.

Clemhout, S., G. Leitmann, and H. Y. Wan (1971), "A Differential Game of Duopoly," *Econometrica*, 39 (November), 911–38.

Cleveland, William S. (1972), "The Inverse Autocorrelations of a Time Series and Their Applications," *Technometrics*, 14, 277–93.

Cogger, Kenneth D. (1981), "A Time-Series Analytic Approach to Aggregation Issues in Accounting Data," *Journal of Accounting Research*, 19 (Autumn), 285–98.

Coleman, Stephen and G. Brown (1983), "Advertising Tracking Studies and Sales Effects," *Journal of the Market Research Society*, 25 (2), 165–83.

Cook, Thomas D. and Donald T. Campbell (1979), *Quasi-Experimentation: Design and Analysis Issues for Field Settings*. Boston: Houghton Mifflin.

Cooley, Thomas F. and Edward C. Prescott (1973), "Varying Parameter Regression: A Theory and Some Applications," *Annals of Economic and Social Measurement*, 2 (October), 463–73.

Cooper, Lee G. (1988), "Competitive Maps: The Structure Underlying Asymmetric Cross Elasticities," *Management Science*, 34 (June), 707–23.

——— and Masao Nakanishi (1988), *Market Share Analysis: Evaluating Competitive Marketing Effectiveness*. Boston: Kluwer Academic Publishers.

Corkindale, David (1984), "Measuring the Sales Effectiveness of Advertising: The Role for an ADLAB in the UK," *Journal of the Market Research Society*, 26 (January), 29–49.

——— and John Newall (1978), "Advertising Thresholds and Wearout," *European Journal of Marketing*, 12 (5), 328–78.

Cournot, Augustin A. (1838), *Recherches sur les Principes Mathématiques de la Théorie des Richesses*. Paris: Hachette.

Cowling, Keith (1972), "Optimality in Firms' Advertising Policies: An Empirical Analysis," in *Market Structure and Corporate Behavior: Theory and Empirical Analysis of the Firm*, Keith Cowling, ed. London: Gray-Mills Publishing, 85–103.

—— and John Cubbin (1971), "Price, Quality and Advertising Competition: An Econometric Investigation of the United Kingdom Car Market," *Economica*, 38 (November), 378–94.

—— and A. J. Rayner (1970), "Price, Quality, and Market Share," *Journal of Political Economy*, 78 (November/December), 1292–309.

Cox, D. R. (1961), "Tests of Separate Families of Hypotheses," *Proceedings of the 4th Berkeley Symposium on Mathematical Statistics and Probability*, Volume 1. Berkeley: University of California Press, 105–23.

—— (1962), "Further Results on Tests of Separate Families of Hypotheses," *Journal of the Royal Statistical Society, Series B*, 24, 406–24.

Cox, Keith K. (1964), "The Responsiveness of Food Sales to Shelf Space Changes in Supermarkets," *Journal of Marketing Research*, 1 (May), 63–67.

—— (1970), "The Effect of Shelf Space Upon Sales of Branded Products," *Journal of Marketing Research*, 7 (February), 55–58.

Curhan, Ronald C. (1972), "The Relationship Between Shelf Space and Unit Sales in Supermarkets," *Journal of Marketing Research*, 9 (November), 406–12.

—— (1974a), "Shelf Space Elasticity: Reply," *Journal of Marketing Research*, 11 (May), 221–22.

—— (1974b), "The Effects of Merchandising and Temporary Promotional Activities on the Sales of Fresh Fruits and Vegetables in Supermarkets," *Journal of Marketing Research*, 11 (August), 286–94.

Dalrymple, Douglas J. and George H. Haines, Jr. (1970), "A Study of the Predictive Ability of Market Period Demand—Supply Relations for a Firm Selling Fashion Products," *Applied Economics*, 1 (January), 277–85.

Davis, G. B. and M. H. Olson (1985), *Management Information Systems: Conceptual Foundations, Structure, and Development*. New York: McGraw-Hill.

Deal, Kenneth R. (1975), "Verification of the Theoretical Consistency of a Differential Game in Advertising," paper presented at the ORSA/TIMS Joint National Meeting, Las Vegas, November.

—— (1979) "Optimizing Advertising Expenditures in a Dynamic Duopoly," *Operations Research*, 27 (July–August), 682–92.

——, Suresh P. Sethi, and Gerald L. Thompson (1979), "A Bilinear-Quadratic Differential Game in Advertising," in *Control Theory in Mathematical Economics*, Lin Pai-Tai and Jon G. Sutinen, eds. New York: Marcel Dekker, 91–109.

de Kluyver, Cornelius A. and Roderick J. Brodie (1987), "Advertising-Versus-Marketing Mix Carryover Effects: An Empirical Evaluation," *Journal of Business Research*, 15 (June), 269–87.

DeSanctis, Geraldine (1984), "A Micro Perspective of Implementation," in *Management Science Implementation*, Randall L. Schultz and Michael J. Ginzberg, eds. Greenwich, CT: JAI Press, 1–27.

DeSarbo, Wayne S., Vithala R. Rao, Joel H. Steckel, Jerry Wind, and Richard Colombo (1987), "A Friction Model for Describing and Forecasting Price Changes," *Marketing Science*, 6 (Fall), 299–319.

Devinney, Timothy M. (1987), "Entry and Learning," *Management Science*, 33 (June), 706–24.

Dhyrmes, Phoebus J. (1962), "On Optimal Advertising Capital and Research Expenditures under Dynamic Conditions," *Econometrica*, 29 (August), 275–79.

di Benedetto, C. Anthony (1985), "A Multiplicative Dynamic-Adjustment Model of Sales Response to Marketing Mix Variables," *Modelling, Simulation, and Control C: Environmental, Biomedical, Human & Social Systems*, 4 (Autumn), 7–18.

————— (1986), *Game Theory in Marketing Management: Issues and Applications*, Marketing Science Institute, Report No. 86–100, March.

————— (1987), "Modeling Rationality in Marketing Decision Making with Game Theory," *Journal of the Academy of Marketing Science*, 15 (Winter), 22–32.

Dickey, David A., William R. Bell, and Robert B. Miller (1986), "Unit Roots in Time Series Models: Tests and Implications," *The American Statistician*, 40 (February), 12–26.

Dijkstra, Theo K. and Frans W. Platt (1986), "On the Use of Audit Data in Marketing Models," paper presented at the Annual EMACS Conference, Helsinki, Finland, June.

Dockner, Engelbert (1984), "Optimal Pricing of a Monopoly Against a Competitive Producer," *Optimal Control Applications & Methods*, 5 (October–December), 345–60.

————— (1985), "Optimal Pricing in a Dynamic Duopoly Game Model," *Zeitschrift fur Operations Research*, 29 (April), B1–B16.

————— and Gustav Feichtinger (1986), "Dynamic Advertising and Pricing in an Oligopoly: A Nash Equilibrium Approach," in *Dynamic Games and Applications in Economics*, Lecture Notes in Economics and Mathematical Systems No. 265, T. Basar, ed. New York: Springer-Verlag, 238–51.

————— and ————— (1988), "Optimal Advertising Policies for Diffusion Models of New Product Innovation in Monopolistic Situations," *Management Science*, 34 (January), 119–30.

————— and Steffen Jørgensen (1988), "Optimal Pricing Strategies for New Products in Dynamic Oligopolies," *Marketing Science*, 7 (Fall), 315–34.

Dodson, Jr., Joe A. and Eitan Muller (1978), "Models of New Product Diffusion Through Advertising and Word of Mouth," *Management Science*, 24 (November), 1568–78.

Doktor, Robert H. and W. F. Hamilton (1973), "Cognitive Style and the Acceptance of Management Science Recommendations," *Management Science*, 19, 884–94.

—————, Randall L. Schultz, and Dennis P. Slevin, eds. (1979), *The Implementation of Management Science*. New York: North-Holland.

Dolan, Robert J. and Abel P. Jeuland (1981), "Experience Curves and Dynamic Demand Models: Implications for Optimal Pricing Policies," *Journal of Marketing*, 45 (Winter), 52–62.

Dorfman, R. and P. O. Steiner (1954), "Optimal Advertising and Optimal Quality," *American Economic Review*, 44 (December), 826–36.

Doyle, Peter and John Saunders (1985), "The Lead Effect in Marketing," *Journal of Marketing Research*, 22 (February), 54–65.

Dubin, Robin A. (1988), "Estimation of Regression Coefficients in the Presence of Spatially Autocorrelated Error Terms," *Review of Economics and Statistics*, 70 (August), 466–74.

Dyson, Freeman (1979), *Disturbing the Universe*. New York: Harper & Row.

Eastlack, Jr., Joseph O. and Ambar G. Rao (1986), "Modeling Response to Advertising and Pricing Changes for 'V-8' Cocktail Vegetable Juice," *Marketing Science*, 5 (Summer), 245–59.

Ebbeler, Donald H. (1974), "On the Maximum R^2 Choice Criterion," Claremont Economic Paper Number 113, The Claremont Colleges, August.

Edlund, Per-Olov (1984), "Identification of the Multiple-Input Box-Jenkins Transfer Function Model," *Journal of Forecasting*, 3, 297–308.

Ehrenberg, A.S.C. (1969), "Laws in Marketing," in *Current Controversies in Marketing Research*, Leo Bogart, ed. Chicago: Markham, 141–52.

––––– (1972), *Repeat-Buying*. Amsterdam: North-Holland.

Ein-Dor, Phillip and Eli Segev (1981), *A Paradigm for Management Information Systems*. New York: Praeger.

Einhorn, H. J. (1982), "Learning from Experience and Suboptimal Rules in Decision Making," in *Judgment under Uncertainty: Heuristics and Biases*, Daniel Kahneman, Paul Slovic, and Amos Tversky, eds. Cambridge: Cambridge University Press, 268–83.

––––– and R. M. Hogarth (1981), "Behavioral Decision Theory: Process of Judgment and Choice," *Annual Review of Psychology*, 53–88.

Eliashberg, Jehoshua and Abel P. Jeuland (1986), "The Impact of Competitive Entry in a Developing Market Upon Dynamic Pricing Strategies," *Marketing Science*, 5 (Winter), 20–36.

–––––, Charles Tapiero, and Yoram Wind (1987), "Innovation Diffusion Models with Stochastic Parameters: Forecasting and Planning Implications," Working Paper No. 87-003, The Wharton School, University of Pennsylvania, January.

Elrod, Terry and Russell L. Winer (1979), "Estimating the Effects of Advertising on Individual Household Purchasing Behavior," in *Proceedings*, Neil Beckwith et al., eds. Chicago: American Marketing Association, 83–89.

Enis, Ben M. and Michael P. Mokwa (1979), "The Marketing Management Matrix: A Taxonomy for Strategy Comprehension," in *Conceptual and Theoretical Developments in Marketing*, O. C. Ferrell, Stephen W. Brown, and Charles W. Lamb, eds. Chicago: 485–500.

Erickson, Gary M. (1981a), "Time-Varying Parameter Estimation as Exploration," *Decision Sciences*, 12 (July), 428–38.

––––– (1981b), "Using Ridge Regression to Estimate Directly Lagged Effects in Marketing," *Journal of the American Statistical Association*, 76 (December), 766–73.

––––– (1985), "A Model of Advertising Competition," *Journal of Marketing Research*, 22 (August), 297–304.

Eskin, Gerald J. (1975), "A Case for Test Market Experiments," *Journal of Advertising Research*, 15 (April), 27–33.

––––– and Penny H. Baron (1977), "Effect of Price and Advertising in Test-Market Experiments," *Journal of Marketing Research*, 14 (November), 499–508.

Evans, G. C. (1924), "The Dynamics of Monopoly," *American Mathematical Monthly*, 31, 77–83.

Farley, John U. and Melvin J. Hinich (1970), "A Test for a Shifting Slope Coefficient in a Linear Model," *Journal of the American Statistical Association*, 65 (September), 1320–29.

———, ———, and Timothy W. McGuire (1975), "Some Comparisons of Tests for a Shift in the Slopes of a Multivariate Linear Time Series Model." *Journal of Econometrics*, 3 (August), 297–318.

——— and H. J. Leavitt (1968), "A Model of the Distribution of Branded Products in Jamaica," *Journal of Marketing Research*, 5 (November), 362–69.

——— and Donald R. Lehmann (1986), *Meta-Analysis in Marketing: Generalization of Response Models*. Lexington, MA: D. C. Heath.

———, ———, and Michael J. Ryan (1981), "Generalizing from Imperfect Replication," *Journal of Business*, 54 (October), 597–610.

——— and Charles S. Tapiero (1981), "Using an Uncertainty Model to Assess Sales Response to Advertising," *Decision Sciences*, 12 (July), 441–55.

Farris, Paul W. and Mark S. Albion (1980), "The Impact of Advertising on the Price of Consumer Products," *Journal of Advertising Research*, 44 (Summer), 17–35.

Feichtinger, Gustav (1982), "Optimal Pricing in a Diffusion Model with Concave Price-Dependent Market Potential," *Operations Research Letters*, 1 (December), 236–40.

——— and Engbert Dockner (1985), "Optimal Pricing in a Duopoly: A Noncooperative Games Solution," *Journal of Optimization Theory and Applications*, 45 (February), 199–218.

———, Alfred Luhmer, and Gerhard Sorger (1988), "Optimal Price and Advertising Policy for a Convenience Goods Retailer," *Marketing Science*, 7 (Spring), 187–201.

Fellner, William (1949), *Competition Among the Few*. New York: Alfred Knopf.

Fildes, Robert (1985), "Quantitative Forecasting—The State of Art: Econometric Models," *Journal of the Operational Research Society*, 36 (July), 549–80.

Findley, James J. and J. D. C. Little (1980), "Experiences with Market Response Analysis," Working Paper, March.

Fischoff, Baruch (1982), "For Those Condemned to Study the Past: Heuristics and Biases in Hindsight," in *Judgment under Uncertainty: Heuristics and Biases*, Daniel Kahneman, Paul Slovic, and Amos Tversky, eds. Cambridge: Cambridge University Press, 335–51.

Fishburn, Peter C. (1970), "Intransitive Indifference in Preference Theory: A Survey," *Operations Research*, 18 (March-April), 207–228.

Fornell, Claes, William T. Robinson, and Birger Wernerfelt (1985), "Consumption Experience and Sales Promotion Expenditure," *Management Science*, 31 (September), 1084–1105.

Fourt, L. A. and J. W. Woodlock (1960), "Early Prediction of Market Success for Grocery Products," *Journal of Marketing*, 24 (October), 31–38.

Frank, Ronald E. and William F. Massy (1967), "Effects of Short-Term Promotional Strategy in Selected Market Segments," in *Promotional Decisions Using Mathematical Models*, Patrick J. Robinson, ed. Boston: Allyn and Bacon, 147–99.

——— and ——— (1970), "Shelf Position and Space Effects on Sales," *Journal of Marketing Research*, 7 (February), 59–66.

——— and ——— (1971), *An Econometric Approach to a Marketing Decision Model.* Cambridge, MA: MIT Press.

Franke, George and Gary Wilcox (1987), "Alcoholic Beverage Advertising and Consumption in the United States, 1964–1984," *Journal of Advertising*, 16 (3), 22–30.

Franz, Charles R., Daniel Robey, and Robert R. Koeblitz (1986), "User Response to an On-line Information System: A Field Experiment," *MIS Quarterly*, 10 (March), 29–47.

Fraser, Cynthia and Robert E. Hite (1988), "An Adaptive Utility Approach for Improved Use of Marketing Models," *Journal of Marketing*, 52 (October), 96–103.

Freeland, James R. and Charles B. Weinberg (1980), "S-Shaped Response Functions: Implications for Decision Models," *Journal of the Operational Research Society*, 31 (11), 1001–7.

Friedman, James W. (1977a), "Cournot, Bowley, Stackelberg and Fellner, and the Evolution of the Reaction Function," in *Economic Progress, Private Values, and Public Policy*, Bela Balassa and Richard Nelson, eds. New York: North-Holland, 139–60.

——— (1977b), *Oligopoly and the Theory of Games.* Amsterdam: North-Holland.

——— (1983), "Advertising and Oligopolistic Equilibrium," *Bell Journal of Economics*, 14 (Fall), 464–73.

Friedman, Lawrence (1958), "Game-Theory Models in the Allocation of Advertising Expenditures," *Operations Research*, 6 (September–October), 699–709.

Fujii, Edwin T. (1980), "The Demand for Cigarettes: Further Empirical Evidence and Its Implications for Public Policy," *Applied Economics*, 12 (December), 479–89.

Gasmi, Farid and Quang H. Vuong (1988), "An Econometric Analysis of Some Duopolistic Games in Prices and Advertising," Working Paper, Bell Communications Research/University of Southern California, May.

Gatignon, Hubert (1984), "Competition as a Moderator of the Effect of Advertising on Sales," *Journal of Marketing Research*, 21 (November), 387–98.

——— and Dominique M. Hanssens (1987), "Modeling Marketing Interactions with Application to Salesforce Effectiveness," *Journal of Marketing Research*, 24 (August), 247–57.

Gaugusch, Julius (1984), "The Non-cooperative Solution of a Differential Game: Advertising versus Pricing," *Optimal Control Applications & Methods*, 5 (October–December), 353–60.

Gaver, Kenneth M., Dan Horsky, and Chakravarti Narasimhan (1988), "Invariant Estimators for Market Share Systems and Their Finite Sample Behavior," *Marketing Science*, 7 (Spring), 169–86.

Gensch, Dennis H. and Ulf Peter Welam (1973), "An Optimal Budget Allocation Model in Dynamic, Interacting Market Segments," *Management Science*, 20 (October), 179–90.

Geweke, John, Richard Meese, and Warren Dent (1983), "Comparing Alternative Tests of Causality in Temporal Systems," *Journal of Econometrics*, 21, 161–94.

Ghosh, Avijit, Scott Neslin, and Robert Shoemaker (1984), " A Comparison of Market Share Models and Estimation Procedures," *Journal of Marketing Research*, 21 (May), 202–10.

Gijsbrechts, Els. and Philippe Naert (1984), "Towards Hierarchical Linking of Marketing Resource Allocation to Market Areas and Product Groups," *International Journal of Research in Marketing*, 1 (2) 97–116.

Ginsberg, William (1974), "The Multiplant Firm with Increasing Returns to Scale," *Journal of Economic Theory*, 9 (November), 283–92.

Ginzberg, Michael J. (1979a), "Improving MIS Project Selection," *Omega*, 7 (6), 527–37.

———— (1979b), "A Study of the Implementation Process," in *The Implementation of Management Science*, R. Doktor, R. L. Slevin, and D. P. Slevin, eds. New York: North-Holland, 85–102.

———— (1980), "An Organizational Contingencies View of Accounting and Information Systems Implementation," *Accounting, Organizations and Society*, 5 (4), 369–82.

———— (1981a), "Early Diagnosis of MIS Implementation Failure: Promising Results and Unanswered Questions," *Management Science*, 27 (April), 459–78.

———— (1981b), "Key Recurrent Issues in the Implementation Process," *MIS Quarterly*, 5 (June), 47–59.

———— (1983), "DSS Success: Measurement and Facilitation," in *Data-Base Management: Theory and Applications*, C. W. Holsapple and A. B. Whinston, eds. Dordrecht, Holland: D. Ridel, 367–87.

————, Henry C. Lucas, Jr., and Randall L. Schultz (1986), "Testing an Integrated Implementation Model with Data from a Generalized DSS," Working Paper, Case Western Reserve University, March.

Givon, Moshe and Dan Horsky (1986), "The Effects of Brand Loyalty and Advertising Goodwill on the Measurement of Advertising Duration," Working Paper, University of Rochester, Graduate School of Management, March.

———— and ———— (1988), "Untangling of Dynamic Effects: Purchase Reinforcement and Carryover Effects of Advertising," Working Paper, University of Rochester, Graduate School of Management, February.

Glaister, Stephen (1974), "Advertising Policy and Returns to Scale in Markets Where Information Is Passed Between Individuals," *Economica*, 41 (May), 138–56.

Gorry, G. A. and Scott Morton (1971), "A Framework for Management Information Systems," *Sloan Management Review*, 13 (Fall), 55–70.

Gould, J. P. (1970), "Diffusion Processes and Optimal Advertising Policy," in *Microeconomic Foundations of Employment and Inflation Theory*, Edmund S. Phelps et al., eds. New York: Norton, 338–68.

Granger, C.W.J. (1969), "Investigating Causal Relations by Econometric Models and Cross-Spectral Methods," *Econometrica*, 37, 424–38.

———— (1980), "Long Memory Relationships and the Aggregation of Dynamic Models," *Journal of Econometrics*, 14, 227–38.

———— (1988), "Some Recent Developments in a Concept of Causality," *Journal of Econometrics*, 39 (September–October), 199–212.

———— and M. J. Morris (1976), "Time Series Modelling and Interpretation," *Journal of the Royal Statistical Society, Series A*, 139, Part 2, 246–57.

—— and Paul Newbold (1974), "Spurious Regressions in Econometrics," *Journal of Econometrics*, 2, 111–20.

—— and —— (1977), *Forecasting Economic Time Series*. New York: Academic Press.

Grass, Robert G. and Wallace H. Wallace (1969), "Satiation Effects of TV Commercials," *Journal of Advertising Research*, 9 (September), 3–8.

Gray, H. L., G. D. Kelly, and D. D. McIntire (1978), "A New Approach to ARMA Modeling," *Communication in Statistics*, B7, 1–77.

Guilkey, David K. and Michael K. Salemi (1982), "Small Sample Properties of Three Tests for Granger-Causal Ordering in a Bivariate Stochastic System," *Review of Economics and Statistics*, 64 (November), 668–80.

Hagerty, Michael R., James M. Carman, and Gary Russell (1988), "Estimating Elasticities with PIMS Data: Methodological Issues and Substantive Implications," *Journal of Marketing Research*, 25 (February), 1–9.

Haley, Russell I. (1978), "Sales Effects of Media Weight," *Journal of Advertising Research*, 18 (June), 9–18.

Hall, Graham and Sidney Howell (1985), "The Experience Curve from the Economist's Perspective," *Strategic Management Journal*, 6, 197–212.

Hanson, Norwood Russell (1961), *Patterns of Discovery: An Inquiry into the Conceptual Foundations of Science*. Cambridge: Cambridge University Press.

Hanssens, Dominique M. (1977), "An Empirical Study of Time-Series Analysis in Marketing Model Building," Unpublished Ph.D. Dissertation, Purdue University, Krannert Graduate School of Management.

—— (1980a), "Bivariate Time Series Analysis of the Relationship Between Advertising and Sales," *Applied Economics*, 12 (September), 329–40.

—— (1980b), "Market Response, Competitive Behavior, and Time Series Analysis," *Journal of Marketing Research*, 17 (November), 470–85.

—— (1982), "Expectations and Shocks in Market Response," University of California, Los Angeles, Working Paper Series, Center for Maketing Studies, Paper No. 123.

—— (1988), "Marketing and the Long Run," University of California, Los Angeles, Working Paper Series, Center for Marketing Studies, Paper No. 164 (Revised), June.

—— and Henry A. Levien (1983), "An Econometric Study of Recruitment Marketing in the U.S. Navy," *Management Science*, 29 (October), 1167–84.

—— and Lon-Mu Liu (1983), "Lag Specification in Rational Distributed Lag Structural Models," *Journal of Business and Economic Statistics*, 1 (October), 316–25.

Harvey, A. C. (1981), *The Econometric Analysis of Time Series*. New York: Halsted Press.

Haugh, Larry D. (1976), "Checking the Independence of Two Covariance-Stationary Time Series: A Univariate Residual Cross-Correlation Approach," *Journal of the American Statistical Association*, 71 (June), 378–85.

—— and George E. P. Box (1977), "Identification of Dynamic Regression (Distributed Lag) Models Connecting Two Time Series," *Journal of the American Statistical Association*, 72 (March), 121–29.

Hausman, J. A. (1978), "Specification Tests in Econometrics," *Econometrica*, 46 (November), 1251–72.

—— and W. E. Taylor (1981), "A Generalized Specification Test," *Economic Letters*, 8, 239–47.

Hayes-Roth, Frederick, Donald Waterman, and Douglas Lenat (1983), *Building Expert Systems*. Reading, MA: Addison-Wesley.

Heckman, James J. (1976), "The Common Structure of Statistical Models of Truncation, Sample Selection, and Limited Dependent Variables and a Simple Estimator for Such Models," *Annals of Economic and Social Measurement*, 5 (Fall), 475–92.

Helmer, Richard M. and Johny K. Johansson (1977), "An Exposition of the Box-Jenkins Transfer Function Analysis with Application to the Advertising-Sales Relationship," *Journal of Marketing Research*, 14 (May), 227–39.

Hendon, Donald W. (1981), "The Advertising-Sales Relationship in Australia," *Journal of Advertising Research*, 21 (February), 37–47.

Hendry, David, ed. (1986), "Economic Modeling with Cointegrated Variables (Special Issue)," *Oxford Bulletion of Economics and Statistics*, 48 (3).

Herniter, Jerome D. (1973), "An Entropy Model of Brand Purchase Behavior," *Journal of Marketing Research*, 10 (November), 361–75.

—— and V. Cook (1970), "A Multidimensional Stochastic Model of Consumer Purchase Behavior," Working Paper, Center for Multitudinal Studies in Business and Economics University of Chicago, June.

Hogarth, Robin M. (1980), *Judgment and Choice: The Psychology of Decision*. New York: John Wiley.

—— (1981), "Beyond Discrete Biases: Functional and Dysfunctional Aspects of Judgmental Heuristics," *Psychological Bulletin*, 90 (September), 197–297.

—— (1982), "On the Suprise and Delight of Inconsistent Responses," in *New Directions for Methodology of Social and Behavioral Science: The Framing of Questions and Consistency of Response*. Robin M. Hogarth, ed. San Francisco: Jossey-Bass, 3–20.

—— and S. Markridakis (1981), "The Value of Decision Making in a Complex Environment: An Experimental Approach," *Management Science*, 27 (January), 93–107.

——, Claude Michaud, and Jean-Louis Mery (1980), "Decision Behavior in Urban Development: A Methodological Approach and Substantive Considerations," *Acta Psychologica*, 45 (August), 95–117.

Hogarty, Thomas F. and Kenneth G. Elzinga (1972), "The Demand for Beer," *Review of Economics and Statistics*, 54 (May), 195–98.

Holthausen, Duncan M., Jr. (1982), "Advertising Budget Allocation under Uncertainty," *Management Science*, 28 (May), 487–99.

Hooley, Graham J., Nick Wilson, and P. Wigodsky (1988), "Modelling the Effects of Advertising: Some Methodological Issues," *Journal of the Market Research Society*, 30 (January), 45–58.

Horsky, Dan (1977a), "Market Share Response to Advertising: An Example of Theory Testing," *Journal of Marketing Research*, 14 (February), 10–21.

——— (1977b), "An Empirical Analysis of the Optimal Advertising Policy," *Management Science*, 23 (June), 1037–49.

——— and Leonard S. Simon (1983), "Advertising and the Diffusion of New Products," *Marketing Science*, 2 (Winter), 1–17.

——— and Karl Mate (1988), "Dynamic Advertising Strategies of Competing Durable Goods Producers," *Marketing Science*, 7 (Fall), 356–67.

Houston, Franklin S. (1977a), "Aggregated and Disaggregated Cumulative Advertising Models," in *Proceedings*, B. A. Bellenger and D. N. Bellenger, eds. Chicago: American Marketing Association.

——— (1977b), "An Econometric Analysis of Positioning," *Journal of Business Administration*, 9 (Fall), 1–12.

——— and Doyle L. Weiss (1974), "An Analysis of Competitive Market Behavior," *Journal of Marketing Research*, 11 (May), 151–55.

——— and ——— (1977), "Cumulative Advertising Effects: The Role of Serial Correlation," *Decision Sciences*, 6, 471–81.

Howard, Ronald A. (1988), "Decision Analysis: Practice and Promise," *Management Science*, 34 (June), 679–95.

Huber, George P. (1983), "Cognitive Style as a Basis for MIS and DSS Designs," *Management Science*, 29 (May), 567–79.

Hulbert, James M. (1981), "Descriptive Models of Marketing Decisions," in *Marketing Decision Models*, Randall L. Schultz and Andris A. Zoltners, eds. New York: Elsevier North-Holland, 18–49.

Huysmans, J.H.B.M. (1970), "The Effectiveness of the Cognitive Style Constraint in Implementing Operations Research Proposals," *Management Science*, 17 (1), 92–104.

Imhof, J. P. (1961), "Computing the Distribution of Quadratic Forms in Normal Variables," *Biometrika*, 48, 419–26.

Ireland, N. J. and H. G. Jones (1973), "Optimality in Advertising: A Control Theory Approach," in *Dynamic Modelling and Control of National Economies*, IEE Conference Publication Number 101, 186–99.

Ives, B. and M. H. Olson (1984), "User Involvement and MIS Success: A Review of Research," *Management Science*, 30 (May), 586–603.

Jacobson, Robert and Franco M. Nicosia (1981), "Advertising and Public Policy: The Macroeconomic Effects of Advertising," *Journal of Marketing Research*, 18 (February), 29–38.

Jacquemin, Alex P. (1973), "Optimal Control and Advertising Policy," *Metroeconomica*, 25, 200–209.

Jagpal, Harsharanjeet S. (1981), "Measuring Joint Advertising Effects in Multiproduct Firms," *Journal of Advertising Research*, 21 (1), 65–69.

——— (1982), "Multicollinearity in Structural Equation Models with Unobservable Variables," *Journal of Marketing Research*, 19 (November), 431–39.

——— and Ivan E. Brick (1982), "The Marketing Mix Decision under Uncertainty," *Marketing Science*, 1 (Winter), 79–92.

——— and Balwin S. Hui (1980), "Measuring the Advertising-Sales Relationship: A Multivariate Time-Series Approach," in *Current Issues and Research in Advertising*. Ann Arbor, MI: Division of Research, Graduate School of Business, 211–28.

―――, Ephraim F. Sudit, and Hrishikesh D. Vinod (1979), "A Model of Sales Response to Advertising Interactions," *Journal of Advertising Research*, 19 (June), 41–47.

―――, ―――, and ――― (1982), "Measuring Dynamic Maketing Mix Interactions Using Translog Functions," *Journal of Business*, 55 (July), 401–15.

Jain, Arun K. and Vijay Mahajan (1979), "Evaluating the Competitive Environment in Retailing Using Multiplicative Competitive Interactive Model," in *Research in Marketing*, 2, Jagdish N. Sheth, ed. Greenwich, CT: JAI Press, 217–57.

Jastram, Roy W. (1955), "A Treatment of Distributed Lags in the Theory of Advertising Expenditures," *Journal of Marketing*, 20 (July), 36–46.

Jedidi, Kamel, Jehoshua Eliashberg, and Wayne DeSarbo (1989), "Optimal Advertising and Pricing for a Three-Stage Time-Lagged Monopolistic Diffusion Model Incorporating Income," *Optimal Control Applications & Methods*, forthcoming.

Jeuland, Abel P. and Robert J. Dolan (1982), "An Aspect of New Product Planning: Dynamic Pricing," in *Marketing Planning Models*, Adris A. Zoltners, ed. Amsterdam: North-Holland, 1–21.

Johansson, Johny K. (1973), "A Generalized Logistic Function with an Application to the Effect of Advertising," *Journal of the American Statistical Association*, 68 (December), 824–27.

――― (1974), "Price-Quantity Relationships Varying across Brands and over Time," paper presented at the ORSA/TIMS National Meeting, San Juan, Puerto Rico, October.

――― (1979), "Advertising and the S-Curve: A New Approach," *Journal of Marketing Research*, 16 (August), 346–54.

Johnston, J. (1984), *Econometric Methods*, 3rd Edition. New York: McGraw-Hill.

Jones, John P. (1984), "Universal Diminishing Returns—True or False? *International Journal of Advertising*, 3 (1), 27–41.

Jones, P. C. (1983), "Analysis of a Dynamic Duopoly Model of Advertising," *Mathematics of Operations Research*, 8 (February), 122–34.

Jørgensen, Steffen (1982), "A Survey of Some Differential Games in Advertising," *Journal of Economic Dynamics and Control*, 4, 341–69.

――― (1983), "Optimal Control of a Diffusion Model of New Product Acceptance with Price-Dependent Total Market Potential," *Optimal Control Applications & Methods*, 4, 269–76.

――― (1986), "Optimal Dynamic Pricing in an Oligopolistic Market: A Survey," in *Dynamic Games and Applications in Economics*, Lecture Notes in Economics and Mathematical Systems No. 265, T. Basar, ed. New York: Springer-Verlag.

Judge, George G., William E. Griffiths, R. Carter Hill, Helmut Lütkepohl, and Tsoung-Chao Lee (1985), *The Theory and Practice of Econometrics*, 2nd Edition. New York: John Wiley.

Judson, Horace Freeland (1979), *The Eighth Day of Creation: Makers of the Revolution in Biology*. New York: Simon & Schuster.

Kadane, Joseph B. and Patrick D. Larkey (1983), "The Confusion Between Is and Ought in Game Theoretic Contexts," *Management Science*, 29 (December), 1365–79.

Kahneman, Daniel, Paul Slovic, and Amos Tversky, eds, (1982), *Judgment Under Uncertainty: Heuristics and Biases.* Cambridge: Cambridge University Press.

Kalish, Shlomo (1983), "Monopolistic Pricing with Dynamic Demand and Production Costs," *Marketing Science*, 2 (Spring), 135–60.

——— (1985), "New Product Adoption Model with Price, Advertising, and Uncertainty," *Management Science*, 31 (December), 1569–85.

Kamien, Morton I. and Nancy L. Schwartz (1981), *Dynamic Optimization: The Calculus of Variations and Optimal Control in Economics and Management.* New York: North-Holland.

Kanetkar, Vinay, Charles B. Weinberg, and Doyle L. Weiss (1986a), "Recovering Microparameters from Aggregate Data for the Koyck and Brand Loyal Models," *Journal of Marketing Research*, 23 (August), 298–304.

———, ——— and ——— (1986b), "Estimating Parameters of the Autocorrelated Current Effects Model from Temporally Aggregated Data," *Journal of Marketing Research*, 23 (November), 379–86.

Karnani, Aneel (1985), "Strategic Implications of Market Share Attraction Models," *Management Science*, 31 (May), 536–47.

Keeney, Ralph L. and Howard I. Raiffa (1976), *Decisions with Multiple Objectives.* New York: John Wiley.

Keim, Robert T. (1976), "Assessing Implementation Attitudes in Traditional Versus Behavioral Model Building: A Longitudinal Investigation with the MAPS Design Technology," Unpublished Ph.D. Dissertation, University of Pittsburgh.

Kemeny, John G. (1959), *A Philosopher Looks at Science.* New York: Van Nostrand Reinhold.

Kendall, Maurice and Alan Stuart (1973), *The Advanced Theory of Statistics.* New York: Hafner.

Kennedy, John R. (1970), "The Effect of Display Location on the Sales and Pilferage of Cigarettes," *Journal of Marketing Research*, 7 (May), 210–15.

Kevles, Daniel (1984), *In the Name of Eugenics.* New York: Knopf.

Kimball, George E. (1957), "Some Industrial Applications of Military Operations Research Methods," *Operations Research*, 5 (April), 201–4.

King, W. R. and J. I. Rodriguez (1978), "Evaluating Management Information Systems," *MIS Quarterly*, 2 (September), 43–51.

——— and ——— (1981), "A Participative Design of Strategic Decision Support Systems: An Empirical Assessment," *Management Science*, 27 (June), 717–26.

Klein, Roger W., Lawrence C. Rafsky, David Sibley, and Robert D. Willig (1978), "Decisions with Uncertainty," *Econometrica*, 46 (November), 1363–83.

Kleinbaum, Robert M. (1988), *Multivariate Time Series Forecasts of Market Share*, Marketing Science Institute Report No. 88-102, April.

Koehler, Gary J. and Albert R. Wildt (1981), "Specification and Estimation of Logically Consistent Linear Models," *Decision Sciences*, 12, 1–31.

Koerts, J. and A.P.J. Abrahamse (1969), *On the Theory and Application of the General Linear Model.* Rotterdam: Rotterdam University Press.

Kohn, Meir G. and Yakir Plessner (1973), "An Applicable Model of Optimal Marketing Policy," *Operations Research*, 21 (March–April), 401–12.

Kotler, Philip (1971), *Marketing Decision Making: A Model-Building Approach*. New York: Holt, Rinehart, and Winston.

――― and Randall L. Schultz (1970), "Marketing Simulations: Review and Prospects," *Journal of Business*, 43 (July), 237–95.

Kotzan, Jeffrey A. and Robert V. Evanson (1969), "Responsiveness of Drug Store Sales to Shelf Space Allocation, *Journal of Marketing Research*, 6 (November), 465–69.

Krishnamurthi, Lakshman, Jack Narayan, and S. P. Raj (1986), "Intervention Analysis of a Field Experiment to Assess the Buildup Effect of Advertising," *Journal of Marketing Research*, 23 (November), 337–45.

――― and S. P. Raj (1985), "The Effect of Advertising on Consumer Price Sensitivity," *Journal of Marketing Research*, 22 (May), 119–29.

――― and Arvind Rangaswamy (1987), "The Equity Estimator for Marketing Research," *Marketing Science*, 6 (Fall), 336–57.

―――, S. P. Raj, and Raja Selvam (1988), "Statistical and Managerial Issues in Cross-Sectional Aggregation," Working Paper, J. L. Kellogg Graduate School of Management, Northwestern University, August.

Kristensen, Kai (1984), "Hedonic Theory, Marketing Research, and the Analysis of Complex Goods," *International Journal of Research in Marketing*, 1 (1), 17–36.

Kuehn, Alfred A. (1961), "A Model for Budgeting Advertising," in *Mathematical Models and Methods in Marketing*, Frank M. Bass et al., eds. Homewood, IL: Richard D. Irwin, 315–48.

――― (1962), "How Advertising Performance Depends on Other Marketng Factors," *Journal of Advertising Research*, (March), 2–10.

―――, Timothy W. McGuire, and Doyle L. Weiss (1966), "Measuring the Effectiveness of Advertising," in *Proceedings*, R. M. Haas, ed. Chicago: American Marketing Association, 185–94.

――― and Doyle L. Weiss (1965), "Marketing Analysis Training Exercise," *Behavioral Science*, 10 (January), 51–67.

Kvålseth, Tarald O. (1985), "Cautionary Note about R^2," *The American Statistician*, 39 (November), 279–85.

Lal, Rajiv and Richard Staelin (1986), "Salesforce Compensation Plans in Environments with Asymmetric Information," *Marketing Science*, 5 (Summer), 179–98.

Lambert, Zarrel V. (1968), *Setting the Size of the Sales Force*. State College, PA.: Pennsylvania State University Press.

Lambin, Jean-Jacques (1969), "Measuring the Profitability of Advertising: An Empirical Study," *Journal of Industrial Economics*, 17 (April), 86–103.

――― (1970a), "Advertising and Competitive Behavior: A Case Study," *Applied Economics*, 2 (January), 231–51.

――― (1970b), "Optimal Allocation of Competitive Marketing Efforts: An Empirical Study," *Journal of Business*, 17 (October), 468–84.

――― (1972a), "A Computer On-Line Marketing Mix Model," *Journal of Marketing Research*, 9 (May), 119–126.

――― (1972b), "Is Gasoline Advertising Justified?" *Journal of Business*, 45 (October), 585–619.

———— (1976), *Advertising, Competition, and Market Conduct in Oligopoly over Time.* Amsterdam: North-Holland.

————, Philippe A. Naert, and Alain Bultez (1975), "Optimal Marketing Behavior in Oligopoly," *European Economic Review*, 6, 105–28.

———— and Robert Peeters (1982), *Anticipating Dynamic Market Response to Brand Advertising: The Case of Automobile Advertising in Belgium*, CESAM, Louvain-la-Neuve, Belgium, December.

Lancaster, Kent M. (1984), "Brand Advertising Competition and Industry Demand," *Journal of Advertising*, 13 (4), 19–24.

Larréché, Jean-Claude (1979), "Integrative Complexity and the Use of Marketing Models," in *The Implementation of Management Science*, Robert Doktor, Randall L. Schultz, and Dennis Slevin, eds. Amsterdam: North-Nolland.

Layton, Allan P. (1984), "A Further Note on the Detection of Granger Instantaneous Causality," *Journal of Time Series Analysis*, 5 (1), 15–18.

Lee, J. and M. G. Brown (1985), "Coupon Redemption and the Demand for Concentrated Orange Juice: A Switching Regression," *American Journal of Agricultural Economics*, 67, 647–53.

Leeflang, Peter S. H. (1977), "A Comparison of Alternative Specifications of Market Share Models," in *Modeling for Government and Business*, C. A. van Bochove, ed. Leiden: Martinus Nijhoff, 247–81.

———— and Jacob J. van Duyn (1982a), "The Use of Regional Data in Marketing Models: The Demand for Beer in the Netherlands, Part 1: Regional Models," *European Research*, 10, 2–9.

———— and ———— (1982b), "The Use of Regional Data in Marketing Models: The Demand for Beer in the Netherlands, Part 2: Pooling Regional Data," *European Research*, 10, 64–71.

———— and Alex J. Olivier (1985), "Bias in Consumer Panel and Store Audit Data," *International Journal of Research in Marketing*, 2 (1), 27–41.

———— and F. W. Platt (1984a), "Linear Structural Relation Market Share Models," paper presented at the Annual EMACS Conference, Nijrode, The Netherlands, April.

———— and ———— (1984b), "Consumer Response in an Era of Stagflation: Preliminary Results," in *Advances in Marketing Research in Theory and Practice* (EMAC/ESOMAR Symposium, Copenhagen, October), 195–227.

———— and Jan C. Reuyl (1984), "On the Predictive Power of Market Share Attraction Models," *Journal of Marketing Research*, 21 (May), 211–15.

———— and ———— (1985a), "Competitive Analysis Using Market Response Functions," *Proceedings*. Chicago: American Marketing Association, 388–95.

———— and ———— (1985b), "Advertising and Industry Sales: An Empirical Study of the West German Cigarette Market," *Journal of Marketing*, 49 (Fall), 92–98.

———— and ———— (1986), "Estimating the Parameters of Market Share Models at Different Levels of Aggregation with Examples from the West German Cigarette Market," *European Journal of Operational Research*, 23, 14–24.

Leitmann, G. and W. E. Schmitendorf (1978), "Profit Maximization Through Advertising: A Nonzero Sum Differential Game," *IEEE Transactions on Automatic Control*, 23 (August), 646–50.

Leone, Robert P. (1983), "Modeling Sales-Advertising Relationships: An Integrated Time Series-Econometric Approach," *Journal of Marketing Research*, 20 (August), 291–95.

—— and Randall L. Schultz (1980), "A Study of Marketing Generalizations," *Journal of Marketing*, 44 (Winter), 101–18.

Lilien, Gary L. (1979), "ADVISOR 2: Modeling Marketing Mix Decisions for Industrial Products," *Management Science*, 25 (February), 191–204.

—— and Philip Kotler (1983), *Marketing Decision Making: A Model-Building Approach*. New York: Harper & Row.

—— and Ambar G. Rao (1976), "A Model for Allocating Retail Outlet Building Resources Across Market Areas," *Operations Research*, 24 (January–February), 1–14.

—— and A. Api Ruzdic (1982), "Analyzing Natural Experiments in Industrial Markets," in *Marketing Planning Models*, Andris A. Zoltners, ed. New York: North-Holland, 241–69.

—— and Eunsang Yoon (1988), "An Exploratory Analysis of the Dynamic Behavior of Price Elasticity over the Product Life Cycle: An Empirical Analysis of Industrial Chemical Products," in *Issues in Pricing*, Timothy M. Devinney, ed. Lexington, MA: Lexington Books, 261–87.

Little, John D. C. (1966), "A Model of Adaptive Control of Promotional Spending," *Operations Research*, 14 (November–December), 1975–97.

—— (1970), "Models and Managers: The Concept of a Decision Calculus," *Management Science*, 16 (April), 466–85.

—— (1975a), "BRANDAID: A Marketing-Mix Model, Part 1: Structure," *Operations Research*, 23 (July–August), 628–55.

—— (1975b), "BRANDAID: A Marketing-Mix Model, Part 2: Implementation, Calibration, and Case Study," *Operations Research*, 23 (July–August), 656–73.

—— (1979a), "Aggregate Advertising Models: The State of the Art," *Operations Research*, 27 (July–August), 629–67.

—— (1979b), "Decision Support Systems for Marketing Managers," *Journal of Marketing*, 43 (Summer), 9–26.

—— and Leonard M. Lodish (1981), "Commentary on 'Judgment-Based Marketing Decision Models,'" *Journal of Marketing*, 45 (Fall), 24–29.

Liu, Lon-Mu and Dominique M. Hanssens (1981), "A Bayesian Approach to Time-Varying Cross-Sectional Models," *Journal of Econometrics*, 15 (April), 341–56.

—— and —— (1982), "Identification of Multiple-Input Transfer Function Models," *Communication in Statistics Theory and Methods*, 11 (3), 297–314.

Ljung, G. M. and George E. P. Box (1978), "On a Measure of Lack of Fit in Time Series Models," *Biometrika*, 65 (2), 297–303.

Lodish, Leonard M. (1976), "Assigning Salesmen to Accounts to Maximize Profits," *Journal of Marketing Research*, 13 (November), 440–44.

—— (1981), "Experience with Decision-Calculus Models and Decision Support

Systems," in *Marketing Decision Models*, Randall L. Schultz and Andris A. Zoltners, eds. New York: Elsevier North-Holland, 99–122.

Lucas, Jr., Henry C. (1975), "Performance and Use of an Information System," *Management Science*, 21 (April), 908–19.

――― (1979), "The Implementation of an Operations Research Model in the Brokerage Industry," in *The Implementation of Management Science*, Robert Doktor, Randall L. Schultz, and Dennis P. Slevin, eds. Amsterdam: North-Holland.

――― (1982), *Information System Concepts for Management*. New York: McGraw-Hill.

――― (1984), "Organization Power and the Information-Services Department," *Communications of the ACM*, 27, 58–65.

――― , Michael J. Ginzberg, and Randall L. Schultz (1989), *Information Systems Implementation: Testing a Structural Model*. Norwood: NJ: Ablex.

――― and J. A. Turner (1982), "A Corporate Strategy for the Control of Information Processing," *Sloan Management Review*, 23 (Spring), 25–36.

Luce, R. D. and Howard Raiffa (1957), *Games and Decisions*. New York: John Wiley.

Lusk, E. J. and M. Kersnick (1979), "The Effect of Cognitive Style and Report Format on Task Performance: The MIS Design Consequences," *Management Science*, 25 (August), 787–98.

Lütkepohl, Helmut (1982), "Non-Causality Due to Omitted Variables," *Journal of Econometrics*, 19, 367–78.

Lynch, Michael (1974), "Comment on Curhan's 'The Relationship Between Shelf Space and Unit Sales in Supermarkets,'" *Journal of Marketing Research*, 11 (May), 218–20.

MacKinnon, James G. (1983), "Model Specification Tests Against Non-Nested Alternatives," *Econometric Reviews*, 2 (1), 85–110.

Maddala, G. S. (1977), *Econometrics*. New York: McGraw-Hill.

Magat, Wesley A., John M. McCann, and Richard C. Morey (1986), "When Does Lag Structure Really Matter in Optimizing Advertising Expenditures?" *Management Science*, 32 (February), 182–93.

――― , ――― , and ――― (1988), "Reply to 'When Does Lag Structure Really Matter ... Indeed?'" *Management Science*, 34 (July), 917–18.

Mahajan, Vijay, Stuart I. Bretschneider, and John W. Bradford (1980), "Feedback Approaches to Modeling Structural Shifts in Market Response," *Journal of Marketing*, 44 (Winter), 71–80.

――― , Arun K. Jain, and Michel Bergier (1977), "Parameter Estimation in Marketing Models in the Presence of Multicollinearity," *Journal of Marketing Research*, 14 (November), 586–91.

――― and Eitan Muller (1986), "Advertising Pulsing Policies for Generating Awareness for New Products," *Marketing Science*, 5 (Spring), 89–106.

――― , Subhash Sharma, and Yoram Wind (1984), "Parameter Estimation in Marketing Models in the Presence of Influential Response Data: Robust Regression and Applications," *Journal of Marketing Research*, 21 (August), 268–77.

Makridakis, S., A. Anderson, R. Carbone, R. Fildes, M. Hibon, R. Lewandowski, J. Newton, E. Parzen, and R. Winkler (1982), "The Accuracy of Extrapolation (Time

Series) Methods: Results of a Forecasting Competition," *Journal of Forecasting*, 1, 111–53.

———— and S. C. Wheelwright (1977), "Forecasting: Issues and Challenges for Marketing Management," *Journal of Marketing*, 41 (October), 24–38.

Manley, John H. (1975), "Implementation Attitudes: A Model and a Measurement Methodology," In *Implementing Operations Research/Management Science*, Randall L. Schultz and Dennis P. Slevin, eds. New York: American Elsevier, 183–202.

Mann, Don H. (1975), "Optimal Advertising Stock Models: A Generalization Incorporating the Effects of Delayed Response to Promotion Expenditures," *Management Science*, 21 (March), 823–32.

Maravall, Augustin (1981), "A Note on Identification of Multivariate Time-Series Models," *Journal of Econometrics*, 16 (June), 237–47.

March, James G. and Herbert A. Simon (1958), *Organizations*. New York: John Wiley.

Marcus, M. Lynne (1983), "Power, Politics, and MIS Implementation," *Communications of the ACM*, 26 (June), 430–44.

Massy, William F. and Ronald E. Frank (1965), "Short-Term Price and Dealing Effects in Selected Market Segments," *Journal of Marketing Research*, 2 (May), 171–85.

McCann, John M. (1974), "Market Response to the Marketing Decision Variables," *Journal of Marketing Research*, 11 (November), 399–412.

McGuiness, Tony and Keith Cowling (1975), "Advertising and the Aggregate Demand for Cigarettes," *European Economic Review*, 6, 311–28.

McGuire, Timothy W., John U. Farley, Robert E. Lucas, and Winston J. Ring (1968), "Estimation and Inferences for Linear Models in Which Subsets of Dependent Variables Are Constrained," *Journal of the American Statistical Association*, 63 (December), 1201–13.

———— and Richard Staelin (1983), "An Industry Equilibrium Analysis of Downstream Vertical Integration," *Marketing Science*, 2 (Spring), 161–90.

———— and Doyle L. Weiss (1976), "Logically Consistent Market Share Models II," *Journal of Marketing Research*, 13 (August), 296–302.

McIntyre, Shelby H. (1982), "The Impact of Judgment-Based Marketing Models," *Management Science*, 28 (January), 17–33.

————, David B. Montgomery, V. Srinivasan, and Barton A. Weitz (1983), "Evaluating the Statistical Significance of Models Developed by Stepwise Regression," *Journal of Marketing Research*, 20 (February), 1–11.

McNiven, Malcolm A. (1980), "Plan for More Productive Advertising," *Harvard Business Review*, 58 (March–April), 130–36.

Meissner, F. (1961), "Sales and Advertising of Lettuce," *Journal of Advertising Research*, 1 (March), 1–10.

Melrose, Kendrick B. (1969), "An Empirical Study on Optimizing Advertising Policy," *Journal of Business*, 42 (July), 282–92.

Mesak, H. I. (1985), "On Modeling Advertising Pulsing Decisions," *Decision Sciences*, 16 (Winter), 25–42.

Metwally, M. M. (1978), "Escalation Tendencies of Advertising," *Oxford Bulletin of Economics and Statistics*, 40 (May), 153–63.

——— (1980), "Sales Response to Advertising of Eight Australian Products," *Journal of Advertising Research*, 20 (October), 59–64.

Mickwitz, Gösta (1959), *Marketing and Competition*. Helsingfors: Centraltrykeriet, 87–89.

Miller, R. E. (1979), *Dynamic Optimization and Economic Applications*. New York: McGraw-Hill.

Mills, Harland D. (1961), "A Study in Promotional Competition," in *Mathematical Models and Methods in Marketing*, Frank M. Bass et al., eds. Homewood, IL: Richard D. Irwin, 271–301.

Mohler, R. R., ed. (1988), *Nonlinear Time Series and Signal Processing*. Berlin: Springer-Verlag.

Monahan, George E. (1983), "Optimal Advertising with Stochastic Demand," *Management Science*, 29 (January), 106–17.

——— (1984), "A Pure Birth Model of Optimal Advertising with Word-of-Mouth," *Marketing Science*, 3 (Spring), 169–78.

——— (1987), "The Structure of Equilibria in Market Share Attraction Models," *Management Science*, 33 (February), 228–43.

——— and Kofti O. Nti (1988), "Optimal Pricing and Advertising for New Products with Repeat Purchases," in *Issues in Pricing*, Timothy M. Devinney, ed., Lexington, MA: Lexington Books.

Montgomery, David B. and Alvin Silk (1972), "Estimating Dynamic Effects of Market Communications Expenditures," *Management Science*, 18, B485–501.

——— and Glen L. Urban (1970), "Marketing Decision Information Systems: An Emerging View," *Journal of Marketing Research*, 7 (May), 226–34.

——— and Charles B. Weinberg (1979), "Strategic Intelligence Systems," *Journal of Marketing*, 43 (Fall), 41–53.

Montgomery, Douglas C. and Ginner Weatherby (1980), "Modeling and Forecasting Time Series Using Transfer Function and Intervention Methods," *AIEE Transactions*, (December), 289–307.

Moore, J. H. and M. G. Chang (1980), "Design of Decision Support Systems," *Data Base*, 12 (Fall), 8–14.

Moore, William L. and Russell S. Winer (1987), "A Panel-Data-Based Method for Merging Joint Space and Market Response Function Estimation," *Marketing Science*, 6 (Winter), 25–42.

Moorthy, K. Sridhar (1984), "Market Segmentation, Self-Selection, and Product Line Design," *Marketing Science*, 3 (Fall), 288–307.

——— (1985), "Using Game Theory to Model Competition," *Journal of Marketing Research*, 22 (August), 262–82.

Moran, William T. (1978), "Insights from Pricing Research," in *Pricing Practices and Strategies*, in Earl L. Bailey, ed. New York: The Conference Board, 7–13.

Morey, Richard C. and John M. McCann (1983), "Estimating the Confidence Interval for the Optimal Marketing Mix: An Application of Lead Generation," *Marketing Science*, 2 (Spring), 193–202.

Moriarty, Mark M. (1975), "Cross-Sectional, Time-Series Issues in the Analysis of Marketing Decision Variables," *Journal of Marketing Research*, 12 (May), 142–50.

—— (1983), "Carryover Effects of Advertising on Sales of Durable Goods," *Journal of Business Research*, 11 (March), 127–37.

—— (1985a), "Transfer Function Analysis of the Relationship Between Advertising and Sales: A Synthesis of Prior Research," *Journal of Business Research*, 13, 247–57.

—— (1985b), "Design Features of Forecasting Systems Involving Management Judgments," *Journal of Marketing Research*, 22 (November), 353–64.

—— and Arthur Adams (1979), "Issues in Sales Territory Modeling and Forecasting Using Box-Jenkins Analysis," *Journal of Marketing Research*, 16 (May), 221–32.

Muller, Robert W., George E. Kline, and Joseph J. Trout (1953), "Customers Buy 22% More When Shelves Are Well Stocked," *Progressive Grocer*, 32 (June), 40–48.

Mukundan, Rangaswamy and Wolfgang B. Elsner (1975), "Linear Feedback Strategies in Non-Zero-Sum Differential Games," *International Journal of Systems Science*, 6 (6), 513–32.

Naert, Philippe A. (1971), "Optimizing Consumer, Intermediary Advertising, and Markup in a Vertical Market Structure," *Management Science*, 18 (December), 90–101.

—— (1971), "Observations on Applying Marginal Analysis in Marketing: Part I," *Journal of Business Administration*, 4 (Fall), 49–67.

—— (1972), "Observations on Applying Marginal Analysis in Marketing: Part II," *Journal of Business Administration*, 4 (Spring), 3–14.

—— and Alain V. Bultez (1973), "Logically Consistent Market Share Models," *Journal of Marketing Research*, 10 (August), 334–40.

—— and Peter S. H. Leeflang (1978), *Building Implementable Marketing Models*. Leiden: Martinus Nijhoff.

—— and Marcel Weverbergh (1981a), "On the Predictive Power Of Market Share Attraction Models," *Journal of Marketing Research*, 18 (May), 146–53.

—— and —— (1981b), "Subjective Versus Empirical Decision Models," in *Marketing Decision Models*, Randall L. Schultz and Andris A. Zoltners, eds. New York: Elsevier North-Holland, 99–122.

—— and —— (1985), "Market Share Specification, Estimation, and Validation: Toward Reconciling Seemingly Divergent Views," *Journal of Marketing Research*, 22 (November), 453–67.

Nakanishi, Masao (1973), "Advertising and Promotional Effects on Consumer Response to New Products," *Journal of Marketing Research*, 10 (August), 242–49.

—— and Lee G. Cooper (1974), "Parameter Estimation for a Multiplicative Competitive Interaction Model—Least Squares Approach," *Journal of Marketing Research*, 11 (August), 303–11.

—— and —— (1982), "Simplified Estimation Procedures for MCI Models," *Marketing Science*, 1 (Summer), 314–22.

Narasimhan, Chakravarti (1984), "A Price Discrimination Theory of Coupons," *Marketing Science*, 3 (Spring), 128–47.

Narasimhan, Ram and Roger G. Schroeder (1979), "An Empirical Investigation of Implementation as a Change Process," in *The Implementation of Management Science*, R. Doctor, Randall L. Schultz, and Dennis P. Slevin, eds. Amsterdam: North-Holland, 63–83.

Nascimento, Fernando and Wilfried R. Vanhonacker (1988), "Optimal Strategic Pricing of Reproducible Consumer Products," *Management Science*, 34 (August), 921–37.

Näslund, B. (1979), "Consumer Behavior and Optimal Advertising," *Journal of the Operations Research Society*, 30, 237–43.

Naylor, T. H. (1983), "Strategic Planning and Forecasting," *Journal of Forecasting*, 2 (April–June), 108–18.

Nelson, Charles R. (1972), "The Prediction Performance of the FRB-MIT-PENN Model of the U.S. Economy," *American Economic Review*, 62, 902–17.

—— and G. W. Schwert (1979), "Tests for Granger/Weiner Causality: A Monte Carlo Investigation," University of Rochester, Graduate School of Management, Working Paper No. 7905.

Nelson, Forrest D. (1976), "On a General Computer Algorithm for the Analysis of Models with Limited Dependent Variables," *Annals of Economic and Social Measurement*, 5 (Fall), 493–509.

—— and L. Olson (1977), "Specification and Estimation of a Simultaneous Equation Model with Limited Dependent Variables," California Institute of Technology, Social Science Working Paper No. 149.

Nerlove, Marc and Kenneth J. Arrow (1962), "Optimal Advertising Policy Under Dynamic Conditions," *Economica*, 29 (May), 129–42.

—— and F. Waugh (1961), "Advertising Without Supply Control: Some Implications for the Study of the Advertising of Oranges," *Journal of Farm Economics*, 43 (4, Part I), 813–37.

Neslin, Scott A. and Robert W. Shoemaker (1983a), "Using a Natural Experiment to Estimate Price Elasticity: The 1974 Sugar Shortage and the Ready-to-Eat Cereal Market," *Journal of Marketing*, 47 (Winter), 44–57.

—— and —— (1983b), "A Model for Evaluating the Profitability of Coupon Promotions," *Marketing Science*, 2 (Fall), 389–405.

Newbold, Paul (1974), "The Exact Likelihood Function for a Mixed Autoregressive-Moving Average Process," *Biometrica*, 61 (3), 423–26.

Newell, Allen and Herbert A. Simon (1972), *Human Problem Solving*. Englewood Cliffs, NJ: Prentice-Hall.

Nguyen, Dung (1985), "An Analysis of Optimal Advertising Under Uncertainty," *Management Science*, 31 (May), 622–33.

Nisbitt, Richard, David H. Krantz, Christopher Jepson, and Geoffry T. Fong (1982), "Improving Inductive Inference," in *Judgment Under Uncertainty: Heuristics and Biases*. Daniel Kahneman, Paul Slovic, and Amos Tversky, eds. Cambridge: Cambridge University Press, 445–59.

Ofir, Chezy and André Khuri (1986), "Multicollinearity in Marketing Models: Diagnostics and Remedial Measures," *International Journal of Research in Marketing*, 3 (3), 181–205.

O'Herlihy, Callaghan (1988), "A Commercial Perspective on Advertising Modelling as Presented by Dr. Hooley et al.," *Journal of the Market Research Society*, 30 (April), 227–31.

Olsder, Gert Jan (1976), "Some Thoughts About Simple Advertising Models as Differential Games and the Structure of Coalitions," in *Directions in Large-Scale Systems*. Y. C. Ho and S. K. Mitter, eds, New York: Plenum Press, 187–205.

Openshaw, S. and P. J. Taylor (1979), "A Million or So Correlation Coefficients: Three Experiments on the Modified Areal Unit Problem," in *Statistical Applications in the Spatial Sciences*, N. Wrigley, ed. London: Pion, 127–44.

Osborne, D. K. (1974), "A Duopoly Price Game," *Economica*, 41 (May), 157–75.

Ottesen, Otto (1980), "A Theory of Short-Run Response to Advertising," in *Research in Marketing*, 4, 181–222.

Ozga, S. (1960), "Imperfect Markets Through Lack of Knowledge," *Quarterly Journal of Economics*, 7 (February), 29–52.

Palda, Kristian S. (1964), *The Measurement of Cumulative Advertising Effects*. Englewood Cliffs, NJ: Prentice-Hall.

——— (1969), *Economic Analysis for Marketing Decisions*. Englewood Cliffs, NJ: Prentice-Hall.

——— and Larry M. Blair (1970), "A Moving Cross-Section Analysis of the Demand for Toothpaste," *Journal of Marketing Research*, 7 (November), 439–49.

Parasuraman, A. and Ralph L. Day (1977), "A Management-Oriented Model for Allocating Sales Effort," *Journal of Marketing Research*, 14 (February), 22–33.

Parfitt, J. H. and B.J.K. Collins (1968), "Use of Consumer Panels for Brand-Share Prediction," *Journal of Marketing Research*, 5 (May), 131–45.

Parker, Thomas H. and Ira J. Dolich (1986), "Toward Understanding Retail Bank Strategy: Seemingly Unrelated Regression Applied to Cross-Sectional Data," *Journal of Retailing*, 62 (Fall), 298–321.

Parsons, Leonard J. (1968), "Predictive Testing: A Simultaneous Equations Model of Sales and Advertising," Unpublished Ph.D. Dissertation, Purdue University, 1968.

——— (1974), "An Econometric Analysis of Advertising, Retail Availability, and Sales of a New Brand," *Management Science*, 20 (February), 938–47.

——— (1975a), "Econometric Approaches to Integrating Marketing Information from Diverse Sources," in *Proceedings*. Chicago: American Marketing Association, 49–53.

——— (1975b), "The Product Life Cycle and Time-Varying Advertising Elasticities," *Journal of Marketing Research*, 9 (November), 476–80.

——— (1976), "A Rachet Model of Advertising Carryover Effects," *Journal of Marketing Research*, 13 (February), 76–79.

——— (1981), "Models of Market Mechanisms," in *Marketing Decision Models*, Randall L. Schultz and Andris A. Zoltners, eds. New York: North-Holland, 77–98.

——— and Frank M. Bass (1971), "Optimal Advertising Expenditure Implications of a Simultaneous-Equation Regression Analysis," *Operations Research*, 19 (May–June), 822–31.

——— and Randall L. Schultz (1976), *Marketing Models and Econometric Research*. New York: North-Holland.

——— and Piet Vanden Abeele (1981), "Analysis of Sales Call Effectiveness," *Journal of Marketing Research*, 18 (February), 107–13.

Patrizzi, Giacomo (1981), "Proper Identification and Optimization Procedures for the Determination of an Optimal Marketing Policy," paper presented at CORS/TIMS/ORSA Meeting, Toronto, May.

Pauli, Hans and R. W. Hoecker (1952), *Better Utilization of Selling Space in Food Stores: Part I: Relation of Size of Shelf Display to Sales of Canned Fruits and Vegetables*, Marketing Research Report No. 30, Washington, DC: United States Government Printing Office.

Pekelman, Dov and Suresh Sethi (1978), "Advertising Budgeting, Wearout, and Copy

Replacement," *Journal of the Operational Research Society,* 29 (July), 651–59.

———— and Edison Tse (1980), "Experimentation and Budgeting in Advertising: An Adaptive Control Approach," *Operations Research,* 28 (March–April), 321–47.

Peles, Yoram C. (1961a), "Economies of Scale in Advertising Beer and Cigarettes," *Journal of Business,* 44 (January), 32–37.

———— (1971b), "Rates of Amortization of Advertising Expenditures," *Journal of Political Economy,* 79 (September–October), 1032–58.

———— (1979), "Econometric Measurement of the Duration of Advertising Effect on Sales," *Journal of Marketing Research,* 16 (August), 286–89.

Peterson, Robert A. and James W. Cagley (1973), "The Effect of Shelf Space Upon Sales of Branded Products: An Appraisal," *Journal of Marketing Research,* 10 (February), 103–4.

Picconi, Mario J. and Charles L. Olson (1978), "Advertising Decision Rules in a Multibrand Environment: Optimal Control Theory and Evidence," *Journal of Marketing Research,* 15 (February), 82–92.

Pierce, David A. (1972), "Residual Correlations and Diagnostic Checking in Dynamic-Disturbance Time Series Models," *Journal of the American Statistical Association,* 67 (September), 636–40.

———— (1977), "Relationships—and the Lack Thereof—Between Economic Time Series, with Special Reference to Money and Interest Rates," *Journal of the American Statistical Association,* 72 (March), 11–22.

———— and Larry D. Haugh (1977), "Causality in Temporal Systems," *Journal of Econometrics,* 5, 265–93.

Pindyck, Robert S. and Daniell L. Rubinfeld (1981), *Econometric Models and Economic Forecasts.* New York: McGraw-Hill.

Pitz, Gordon F. and Natalie J. Sachs (1984), "Judgment and Decision: Theory and Application," *Annual Review of Psychology,* 35, 139–63.

Plat, F. W. and Peter S. H. Leeflang (1986a), "Competitive Analysis in Segmented Markets," Research Memorandum, Institute of Economic Research, Faculty of Economics, University of Groningen, The Netherlands.

———— and Peter S. H. Leeflang (1986b), "Decomposing Sales Elasticities in Segmented Markets," Research Memorandum, Institute of Economic Research, Faculty of Economics, University of Groningen, The Netherlands.

Plosser, Charles I. and G. William Schwert (1977), "Estimation of Non-Invertible Moving Average Processes: The Case of Overdifferencing," *Journal of Econometrics,* 6, 199–224.

Poirier, Dale J. (1973), "Piecewise Regression Using Cubic Splines," *Journal of the American Statistical Association,* 68 (September), 515–24.

Pollay, Richard W. (1979), "Lydiametrics: Applications of Econometrics to the History of Advertising," *Journal of Advertising History,* 1 (January), 3–18.

Popper, Karl R. (1961), *The Logic of Scientific Discovery.* New York: Basic Books.

Prasad, V. Kanti and L. Winston Ring (1976), "Measuring Sales Effects of Some Marketing Mix Variables and Their Interactions," *Journal of Marketing Research,* 13 (November), 391–96.

Pratt, John W. and Robert Schlaifer (1988), "On the Interpretation and Observation of Laws," *Journal of Econometrics,* 39 (September–October), 23–54.

Preston, Lee E. and Norman R. Collins (1966), *Studies in a Simulated Market*. Berkeley, CA: Institute of Business and Economic Research, University of California.

Progressive Grocer (1963–1964), "The Colonial Study," 42 (September), 43 (March).

Quenouille, M. H. (1957), *The Analysis of Multiple Time Series*. New York: Hafner.

Radnor, Michael and Alden S. Bean (1974), "Top Management Support For Management Science," *Omega*, 2 (1), 63–75.

Raiffa, Howard and R. Schlaiffer (1961), *Applied Statistical Decision Theory*. Boston: Harvard University Press.

Raman, Kalyan (1987a), "Dynamic Optimization of the Marketing Mix in a Stochastic Environment," Department of Marketing and Transportation, Auburn University.

—— (1987b), "Stochastic Optimal Control of Monopoly Pricing Models with Dynamic Demand and Production Cost," Department of Marketing and Transportation, Auburn University.

Ramsey, James B. (1969), "Tests for Specification Errors in Classical Least-Squares Regression Analysis," *Journal of the Royal Statistical Society, Series B*, 21, 350–71.

—— (1972), "Limiting Functional Forms for Market Demand Curves," *Econometrica*, 40 (March), 327–41.

—— (1974), "Classical Model Selection Through Specification Error Tests," in *Frontiers in Econometrics*, Paul Zarembka, ed. New York: Academic Press, 13–48.

Rangan, V. Kasturi (1987), "The Channel Design Decision: A Model and an Application," *Marketing Science*, 6 (Spring), 156–74.

Rao, Ambar G. (1970), *Quantitative Theories in Advertising*. New York: John Wiley.

—— and Peter B. Miller (1975), "Advertising/Sales Response Functions," *Journal of Advertising Research*, 15 (April), 7–15.

—— and Melvin F. Shakun (1972), "A Quasi-Game Theory Approach to Pricing," *Management Science*, 18 Part 2 (January), P110–23.

Rao, Ram C. (1984), "Advertising Decisions in Oligopoly: An Industry Equilibrium Analysis," *Optimal Control Applications & Methods*, 5 (October–December), 331–44.

—— (1986), "Estimating Continuous Time Advertising-Sales Models," *Marketing Science*, 5 (Spring), 125–42.

—— and Frank M. Bass (1985), "Competition, Strategy, and Price Dynamics: Theoretical and Empirical Investigation," *Journal of Marketing Research*, 22 (August), 283–96.

—— and Ronald E. Turner (1984), "Organization and Effectiveness of the Multiproduct Salesforce," *Journal of Personal Selling and Sales Management*, (May), 24–30.

Rao, Vithala R. (1972), "Alternative Econometric Models of Sales-Advertising Relationships," *Journal of Marketing Research*, 9 (May), 177–81.

——, Jerry Wind, and Wayne S. DeSarbo (1988), "A Customized Market Response Model: Development, Estimation, and Empirical Testing," *Journal of the Academy of Marketing Science*, 16 (Spring), 128–40.

Rasmussen, A. (1952), "The Determination of Advertising Expenditure," *Journal of Marketing*, 16 (April), 439–46.

Reibstein, David J. and Hubert Gatignon (1984), "Optimal Product Line Pricing: The Influence of Cross-Elasticities," *Journal of Marketing Research*, 21 (August), 259–67.

Reuijl, Jan C. (1982), *On the Determination of Advertising Effectiveness*. Boston: Kluwer Academic Publishers.

Roberts, David L. and Stephen Nord (1985), "Causality Tests and Functional Form Sensitivity," *Applied Economics*, 17, 135–41.

Robey, Daniel (1979), "User Attitudes and Management Information System Use," *Academy of Management Journal*, 22 (September), 527–38.

——— (1983), "Cognitive Style and DSS Design: A Comment on Huber's Paper," *Management Science*, 29 (May), 580–82.

——— (1984), "Conflict Models in Implementation Research," in *Management Science Implementation*, Randall L. Schultz and Michael J. Ginzberg, eds. Greenwich, CT: JAI Press, 89–105.

——— and M. M. Bakr (1978), "Task Redesign—Individual Moderating and Novelty Effects," *Human Relations*, 31 (August), 689–701.

——— and W. Taggert (1981), "Measuring Manager's Minds: The Assessment of Style in Human Information Processing," *Academy of Management Review*, 6 (July), 375–84.

——— and R. L. Zellner (1978), "Factors Affecting Success and Failure of an Information System for Product Quality," *Interfaces*, 8 (2), 70–75.

Robinson, Bruce and Chet Lakhani (1975), "Dynamic Price Models for New-Product Planning," *Management Science*, 21 (June), 1113–22.

Rodriguez, J. L. (1977), "The Design and Evaluation of a Strategic Issue Competitive Information System," Ph.D. Dissertation, University of Pittsburgh.

Rosenberg, Barr (1973), "The Analysis of a Cross-Section of Time Series by Stochastically Convergent Regression," *Annals of Economic and Social Measurement*, 2 (October), 399–428.

Rosenbleuth, Arturo and Norbert Wiener (1945), "The Role of Models in Science," *Philosophy of Science*, 12 (October), 316–21.

Rosett, Richard N. (1959), "A Statistical Model of Friction in Economics," *Econometrica*, 27 (April), 263–67.

——— and Forrest D. Nelson (1975), "Estimation of the Two-Limit Regression Model," *Econometrica*, 43 (January), 141–46.

Russell, Gary J. (1988), "Recovering Measures of Advertising Carryover from Aggregate Data: The Role of the Firm's Decision Behavior," *Marketing Science*, 7 (Summer), 252–70.

——— and Ruth N. Bolton (1988), "Implications of Market Structure for Elasticity Structure," *Journal of Marketing Research*, 25 (August), 229–41.

Rust, Roland T. (1988), "Flexible Regression," *Journal of Marketing Research*, 25 (February), 10–24.

——— and David C. Schmittlein (1985), "A Bayesian Cross-Validated Likelihood Method for Comparing Alternative Specifications of Quantitative Models," *Marketing Science*, 4 (Winter), 20–40.

Ruud, Paul A. (1984), "Tests of Specification in Econometrics," *Econometric Reviews*, 3 (2), 211–42.

Ryans, Adrian B. and Charles B. Weinberg (1979), "Territory Sales Response," *Journal of Marketing Research*, 16 (November), 453–65.

Saghafi, Massoud M. (1988), "Optimal Pricing to Maximize Profits and Achieve Market-Share Targets for Single-Product and Multiproduct Companies," in *Issues in Pricing*, Timothy M. Devinney, ed. Lexington, MA: Lexington Books, 239–53.

Salmon, Wesley C. (1967), *The Foundations of Scientific Inference*. Pittsburgh: University of Pittsburgh Press.

Samuels, J. M. (1970/1971), "The Effect of Advertising on Sales and Brand Shares," *European Journal of Marketing*, 4 (Winter), 187–207.

Sanders, G. Larry (1984), "MIS/DSS Success Measure," *Systems, Objectives, Solutions*, 4, 29–34.

Sasieni, Maurice W. (1971), "Optimal Advertising Expenditure," *Management Science*, 18 (December), 64–72.

——— (1982), "The Effects of Combining Observation Periods in Time Series," *Journal of the Operational Research Society*, 33, 647–53.

Saunders, John (1987), "The Specification of Aggregate Market Models," *European Journal of Marketing*, 21 (2), 5–47.

Savage, Leonard J. (1954), *The Foundations of Statistics*. New York: John Wiley.

Sawyer, Alan and Scott Ward (1979), "Carryover Effects in Advertising Communication," in Jagdish N. Sheth, ed., *Research in Marketing*, 2, JAI Press, 259–314.

Schmalensee, Richard (1972), *The Economics of Advertising*. New York: North-Holland.

——— (1976), "A Model of Promotional Competition in Oligopoly," *Review of Economic Studies*, 43 (October), 493–507.

——— (1978), "A Model of Advertising and Product Quality," *Journal of Political Economy*, 86 (June), 485–503.

Schmidt, Peter (1973), "Calculating the Power of the Minimum Standard Error Choice Criterion," *International Economic Review*, 14 (February), 253–55.

Schultz, Randall L. (1971a), "Market Measurement and Planning With a Simultaneous-Equation Model," *Journal of Marketing Research*, 8 (May), 153–64.

——— (1971b), "The Measurement of Aggregate Advertising Effects," *Proceedings*. Chicago: American Marketing Association, 220–24.

——— (1973), "Methods for Handling Competition in Dynamic Market Models," *European Journal of Marketing*, 7 (Spring), 13–27.

——— (1974), "The Use of Simulation for Decision Making," *Behavioral Science*, 19 (September), 344–50.

——— (1975), "The Legitimacy of Management Science," *Interfaces*. 5 (August), 26–28.

——— (1984), "The Implementation of Forecasting Models," *Journal of Forecasting*, 3 (January–March), 43–55.

——— and Joe A. Dodson, Jr. (1974), "A Normative Model for Marketing Planning," *Simulation and Games*, 5 (December), 363–82.

——— and ——— (1978), "An Empirical-Simulation Approach to Competition," *Research in Marketing*, 1, 269–301.

——— and Michael J. Ginzberg, eds. (1984), *Management Science Implementation*. Greenwich, CT: JAI Press.

———, ———, and Henry C. Lucas, Jr. (1984), "A Structural Model of Implementation," in *Management Science Implementation*, Randall L. Schultz and Michael J. Ginzberg, eds. Greenwich, CT: JAI Press, 55–87.

——— and Dominique Hanssens (1976), "Logical Implications of Competitive Behavior: An Approach to Model Specification," Krannert Graduate School of Management, Purdue University, Institute Paper No. 561, July.

——— and Michael J. Henry (1981), "Implementing Decision Models," in *Marketing Decision Models*, Randall L. Schultz and Andris A. Zoltners, eds. New York: Elsevier North-Holland, 275–96.

——— and Dennis P. Slevin (1972), "Behavioral Considerations in the Implementation of Marketing Decision Models," in *Proceedings*. Chicago: American Marketing Association, 494–98.

——— and ——— (1975), "Implementation and Organizational Validity: An Empirical Investigation," in *Implementing Operations Research/Management Science*, Randall L. Schultz and Dennis P. Slevin, eds. New York: American Elsevier, 153–72.

——— and ——— (1983), "The Implementation Profile," *Interfaces*, 13, 87–92.

——— and Edward M. Sullivan (1972), "Developments in Simulation in Social and Administrative Science," in *Simulation in Social and Administrative Science*, Harold Guetzkow, Philip Kotler, and Randall L. Schultz, eds. Englewood Cliffs, NJ: Prentice-Hall, 3–47.

——— and Wilfried R. Vanhonacker (1978), "A Study of Promotion and Price Elasticity," Institute Paper No. 657, Krannert Graduate School of Management, Purdue University, March.

——— and Dick R. Wittink (1976), "The Measurement of Industry Advertising Effects," *Journal of Marketing Research*, 13 (February), 71–75.

——— and Andris A. Zoltners (1981), *Marketing Decision Models*. New York: Elsevier North-Holland.

Schwert, G. William (1979), "Tests of Causality: The Message in the Innovations," *Journal of Monetary Economics*, 10, 55–76.

Scitovsky, Tibor (1978), "Asymmetries in Economics," *Scottish Journal of Political Economy*, 25 (November), 227–37.

Sethi, Suresh P. (1973), "Optimal Control of the Vidale-Wolfe Advertising Model," *Operations Research*, 21 (July–August), 998–1013.

——— (1974a), "Optimal Institutional Advertising: Minimum-Time Problem," *Journal of Optimization Theory and Applications*, 14 (August), 213–31.

——— (1974b), "Some Explanatory Remarks on the Optimal Control of the Vidale–Wolfe Advertising Model," *Operations Research*, 22 (September–October), 1119–20.

——— (1974c), "Sufficient Conditions for the Optimal Control of a Class of Systems with Continuous Lags," *Journal of Optimization Theory and Applications*, 13 (May), 545–52.

——— (1975), "Optimal Control of a Logarithmic Advertising Model," *Operations Research Quarterly*, 26 (June), 317–19.

——— (1977a), "Dynamic Optimal Control Models in Advertising: A Survey," *Siam Review*, 19 (October), 685–725.

——— (1977b), "Optimal Advertising for the Nerlove-Arrow Model Under a Budget Constraint," *Operations Research Quarterly*, 28 (3), 638–93.

——— (1979), "A Note on the Nerlove-Arrow Model under Uncertainty," *Operations Research*, 27 (July–August), 839–42.

—— (1983), "Optimal Long-run Equilibrium Advertising Level for the Blattberg-Jeuland Model," *Management Science*, 29 (December), 1436–43.

Sexton, Donald E. (1970), "Estimating Marketing Policy Effects on Sales of a Frequently Purchased Branded Product," *Journal of Marketing Research*, 7 (August), 338–47.

—— (1972), "A Microeconomic Model of the Effects of Advertising," *Journal of Business*, 45 (January), 29–41.

Shakun, Melvin F, (1965), "Advertising Expenditures in Coupled Markets—A Game-Theory Approach," *Management Science*, 11 (February), B42–47.

—— (1966), "A Dynamic Model for Competitive Marketing in Coupled Markets," *Management Science*, 12 (August), B525–29.

—— (1968), "Competitive Organizational Structures in Coupled Markets," *Management Science*, 14 (August), B663–73.

Shane, H. D. (1977), "Mathematical Models for Economic and Political Advertising Campaigns," *Operations Research*, 25, 1–14.

Sharma, Subhash and William L. James (1981), "Latent Root Regression: An Alternate Procedure for Estimating Parameters in the Presence of Multicollinearity," *Journal of Marketing Research*, 18 (May), 154–61.

Shipchandler, Zoher E. and James S. Moore (1988), "Examining the Effects of Regression Procedures on the Temporal Stability of Parameter Estimates in Marketing Models," *Journal of the Academy of Marketing Science*, 16 (Fall), 79–87.

Shocker, Allan and V. Srinivasan (1974), "A Consumer-Based Methodology for the Identification of New Product Ideas," *Management Science*, 20 (February), 921–37.

Shoemaker, Robert W. (1986). "Comment on 'Dynamics of Price Elasticity and Brand Life Cycles: An Empirical Study,'" *Journal of Marketing Research*, 23 (February), 78–82.

—— and Lewis G. Pringle (1980), "Possible Biases in Parameter Estimation with Store Audit Data," *Journal of Marketing Research*, 16 (February), 91–96.

Shubik, Martin (1975), *The Uses and Methods of Gaming*. New York: Elsevier.

—— (1982), *Game Theory in the Social Sciences: Concepts and Solutions*. Cambridge, MA: MIT Press.

Sickles, Robin C. and Peter Schmidt (1978), "Simultaneous Equations Models with Truncated Dependent Variables: A Simultaneous Tobit Model," *Journal of Economics and Business*, 31 (Fall), 11–21.

——, Peter Schmidt, and Ann D. White (1979), "An Application of the Simultaneous Tobit Model: A Study of the Determinants of Criminal Recidivism," *Journal of Economics and Business*, 31 (Spring), 166–71.

Silk, Alvin J. and Glen L. Urban (1978), "Pre-Test Market Evaluation of New Packaged Goods: A Model and Measurement Methodology," *Journal of Marketing Research*, 15 (May), 171–91.

Simon, Herbert (1953), "Causal Ordering and Identifiability," in *Studies in Econometric Method*, W. C. Hood and T. C. Koopmans, eds. New York: John Wiley, 49–74.

—— (1965), *The Shape of Automation for Men and Management*. New York: Harper & Row.

—— (1968), "On Judging the Plausibility of Theories," in *Logic, Methodology, and Philosophy of Science III*, B. Van Rootselaar and S. F. Staal, eds. Amsterdam: North-Holland, 439–59.

—— (1983), *Reason in Human Affairs*. Stanford, CA: Stanford University Press.

Simon, Hermann (1979), "Dynamics of Price Elasticity and Brand Life Cycles: An Empirical Study," *Journal of Marketing Research*, 16 (November), 439–52.

――― (1982), "ADPULS: An Advertising Model with Wearout and Pulsation," *Journal of Marketing Research*, 19 (August), 352–63.

――― and Karl-Heinz Sebastian (1987), "Diffusion and Advertising: The German Telephone Campaign," *Management Science*, 33 (April), 451–66.

Simon, Julian L. (1965), "A Simple Model for Determining Advertising Appropriations," *Journal of Marketing Research*, 2 (August), 285–92.

――― (1969a), "The Effect of Advertising on Liquor Brand Sales," *Journal of Marketing Research*, 6 (August), 301–13.

――― (1969b), "A Further Test of the Kinky Oligopoly Demand Curve," *American Economic Review*, 59 (December), 971–75.

――― (1970), *Issues in the Economics of Advertising*. Urbana, IL: University of Illinois Press.

――― and Johan Arndt (1980), "The Shape of the Advertising Function," *Journal of Advertising Research*, 20 (August), 11–28.

Sims, Christopher A. (1972), "Money, Income and Causality," *American Economic Review*, 62 (September), 540–52.

Sjöberg, L. (1982), "Aided and Unaided Decision Making: Improving Intuitive Judgment," *Journal of Forecasting*, 1 (October–December), 349–62.

Smith, A.F.M. and D. J. Spiegelhalter (1980), "Bayes Factors and Choice Criteria for Linear Models," *Journal of the Royal Statistical Society, Series B*, 42 (2), 213–20.

Snetsinger, Douglas W. (1985a), "Multiproduct Firm Competition: The Role of Product and Advertising Policies," AMA Doctoral Dissertation Competition Abstract, April.

――― (1985b), "Reaction to Advertising of New Brands: A Vector ARMA Modeling Approach," Working Paper Series No. 9184, Wilfrid Laurier University.

Sorensen, Richard E. and Dale E. Zand (1975), "Theory of Change and Effective Use of Management Science," *Administrative Science Quarterly*, 20 (December), 532–45.

Souder, Wm. E., P. M. Maher, N. R. Baker, C. R. Shumway and A. H. Rubenstein (1975), "An Organizational Intervention Approach to the Design and Implementation of RED Project Selection Models," in *Implementing Operations Research/Management Science*, Randall L. Schultz and Dennis P. Slevin, eds. New York: American Elsevier, 133–152.

Spitzer, John J. (1978), "A Monte Carlo Investigation of the Box-Cox Transformations in Small Samples," *Journal of the American Statistical Association*, 73 (September), 488–95.

Sprague, Ralph H. and Eric D. Carlson (1982), *Building Effective Decision Support Systems*. Englewood Cliffs, NJ: Prentice-Hall.

Srinivasan, V, (1976), "Decomposition of a Multiperiod Media Scheduling Model," *Management Science*, 23 (December), 349–60.

――― (1981), "An Investigation of the Equal Commission Rate Policy for a Multiproduct Salesforce," *Management Science*, 27 (July), 731–56.

――― and Helen A. Weir (1988), "A Direct Approach to Inferring Microparameters of the Koyck Advertising-Sales Relationship from Macro Data," *Journal of Marketing Research*, 25 (May), 145–56.

Stackelberg, Heinrich von (1934), *Marktform und Gleichgewicht*. Vienna: Julius Springer.

Staelin, Richard and Ronald E. Turner (1973), "Error in Judgmental Sales Forecasts: Theory and Results," *Journal of Marketing Research*, 10 (February), 10–16.

Steiner, Robert L. (1987), "The Paradox of Increasing Returns to Advertising," *Journal of Advertising Research*, 27 (February–March), 45–53.

Stigler, George J. (1947), "The Kinky Oligopoly Demand Curve and Price," *Journal of Political Economy*, 55, 432–49.

———— (1952), *Theory of Price*. New York: Macmillan.

———— (1961), "Economics of Information," *Journal of Political Economy*, 69 (June), 213–25.

Stone, M. (1977), "An Asymptotic Equivalence of Choice of Model by Cross-Validation and Akaike's Criterion," *Journal of the Royal Statistical Society, Series B*, 39 (1), 44–47.

———— (1979), "Comments on Model Selection Criteria of Akaike and Schwartz," *Journal of the Royal Statistical Society, Series B*, 41 (2), 276–78.

Stöwsand, Heino and Wilfried Wenzel (1979), "Market Mechanics: A Study to Measure the Effect of Marketing Instruments on the Market Position of Fast-Moving Consumer Goods," *Journal of Business Research*, 7, 243–57.

Sturgess, Brian and Peter Wheale (1985), "Advertising Interrelations in an Oligopolistic Market: An Analysis of Causality," *International Journal of Advertising* 4 (4), 305–18.

Sunoo, Don and Lynn Y. S. Lin (1978), "Sales Effects of Promotion and Advertising" *Journal of Advertising Research*, 18 (October), 37–40.

Swamy, P.A.V.B. (1971), *Statistical Inference in Random Coefficient Models*. New York: Springer-Verlag.

———— and Peter von zur Muehlen (1988), "Further Thoughts on Testing for Causality with Econometric Models," *Journal of Econometrics*, 39 (September–October), 105–47.

Swanson, E. B. (1974), "Management Information Systems: Appreciation and Involvement," *Management Science*, 21 (October), 178–88.

———— (1982), "Measuring User Attitudes in MIS Research: A Review," *Omega*, 10 (2), 157–65.

Sweeney, Dennis J., P. Abad, and Ronald J. Dornoff (1974), "Finding an Optimal Dynamic Advertising Policy," *International Journal of Systems Science*, 5 (10), 987–94.

Sweezy, Paul M. (1939), "Demand Under Conditions of Oligopoly," *Journal of Political Economy*, 47, 568–73.

Takada, Hirokazu (1986), "Analysis of Competitive Marketing Behavior Using Multiple Time Series Analysis and Econometric Methods," Working Paper, University of California, Riverside, Graduate School of Management.

Tapiero, Charles S. (1975a), "Random Walk Models of Advertising, Their Diffusion Approximation and Hypothesis Testing," *Annals of Economic and Social Measurement*, 4 (Spring), 293–309.

———— (1975b), "On-Line and Adaptive Optimal Advertising Control by a Diffusion Approximation," *Operations Research*, 23 (September–October), 890–907.

———— (1977a), *Managerial Planning: An Optimal and Stochastic Approach*. New York: Gordon Breach.

——— (1977b), "A Stochastic Model of Sales Response to Advertising," *Metroeconomica*, 24, 159–67.

——— (1979), "A Generalization of the Nerlove-Arrow Model to Multifirm Advertising under Uncertainty," *Management Science*, 25 (September), 907–15.

——— (1982), "A Stochastic Model of Consumer Behavior and Optimal Advertising," *Management Science*, 28 (September), 1054–64.

———, Jehoshua Eliashberg, and Yoram Wind (1987), "Risk Behavior and Optimal Advertising with Stochastic Dynamic Sales Response," *Optimal Control Applications & Methods*, 8, 299–304.

——— and John U. Farley (1975), "Optimal Control of Sales Force Effort in Time," *Management Science*, 21 (May), 976–85.

Taylor, Fredrick, W. (1911), *The Principles of Scientific Management*. New York: Harper & Row.

Tellis, Gerard J. (1988), "The Price Sensitivity of Selective Demand: A Meta-Analysis of Econometric Models of Sales," *Journal of Marketing Research*, 25 (November), 391–404.

——— and Claus Fornell (1988), "The Relationship Between Advertising and Product Quality over the Product Life Cycle: A Contingency Theory," *Journal of Marketing Research*, 25 (February), 64–71.

Telser, Lester G. (1962a), "The Demand for Branded Goods as Estimated from Consumer Panel Data," *Review of Economics and Statistics*, 44 (August), 300–324.

——— (1962b), "Advertising and Cigarettes," *Journal of Political Economy*, 70 (October), 471–99.

Teng, Jinn-Tsair and Gerald L. Thompson (1983), "Oligopoly Models for Optimal Advertising When Production Costs Obey a Learning Curve," *Management Science*, 29 (September), 1087–1101.

Theil, Henri (1971), *Principles of Econometrics*. New York: John Wiley.

Thisted, Ronald and C. Morris (1980), "Theoretical Results for Adaptive Ordinary Ridge Regression," Technical Report No. 94, Department of Statistics, University of Chicago.

Thompson, Gerald L. and Jinn-Tsair Teng (1984), "Optimal Pricing and Advertising Policies for New Product Oligopoly Models," *Marketing Science*, 3 (Spring), 148–68.

Tiao, George C. and George E. P. Box (1981), "Modeling Multiple Time Series with Applications," *Journal of the American Statistical Association*, 76 (December), 802–16.

——— and Ruey S. Tsay (1983), "Multiple Time Series Modeling and Extended Sample Cross-Correlations," *Journal of Business and Economic Statistics*, 1 (January), 43–56.

——— and W. Wei (1976), "Effect of Aggregation on the Dynamic Relationship of Two Time Series Variables," *Biometrica*, 63 (December), 513–23.

Tobin, James (1958), "Estimation of Relationships for Limited Dependent Variables," *Econometrica*, 26 (January), 24–36.

Totten, John C. and Martin P. Block (1987), *Analyzing Sales Promotion*. Chicago: Commerce Communications.

Tsay, Ruey S. (1985), "Model Identification in Dynamic Regression (Distributed Lag)

Models," *Journal of Business and Economic Statistics*, 3 (July), 228–37.

——— and George C. Tiao (1984), "Consistent Estimates of Autoregressive Parameters and Extended Sample Autocorrelation Functions for Stationary and Nonstationary ARMA Models," *Journal of the American Statistical Association*, 79 (March), 84–96.

Tsurumi, Hiroki (1973), "A Comparison of Alternative Optimal Models of Advertising Expenditures: Stock Adjustment Versus Control Theoretic Approaches," *Review of Economics and Statistics*, 55 (May), 156–68.

——— and Yoshi Tsurumi (1971), "Simultaneous Determination of Market Share and Advertising Expenditure under Dynamic Conditions: The Case of a Firm Within the Japanese Pharmaceutical Industry," *Kikan riron-keizaisaku*, 22 (December), 1–23.

Tull, Donald S. (1955), "A Re-Examination of the Causes of the Decline in Sales of Sapolio," *Journal of Business*, 28 (April), 128–37.

———, Van R. Wood, Dale Duhan, Tom Gillpatrick, Kim R. Robertson, and James G. Helgeson (1986), "'Leveraged' Decision Making in Advertising: The Flat Maximum Principle and Its Implications," *Journal of Marketing Research*, 23 (February), 25–32.

Turner, Ronald E. (1971), "Market Measures from Salesmen: A Multidimensional Scaling Approach," *Journal of Marketing Research*, 8 (May), 165–72.

——— and Charles P. Neuman (1976), "Dynamic Advertising Strategy: A Managerial Approach," *Journal of Business Administration*, 7 (Spring), 1–21.

——— and John C. Wiginton (1976), "Advertising Expenditure Trajectories: An Empirical Study for Filter Cigarettes 1953–1965," *Decision Sciences*, 7 (July), 496–507.

Tversky, Amos and Daniel Kahneman (1981), "The Framing of Decisions and the Psychology of Choice," *Science*, 211 (January 30), 453–8.

——— and ——— (1982), "Judgment Under Uncertainty: Heuristics and Biases," in *Judgment Under Uncertainty: Heuristics and Biases*, Daniel Kahneman, Paul Slovic, and Amos Tversky, eds. Cambridge: Cambridge University Press, 3–20.

Tybout, Alice M. and John R. Hauser (1981), "A Marketing Audit Using a Conceptual Model of Consumer Behavior: Application and Evaluation," *Journal of Marketing*, 45 (Summer), 82–101.

Urban, Glen L. (1969), "A Mathematical Modeling Approach to Product Line Decisions," *Journal of Marketing Research*, 6 (February), 40–47.

——— (1975), "PERCEPTOR—Model for Product Positioning," *Management Science*, 21 (April), 858–71.

——— and John R. Hauser (1980), *Design and Marketing of New Products*. Englewood Cliffs, NJ: Prentice-Hall.

Vandaele, Walter (1983), *Applied Time Series and Box-Jenkins Models*. New York: Academic Press.

Vanhonacker, Wilfried R. (1983), "Carryover Effects and Temporal Aggregation in a Partial Adjustment Framework," *Marketing Science*, 2 (Summer), 297–317.

——— (1984), "Estimation and Testing of a Dynamic Sales Response Model with Data Aggregated Over Time: Some Results for the Autoregressive Current Effects Model," *Journal of Marketing Research*, 21 (November), 445–55.

—— (1987), "Estimating the Duration of Dynamic Effects with Temporally Aggregated Observations," *Journal of Statistical Computation and Simulation*, 27 (April), 185–209.

—— (1988), "Estimating an Autoregressive Current Effects Model of Sales Response When Observations Are Aggregated over Time: Least Squares Versus Maximum Likelihood," *Journal of Marketing Research*, 25 (August), 301–7.

—— and Diana Day (1987), "Cross-Sectional Estimation in Marketing: Direct Versus Reverse Regression," *Marketing Science*, 6 (Summer), 254–67.

Van Wormer, Theodore A. and Doyle L. Weiss, (1970), "Fitting Parameters to Complex Models by Direct Search," *Journal of Marketing Research*, 7 (November), 503–12.

Verma, Vinod K. (1980), "A Price Theoretic Approach to the Specification and Estimation of the Sales-Advertising Function,.. *Journal of Business*, 53 (July), S115–37.

Vertinsky, I., R. J. Barth, and V. F. Mitchell (1975), "A Study of OR/MS Implementation as a Social Change Process," in *Implementing Operations Research/Management Science*, Randall L. Schultz and Dennis P. Slevin, eds. New York: American Elsevier, 253–70.

Vidale, M. L. and H. B. Wolfe (1957), "An Operations Reseach Study of Sales Response to Advertising," *Operational Research Quarterly*, 5 (June), 370–81.

von Neumann, John and Oscar Morgenstern (1947), *Theory of Games and Economic Behavior*. Princeton, NJ: Princeton University Press.

Vuong, Quang H. (1989), "Likelihood Ratio Tests for Model Selection and Non-Nested Hypotheses," *Econometrica*, forthcoming.

Waid, Clark, Donald F. Clark, and Russell L. Ackoff (1956), "Allocation of Sales Effort in the Lamp Division of General Electric Company," *Operations Research*, 4 (December), 629–47.

Wall, Kent D. (1976), "FIML Estimation of Rational Distributed Lag Structural Form Models," *Annals of Economic and Social Measurement*, 5 (Winter), 53–64.

Wallace, T.D. (1972) "Weaker Criteria and Tests for Linear Restrictions in Regression," *Econometrica*, 40 (July), 689–98.

Ward, Ronald W. (1975), "Revisiting the Dorfman-Steiner Static Advertising Theorem: An Application to the Processed Grapefruit Industry," *American Journal of Agricultural Economics*, (August), 500–504.

Watson, James D. (1968), *The Double Helix*. New York: Atheneum Publishers.

Weinberg, Charles B. and Doyle L. Weiss (1982), "On the Econometric Measurement of the Saturation of Advertising Effects on Sales," *Journal of Marketing Research*, 9 (November), 585–91.

—— and —— (1986), "A Simpler Estimation Procedure for a Micromodeling Approach to the Advertising-Sales Relationship," *Marketing Science*, 5 (Summer), 269–72.

Weiss, Doyle L. (1968), "The Determinants of Market Share," *Journal of Marketing Research*, 5 (August), 290–95.

—— (1969), "An Analysis of the Demand Structure for Branded Consumer Products," *Applied Economics*, 1 (January), 37–44.

————, Franklin S. Houston, and Pierre Windal (1978), "The Periodic Pain of Lydia E. Pinkham," *Journal of Business*, 51, 91–101.

————, Charles B. Weinberg, and Pierre M. Windal (1983), "The Effects of Serial Correlation and Data Aggregation on Advertising Measurement," *Journal of Marketing Research* 20, (August), 268–79.

———— and Pierre M. Windal (1980), "Testing Cumulative Advertising Effects: A Comment on Methodology," *Journal of Marketing Research*, 17 (August), 371–78.

Welam, Ulf Peter (1982), "Optimal and Near Optimal Price and Advertising Strategies," *Management Science*, 28 (November), 1313–27.

Welsch, Gemma M. (1981), "A Multidimensional Measure of Perceived Decision Support System Implementation Success," paper presented at the First International Conference on Decision Support Systems, Atlanta, Georgia, June.

Wernerfelt, Birger (1986), "A Special Case of Dynamic Pricing Policy," *Management Science*, 32 (December), 1562–66.

Wichern, Dean W. and Richard H. Jones (1977), "Assessing the Impact of Market Disturbances Using Intervention Analysis," *Management Science*, 23 (November), 329–37.

Wierenga, Berend (1981), "Modelling the Impact of Advertising and Optimising Advertising Policy," *European Journal of Operational Research*, 8, 235–48.

Wildt, Albert R. (1974), "Multifirm Analysis of Competitive Decision Variables," *Journal of Marketing Research*, 11 (November), 50–62.

———— (1976), "The Empirical Investigation of Time-Dependent Parameter Variation in Marketing Models," *Proceedings*. Chicago: American Marketing Association.

———— (1977), "Estimating Models of Seasonal Market Response Using Dummy Variables," *Journal of Marketing Research*, 14 (February), 34–41.

————, James D. Parker, and Clyde E. Harris (1987), "Assessing the Impact of Sales-Force Contests: An Application," *Journal of Business Research*, 15 (April), 145–55.

———— and Russell S. Winer (1983), "Modeling and Estimation in Changing Market Environments," *Journal of Business*, 56 (July), 365–88.

Wilson, Nick and Graham J. Hooley (1988), "Advertising Effects: More Methodological Issues: A Reply," *Journal of the Market Research Society*, 30 (April), 231–34.

Wind, Yoram, Vijay Mahajan, and Richard Cardozo (1981), *New Product Forecasting: Models and Applications*. Lexington, MA: Lexington Books.

Windal, Pierre M. and Doyle L. Weiss (1980), "An Iterative GLS Procedure for Estimating the Parameters of Models with Autocorrelated Errors Using Data Aggregated over time," *Journal of Business*, 53 (October), 415–24.

Winer, Russell S. (1979), "An Analysis of the Time Varying Effects of Advertising: The Case of Lydia Pinkham," *Journal of Business*, 52 (October), 563–76.

———— (1983), "Attrition Bias in Econometric Models Estimated by Panel Data," *Journal of Marketing Research*, 20 (May), 177–86.

———— (1985), "A Price Vector Model of Demand for Consumer Durables: Preliminary Developments," *Marketing Science*, 4 (Winter), 74–90.

———— (1986), "A Reference Price Model of Brand Choice for Frequently Purchased Products," *Journal of Consumer Research*, 13 (September), 250–56.

Wittink, Dick R. (1973), "Partial Pooling: A Heuristic," Institute Paper No. 419, Krannert Graduate School of Industrial Administration, Purdue University, July.

—— (1977a), "Advertising Increases Sensitivity to Price," *Journal of Advertising Research*, 17 (April), 39–42.

—— (1977b), "Exploring Territorial Differences in the Relationship Between Marketing Variables," *Journal of Marketing Research*, 14 (May), 145–55.

—— (1983a), "Standardized Regression Coefficients: Use and Misuse," Graduate School of Management, Cornell University, September.

—— (1983b), "Autocorrelation and Related Issues in Applications of Regression Analysis," Graduate School of Management, Cornell University, October.

—— (1987), "Causal Market Share Models in Marketing: Neither Forecasting nor Understanding?" *International Journal of Forecasting*, 3 (3/4), 445–48.

Wolffram, Rudolf (1971), "Positivistic Measures of Aggregate Supply Elasticities: Some New Approaches—Some Critical Notes," *American Journal of Agricultural Economics*, 53, 356–59.

Wrather, C. and P. L. Yu (1979), "Advertising Games in Duopoly Market Expansion," in *Control Theory in Mathematical Economics*, Pan-Tai Liu and Jon G. Sutinen, eds. New York: Marcel Dekker, 111–49.

Yi, Youjae (1988), "Assessing Main Effects in Interactive Regression Models," *Proceedings*. Chicago: American Marketing Association, 298.

Yokum, J. Thomas and Albert R. Wildt (1987), "Forecasting Sales Response for Multiple Time Horizons and Temporally Aggregated Data: A Comparison of Constant and Stochastic Coefficient Models," *International Journal of Forecasting*, 3 (3/4), 479–88.

Young, Kan H. and Lin Y. Young (1975), "Estimation of Regression Involving Logarithmic Transformation of Zero Values in the Dependent Variable," *The American Statistican*, 29 (August), 118–20.

Young, Trevor (1982), "Addiction Asymmetry and the Demand for Coffee," *Scottish Journal of Political Economy*, 29 (February), 89–98.

—— (1983), "The Demand for Cigarettes: Alternative Specifications of Fujii's Model," *Applied Economics*, 15 (April), 203–11.

Yule, G. U. (1926), "Why Do We Sometimes Get Nonsense Correlations Between Time Series? A Study in Sampling and the Nature of Time Series," *Journal of the Royal Statistical Society*, 89, 1–64.

Zellner, Arnold (1971), *An Introduction to Bayesian Inference in Econometrics*. New York: John Wiley.

—— (1988a), "Bayesian Analysis in Econometrics," *Journal of Econometrics*, 39 (January), 27–50.

—— (1988b), "Causality and Causal Laws in Econometrics," *Journal of Econometrics*, 39 (September–October), 7–21.

——, J. Kmenta, and J. Dréze (1966), "Specification and Estimation of Cobb-Douglas Production Function Models," *Econometrica*, 34 (October), 784–95.

—— and Franz Palm (1974), "Time Series Analysis and Simultaneous Equation Regression Models," *Journal of Econometrics*, 2, 17–54.

Zentler, A. P. and Dorothy Ryde (1956), "An Optimal Geographic Distribution of Publicity Expenditure in a Private Organization," *Management Science* 4 (July), 337–52.

Zielske, Hugh A. (1986), "Comments," *Marketing Science*, 5 (Spring), 109.

Zmud, Robert W. (1979), "Individual Differences and MIs Success: A Review of the Empirical Literature," *Management Science*, 25 (October), 966–69.

Zoltners, Andris A. (1981), "Normative Marketing Models," in *Marketing Decision Models*, Randall L. Schultz and Andris A. Zolthers, eds. New York: North-Holland, 55–76.

――――― and Prahakant Sinha (1980), "Integer Programming Models for Sales Resource Allocation," *Management Science*, 26 (March), 242–60.

Author Index

Subject Index